Indexed in special indexes

HENRY JAMES'S MAJOR NOVELS:

Essays In Criticism

HENRY JAMES'S
MAJOR NOVELS:
Essays in Criticism

EDITED WITH AN INTRODUCTION BY

LYALL H. POWERS

EAST LANSING
MICHIGAN STATE UNIVERSITY PRESS

1973

For my Father

Contents

THE ESSAYS

Preface

This collection presents a series of critical studies of Henry James's twelve major novels; each essay is concerned principally with one novel. Six of the novels have a single essay devoted to them; six have two essays devoted to them. It seemed to me that those novels which have come to be recognized as James's best, or which have been the occasion of the most critical attention, or have proved most puzzling, should be represented by two essays. I have not included works like *The Reverberator*, which is interesting in its relation to *The Bostonians*, for instance, yet of secondary merit; or short novels like *The Europeans* and the excellent *Washington Square*.

With one exception, all of the essays have been published within the past twenty years, and over half of them within the last decade. They have been selected solely on the basis of suitability and intrinsic merit. I have made no attempt to represent recognized authorities on James (although several of them are included), nor have I tried to indicate trends in, or the range of, James criticism (in those instances where a novel is treated in two essays, they are in no sense a "pair"—complementing each other or demonstrating opposed views, etc.). In every case I have attempted simply to provide the clearest and most persuasive, the most perceptive and satisfying critical explication and appreciation that is presently available.

The variety and range of this collection, however, is representative of the kind of criticism to which James's fiction has been subject. Some of the essays are strictly explicative—F. C. Crews' on *The Ambassadors*, my own on *The Portrait of a Lady*, and H. K. Girling's on *The Golden Bowl*, which examines one aspect of the narrative technique as a means of illuminating the central concern of the novel. In other essays the explication serves to relate the novel in question to major motifs of European literature of the nineteenth and twentieth centuries—e.g. Edward Engelberg's on *Roderick Hudson*, Lionel Trilling's and Frederick J. Hoffman's on *The Princess Casamassima*.

Taken as a whole, the essays indicate very well the major motifs, the recurring concerns, of James's novels; the general "dialectical" nature of his fiction is specified in Trilling's essay on *The Bostonians*—from which I quote in the Introduction. And this is touched on specifically in J. J. Firebaugh's essay on *The Awkward Age*— and implicitly in several other essays. The importance of *consciousness* as opposed to *conscience* (another prominent theme treated dialectically in James, and recently attracting more and more the notice of critics), and the connection of this theme in James with its appearance in Matthew Arnold, is directly the subject of Engelberg's essay on *Roderick Hudson* and central in Austin Warren's essay on *The Ambassadors* and in Mrs. Krook's essays on *The Wings of the Dove* and *The Golden Bowl;* it is also treated to some extent in my essay on *The Tragic Muse*. Associated with consciousness is the theme of vision (something of a Blakean theme), which is a major concern of Crews' essay on *The Ambassadors* as it is of Firebaugh's on *The Awkward Age* and of both essays (Leon Edel's and Tony Tanner's) on *The Sacred Fount;* it also plays a part in James W. Gargano's essay on *What Maisie Knew*. The "religious" dimension of James's fiction is examined in Mrs. Krook's essays—especially that on *The Wings of the Dove*—and in my essay on *The Portrait of a Lady* as well as, to some extent, in Arnold Kettle's on *The Portrait* and Firebaugh's on *The Awkward Age*. Thus, while the individual essayists are not themselves interested primarily in tracing the development or incidence of recurrent themes, the essays taken as a group do faithfully indicate the principal themes; and of course most of the essays make usual reference to other works of James's than the novel with which they are particularly concerned. This collection, consequently, is not simply a gathering of discrete studies: it is more than a sum of its parts.

A basic assumption that lies behind such a collection as this is that James is in no sense an "easy" writer, that his novels are complex and often difficult, and that an intelligent elucidation of the difficulties may aid the reader in appreciating more fully the accomplishment—the beauty and significance—of James's major fiction. We ought not to forget James's admonitory admission: "Attention of perusal, I thus confess by the way, is what I at every point . . . absolutely invoke and take for granted. . . ."[1] I hope, then, that this series of essays will prove to be a helpful guide and that it will assist attention of perusal and stimulate the reader to return to the novels refreshed and enlightened.

[1] Preface to *The Wings of the Dove, The Art of the Novel,* ed. R. P. Blackmur (New York, 1953), p. 304.

Introduction

The comparative popularity that Henry James's works now enjoy is a phenomenon of only the past few years; one might date it from World War II or, perhaps, from his own centenary in 1943. Although James suffered throughout his life from popular neglect, he never despaired. When writing to his friend William Dean Howells (in 1888) to confess that the demand for his works had been reduced to zero, he was yet able to express optimism for the future: "Very likely too, some day, all my buried prose will kick off its various tombstones at once." That expression was to prove prophetic: the tombstones have been roundly kicked, and the buried prose strides boldly abroad in the public realm. James has indeed come to life for the general reader. Almost all of his work has been republished in recent years, much of it in inexpensive editions; most notably, the original edition of his novels and tales (the New York Edition) has been reissued and a complete edition of his tales published—both under the able editorship of Leon Edel.

Henry James was never absolutely neglected, of course: there were always the perceptive few who had high regard for his accomplishments; and in later years he was to enjoy the respect of a group of young admirers for whom he came to be—as Ford Madox Ford called him—the Master. In addition to such intelligent essays as Howells' "Mr. Henry James's Later Work" (1903) and Herbert Croly's "Henry James and his Countrymen" (1904), a full study of his novels appeared a decade before his death—Elizabeth Cary's *The Novels of Henry James* (1905). In 1916, the year of his death, there appeared both Ford Madox Ford's *Henry James: A Critical Study* and Rebecca West's *Henry James;* and only two years later Joseph Warren Beach's classic study *The Method of Henry James* was published. In that year (1918) two magazines, *The Egoist* and *The Little Review*, each devoted a whole issue to commemorative essays on James; *Hound and Horn* did the same in 1934, as did *The New Republic* and *The Kenyon Review* in 1943.

It is not a simple matter to account for James's new found popularity. Two burning issues that once stood in the way of just appreciation of his work have for the most part been laid to rest: 1) the question raised by Van Wyck Brooks and V. L. Parrington, for instance, of the evil results of James's failure of patriotism— i.e., his removal to Europe for most of his productive life; and 2) the question of his failure of social consciousness—his "snobbishness," his role as "culture hound"—which characterized Jamesian criticism of the thirties. It may be that James's "psychological realism" is now more accessible to the general reader, who is more "psychologically" sophisticated in our Freudian-oriented world. In his essay of 1884, "The Art of Fiction," James confessed his delight in the psychological interest of fiction that was to characterize his own work:

> A psychological reason is, to my imagination, an object adorable pictorial; to catch the tint of its complexion—I feel as if that idea might inspire one to Titianesque efforts. There are few things more exciting to me, in short, than a psychological reason, and yet, I protest, the novel seems to me the most magnificent form of art.

It may be that another kind of sophistication has been fostered by the new critical approach to literature, which encourages especially the appreciation of technique—of formal structure, patterns of imagery, symbolism, in a word of that aspect of the art of fiction that was so dear to James himself. It may be, too, that contemporary readers now find attractive the world of which James wrote, a world in which traditional and established values were still operative, in which assumptions about absolute good were still generally tenable. It may also be that for readers of our age of anxiety and automation, when many gods have already failed, the religious humanism with which James's fiction is informed—a devout respect for individual human integrity—exerts a strong appeal.

In any case, the vogue continues. Henry James is now largely with us, and because of that fact he may be more easily appreciated and more accurately assigned his proper position in American literature. If he did not write *the* great American novel, he did write a number of novels that rank with the greatest—*The Ambassadors, The Portrait of a Lady, The Golden Bowl, The Wings of the Dove,* and perhaps *The Princess Casamassima* or even the early *Roderick Hudson.* In addition to the novels, many of his novelettes and tales are recognized now as among the best of those genres in American literature. There is also his critical writing—both theoretic and practical—on the art of fiction. The general excellence of much of that criticism has been admitted, and R. P. Blackmur has called James's eighteen prefaces to the New York Edition of his novels and tales "the most sustained and I think the most eloquent piece of literary criticism in existence." Finally, James has exerted an important influence on the development of modern fiction: his experiments in narrative technique, especially in the use of point of view (which reached its apogee in *The Ambassadors),* have contributed much to the development of stream of consciousness and internal monologue as principal techniques of the modern novel. Conrad, Ford, Woolf, Richardson, Joyce, Faulkner are all to some degree in his debt. He can now be seen as a dominant figure: if not the Master of American Prose Fiction, James is nevertheless unmistakably a lion in our path.

II

The basis of James's view of humanity is a belief in the supreme value of the individual, in the right of the individual to full development of his potential; consequently, he views as evil all that tends to violate individual integrity and to prevent or restrict human development. Henry James nowhere makes explicit claim for the innate divinity of the individual human being, as Emerson does, yet his tacit assumption seems to be close to that idea. The typical Jamesian protagonist is a creature innately good but in some degree undeveloped: he is inexperienced and ignorant of the world in which he finds himself and is in a real sense naive and innocent. The question always is whether the protagonist will be able to benefit from the new experiences offered him, whether, that is, he will be able to develop and mature as a result of the opportunity thus presented. The sign of maturity in the Jamesian protagonist is clear vision—the ability to see and know the truth about things as they really are, to recognize the evil in the world for what it is, to understand the significance of conventional ways of behavior and discover the morality beneath the manners. Confronting the world is, of course, an experience fraught with danger, yet it seems always to be assumed that the protagonist will succeed if he trusts his own inner promptings and keeps his eyes open. In this he must beware of deception, and particularly of self-deception, for self-trust obviously depends on self-knowledge. He must also resist the temptation to turn away from the experience offered, to refuse to see and learn; otherwise he will remain, like Blake's Thel, a figure of arrested development—which is to deny one's humanity.

Daisy Miller is perhaps the most familiar example of the Jamesian heroine who comes to grief through willful refusal to learn: she simply will not "see." Isabel Archer, in *The Portrait of a Lady*, suffers from a similar stubbornness coupled with a failure to harken to the moral promptings of her own nature—to trust her "moral spontaneity," as James would call it. These innocents are in part responsible for the dilemma that strikes them: they earn their fate. Christopher Newman, of *The American*, is in some sense the male counterpart of Isabel: for all his attested shrewdness in the American business world he is clearly a *naif* in the great old world of Europe—as his very name implies. Newman must face the test of his new experience, must learn the ways of the world in which he finds himself, and especially must recognize the constricting evil that is beautifully hidden beneath its charming social conventions. By trusting his own essential moral nobility, once he has learned to see things clearly, Christopher Newman is finally able to achieve that maturity which permits him to scorn revenge and destroy the evidence against the Bellegardes. The similar importance of cleared vision to the hero of *The Ambassadors* is a major point of F. C. Crews' essay in this collection. For all his comparatively advanced age, Lambert Strether is morally naive and his confrontation with the world is literally shocking for him. His good will—a kind of middle-aged moral spontaneity—and his eager willingness to learn help to see him through to his clarified conclusion.

James shared with Hawthorne a keen sense of the evil of human beings' manipulation of their fellow men—the inhuman use of others for ignoble and selfish ends. Consequently many of James's

evil characters seem descendents of Hawthorne's Roger Chillingworth insofar as their function as manipulators is concerned.
"Emotional Cannibalism" is the very apt title which Mr. Osborne
Andreas has given to this dominant theme in James.[1] This theme
of evil is well depicted in *The Portrait of a Lady,* where Gilbert
Osmond has virtually manipulated the life out of his daughter,
Pansy, has seriously harmed his former mistress, Serena Merle,
and threatens his wife, Isabel, with a similar fate. Another such
character is the severe Olive Chancellor, whose latent lesbianism
is to some extent responsible for her control and manipulation of
Verena Tarrant in *The Bostonians.* Little Maisie is a kind of pawn
(in *What Maisie Knew),* pushed about in the evil game in which
her parents and their lovers are involved; and Nanda Brookenham
(The Awkward Age) is threatened with the same kind of abuse. In
every instance the evil arises from a failure to respect the value
of the individual and his right to unimpeded personal development

The opponent of free individual development is often, in James's work, the restrictive force of institutions, of the dictates of
convention. Roderick Hudson's difficulties stem in part from the
conventions of the New England society which produced him, and
he is unable to free himself from this convention by expatriation
for the simple reason that a representative of that society makes
his expatriation possible—Rowland Mallett. Furthermore, Roderick's choice (between remaining dutifully faithful to ties with
home—and with its conventions—and "irresponsibly" following
his own bent) is dramatically represented by the two women in his
life, Mary Garland and Christina Light. Nick Dormer's case (in
The Tragic Muse) involves him in the institution of public service
as a member of the House of Commons; he must learn the necessity of replacing his sense of duty to that institution with the sense
of his higher duty to himself. In *The Awkward Age* little Aggie, the
obverse of Nanda Brookenham, is a victim of the European convention which controls the upbringing of young ladies to preserve
them in as complete ignorance as possible. Once freed from this
domination, Aggie bursts upon the world of Mrs. Brook and her
cronies like a little fury. The life has not been squeezed out of her,
as it nearly has out of Pansy Osmond, but it has been so repressed
as to be severely twisted and misshapen. Frequently, the institution that threatens individual freedom is the Church. In his use of

the forms of religion to represent what he considers to be the stifling control of people, James is similar to William Blake.

> *I went to the Garden of Love,*
> *And saw what I never had seen:*
> *A Chapel was built in the midst,*
> *Where I used to play on the green.*
>
> *And the gates of this Chapel were shut,*
> *And 'Thou shalt not' writ over the door;*
> *So I turn'd to the Garden of Love*
> *That so many sweet flowers bore;*
>
> *And I saw it was fillèd with graves,*
> *And tomb-stones where flowers should be;*
> *And priests in black gowns were walking their rounds,*
> *And binding with briars my joys and desires.*

The strong opposition in Blake's writing between the evil of duty—imposed from without by the father-priest-king—and the good of following the dictates of one's desires ("Jesus was all virtue, and acted from impulse, not from rules.") is also present in James. Sometimes the situation which confronts the Jamesian protagonist presents him with the opportunity for evil use of himself: he is often faced with the alternatives of love and duty, of choosing between what his inmost being desires and what he believes it is his duty to do. Closer at hand than Blake, certainly, was the Jameses' friend Ralph Waldo Emerson, the advocate of self-reliance, who would write "Whim" over his door and whose sentiments in *Works and Days* find an echo in James's writing. The whole idea of self-reliance and the religious and philosophical basis on which it rested were strongly present in the atmosphere which nurtured Henry James. Emerson was simply part of an American tradition which began at least with Jonathan Edwards' belief in the sweetness of indwelling grace and extended to include Henry James, Sr. and Josiah Royce. Especially important is the distinction between what one is and what one does. Often the alternatives facing the protagonist in James's fiction are 1) his duty to do something specific, and 2) his penchant to *do* nothing at all but simply to *be* himself. This idea may have come immediately from his father. In *Notes of a Son and Brother* Henry recalls the paternal advice given him and William in their youth: "What we

were to do . . . was just to *be* something, something unconnected
with specific doing, something free and uncommitted, something
finer in short than being *that*, whatever it was, might consist of."²

In any case, the conflict is typical of James's fiction. Verena
Tarrant's dilemma in *The Bostonians* is complicated by the fact
that, in spite of Basil Ransom's strong attraction for her, she believes it her duty to follow the line indicated to her by Olive
Chancellor. Hyacinth Robinson's problem, in *The Princess Casamassima*, is even more complicated in that he is never fully able
to understand what his desires are or who really would be the
objects of those desires if he did understand them. Hyacinth's
problem is to discover who he is; his world not only offers him no
help but actually makes the discovery more difficult by confusing
all the issues. Ought his sympathies to be with "the people" in
their struggle?—yes, through all the weight of hereditary pressure
from his maternal line; but his taste is not theirs, and anyway many
of the representatives of the people are aristophiles and eager to
maintain the *status quo*. On the other hand, his own sensibility and
his taste incline him to the aristocratic world—the world to which
his father supposedly belonged (Hyacinth cannot even be sure of
that!), and which is so glamorously represented by the Princess
Casamassima. Yet this most glamorous representative is herself
intimately allied with the mysterious Hoffendahl and the anarchist
movement. Hyacinth's dilemma is as acute as Quentin Compson's
in Faulkner's *The Sound and the Fury*, and his solution in suicide
quite as understandable. As was the case with Verena Tarrant and
with Hyacinth Robinson, Nick Dormer must discover who he
really is—his essential being—and then *be* himself. When Nick
presents Gabriel Nash with all the arguments on the side of duty
and challenges him with "Don't you recognize in any degree the
grand idea of duty?" Nash's strategy is to oppose that idea of duty
with the more exalted idea of duty to one's self, to "The conscience that's in us—that charming conversible infinite thing, the
intensest thing we know. . . . One must do one's best to find out
the right, and your criminality appears to be that you've not taken
the commonest trouble."³ Self-knowledge precedes and makes
possible self-trust.

James uses this method of dialectic—of suspending his "argument" between two polar opposites—to develop the thematic concerns of many of his stories of writers and artists. The opposition

here is between the aesthetic and the utilitarian, between the beautiful and the merely useful and practical. The theme usually involves the artist who faithfully pursues his art yet appears never to succeed in the eyes of the world. It is interesting, in this connection, to recall a statement James made in a letter to his brother William (July 23, 1890) about his own position as an artist: "One must go one's way and know what one's about and have a general plan and a private religion—in short have made up one's mind as to *ce qui en est* with a public the draggling after which simply leads one in the gutter. One has always a 'public' enough if one has an audible vibration—even if it should only come from one's self."[4] Roderick Hudson and, to a considerable extent, Nick Dormer of *The Tragic Muse* are representative of the beleaguered artist; the former a tragic example, the latter (I suppose) a happy one.

In a number of stories, from as early as "The Madonna of the Future" (1873), James dealt specifically with the dilemma of the artist. Many of these stories appeared during that period of James's life when he seemed to be passing through a crisis similar to that which he presents variously in his fiction. (In several instances, the hero is of the age James was when he wrote the story.) From about the middle eighties until the turn of the century James was bent on capturing the public ear, on making a concerted effort to gain, if not "popularity," then at least some broader recognition of his artistic achievement. It is not surprising, therefore, that his concern over the situation he was directly facing should find its way into several of his works of those years. The particular problem, the confrontation of art and the world (to use the terms James used in his preface to *The Tragic Muse)*, informs all of these stories.

They may be divided into two groups: 1) those dealing with the social demands made on the artist by the thoughtless world— the *lionization* stories, as the group might be called, of which "The Death of the Lion" is paradigmatic; and 2) those dealing with the impatient demands of the world that the artist produce punctually and in some abundance—that he do his public duty, so to speak, and have plenty to show to justify his existence. "The Tree of Knowledge" well exemplifies this group. In both cases the implicit plea is that the artist be left free—and "irresponsible"— to be himself and to listen to no voice but that of his muse, to recognize no duty beyond that owed to his artistic self. Perhaps this plea for the artist is nowhere made so clearly as in *The Tragic Muse.* There Gabriel Nash assures the perplexed Nick Dormer that his first responsibility, his chief duty, is to his essential self. Whether one sees Gabriel Nash as a soft satire of the aesthete of the nineties or not, he is unmistakably arguing for the right of the artist; he is on the side James himself certainly espoused, "the side of the angels." The problem of the artist often resolves itself into the opposition of *being* to *doing:* the natural demand of the artistic soul to *be* what it must is confronted with the world's demand that the artist *do* something (something useful or popularly pleasing, etc.). The terms of this particular opposition (and we find them especially in the second group of stories mentioned above) echo a statement of Emerson's (In *Works and Days):* " 'Tis not important how the hero does this or this, but what he is. What he is will appear in every gesture and syllable." Furthermore, such an idea as this had been instilled in James by his father.

We recognize here again James's familiar theme of self-knowledge and self-trust: he insists on the importance of discovering one's true identity, one's essential being, and remaining faithful to that in the face of whatever slings and arrows the world may launch. The recognition of this theme—fundamental, I suppose, in James's system—permits us to see the close connection between his stories of artists and his stories of "lay" heroes. R. P. Blackmur well says, "James made of the theme of the artist a focus for the ultimate theme of human integrity, how it is conceived, how it is destroyed, and how, ideally, it may be regained."[5] Especially close is the connection between the artist stories and the large group of stories that belong under the general heading of the International Theme—those stories which deal with the confrontation of America and Europe. In the usual pattern of the International story the characteristic elements are American innocence, naivete, and cultural ignorance (not to say bad taste) in contrast with European experience, tradition, and *savoir-faire.* Sometimes James's intention seems to have been simply to write a comedy of manners, an ambiguous and ambivalent little social satire, as in "Pandora" (1884), where the refreshing innocence, the charming but occasionally alarming naivete of the heroine puzzles the traditional, properly conventional but somewhat stuffy and humorless Count Vogelstein. James uses the point of view of this foreign observer to cast a searching light on Washington society of roughly a cen-

tury ago. The satire cuts (not very deeply) both ways: both Vogelstein and Pandora (and the society which makes her success possible) are its targets. Conversely, our sympathy is drawn to both the
German diplomat and the American "self-made girl." An amusing
tale. But often James's intention was more serious. In "Daisy
Miller" (1879)—to which "Pandora" was a companion-piece—
rather more is at stake than the portrayal of social and cultural
differences: in Daisy's case, the difference in social behavior which
she encounters in Europe virtually kills her. She is not merely an
innocent victim, of course; Winterbourne and Mrs. Walker both
try valiantly and vainly to help Daisy understand her precarious
position. But Daisy remains wilfully ignorant of her offenses
against social decorum and thus in a sense earns her tragic end.

Especially on the large full canvasses of his novels can be seen
the more serious intent in James's handling of the International
Theme. There the subject assumes almost a metaphoric quality, as
James's ultimate concern was less with how society looks and
much more with how man *is*, or ought to be. On this matter Mrs.
Dorothea Krook writes, "James's handling of the international
theme . . . makes it serve the double purpose of every great dramatist: that of a radical criticism of society at the turn of the last
century on the one hand, and, on the other, of a 'criticism of life'
in Matthew Arnold's sense—a radical exposure, sometimes in its
comic aspect, more often in its tragic aspect, of some of the fundamental and permanent predicaments of human life."[6] The American hero, whatever his age, is essentially the new man which the
hero's name in *The American* announces him to be; and if his
America is not, after all, a New World Paradise, he is himself
innately good, good-hearted and well intentioned. Yet he is often
woefully ignorant, or his head is filled with a bizarre system of
values. His confrontation with Europe presents him with the experience which his own fresh young America could not hope to offer
him, experience of a world ages old, heavy with tradition, deeply
knowing, girded by convention—and fraught with evil. The
American hero must face that experience of the Old World, it
would seem, as a necessary step toward real maturity. It is a
dangerous step, of course, and he risks destruction, or at least
corruption. If, however, he can learn to understand the ways of the
world and to evaluate them correctly, if in particular he can learn
to recognize evil for what it is—and in Europe evil is often sugar-

coated with the finest manners and the most proper behavior and the most exquisite taste—then the hero emerges beyond that experience as a better and wiser soul. Even then, however, he often appears to have failed; Newman doesn't get the wife he came for and even tears up his ace in the hole that might have turned the trick against the Bellegardes; Isabel Archer marries the wrong man, and even though she does come to recognize that fact, she seems finally to have nowhere to turn but back to the sorry bed she has made and now must lie in; Lambert Strether fails in his ambassadorial commission and loses even the little he came with —his job in Woollett. Yet each of these representative characters, who have failed in the eyes of the world, has nevertheless succeeded in another sense, each has won a moral (not a Pyrrhic) victory. Those heroes who emerge at the other side of their experience—with heads perhaps bloody, but finally unbowed—have triumphed by remaining faithful to their essential being while learning, however painfully, the ways of the world in which we are all obliged to live. These American heroes, then, are very like the artist-heroes of James: in one sense the "world" has beaten them, for they do not succeed in the terms that the world understands; yet in the other sense they have succeeded admirably by keeping faith with the divinest thing they know—"the conscience that's in us," as Gabriel Nash phrases it, "that charming conversible infinite thing, the intensest thing we know."

In both kinds of story James is preoccupied with man's problem of "how to be," and the answer implicitly offered in the stories is that the solution to the problem does not lie in simply learning a pattern of behavior or conforming to a code of manners: James would reject the Decalogue and ask, like Auden, for an improved *ordre du coeur.* James's regenerate man is free of the law. And what matters supremely is not what he does, but what he is. It would seem that ultimately James's understanding of the term "artist" was very like his father's:

> But now observe that when I speak of the aesthetic man or Artist, I do not mean the man of any specific function, as the poet, painter, or musician. I mean the man of whatsoever function, who in fulfillment of it obeys his own inspiration or taste, uncontrolled either by his physical necessities or his social obligations. He alone is the Artist, whatever be his manifest vocation, whose action obeys his own internal taste or attraction, uncontrolled by necessity or duty. The action

may perfectly consist both with necessity and duty . . . but these must not be its animating principles, or he sinks at once from the Artist into the artisan.[7]

It is almost as though Henry, Sr. had been advocating reliance on "moral spontaneity."

A common complaint of the disgruntled reader who has found James's writing rougher going, more demanding, than he is used to is that his stories seem to have nothing to do with two of the most common "drives" in life—sex and money. It is quite true, of course, that as a general rule James's fiction is not concerned primarily with "jobs," with the business of earning a living, and that he does not spend many words describing people engaged in what he called "the great relation of men and women, the constant world renewal." One gets the impression, so the argument goes, that James's characters are all of independent means and spend long week-ends at country houses—talking. That description might possibly fit *The Sacred Fount* (if Mrs. Brissenden is right about the narrator), but it is quite inadequate to account for anything but the most superficial aspects of his other major novels and some ninety percent of his short fiction. While the hero's "job" may well be scanted (the case of Hyacinth Robinson is something of an exception even to that), the question of the living to be earned is often a principal concern of the novels. Certainly the question is an important one for Roderick Hudson until Rowland Mallett undertakes to become his patron and benefactor; it is important also for Basil Ransom, who must be able to support Verena Tarrant after he has won her—and is even a condition of his earnest pursuit—from the clutches of Olive Chancellor; it is a central issue in the life of Merton Densher, in *The Wings of the Dove;* and it complicates Lambert Strether's decision in *The Ambassadors.*

Money, indeed, plays a central role in James's fiction. A constant theme in his stories is the demonstration of the maxim "the love of money is the root of all evil." Money is a kind of synecdoche: it stands, often, for material goods generally and is thus something of a "natural" symbol. In story after story the evil of the cash nexus for human intercourse is laid bare and searchingly scrutinized. It is at the heart of *The American* in the frustrated

affair of Christopher Newman and the impounded Claire de Cintré; it poisons the relationship of Roderick Hudson and Rowland
Mallett; one is tempted to say that it accounts completely for
Gilbert Osmond in *The Portrait of a Lady;* the purchase of Verena
Tarrant by Olive Chancellor, the use of Milly Theale ("heiress of
all the ages") by Kate Croy and Merton Densher, and the marriages of the Ververs in *The Golden Bowl*—all these exemplify the
evil of cupidity as it makes money the term and the motivation of
human behavior. It is a mistake to say that James considers money
itself to be evil: the possession of money is regularly equated
(naturally enough) with the possession of freedom. The possession
of money, of personal freedom, qualifies one especially well as an
object of desire for the Emotional Cannibals—fair game, as who
should say.

The question of James's treatment of sex is somewhat more
complicated. To begin with, we must consider James's attitude to
the treatment of sex in art. It is well known that he regularly
claimed for the artist complete freedom in the selection of subject,
insisting that our judgment be based on what is made of that
subject, on how well it is handled. If on the one hand he would
complain of the moral timidity of writers in English, he would on
the other caution his French colleagues about the danger of being
preoccupied with "the carnal side of man." In "The Art of Fiction" James says that many have been struck with

> the moral timidity of the usual English novelist; with his (or with her)
> aversion to face the difficulties with which on every side the treatment
> of reality bristles. He is apt to be extremely shy . . . and the sign of
> his work, for the most part, is a cautious silence on certain subjects.
> In the English novel (by which of course I mean the American as well)
> . . . there is a traditional difference between that which people know
> and that which they agree to admit that they know, that which they
> see and that which they speak of, that which they feel to be a part of
> life and that which they allow to enter into literature.

And he wrote in a letter to Howells that the current production
of literature seemed to come from "seamstresses and eunuchs."
Still, he was to express in his essay of 1888 on Maupassant the
directly complementary opinion. "The carnal side of man appears
the most characteristic if you look at it a great deal," he admits;
then he adds, "The more you look at the other, the less the whole
business . . .—the business, as I may say, of the senses, will strike

you as the only typical one." To add to this, we have James's later words of stronger warning, from "The Present Literary Situation in France" (1899); there he reminds us that passion

> lives a great variety of life, burns with other flames and throbs with other obsessions than the sexual. In some of these connections it absolutely *becomes* character; whereas character, on the contrary, encounters in the sexual the particular air, the special erotic fog, that muffles and dampens it.

One reason for James's reticence about "the constant world renewal" is clearly aesthetic—the threat of "the special erotic fog." Nevertheless, sex is seldom far below the surface nor far from the center of James's novels: Roderick Hudson's excursions to Baden-Baden lead him to the den of Venus; *What Maisie Knew* and *The Awkward Age* both depend on a series of adulterous associations for their plot; Kate Croy's surrender to Merton Densher is her means of persuading him to carry out her scheme to procure Milly Theale's millions (and while the act of surrender itself is not specifically treated in the novel, the result of that surrender is quite amply presented in Densher's peculiar consciousness of the atmosphere of his rooms subsequent to that tremendous event); nor can we fail to notice the sexually charged atmosphere of the scenes of intimacy between Amerigo and Charlotte in *The Golden Bowl.* It is not the fact of sex that interested James artistically, but rather the *effect* of that fact on his characters.

The possible objection to James's treatment of the subject of sex is that he almost never considers it as an integral part of human love. *(The Golden Bowl* is a marked exception to this, and will be discussed later.) A latent Puritanism may have been responsible for this aspect of his writing, or a personal distrust of physical involvement. In any case, he was apparently interested in getting a particular dramatic effect from the treatment of sex in his work —in using it effectively for other significance. The fact of sexual possession, of physical possession, may be very well employed to express the "cannibalism" of human relationships. Sex seems to fit into James's peculiar symbology in this way: he was regularly involved in distinguishing between obsession with material values and concern for spiritual values; he often chose, therefore, to express this distinction in terms of an opposition between physical (i.e., sexual) love and spiritual love—the opposition of *eros* and *agape.* Obvious examples of this tactic are to be found in *The Portrait of a Lady*—where the selfless spiritual love of Ralph Touchett is sharply contrasted to the selfish, possessive, and materialistic "love" of Gilbert Osmond (on the one hand) and to the sexually colored offering of both Lord Warburton and especially Caspar Goodwood (on the other)—and in *The Wings of the Dove*, where Merton Densher's alternatives seem ultimately reduced to Kate Croy as representative of purely physical love and Milly Theale as representative of purely spiritual love. It might be pointed out, however, that James has in common with D. H. Lawrence a deep distrust of the love that is possessive, selfish, destructive, and an abiding faith in that love which contributes to the wholeness of the individual: the difference is that "star equilibrium" was differently understood and expressed by the two writers.

It is apparent, in this brief discussion of some of the principal themes of Henry James, that his fiction often exhibits a dialectical nature, that it expresses its main concerns by means of marked antitheses. In his essay on *The Bostonians* (included in this collection), Lionel Trilling makes this observation:

> It may be said of James—with, of course, some risk of excessive simplification—that virtually all his fiction represents the conflict of two principles, of which one is radical, the other conservative. The two principles are constant, although circumstances change their particular manifestations and the relative values which they are to be judged to have. They may be thought of as energy and inertia; or spirit and matter; or spirit and letter; or force and form; or creation and possession; or Libido and Thanatos. In their simpler manifestations the first term of the grandiose duality is generally regarded with unqualified sympathy and is identified with the ideality of youth, or with truth, or with art, or with America; the second term is regarded with hostility and represented as being one with age, or convention, or philistinism, or decadent Europe.

While the observation is, of course, quite sound, one feels that James's fiction tends to be seeking some possible resolution of the conflict—not the triumph of one antithetical element over the other. To put it figuratively, James seems to have been trying to marry his innocent American to his cultivated European, to find for Merton Densher a mate who combines the virtues of both Kate Croy and Milly Theale, or to depict the artist who faithfully pursues his "sacred" vocation yet manages at the same time to *do* what is acceptable in the eyes of the world. Just as we should all probably confess to a preference for "naturalness" over mere good manners, so did James; yet he also recognized the beauty of proper civilized behavior and, indeed, its usefulness to civilization. That one's manners faithfully express one's natural goodness, that one adapt one's moral spontaneity to conventional behavior, would be the ideal resolution—a truly satisfactory marriage of Isabel Archer and Gilbert Osmond. If we feel, as James apparently did, that the "spiritual love" represented by Milly Theale is superior to the merely physical love represented by Kate Croy, we can hardly escape the strong regret that Merton Densher cannot enjoy both kinds of love at once: *must* it be a choice? One of the remakable achievements of *The Golden Bowl* is that it effects, in the marriage of Maggie Verver and Prince Amerigo, the very resolution that much of James's earlier work seems to have been implicitly seeking. This young American marries her European and it is ultimately a successful marriage. The sacrifice here is merely (if one may say that) of one kind of selfishness: there is self-denial, to be sure, but it is quite different from that exhibited by Milly Theale and Ralph Touchett. And Maggie is permitted to enjoy the result of this sacrifice fully in *this* life: she has won Amerigo. Her winning Amerigo does not mean his defeat, but his improvement. The success of this union, furthermore, means also the triumphant fusion of physical and spiritual love. The Principino is then a most significant symbolic character. (The number of infants "visibly" born in James's fiction can probably be counted on the thumb of one hand.) But this point is most persuasively presented by Mrs. Krook in her essay on *The Golden Bowl*, included in this collection.

The Golden Bowl is not therefore to be considered James's one "successful" novel. The dramatic tension of the unresolved antinomies sufficiently accounts for the effectiveness of the other novels; they are concerned with giving artistic definition to certain crucial problems that characterize the human condition—and that is really all we may properly demand from an artist.

These are some of the principal themes of James's works of fiction—the valuable "message" they implicitly carry, the particular vision of truth they artistically offer. The "message" is not especially new, the vision of truth not absolutely peculiar. Yet the

means James has employed to convey these messages of truth—
his artistic achievement—is what makes his work paticularly valuable to us. The form has revitalized the content.

III

In James's writing, his "world view" remains surprisingly constant from the beginning of his career to its end. What he had to
say, he seems to have known from the outset. There are modifications, of course, but no principal changes in the attitudes embodied
in his work. The manner of expressing these attitudes, however,
underwent constant development. The history of James's career is
to a large extent a record of experiment in narrative means, in
literary technique. Anthologies usually couple Henry James and
William Dean Howells as exemplars of American Realism. There
is some justice in that grouping—and certainly not simply because
of the life-long association of the two men. James admired the
masterful realism of Balzac's fiction, and his appreciation of Hawthorne was tempered by the qualification that he was not enough
of a realist. George Eliot's attraction for James is partly explained
by her position as English Realist or Naturalist (Ferdinand
Brunetière's opinion was that Eliot had first raised the flag of
Naturalism in England). Ivan Turgenev, the fourth of his "masters," introduced James to the Flaubert group (Zola, Daudet,
Maupassant, etc.), which he called alternately "the new votaries
of realism," and "the grandsons of Balzac." Early and late James's
criticism sounds a strong note of approval of the "represented
real"; he always cherished the "air of reality" in the fiction he
admired. In his first major essay in criticism, "The Art of Fiction"
(1884), he wrote—

> the importance of exactness, of truth of detail, . . . the air of reality
> (solidity of specification) seems to me to be the supreme virtue of a
> novel—the merit on which all its other merits . . . helplessly and
> submissively depend. If it is not there they are all as nothing, and if
> these be there, they owe their effect to the success with which the
> author has produced the illusion of life. The cultivation of this success,
> the study of this exquisite process, form, to my taste, the beginning
> and end of the art of the novelist.

And in "The New Novel," published just two years before his
death, James mentions the value of "hugging the shore of the

real." He therefore heartily approved of the notebook. He found
the success of the palpable provable world of Balzac and of Zola
to depend upon their accurate note-taking; and he kept a notebook
himself.

Yet James, like Maupassant, would carefully distinguish between *reproduction* and *representation:* he well knew that art must
be mimetic. And his late comments on Balzac and Zola lament the
dependence of those writers on their notes, on their abundance of
factual data: the danger, James saw, lay in the weight of the notes,
in the threatened depression of fact. The novelist must not be
mastered by his notes, for he is to be judged (James rightly felt)
by what he is able to do with them. The artist must travel light if
he is to enjoy real artistic mobility.

James's efforts in his own work were constantly directed toward
producing the illlsion of reality, and his means were not merely
what we usually think of as the Realist's careful notation. His
efforts were guided by James's basic assumption that fiction is
indeed an art, and, therefore, that it should be amenable to those
general laws which govern all art. That assumption specifically
meant, to James, that in addition to the usual considerations of
composition, of proportion and construction, the work of art
should be sufficient in itself—perfect and independent. James's
interest in the dramatic mode of expression, which dated from his
earliest years, had an important influence on his ideas about the
art of fiction. A familiar word of advice that he was constantly
writing to himself was the double-barreled exhortation "Dramatize, dramatize!" which echoes throughout his notebooks. And
this interest in the dramatic is closely associated with his appreciation of Maupassant's achievement in the short story—his ability
to create hard little gems, creations of closely interwoven texture
in which every bit of the machine was devoted to the single business of realizing the story's aim and end. James delighted in their
aspect of "perfection," the uninterrupted surface (the absence
of explanatory comment), which these stories—like the drama—
offered to the audience. The other word of advice which James
frequently penned to himself in his notebooks was "à la Maupassant"—the manner in which he must handle the story in question,
or the particular piece of the novel currently under his hand. The
idea that the work of literary art should seem self-sufficient, perfectly self-reliant and autonomous, and have its own independent

existence, that (in a word) it should seem in no way to rely on the manipulation and support of its author, came more and more to dominate James's aesthetic. Let the writer show us, let him not tell us; that became James's principal imperative.

> We take for granted by the general law of fiction a primary author, take him so much for granted that we forget him in proportion as he works upon us, and that he works upon us most in fact by making us forget him.   ("The New Novel")

He felt strongly that all of the artist's control of the work must be implicit, must be built in as part of the work itself, and must never appear in any other way. The author must not appear to plead for or explain his work: the work must be expressive, not explanatory but self-explanatory. James's view of the writer's relation to his work was a near approximation to that of Flaubert, which found its echo in the aesthetic of Joyce's Stephen Dedalus: the artist must be, in his work, like God in the creation, invisible and all-powerful; let him be felt everywhere, but let him not be seen.[8]

It is certainly true that James is not absent from his stories. He is there, all right, chatting about "our hero" or about "this story"; but his role is usually that of a commentator—almost never that of manager, director, creator. Far from harming the illusion, these intrusions tend rather to increase and strengthen the air of reality of the story, just as Hawthorne's technique of denying his authority for the "wonders" he has to relate in his tales and romances serves to heighten their credibility. Indeed, the very nature of the intrusions emphasizes the commentator's lack of authority and responsibility for what he has to relate. The comments, further-more, usually lack sufficient bias even to qualify as a point of view.

The phrase "point of view" is, of course, a familiar one in the vocabulary used to discuss James's fiction and, indeed, much prose fiction since his time. It is applicable to his work in two ways. In the first place it refers to the handling of a given "germ" for a story, the genial anecdote, as James might call it. His usual practice was to turn the little gem over and about in his palm, considering its various facets, determining which face should be turned to the reader's eye. This is very like the painter's deciding on his "view." We find in the Notebooks ample evidence of James's preliminary handling of a subject to select the point of view from which it should be approached. The second application of the phrase con-cerns the building of the story from the initial germ: once the subject had been properly placed, James would then frame it in the eye of one or more of the characters involved in the story—sometimes simply by means of a first-person narrator. The story is then told or presented to the reader from the "point of view" of those "focussing" characters. Well handled, this technique affords a pair of advantages: it permits the author to remain "in the wings" as the actors in his drama take care of the exposition themselves; further, the point of view expressed may be made to characterize and develop that character whose view of things we are at the moment receiving—a kind of reflexive illumination. The dramatic immediacy achieved by the technique of point of view, James valued highly.

In the Prefaces James wrote for the collected edition (the New York Edition) of his works early in this century, we find much illuminating comment on the technique of point of view. The Preface to *What Maisie Knew*, in particular, is rich in such comment. On his decision to present the whole story from Maisie's point of view, James had this to say:

> The one presented register of the whole complexity would be the play of the child's confused and obscure notation of it, and yet the whole, as I say, should be unmistakably, should be honourably there, seen through the faint intelligence, or at least attested by the imponderable presence, and still advertising its sense.

> I lose myself, truly, in appreciation of my theme on noting what she does by her 'freshness' for appearances in themselves vulgar and empty enough. They become, as she deals with them, the stuff of poetry and tragedy and art; she has simply to wonder, as I say, about them, and they begin to have meanings, aspects, solidities, connexions —connexions with the "universal!"—that they could scarce have hoped for. . . .

The light which Maisie's vision throws on the whole sordid minuet of the Farranges and their various partners is greatly responsible for the "interest" of the story; and of course that light is reflexive and illuminates Maisie quite as much as it does her situation. A different use of point of view is exemplified by *The Awkward Age*. There, instead of a single central intelligence lighting up the goings-on, we have the central subject lighted by a series of circumferent points of view. James described his technical arrangement this way:

I drew on a sheet of paper . . . the neat figure of a circle consisting of a number of small rounds disposed at equal distance about a central object. The central object was my situation, my subject itself, to which the thing would owe its title, and the small rounds represented so many distinct lamps, as I liked to call them, the function of each of which would be to light with all due intensity one of its aspects.

Usually James's use of point of view has something of both of these examples, which is to say that he does not regularly restrict himself to the single view (as in *Maisie)* or employ the series of circumferent illuminators: his most common method is to employ the view of two or three principal characters, and with that, occasionally and briefly, the view of one or other of the minor characters involved. The purpose of this narrative technique was always to help create a work of art that would appear to be independent, self-sufficient, self-expressive, and as dramatically immediate as a play upon the stage, or as life itself.

It is a safe enough generalization to say that all of James's technical devices were aimed at achieving that end of discrete independence for the work of fiction—of cutting the artistic umbilical cord between creator and creature. For if the artist is to abdicate as omniscient and omnipotent controller, he must yet be able to function as the Deistic god. He must make his created machine capable of running itself. He must find the surest means of expressing the values and significance of his work—means that will function in his place. The necessary technical means available to the artist include, of course, devices of imagery and symbolism. These impressionistic devices are not used simply to illuminate a given scene or a particular character: they can assume the burden of expressing the value and significance of the simple plot itself. That expressiveness relieves the author of his traditional task of explaining and evaluating for the reader. But it has another virtue. While the strict Realist might restrain himself to the point of giving merely the factual details of scene or character or situation with quasi-scientific accuracy and objectivity and thus arrive at an approximation of one kind of truth, the impressionistic writer has discovered that he can as well (if not better!) convey the truth of a scene or character or situation by means of impressionistic analogy, through image and symbol. He thus avails himself of the value that oblique metaphoric expression always offers.

James was alive to these advantages and as his career developed he tended to make more and more use of extended metaphor, developed patterns of imagery, and symbolism. A study of James's revisions of his novels and stories as he prepared them for the New York Edition indicates that he picked up undeveloped figures and extended their usefulness, developed them into motifs of expression, removed merely adequate imagery to replace it with images that matched others in the story so as to create a network or pattern of significant imagery.

A frequent motif in James's fiction is the pattern of religious imagery and symbolism. Whatever his attitude to the fine old cathedrals he knew in Europe, James tended to employ the structures and institutions of the Church in his fiction to a great extent for the purpose of emphasizing the evil behavior of his creatures. For example, the convent often appears in the role of prison (or something very like it), most obviously in *The American* and *The Portrait of a Lady*. In order that Claire de Cintré be placed quite definitely beyond the reach of Newman, she is entered into the Carmelite convent, significantly located in the *rue d'Enfer;* and Osmond keeps his daughter Pansy cooped up in a convent to make her behave, until she literally cries "Enough!" In both of these cases, clearly, the convent is used to restrict the natural development of the two girls, as though to symbolize the de-humanizing effect of convention, for in each case the particular threat to the incarcerated character is a suitor who is "unsatisfactory" according to conventional standards. Elsewhere, convent training for young ladies is presented as a singularly inappropriate means of preparing them for life in the world—so inappropriate, in fact, as to qualify the young ladies as vulnerable victims for the various types of cannibals they are soon to meet. ("Madame de Mauves" is one example among many of this use of the convent.) Again the convent symbolizes the pressure of social convention as restrictive of fruitful human life. *The Portrait of a Lady* offers us a good example of extensive use of a pattern of religious imagery; there its purpose is to express the evil that can arise from the institutions and conventions of our civilised world, and thus even the "nun-like forehead" of Lord Warburton's sister serves to express the threat Isabel feels to be lurking behind the offer of marriage into that family. The religious imagery is thus part of the narrative irony.

On the other hand, James often makes use of a pattern of religious imagery to emphasize the high value of dedication to a worthy pursuit—most often in his stories of writers and artists. Religious imagery, indeed, is a regular feature of James's technique of characterization of the artist who is frequently said to be "on the side of the angels," and whose work "addresses itself to the angels" and occasionally affects his sympathetic public as though they had been brushed with an angel's wing. One of James's stories about disappointed artists even announces the angelic motif in its title, "Broken Wings." The hero of *The Tragic Muse*, Nick Dormer, is dissuaded from his political career and urged to follow his artistic bent by the appropriately named Gabriel Nash.

The fact that James uses this kind of imagery to express positively particular values, on the one hand, and ironically to express mistaken devotion to worldliness, materialism, selfishness, on the other, need not lead at all to any confusion of response on the reader's part. The pattern of imagery serves to reinforce the evaluation of behavior already recognizable as praiseworthy (in the one case) or as reprehensible (in the other): the imagery provides emphasis and emotional appeal. One distinction is possible, however: used to underline evil behavior, the imagery tends to be "institutional" and public; used to underline praiseworthy behavior, it tends to be personal and private. One might say that in the former the imagery is rather "high church" or Catholic, and in the latter "low church" or Protestant.

It may be that the best example of James's use of image patterns and extended metaphor as narrative devices is offered by *The Ambassadors*. In that novel, for instance, two closely related motifs persist throughout the narrative—a "portrait" motif and a "theater and drama" motif. Now *The Ambassadors* is much concerned with the distinction between appearance and reality, and Strether's problem in the novel is to learn to make that distinction. His problem is complicated by the dazzling appearance of life in Europe, and even further by his desire to see things as he wants them to be. Thus, his first social experience, dining with Maria Gostrey, presents itself to Strether as a "high picture." This pictorial dinner is followed by an excursion to the theater. There Strether is so taken by the wonderful appearance presented by the figures in the audience that he feels unable to distinguish between "real" life and "represented" life: he confuses the actors on the stage with the people in the boxes and stalls, and is unsure of which is more real. (A further note of interest is that the plot of the play being performed, involving a woman in yellow and a young man in evening dress, casts an oblique but very keen light on the situation in which Strether knows Chad Newsome is involved.) The two motifs are thus initially stated, and as the novel continues they are gradually developed. Their obvious function is, of course, to emphasize Strether's difficulty in seeing what is actually going on. Picture and theater symbolize life artfully but artificially represented—not real life—and therefore these motifs in the novel help us feel that Strether's tendency to see life as picture and drama is a fault of blurred vision.

The motifs are, as I say, part of the narrative technique, but they actually merge with the very subject of the story: Chad and Marie de Vionnet *are* play-acting, of course, and their performance is directed preeminently at Strether. It is designed for his satisfaction. Marie de Vionnet admits the fact openly to Strether late in the novel. Strether himself recognizes that his great enjoyment of the performance put on by Chad and Marie consists in his thus being able to relive vicariously his lost youth: Strether can "identify" completely with the drama he sees. The shock of recognition occurs when Strether detects the smudge of mortality across the surface of his Lambinet—that smudge which is like the blood on Lucy Honeychurch's Italian postcards in E. M. Forster's *A Room With A View*—when he *sees*, at last, that his picture is alive and real and mortal and as capable of sin as human mortals are by very definition.

The important point to notice is the absolute appropriateness of technique to subject in *The Ambassadors*. One can easily understand why James felt this one to be "the best 'all round' of my productions." The story is given to us almost exclusively from Strether's point of view—it frames the story. This is singularly appropriate in that *The Ambassadors* is the story of Strether's late experience of Europe—of the "typical tale of Paris." Furthermore, the point of the story is, as I have said, the difficulty of *seeing* clearly, of distinguishing between appearance and reality in a highly conventional and mannered society. Strether's tendency to see that world as a lovely picture or an artfully acted drama—his point of view—at once illuminates his own romantically inadequate vision (that is, characterizes him) and also ironically illuminates the character of the actors in that drama (ironically, since Strether does not realize that the life he is permitted to see is in fact as artificial as his view of it suggests). Thus the technique of narration is virtually identical with the subject narrated: here is an almost perfect fusion of form and content, of manner and matter.

James had arrived at the perfection I claim for *The Ambassadors* through a series of experiments both with point-of-view and with first-person narration. In such short stories as "The Liar" and the unfamiliar "The Solution," in *What Maisie Knew* (to some extent), and in *The Turn of the Screw* and *The Sacred Fount*, we have examples of what might be called "ironic point-of-view": the controlling focus or central intelligence either knows less than is needed for the conclusions he reaches and the inferences he draws, or simply does not see things clearly and correctly, or both, and is hence bound to be mistaken. This is not to say that the stories I mention are little more than a kind of joke on the central character. There is too much at stake in each one of them, principles too important, for us to dismiss them as mere jokes. It is a case, rather, of exploring the use of the irony of reflexive illumination as a realistic means of characterization: a case of employing the truth that "what Peter says about Paul tells us more about Peter than it does about Paul." What Lambert Strether tells us about Chad and Marie tells us more (ultimately) about him than about them. In a very real sense, the story of *The Ambassadors* is what Strether sees. It is true that the reader can see around Strether, has a clearer (because not romantically and nostagically clouded) view of the goings-on in "Europe" than Strether has. Yet the point of interest from first to last is what Strether will make of the whole situation —or rather what it will make of him. The story is *what Strether sees;* our interest is in *how Strether sees it.* There is but a short step, then, from James's achievement in *The Ambassadors* to the full-blown stream-of-consciousness technique of the modern novel— of, say, Joyce's *Ulysses.* And it is the remarkable technical accomplishments of Henry James that account for his importance in the development of the modern novel, particularly of the *art novel*, as it has come to be called.

One additional comment ought to be made on a feature of James's style that is often considered perplexing and occasionally annoying. We might call it simply the famous Jamesian ambiguity

—a refusal to "say what he means." James's ambiguous style, seen in its full flower in his latest works, is comprised of involved sentence structure, amphibology, and a general tendency to "circle about" the specific subject rather than to put the finger squarely upon it. Even passages of direct discourse can be tantalizingly evasive. Here, for example, is a passage from *The Wings of the Dove*, in which Maud Lowder and Susan Stringham are discussing Milly Theale's illness and possible cure, according to her physician Sir Luke Strett:

"What then is it?"

"It isn't, at least," Mrs. Stringham explained, "the case she believed it to be—though it at any rate *might* be—when, without my knowledge, she went to see him. She went because there was something she was afraid of, and he examined her thoroughly—he has made sure. She's wrong—she hasn't what she thought."

"And what did she think?" Mrs. Lowder demanded.

"He didn't tell me."

"And you didn't ask?"

"I asked nothing," said poor Susie—"I only took what he gave me. He gave me no more than he had to—he was beautiful," she went on. "He *is*, thank God, interested."

"And what is the rest?" Mrs. Lowder asked.

"I don't know. *His* business. He means to keep hold of her."

"Then why do you say it isn't a 'case'? It must be very much of a one."

Everything in Mrs. Stringham confessed to the extent of it. "It's only that it isn't *the* case she herself supposed."

"It's another?"

"It's another."

"Examining her for what she supposed, he finds something else?"

"Something else."

"And what does he find?"

"Ah," Mrs. Stringham cried. "God keep me from knowing!"

"He didn't tell you that?"

But poor Susie had recovered herself. "What I mean is that if it's there I shall know in time. He's considering, but I can trust him for it—because he does, I feel, trust me. He's considering," she repeated.

"He's, in other words, not sure?"

"Well, he's watching. I think that's what he means. She's to get away now, but to get back to him in three months.

"Then I think," said Maud Lowder, "that he oughtn't meanwhile to scare us."

It roused Susie a little, Susie being already enrolled in the great doctor's cause. This came out at least in her glimmer of a reproach. "Does it scare us to enlist us for her happiness?"

Mrs. Lowder was rather stiff for it. "Yes; it scares *me.* I'm always scared—I may call it so—till I understand. What happiness is he talking about?"

Mrs. Stringham at this came straight. "Oh, you know!"

She had really said it so that her friend had to take it; which the latter in fact after a moment, showed herself as having done. A strong light humour in the matter even perhaps suddenly aiding, she met it with a certain accommodation. "Well say one seems to see. The point is—" But, fairly too full now of her question, she dropped.

(Book Seventh, chap. XXII)

Such a style as James's admittedly makes demands on the reader, demands more severe, perhaps, than had ever been made before by the art of fiction. It is a way, however, of engaging the reader—if he will—directly and deeply, implicating him immediately in the problems of the story: he must cooperate and contribute his creative share to the experience the novels offer him. And the rewards are commensurate with the demands, for his experience will be all the richer for the deep involvement required. Furthermore, the reader will discover that the oblique expression, and the resulting ambiguous aspect of the life fictionally presented, is ultimately more satisfactorily faithful to life as he honestly knows it than a clear and unambiguous simplification could possibly be. Life's very perplexing complexity is thus represented in all its richness.

The importance of the significant concerns of James's fiction—the serious themes that characterize his stories—and the importance of his considerable technical achievement in the art of fiction combine to argue for Henry James a most prominent place in the ranks of the writers of fiction in English. He merits our interest and rewards our study. It is with a view to furthering that interest and aiding that study that I have gathered the collection of essays which follow.

LYALL H. POWERS
Ann Arbor, 1970

NOTES

1. *Henry James and the Expanding Horizon* (University of Washington Press 1948), chap. I and passim.
2. *Autobiography of Henry James*, ed. F. W. Dupee (New York 1956), p. 208; cf. L. H. Powers, "Henry James's Antinomies," *University of Toronto Quarterly*, XXXI (January 1962), 125-135.
3. New York Edition, vol. VIII, p. 25.
4. *The Letters of Henry James*, ed. Percy Lubbock (New York 1920), I, 170.
5. "In the Country of the Blue," *Kenyon Review*, V (Autumn 1943), 595.
6. *The Ordeal of Consciousness in Henry James* (Cambridge 1962), p. 10.
7. Henry James, Sr., *Moralism and Christianity*, quoted in Frederick H. Young, *The Philosophy of Henry James, Sr.* (New York 1951), p. 185.
8. "L'artiste doit être, dans son oeuvre, comme Dieu dans la création, invisible et tout-puissant; qu'on le sente partout, mais qu'on ne le voie pas." (Letter to Mlle Leroyer de Chantepie, Paris, 18 March 1875.) Cf. Dedalus: "The artist, like the God of the creation, remains within or behind or beyond or above his handiwork, invisible, refined out of existence, indifferent, paring his fingernails."

RODERICK HUDSON

1876

"James and Arnold: Conscience and Consciousness in a Victorian *Künstlerroman*"

EDWARD ENGELBERG*

In his recent study of the artist-hero in fiction, Maurice Beebe examines the scores of novels in nineteenth-century English fiction which might be considered, even in the remotest way, as dealing with the "Artist-Hero," or simply with artist types.[1] With the exception of Henry James, Beebe's list is unimpressive. Almost all the novels he cites, from Disraeli's *Contarini Fleming* to Thackeray's *The Newcomes*, remain unread today. Not until the turn of the century—and perhaps not really until Joyce's *Portrait*—did the English novel concern itself with the "Artist-Hero"—except, of course, for Henry James. In view of the central place which the *Künstlerproblem* occupied in the German Romantic tradition (Eichendorff, Novalis, Tieck, Hoffmann, not to speak of Goethe) and in mid-century France, this belated interest in the Artist as Hero in English fiction is curious; it may well be due to the traditionally low place assigned to the novel in England, even amongst its own practitioners. Before the ascendancy of Henry James, James Joyce, and Virginia Woolf, who in England would have argued that the novel was as worthy of our serious interest as, say, the drama, the epic, the narrative, or the lyric poem?

*From *Criticism*, X (Spring 1968) 93-114. Reprinted by permission of Wayne State University Press.

[3]

Beebe links the *Künstlerroman* to the *Bildungsroman* (the "Apprentice" novel) and to the "Confessional Novel," forms in which English fiction fares much better, with books like *David Copperfield* as prototypes and progenitors. But I feel that there is a certain blurring in the way these links are established. The *Bildungsroman*, in the German tradition,[2] is almost antithetical to the *Künstlerroman:* from Goethe's *Wilhelm Meister* through Keller's *Grüne Heinrich* to Mann's *Magic Mountain,* the *Bildungsroman* has tended to portray the education of a *would-be* artist, a young man who comes to his senses, ceases to dabble in areas in which he discovers he has no talent, and associates himself with some useful activity in the social community—as surgeon, civil servant, engineer, soldier. This "anti-*Künstlerroman*" was scorned even by some of Goethe's admirers, especially Novalis, who wrote his anti-*Meister* (he considered that book to be a betrayal of Art), *Heinrich von Ofterdingen,* in which Poetry is, as with Shelley, not merely a civilizing force but the very unifying power of the universe, the victor over all positivistic-rationalistic values in a spiritual realm beyond death. Thus, in German fiction at least, there are two opposing artist-themes: stories of young men who renounce their artistic pretensions to become useful members of society and stories of young men who pursue the Ideal of Art, renouncing the "useful" for what they often feel is the truer reality, the "visionary."

Obviously, these distinctions are complex and one can infer endless implications from them. My aim has been merely to place James's first novel (he virtually disowned *Watch and Ward*) *Roderick Hudson,* his *Künstlerroman,* into a context. I feel justified in claiming that, from a modern perspective, James's novel is the first in English fiction to take the "artist's dilemma" seriously, and that in so doing, James prepared the way for a significant progeny. From *The Picture of Dorian Gray* (1891) onwards artists have abounded in English fiction. Throughout this essay I will consider James as an English writer, and while both Poe and Hawthorne are two prominent American writers who dealt with the Artist-Problem, neither sustained a full-scale novel on the theme. Hawthorne's *The Marble Faun* is only incidentally about Art; nevertheless, it is true that American writers, more influenced by Germans like E.T.A. Hoffmann perhaps, took up the Artist as Hero earlier and more frequently than their English cousins.

The "artist's dilemma" in *Roderick Hudson* encompasses the whole debate over the artist and his function from Romanticism to Realism—and beyond. Many Romantics—Shelley, Hugo, Novalis, Wordsworth—had faith that the august Imagination could conquer Life. Such faith became transvaluated so that—as Goethe at times complained—Life was being ignored in the very process of being pursued. The Imagination became an agent not of wider perception but of narrowing containment: it often died for lack of sustenance. When "consciousness" enlarged itself by focusing on a single line of vision (love, hate, pleasure) it also, paradoxically, became exclusive, narrow, obsessive. As many Romantics discovered (and later the Symbolists and Decadents in a different era), Imagination cannot sustain itself on itself: it needs to be stimulated from without, freely and—as Nietzsche finally warned—guiltlessly.

I

Roderick Hudson begins his artistic career with vast, abstract conceptions, with the help of which he does some very fine work. But conceptions soon cease to stimulate, and Roderick turns to Life, to experience, for his "ideas." But between Roderick and Life there appear a number of formidable obstacles and his struggles to overcome these result in the familiar curve of Romantic genius: decline, dissipation, despair, a state in which Imagination is totally disabled. It appears that Roderick's pursuit of ideals in fleshly form is the prime cause of his demise, but James, both in his Preface to the New York Edition and in his revisions, makes clear that this is too simple a view of the matter. The Romantic's urge for vague and infinite abstractions; the Realist's awareness that such a course is futile; and the artist's struggle to resolve this impasse: these are all carefully delineated in the novel. What makes *Roderick Hudson* a special "case" is not the treatment of a Romantic artist who fails (romantically), but the special conflict leading to that failure, both within and without the hero. Most commentators blame this collapse on the enchanting but fatal charms of Christina Light, with whom Roderick falls in love, and almost all of these—including Beebe—champion Rowland over Roderick, see Christina Light as a *femme fatale*, and sum up the theme of the novel as a kind of object-lesson about "a romantic artist, divided between sex and art."³ However, in his own Introduction to the New York Edition, James cautions against such a view: "Everything occurs . . . too punctually and moves too fast," and "the determinant function attributed to Christina Light, the character of well-nigh sole agent of [Roderick's] catastrophe that this unfortunate young woman has forced upon her, fails to commend itself to our sense of truth and proportion."⁴ Still, Roderick Hudson is a failure: he is a man caught in the encirclement of a very un-Hegelian dialectic; thesis and antithesis produce no synthesis, only pain, suffering, and finally death.

One way to describe this dialectic is Romanticism *versus* Realism. Certainly the consistent change of a word like "picturesque" (in the early versions) to the word "romantic" for the 1907 New York Edition provides some evidence for James's apparent desire to underscore the novel's involvement in Romanticism, particularly as James saw the book retrospectively.⁵ Another possible approach to the dialectic of the novel is the strongly suggested Faustian theme: defiant action and defiant despair. A year before writing *Roderick Hudson*, James reviewed a French translation of *Faust.*⁶ Several indirect and direct allusions to *Faust* found their way into the novel: the young man who sculpts a Water-Drinker called "Thirst"—for "knowledge," he says; the betrayal of the fiancée; the pursuit of Ideal Beauty in a woman; the Baden-Baden episode, even the final thunderstorm, a kind of *Walpurgisnacht.* There are references to the sculptor Gloriani as resembling Mephisto and to the black poodle in Goethe's *Faust.* All these allusions, however, do not add up, except in a general way. Indeed, Roderick is less a Goethean Faust and more a Byronic Manfred, whom Gérard de Nerval called the "personification of remorse." As a variation of the Faust-Manfred theme, Roderick may be seen as suffering from an Imagination too quickly spent, for, like Coleridge's, Roderick's decline of genius is not merely a dissipation of character but a paralysis of creativity: "My mind is like a dead calm in the tropics, and my imagination as motionless as the blighted ship in the 'Ancient Mariner!' " (231). Here in his dejection Roderick echoes Coleridge:

> *But oh! each visitation*
> *Suspends what nature gave me at my birth,*
> *My shaping spirit of Imagination . . .*

But there is yet another, and a far more explicit set of terms to describe Roderick's dialectic, for the terms are James's own as he undoubtedly took them from Matthew Arnold: Hebraism (conscience) *versus* Hellenism (consciousness). From this dialectic there can never result any synthesis, only mutual annihilation.

II

In Chapter VI of *Roderick Hudson* James describes an elaborate party of artists and friends who have come to be guests at Roderick's debut as a sculptor. They are rewarded with life-sized statues of Adam and Eve and with a confident and ebullient young genius. It is Roderick's high point (a figure of speech that fits in several ways). On this occasion he announces a creed which to any English reader would undoubtedly have been a topical allusion: ". . . I'm a Hellenist; I'm not a Hebraist!" (115). That James was here alluding to Arnold's famous distinction is almost certain, although James reinterprets Arnold's terms and applies them to serve his own purposes. Encouraged by Henry James Sr., James had from early youth been a sympathetic reader of Arnold. We also have evidence that in the year *Culture and Anarchy* (which contains the section on "Hebraism and Hellenism") was published in book form, 1869, James was in London, where he probably first heard of the new book, then the talk of the hour: it was his "thrilling opportunity to sit one morning, beside Mrs. Charles Norton's tea-urn . . . opposite to Frederic Harrison, eminent to [him] at the moment as one of the subjects of Matthew Arnold's early fine banter. . . ."[7] James's first review of Arnold (the *Essays in Criticism*, First Series) was published in the *North-American Review*, July, 1865. In his biography of James, Leon Edel records a meeting between James and Arnold in 1873. Though the personal confrontation was a disappointment (due apparently to the "little glass [Arnold] screws into one eye"), Edel stresses the intellectual kinship between the two men. He also records a letter from Arnold to James in 1879, congratulating James on the achievement of *Roderick Hudson*. Clearly, Arnold was an early, strong influence, and, I should think, a permanent one.[8]

For Arnold, Hebraism and Hellenism were the anti-poles of Western history: "doing" and "thinking," "energy" and "intelligence." "The uppermost idea with Hellenism is to see things as they really are; the uppermost idea with Hebraism is conduct and obedience." What characterizes the spirit of Hellenism is *"spontaneity of consciousness";* what characterizes Hebraism is *"strictness of conscience."* The ideal of Hellenism is the perception of Beauty, but its attainment is impeded by a Hebraistic sense of sin, an obstacle which Arnold noted was greatly strengthened during the Puritan reactions against the excesses and moral deficiencies of the Renaissance. Although neither Roderick Hudson nor his patron, Rowland Mallet, perfectly fits one or the other of Arnold's principles, each behaves according to certain basic patterns which a knowledge of Arnold's dualism helps to illuminate. Rowland, by and large, is a Puritan, a man long habituated to "conscience" of the kind Arnold meant by "Hebraism"; Roderick is largely a creature of consciousness, and his own aesthetic aims toward the perfection of Ideal Beauty identify him as something of an Arnoldian Hellenist. (It is true that Roderick's Hellenism is very Romantic and less "classical" than Arnold's, and that unlike Shelley, whom Trelawney took to see the dirty Grecian ships, Roderick never discovers that Hellenism can be Hell.) These distinctions are not, of course, rigid in the novel, and the complexities of character and story happily prevent one from forcing an almost allegorical interpretation on the book. Still, in that very complexity James seems to have caught the duality of the problem with a very firm grip: the century was, after all, characterized by a mixture of inclinations between Hebraism and Hellenism. Goethe, Schiller, Wordsworth, Shelley, Carlyle, Hopkins, Ruskin, Nietzsche, Tolstoy, and, indeed, Arnold and James—were they not all (sometimes alternately) moral aesthetes or aesthetic moralists?

From the first pages of the novel, James makes us aware of Rowland Mallet's conflict between his Puritan heritage and his acquired taste for a form of irresponsible dilettantism: "[Europe is] always lotus-eating" (7). Rowland had a "lively suspicion of his [own] uselessness," which coincides with his cousin Cecilia's suggestion that there may be some positive harm in a man who is *not* doing some "positive good" (2-3). This inner state of disaffection puts Rowland on the track of some "errand"—something to *do:* and in his "frequent fits of melancholy," he declared that he was "neither fish nor flesh . . . neither an irresponsibly contemplative nature nor a sturdily practical one. . . ." Indeed, the two impulses divide him to make an "awkward mixture of moral and

aesthetic curiosity," and Rowland can obtain "happiness" only in
one of two directions: "either in action of some thoroughly keen
kind in behalf of an idea, or in producing a masterpiece in one of
the arts" (16). Since he confesses himself as being incapable of
achieving either, being "a man of genius half-finished" with "the
faculty of expression . . . wanting," but "the need of expression"
remaining, the reader is very early alerted to Rowland's fate,
which Rowland himself predicts: to "spend [his] days groping for
the latch of a closed door" [8] (like Morris Townsend in *Washington Square*). For all his knowledge of the arts and his immersion
in the "antique" world, Rowland's conception of the artist—which
is central to the shaping of Roderick's fate—is a "strong conviction that the artist is better for leading a quiet life," a philosophy
which he promises to "preach to [his] gifted pupil [Roderick Hud-
son]" (49). The artist, then, must *do:* what is to feed the imagination toward execution is a question that does not exist for
Rowland; or, to put it more positively, any contact with Life as a
source of stimulation will, in Rowland's view, merely contaminate
the artist.

Rowland's sole prescription for artistic success is Work:
"You've only to work hard," he tells Roderick before they set sail
for Europe (37); and, much later, after a stormy scene during
which Roderick pleads the special case of genius, Rowland's only
response is: "tumble to work somehow . . ." (232). Rowland even
advises Roderick to continue working on commissions which now
revolt the artist, for virtue lies in the act, in "the resolution *not* to
chuck [it]," in making "the effort necessary at least for finishing
[the] job," after which one is free to destroy it, the moral fiber
having been tested by chafing it against the grain (305). When
Roderick's collapse is imminent and he pleads for Rowland's companionship, the latter offers to bargain his affection on familiar
terms: "If I go with you, will you try to work?" To this he gets a
bitter reply: " 'Try to work!' [Roderick] cried, 'Try—try! work—
work! . . . Do you suppose I'm trying *not* to work?' " (441). James
may very well have been divided on the question himself: all artists
have found, sometimes to their bitter dismay, that work is an
inseparable adjunct to creativity. Nor am I suggesting that, in the
special case of this novel, Rowland's advice was always and altogether wrong. But James also courts sympathy for the artist's
desperate need to rejuvenate himself, an activity of "play" and

"purposelessness" (using Kantian terms) with which Rowland's "Work" has little in common. The somewhat sudden decline of Roderick's creative productivity, James shows very clearly, is not due to a lack of work—as Rowland repeatedly thinks.

The chronology of the story is here very important. Despite Rowland's repeated insinuations that it was Christina Light whose fatal charms paralyzed Roderick's genius, events do not bear this out. After the initital vision of Christina ("Immortal powers . . . what a vision!" [95]), before he even knows her name, follows a great and happy period of inspiration and a good deal to show for it, namely the Adam and Eve. The dissipation of Roderick's powers begins almost immediately after his great success and *before* he meets Christina Light again. The fact is that Christina, when she becomes "involved" with Roderick, acts as a potential stimulant for his imagination, not as a deterrent; and what leads Roderick to the escapade in Baden-Baden is the weight of "conscience," the claustrophobic pressures of "creating" in a dingy Roman studio, where his imagination feels—as well it might—imprisoned. The later appearance of Christina is truly a "light" in contrast to the darkness of the studio which has made the young genius as impatient as it had Goethe's Faust in his solitary study, *"unruhig auf seinem Sessel am Pulte."*

At the party where Roderick displays his life-sized Adam and Eve, proclaiming himself a "Hellenist," there is one man who understands Roderick's plight—his aesthetic opponent, the sculptor Gloriani. These first fruits of Roderick's Hellenism are admired by the young, seasoned Italian, but he is also sardonic: is the young man to proceed "straight through the Bible" now that he has begun with the Creation? Roderick replies that he does not care for "Old Testament people," though he concedes he may make a David, treat it "as a young Greek," Roderick stressing that his interests lie with the "Christian, or still better the pagan, form" (a sentiment James added in the revision of 1907). From David, "a beautiful runner at the Olympic games," Roderick intends to go forward and create a "ripping Christ," not a Christ of tradition but "More idealistic! . . . The perfection of form . . . to symbolise the perfection of spirit." Will there be a Judas? He is being teased. "Never! I mean never to make anything ugly, and I'm a Hellenist . . ." (114-115).

Such a notion of Greek sculpture had its historic anchoring, and evidently James was not unaware of it: to counter Roderick's Hellenism he creates Gloriani, strictly a Realist, both as a man and an artist. By the time James wrote *Roderick Hudson*, the conception of Greek sclupture was an old matter of dispute, but still a lively one. Winckelmann had established a view of Greek art that radpidly spread from the continent to England and stubbornly prevailed for better than a century. Greek art was ideal, circumventing the realistic and incidental; it was the product, not of imitation but of the artist's grand conceptualization, the contemplation of a sort of divine essence, the result of which was abstract form. No Greek could bring his noble soul to create anything ugly (though Lessing had vigorously disputed this in the *Laocöon*), and Beauty, based on the ethical conception of nobility, was the chief aim of the artist. This was the Romantic Hellenism which held sway through the time of Pater, who celebrated Winckelmann in his famous essay in *The Renaissance*. Pater undoubtedly understood Hellenism better than did Roderick Hudson, who thinks he will yet concede once more beyond the David to the Old Testament and make a Cain, though not ugly, but a "handsome fellow . . . lift[ing] up the murderous club with the beautiful movement of the fighters in the Greek friezes . . ." (115). Evidently Roderick is reluctant to surrender the Old Testament; but what is interesting is his notion that he can transform his Hebraic subjects into Hellenistic ideals: it is a conflict which appears unresolved within himself. And Adam, Eve, Cain, and David are a mixed company, topped by a Christ; as if he were intent on working his way through innocence, the fall, and ultimate redemption.[9]

Gloriani warns Roderick against "trying to be Greek" (115) and encourages the suggestion of a Judas, to which Roderick answers, in the revision, that such a figure might have "a great deal of character" but not of the sort he cares for: "I care only for beauty of Type" (116). Roderick complains that his contemporaries have forsaken the "beauty in the large ideal way," and that he means to restore it, to "go in for big things; that's my notion of my art. I mean to do things that will be simple and sublime" (116), an unconscious echo perhaps of Winckelmann's famous phrase about Greek sculpture—"noble simplicity and calm grandeur." For the 1907 revision James puts into Roderick's mouth a pure late Jamesian language to propose what the young sculptor means to do: "I want to thrill you, with my cold marble, when you look. I want to

produce the sacred terror. . . ." This remark is uncharitably received by his guests; after all, the Greeks had their belief in the
gods. But Rome today, where "we sit talking nineteenth-century
English[?]" "Mr. Hudson," ventures one guest, "may be a new
Phidias, but Venus and Juno—that's you [referring to another
guest] and I—arrived to-day in a very dirty cab; and were cheated
by the driver too" (117).

Against the Idealistic Roderick, James marshalls all the resources of the New Realism (including cynicism), embodying
them in a point of view which admires the naiveté and spontaneity
of a nineteenth-century Hellenistic Imagination, while recognizing all the inherent weaknesses and dangers of an epigone. When
Rowland asks Gloriani to judge a photograph of the "Water
Drinker," an early piece done in Northampton, the experienced
sculptor admires but issues a warning that Roderick won't be able
to keep up this sort of thing; to which Roderick replies that he
won't merely keep it up but do even better. Gloriani's answer is
straight to the point:

> "You'll do worse. You'll do it on purpose. This thing wasn't done on
> purpose. It couldn't have been. You'll have at any rate to take to
> violence, to contortions, to romanticism, in self-defence. Your beauty,
> as you call it, is the effort of a man to quit the earth by flapping his
> arms very hard. He may jump about or stand on tiptoe, but he can't
> do more. Here you jump about very gracefully, I admit; but you can't
> fly; there's no use trying." (119)

It takes only a week for Gloriani's prophecy to come true;
Roderick suddenly becomes restless and he ceases to work. Here
occurs the interlude at Baden-Baden (Roderick is reluctantly
released by Rowland to make the trip himself and James never
reports what happens except indirectly). When he returns he
seems to have forgotten all his grand abstractions—Hebrew,
Christian, Pagan. Instead he sculpts "a woman leaning lazily back
in her chair, with her head inclined in apparent attention, a vague
smile on her lips and a pair of remarkably beautiful arms folded
in her lap." Rowland "was not sure he liked it" because it "differed
singularly from anything his friend had yet done" (143). But
Gloriani likes this "Lady conversing affably with a Gentleman,"
admires it, is happy that Roderick is "coming round": had he not
prophesized he "couldn't keep up that flapping of his wings in the

blue, and . . . [would have to] come down to earth" (146)? Rowland
remains unconvinced; he does not like this fruit of experience at
Baden-Baden. "That's because you yourself try to sit like an angel
on a cloud," replies Gloriani; "This . . . is full of possibilities, and
he'll pull some of them off; but it isn't the *sancta simplicitas* of
a few months ago. . . . I congratulate him on having found his
feet . . ." (147). Baden-Baden, then, has not been merely an episode
of debauchery, nor has it led to declining creative powers. On the
contrary, experience with Life has put to rest some of Roderick's
grandiose Abstractions ("I mean to do the Morning . . . Night
. . . Ocean . . . Mountains . . . Moon . . . West Wind" [118]), and
it has inspired a new inventiveness and a new Art.

It is true that Roderick himself is moodily unhappy about his
work: the newly acquired art is too close to the art Gloriani has
championed and Roderick had scoffed at. The "reclining lady"
Roderick finds "curiously, almost interestingly bad," "false from
the first," having "fundamental vices." The trouble appears to be
not so much the art but the manner of sustaining it. "I haven't a
blamed idea. I think of subjects, but they remain idiotic names.
They're mere words—they're not images" (149).

Words, not images: Roderick has not yet learned the fundamental lesson of the artist as James conceived it, that abstractions need
to be embodied in concretions which are in turn rooted in reality.
The Word is never equal to the Image. James by no means under-
stimated the value of "ideas" in Art, saying in his *Notebooks* that
"one does nothing in art or literature unless one has some general
ideas. . . ."[10] But even the "idea"—which Roderick invokes as if
it alone would have him—is insufficient. Moments after his moody
disapproval of himself, his failure to make words into images,
Christina Light enters his life for a second time. This time she is
no vision; nor is she an idea, nor an image—she is flesh and blood,
a human being.

It should be no surprise that Roderick immediately wishes to
sculpt Christina Light, for her idea and image are rooted in a real
person. "Didn't you hear him?" Christina asks Rowland:
"Mademoiselle, you almost come up to one of my dreams. . . . That
almost should be rewarded" (168). And that *almost* would have
been impossible prior to Baden-Baden; that *almost* is testimony to
a changing aesthetic, one which produces finally a bust of Christina which has neither the pure naiveté of the earlier work nor the

apparent vulgarity which Roderick suspected in the too noncha-
lant work of the reclining lady. Christina's bust "was thoroughly
a portrait,—not a vague fantasy executed on a graceful theme. . . .
The resemblance was close and firm; inch matched with inch, item
with item, grain with grain, yet all to fresh creation" (182). Like the
novelist James describes in *The Art of Fiction*, Roderick had succeeded at the great task of art; he had "converted . . . ideas into
a concrete image and produced a reality," without sacrificing either conception or "exactness . . . truth of detail," which James
never meant, in his own words, to "minimize."

This is the young artist's moment of crisis; the transition from
abstraction to concretion marks a crucial advance in both the man
and the artist. While it might be misleading to claim that Christina
Light has caused this momentous change, it is quite accurate to say
that she has at least served as its instrument. Beyond this point
Roderick does not develop, partly because he himself resists, but
mostly because Rowland, among others, prevents him. Much
later, far into his decline, he speaks again in St. Peter's of "grand
form," sublimity, "magnificent forms" (337), and still later,
"Before Michael Angelo's statues and pictures of the early Tus-
cans [he picks up] the thread of his old love of ideas" (445-446).
What happens to Roderick between the momentary triumph of
creating Christina Light's bust and his regression to *thinking* of
Abstractions comprises the "reversal" of the novel, the conflict
between Hebraism and Hellenism, Conscience and Consciousness.

III

Although Rowland has an "uncomfortably sensitive conscience" (1), his consciousness is another matter; we must not
confound, as he does, a Hebraistic sense of sin with a Hellenistic
capacity to see the object as it really is. Rowland is a connoisseur,
that is all; and even in this role his Puritan taste remains an
unconscious censor. He tells his cousin Cecilia that to care for
something or someone is now his only aim, for as a man he is
totally insufficient: his search is for love. James allows Rowland to
fall in love (in the Jamesian manner) with Roderick's American
fiancée at the very start of the novel, yet he proceeds to have

Rowland remove not only the future bridegroom but himself. While the young James might well have been struggling with plot and structure, there is already the self-punitive economics as well as the punishment-of-others at work in his character of Rowland. Eventually it is Roderick, not Mary Garland, who becomes the object of Rowland's love (a prefiguring of a theme taken up by James in many later stories). Rowland's relationship to Roderick is essentially that of the former being nourished by the latter; as "experience" it is surrogate, or, in the phrase of Osborne Andreas (though not in relation to this novel), a form of "emotional cannibalism." Andreas perceives that "The conclusion in James's stories of emotional cannibalism is that inevitable defeat lies in wait for him who seeks to procure from other people that strength which can only come from within"; "to make . . . use of other people is to consume them, and both the user and the used, the consumer and the consumed, are depleted by it." (Andreas inexplicably ignores *Roderick Hudson* as a prime instance of this Jamesian theme.)[11]

In fairness, Rowland does not undertake his mission of "educating" Roderick lightheartedly: "when he reflected that he was really meddling . . . he gasped, amazed at his temerity" (67). Yet this very sense of responsibility nails down his relationship to Roderick with ambiguously gained rights. "If anything happens to you I'm accountable," and he speaks deep from his "moral passion"; for Roderick it feels like the boot upon his chest: "That's a view . . . I can't accept. . . . I know all I owe you. . . . But I'm not a small boy . . . and whatever I do I do with my eyes open. When I do well the merit's my own; if I do ill the fault's my own" (220). Rowland is bitter at such a declaration of independence: "If I hadn't been meddlesome I should never have cared a fig for you" (220) he reasons, to which Roderick, after some pause, gives his most articulate reply:

> "I think when you expect a man to produce beautiful and wonderful works of art you ought to allow him a certain freedom of action . . . to give him a long rope . . . to let him follow his fancy and look for his material wherever he thinks he may find it. . . . An artist can't bring his visions to maturity unless he has a certain experience. You demand of us to be imaginative, and you deny us the things that feed the imagination. . . . When you've an artist to deal with you must take him

as he is, good and bad together. . . ; if you want them to produce you must let them conceive. If you want a bird to sing you mustn't cover up its cage." (224).

When it is the artist's turn to reproach his sponsor, he asks bitterly: "What am I . . . but a desperate experiment?" (231). The word "desperate" James added in the 1907 revision perhaps to balance the characteristic noun of the century—experiment—with an adjectival corrective from the world of feeling (Hawthorne had written a score of stories about "desperate experiments"). Roderick prepares his brief against the future with a typically Romantic weaponry: "Do I more or less idiotically succeed—do I more or less sublimely fail? I seem to myself to be the last circumstance it depends on" (231). The Romantic hero invariably feels that "circumstance" is his greatest enemy, and he himself the least effective of circumstances. Although only ten pages earlier Roderick had in effect accepted the responsibility for success or failure, he now implies that *Zeitgeist* will play the ultimate role in his fate.

In making of Roderick a self-conscious Romantic increasingly aware that he is an anachronism presiding over his own extinction, James has opened the question of free will, essential in the case of the artist who must decide whether he can triumph over such preying monsters as Ennui, one thoroughly catalogued and described by a variety of nineteenth century writers.[12]

"Live!" It was the great cry of the century; and the clutching to the bosom of Time, the Keatsian fear of the temporal, gives way —must give way (even in Keats), for the sake of survival, to the "breathing human passion . . . / . . . heart high-sorrowful and cloy'd,/ A burning forehead, and a parching tongue," or to "The weariness, the fever, and the fret." It gives way to the even greater fear of a paralysis of the Imagination itself. The Romantics were not always morbidly anxious to die—that has been in part the romanticizing of Romanticism; the Romantic often wished very much to live, if he could find terms adequate enough to appropriate experience as a successive number of terminations and reimmersions, not merely a long straight path toward longevity itself. "Our physical life is a perpetual motion": and within that motion Pater sought to find the fixity of ceaselessness, the paradox of Zeno's arrow transferred from physics to metaphysics: "experience seems to bury us under a flood of external objects, pressing upon us with a sharp and importunate reality. . . ." To relieve the pressure, to make the "reality" bearable, we must corner the moment—not, indeed, as Pater's young readers appeared to have thought, in order to indulge our senses for the sake of a fleeting pleasure; but, quite the opposite, the moment would be arrested and enriched to combat and outmaneuver static reality, which seemed so insistently to front itself as a finite goal toward which the earnest travel and at which the wise arrive. Zeno's arrow was the issue: "How shall we pass most swiftly from point to point, and be present always at the focus where the greatest number of vital forces unite in their purest energy?" That is, how shall we *survive* the many deaths of aliveness we must live through? It was a paradox: "expanding [the] interval," answers Pater, is "our one chance," and the metaphor itself is painfully self-contradictory. If there was a false way of life for Pater it was surely the way of *fleeting* emotions, moments devoured for transitory pleasures; to expand the interval was merely to recognize that Time was also Space. But free will would need to assert itself if one wanted to "live."

James did not, I think, quite realize the issue in this way, for his complaint that Roderick collapses too fast betrays a measure of naiveté about Time as it relates to the subject he treated: the life and death of an artist. Yet James sufficiently recognized the necessity to expand the interval; for James "Live!" was to mean finally the art of living not measured temporally, by duration, but spatially, by the capaciousness with which the educated sensibility could take measure of the life before it. If Roderick Hudson goes to death too rapidly, Lambert Strether in *The Ambassadors* comes to life even more rapidly—but there is no record of James's complaint on that score. For James "consciousness" seems almost always *intended* at least as the liberated state; yet in this novel, as elsewhere, it is clear that consciousness, in the end, can be a dangerous, even barren, condition. In spite of James's insistence on living to one's greatest capacity, few of his heroes, even when they achieve such desired awareness, are permitted to enjoy the fruits of their struggle. From Roderick and Rowland to Isabel Archer, from Strether to the Ververs, conscience prevents, thwarts, aborts: renunciation is James's ultimate virtue, but it is an expense of spirit, a waste, a highly questionable triumph at best.

Some critics see *Roderick Hudson* as a fictionalized biographical novel in which James erects a "split personality" structure. James is here regarded as questioning his own future as an artist, Roderick and Rowland representing two parts of himself: the straying artist, who becomes ensnared by vulgar Life and the Conscience which attempts to prevent this by emphasizing the dedication to Art required of the genuine Artist.[13]

But the renunciation of the artist in *Roderick Hudson* is not, as has so often been suggested, Roderick's fickleness toward the Muse and his involvement in a hopeless love affair. Like so many nineteenth-century heroes, Roderick is fatherless, and his mother, weak in character, possessive, desperate to preserve herself, joins with the now discarded fiancée and the disenchanted patron to unman the young sculptor. For James makes it rather clear that Roderick—though he may have all the predisposition for it—is, ultimately unmanned. Toward the end of the novel, in a move of questionable motives, Rowland brings mother and fiancée to "rescue" the failing son and bridegroom-to-be. In his pursuit of the beautiful Christina Light, Roderick is thwarted by the young lady's mother, the disowned father, and Rowland himself. Moody, inert, at times full of heat and passion, Roderick rather rapidly (as James noted) falls apart. When the mother and Mary Garland arrive, the young man submits, though here and there are occasional rebellions, furtive, instinctual—the instinct in the wriggling butterfly pinned live against the collector's velvet. Mrs. Hudson has always demanded that Roderick deliver to her an emotional response worth two sons—one for himself and one for the favorite, lost in the Civil War. "I have to fill a double place," Roderick tells Rowland; "I have to be my brother as well as myself. . . . I must be to her everything that he would have been" (41-42). Under such a burden, Roderick buckles, and he reverts, in classic fashion, to childhood: "He said little. . . . [but] he clearly liked again, almost as he had liked it as a boy, in convalescence from measles, to lounge away the hours in an air so charged with feminine service" (353).

In submitting—in renouncing—Roderick is by no means unaware of the tightening cords. His mother's effect upon him is silently absorbed, and he attempts to propitiate her by "doing" her bust, as if it were an act of exorcism. But Mary's effect (and Rowland's) is felt and expressed—far more strongly in the 1907 revision, James accenting the "cannibalism" theme in human relationships which he had by 1907 so thoroughly explored: "She thinks all the world of me," Roderick says of his American fiancée; "She likes me as if I were good to eat. She's saving me up, canni-bal-fashion, as if I were a big feast" (356). The cannibalism meta-phor clarifies what James must have felt, in revising, was the true meaning of the story of his *Künstlerroman:* prevented from using Life as experience for Art, the artist will be devoured by Life. Feelings of helplessness, excessive self-pity, regressive and petu-lant moods, passion and quiescence alternating—all are symptoms of Romantic Genius whose consciousness of Life has brought him not freedom but imprisonment. Certainly Roderick still belongs in the tradition of Werther: the gesture toward sublimity, the empty response, the paralysis of imagination, the tendency to self-drama-tize, the fears of a devouring world, and the final plunge into the abyss (which incidentally Roderick takes during the inevitable Alpine thunderstorm, rejecting Werther's more orderly suicide by revolver). The end of the novel moves swiftly toward the dénoue-ment.

During the last interview between Roderick and Rowland the pains of the sufferer—that final mark of the sensitized aesthete—are fully bared: Rowland confesses his love for Mary Garland, prompted by Roderick's final bitter outburst aginst his patron. Roderick has asked Rowland for money to follow Christina to Interlaken, but this suddenly strikes his heart with revulsion, the economic aspect of his relationship to Rowland (a theme James was to explore many times in later works) mirroring itself in the most vulgar images, translating itself from the currency of coin to the currency of emotions and spiritual loans:

> ". . . what I resent is that the range of your vision should pretend to be the limit of my action. You can't feel for me nor judge for me, and there are certain things you know nothing about. I have suffered, sir. . . . I've suffered damnable torments. Have I been such a placid, contented, comfortable creature these last six months that when I find a chance to forget my misery I should take such pains not to profit by it? You ask too much . . . for a man who himself has no occasion to play the hero. I don't say that invidiously; it's your disposition, and you can't help it. But decidedly there are certain things you know nothing about." (504).

This attack against Rowland—and those against Mary Garland—is strengthened in the 1907 revision, where Mary herself blames Rowland for having in part destroyed her lover. When it becomes clear that Roderick will not return from the night of the storm,

"Mary stood there at first without a word, only looking hard at [Rowland]" (517)—a hard look she does not give in the earlier versions. Hebraism, too, James seems to have felt, needed its atonement. And if Hellenism failed Roderick, he dies like a hero, imperfect but admirable. There is a suggestion of the Icarus myth in the circumstances and descriptions of Roderick's death, a myth so thoroughly Romantic but already foreshadowing a more famous portrait of the artist. In any case, in James's *Künstlerroman* the artist is a victim.

Alone amidst the stony Alps the morning after the storm, Rowland searches for his lost friend. "The silence everywhere was horrible; it mocked at his impatience, it was charged with cruelty and danger. In the midst of it . . . sat a hideous *crétin* who grinned at him over a vast goitre. . . ." Looking down into the "ugly chasms" below, Rowland "was to consider afterwards, uneasily, how little he had heeded his foothold." Rowland's sense of guilt works hard upon his imagination: with a bright sun penetrating the "depths and heights" of a lonely and "stony Alpine void" Rowland feels "sick to his innermost soul" (522). Finally, in a gorge, he and a friend find "a vague white mass" but James almost ritualistically avoids gory details. This Icarus "had fallen from a great height, but he was singularly little disfigured. The rain had spent its torrents upon him, and his clothes and hair were as wet as if the billows of the ocean had flung him upon the strand" (523-524).

Though attacked by some as melodrama,[14] the final pages of this novel, seen in the perspective I have tried to place them, reinforce the elegiac note of the last Romantic's death and the survivor's guilt for his victim. Again James added sentences for the 1907 edition to strengthen Rowland's guilty conscience as an instrument of Roderick's death. Alone, waiting for the stretcher-bearers to take Roderick to the village, Rowland feels at the very least an actor in a tragedy of Fate:

> The great gaunt wicked cliff above them became almost company to him, as the chance-saved photograph of a murderer might become for a shipwrecked castaway a link with civilisation: it had but done its part too, and what were they both, in their stupidity, he and it, but dumb agents of fate? (525)

Of the surrogate nature in his relationship to Roderick, Rowland is now aware, for he now "understood how up to the brim, for two

years, his personal world had been filled [with Roderick]." This
world now comes to a close in the appropriate metaphor of the
stage (added for the 1907 edition), for the world seems to Rowland
now "as void and blank and sinister as a theatre bankrupt and
closed" (526).

Rowland had predicted he would spend his life "groping for the
latch of a closed door," and so he shall. His "patience" (back in
America) is that of endurance and penitence, not of hope; and
James could not resist sanctifying Roderick's memory by adding
a final sentence in the 1907 revision: "And then [Rowland] talks
to [cousin Cecilia] of Roderick, of whose history she never wearies
and whom he never elsewhere names" (527). Thus Rowland continues to live a surrogate life; his fate was to have failed in sustaining himself, even through others. In spite of vast economic
advantages he is driven to seek domination over another: it is a
sinister parable in nineteenth-century literature, and James was
not alone in being fascinated by it. When the patron becomes the
conscience of his protégé's consciousness, neither can prevail.

IV

The aim of this essay has not been to explicate James's novel for
its own sake, but, quite frankly, to use it illustratively as an exem-
plum of late Victorian ambiguity about Romanticism fictionalized
in the first serious *Künstlerroman* in English. Part of the Victorian
ambiguity about Romanticism was, of course, the ability of the
Victorians to talk with two voices. Their pursuit of Beauty was
fraught with a pervasive Conscience; their Palace of Art was a
consciously perilous place for any prolonged sojourn. To cultivate
Art with a Conscience can lead to more serious problems than to
cultivate it without one. Just before embarking for Rome, Roderick, intoxicated by the thought of his liberation from New England, sings a snatch from Tennyson's *The Princess:*

> The splendour falls on castle walls
> And snowy summits old in story . . .

The snowy summits are prophetic, but James does not quote the
refrain: "Blow, bugle; answer echoes, dying, dying, dying."

Hebraism and Hellenism, Conscience and Consciousness, play
a central role in the lives of countless nineteenth-century heroes

and their authors. As consciousness is permitted to expand, experience often corrupts it (Rowland Mallet's fears are not entirely unfounded); then conscience, or guilt, begins to destroy from within and from without. The Romantics never fully resolved this problem—how to allow a receptive consciousness to lead to fruitful experience and free will (many of Ibsen's early plays are variations on this particular theme, especially of course *Peer Gynt* and *Brand*). Schopenhauer's blind and malign Will (though often misunderstood) was ubiquitous, haunting scores of heroes in fiction and drama and turning them into helpless victims. It was not until 1887 that Nietzsche struck out in *The Genealogy of Morals*, attacking the whole Judaic-Christian system of "guilt" and "conscience." Throughout the nineteenth century the Faustian urge to "experience" seems converted (or perverted) into the compulsive urge to repent (even as Faust himself repents). Something holds back; something negates what is being affirmed: from *Werther* to the last of the Buddenbrooks the theme of Conscience *versus* Consciousness is a source of art itself.

I began this essay by drawing some distinctions between the *Bildungsroman* and the *Künstlerroman*, the novel in which the hero is often educated *away from* Art and the novel in which the hero reaches the Kingdom of Art through a renunciation of the everyday world. I have also suggested from the outset that *Roderick Hudson*, as a *Künstlerroman*, is deeply concerned with the problem of the Artist's Imagination and its susceptibility (in the Romantic tradition) to becoming sterile or crippled. This theme of the vulnerable Imagination James treated largely, I think, by adapting Arnold's distinctions between Hebraism and Hellenism, for here he seemed to have found the perfect dialectic for describing his hero's conflict. As a late Romantic, an epigone, Roderick is already overtaken by a new art and a new time, a situation that makes Roderick's struggle to reach a compromise with Reality pathetic and futile. Hebraism—work, conscience, renunciation—served James perfectly in fashioning his Puritan Hebraist, Rowland; while Hellenism, freedom, spontaneity, the free pursuit of Beauty created the perfect foil in drawing the portrait of his artist-hero.

The "situation" of the novel—something James was interested in creating with extreme care even as early as his first serious novel—was therefore well set. Roderick, the artist with talent and Imagination, would be unable to resolve what had become for a Romantic sensibility an unresolvable conflict: how to permit Consciousness to have a fruitful traffic with Life. But to make the issue less predictable, James introduced Rowland, who acts the role of censorious Conscience. Of one thing James seems certain: from the perspective of Victorian England, the Artist who is indecisively caught between Life and the Studio, between Spontaneity and Work, walks a precarious tightrope which by 1875 he can no longer hope to negotiate safely. Hence Roderick declines, not because he is ensnared by a *femme fatale*, not because he is corrupted by too much experience, but because he is stranded in Limbo: stimulated neither by Life nor by Imagination. Undoubtedly James envisioned the Artist as one who must be close to Life without being corrupted by its vulgarities and sufficiently dedicated to the Muse without becoming lost in the misty regions of unattainable Abstractions. In *The Art of Fiction* James wrote: "All life belongs to you [the novice novelist], and do not listen either to those who would shut you up into corners of it and tell you that it is only here and there that art inhabits, or to those who would persuade you that this heavenly messenger wings her way outside of life altogether, breathing a superfine air, and turning her head from the truth of things."

James was a Romantic Pragmatist, something which Roderick tries but fails to become. What finally frustrates Roderick is not only Rowland, the Puritan Hebraist (his alter-Conscience), but his illusory belief that the Artist's Consciousness can go slumming and then return to its rarefied Heaven. Clearly once the Artist has had true intercourse with Life he has fallen and no return to innocence is possible. To see the object as it is requires, at least for the Artist, a seeking out, a process of "doing." Thus, whether or not he intended it, James's novel is a critique of Arnold's distinctions, for implicitly James insists that the Artist cannot survive them.

Arnold's opposition between Hebraism and Hellenism, Conscience and Consciousness, was well-intentioned; and it served for a time as a useful historical paradigm that highlighted the negative of a striving society too dedicated to the virtues of a materialistic "doing." Yet he was perhaps too optimistic in thinking that he might divide and conquer a habit which he had recognized and berated in the Romantics even before he saw and feared the worst in the conduct of his contemporaries. For between "Knowing" and "Doing" there can never be a true choice, only a continual oscillation.[15] Doing, when translated to the life of an Artist, must always precede Knowing or Being (Arnold was no Existentialist);[16] and the road to Hellenism leads from the Imagination to Baden-Baden, to Christina Light, to Life and Experience. Like Emerson's, Arnold's moral vision was sometimes misleading and incomplete; in separating Hebraism from Hellenism, Doing from Knowing, Conscience from Consciousness, he perhaps ultimately rendered a disservice to the culture of his day.[17] When Hamlet says that "Conscience doth make cowards of us all" he does not mean a "bad conscience" but "Consciousness." These two words, which the nineteenth century separated, had in Shakespeare's day basically the same meaning: "knowledge within oneself." Such courage to behold oneself is neither Doing nor Knowing but both.[18] A good deal of agony has been expended in returning to that identity of meaning, and we are not yet arrived.[19]

NOTES

1 Maurice Beebe, *Ivory Towers and Sacred Founts: The Artist as Hero in Fiction from Goethe to James Joyce* (New York, 1964). In his section on the English "apprentice" novel (pp. 79-100), Beebe draws upon Susanne Howe's *Wilhelm Meister and his English Kinsmen: Apprentices to Life* (New York, 1930). Beebe's title refers to the "divided Self" of the Artist who chooses either the Sacred Fount, art as "essentially a re-creation of experience," or the Ivory Tower, the tradition which "insists that the artist can make use of life only if he stands aloof" (p. 13). In general, this distinction applies to *Roderick Hudson* (though Beebe does not treat this novel from that perspective); using terms taken from James's novel (derived from Arnold), I develop a different point of view.

2 Beebe's study is surprisingly scant in dealing with nineteenth-century German writers. With the exception of *Werther* and *Wilhelm Meisters Lehrjahre*, the *Künstlerproblem* in German literature is all but ignored. E.T.A. Hoffmann's many tales about Art and Artists are not even mentioned.

3 Oscar Cargill, *The Novels of Henry James* (New York, 1961), p. 29. Cargill offers the best review of opinions on *Roderick Hudson*, pp. 19-40. In his Introduction to the Harper Torchbook edition of *Roderick Hudson* (New

York, 1960), Leon Edel writes that ". . . James [is] concerned with sex. . . . Roderick allows his terrible passion to destroy his art" (p. vii). However, in his biography of James (*Henry James, The Conquest of London, 1870-1881* [Philadelphia and New York, 1962], pp. 175-180), Edel modifies this view, insisting that a mere art-sex conflict ignores "the complexity of the story fabric . . ." (p. 175).

4 The New York Edition of *The Novels and Tales of Henry James* (New York, 1907-1909), I, XIX-XX. All references are to this edition. *Roderick Hudson* was published in 1907.

5 The present essay is not concerned with the textual problems of James's revisions. James first serialized the novel in *The Atlantic Monthly* (1875), first published it as a book in 1876, and then revised the novel for subsequent editions in 1879, 1882, and, of course, the New York Edition, 1907-1909. See Hélène Harvitt, "How Henry James Revised *Roderick Hudson;* A Study in Style," *PMLA*, XXXIX (1924), 203-227 (a very unenlightening study); Raymond D. Havens, "The Revision of *Roderick Hudson,*" *PMLA*, XL (1924), 433-434 (a correction of some errors in the Harvitt essay). The issue has again gained currency because F.R. Leavis quoted in *The Great Tradition* excerpts from the New York Edition that aimed to show the young Henry James's stylistic talents. See J.C. Maxwell, *Durham University Journal,* XXIII (1961-1962), 79-80, and Bruce Harkness, "Bibliography and the Novelistic Fallacy," *Studies in Bibliography,* XII (Charlottesville, 1959), 59-60. Harkness quotes Gordon N. Ray, who attackes Leavis, in "The Importance of Original Editions," in *Nineteenth-Century English Books* (1952).

6 "Dumas Fils and Goethe," *The Nation* (October, 1873), reprinted in *Literary Reviews and Essays,* ed. Albert Mordell (New York, 1957), pp. 110-118.

7 Henry James, *Autobiography,* ed. F. W. Dupee (New York, 1956), p. 562 and Notes, p. 609.

8 "In Matthew Arnold the young Henry James had found an intellectual kinsman. . . ," Edel, *The Conquest of London,* p. 123. The entire episode of the meeting between James and Arnold is described on pp. 122-125. The reference to Arnold's letter is on p. 394.

9 F. O. Matthiessen sees Roderick's productions as "an allegory of the life of an artist," in "James and the Plastic Arts," *Kenyon Review,* V (Autumn, 1943), 537.

10 *The Notebooks of Henry James,* ed. F. O. Matthiessen and Kenneth B. Murdock (New York, 1955), p. 69.

11 Osborne Andreas, *Henry James and the Expanding Horizon* (Seattle, 1948), p. 53; see also William H. Gass, "The High Brutality of Good Intentions," *Accent* (Winger, 1958), p. 67; Cargill p. 26, Note 32; p. 37; p. 31.

12 The question of "free will"—or the lack of it—is interestingly explored by Viola R. Dunbar, "The Problem in *Roderick Hudson,*" *MLN,* LXVII (February, 1952), 109-113. However, she tends to place all the blame for failure on

Roderick's passivity, not taking into account Rowland's role in the novel. In his final revision, James made changes which show that he wished to distribute blame among Roderick, Rowland, and Fate as well.

13 Supporters of the "split personality" approach include Cornelia P. Kelley, *The Early Development of Henry James* (Urbana, 1930); Stephen Spender, "The School of Experience in the Early Novels," *Hound and Horn*, VII (April-June, 1934), 420 ff; Leon Edel, Introduction to *Roderick Hudson* (Harper Torchbooks), p. xiii, and *The Conquest of London*, pp. 177-178; and Maxwell Geismar, *Henry James and the Jacobites* (Boston, 1963), p. 20. Undoubtedly the novel is autobiographical, but Roderick and Rowland, when put together, do not add up to Henry James.

14 For Example, Cargill, p. 36.

15 James was all his life writing about artists. The standard discussion of this theme is F. O. Matthiessen's Introduction to *Stories of Artists and Writers*, New Directions (n.d.), pp. 1-17. Lyall H. Powers has written several fine studies on the "artist-theme" in James: "Henry James and the Ethics of the Artist: 'The Real Thing' and 'The Liar,' " *University of Texas Studies in Literature and Language*, III (Autumn, 1961), 360-368, and especially "Henry James's Antinomies," *UTQ*, XXXI (January, 1962), 125-135.

16 See William Barrett, *Irrational Man: A Study in Existential Philosophy* (New York, 1958, 1962), pp. 69-71, for an interesting account of how Arnold fits into the general "Existentialist" situation of our time.

17 To be fair to Arnold, he makes it clear that he conceives of Hebraism and Hellenism dialectically; that both philosophies have as their aim "man's perfection or salvation," and that after a suitable period of Hellenism, he would fully expect Hebraism to return as the corrective swing of the pendulum. But for his time he wanted Hellenism and, in the tradition of Goethe, a Hellenism both guiltless and free, yet full of "order" and "authority."

18 In a section on Zola entitled "Conscience and Consciousness" appearing in *The Gates of Horn: A Study of Five French Realists* (New York, 1963), Harry Levin points out the "interrelated meanings" in the French *conscience*, signifying both "moral compunction" (as in English) or simply consciousness in the broader sense. Of course, only one word in French—*conscience*—covers both meanings (p. 371). In Italian as well as in Spanish Conscience and Consciousness may also be used interchangeably: *coscienza* and *conciencia* respectively. (See, for example, the title of Italo Svevo's novel *La Coscienza di Zeno*.) In German, however, there are distinctions though the words are cognate: we have *Gewissen* (conscience), *wissen* (to know), and *Bewusstsein* (consciousness). Significantly, then, in later English and in German, where the language clearly provides two words, two concepts as well have been developed (illustrated best by Arnold and Nietzsche).

19 On the ubiquitous New England Conscience, Austin Warren remains the expert analyst: especially relevant is his essay "The New England Conscience,

Henry James, and Ambassador Strether," *Minnesota Review*, II (Winter, 1962), 149-166. Seeing *The Ambassadors* as a *Bildungsroman* (p. 158), Warren feels it was James's intent to educate Strether's conscience, to make his story "the development of conscience into consciousness . . ." (p. 157). As I have suggested throughout, it is precisely this New England Conscience which so interestingly parallels Arnold's conception of "Hebraism."

THE AMERICAN

1877

"The American"

CONSTANCE ROURKE*

The Civil War has been considered a prime destructive agent in the life of the nation, warping or even destroying a native culture. But the literature of the '50's had never been truly complete. Uncalculating digressions might have followed even though there had been no catastrophe. In spite of the disruption of the War a determined experiment continued through the '60's, '70's, and '80's. The international scene became a great American scene, even in a sense *the* great American scene.

Few ideas had disturbed the American mind more than those which had to do with the European relationship. In the '60's the early commentaries of European travelers still rankled: Tuckerman gathered them into a compendious volume, with rejoinders. But the old fable had undergone a change. In its last notable version, *Our American Cousin*, the nationalistic hero had exhibited his character and enjoyed his adventures in England, and possessed an English heritage. He was in fact one of those "dispossessed princes and wandering heirs" of whom Henry James was to write. In spite of the burlesque the gesture of disseverance had grown less positive in Mark Twain's long skits. The American went abroad, often to stay; sentiment overspread his return to "our old home," and that preoccupation with art which had been satirized in *Innocents Abroad* became one of his larger preoccupations.

This was mixed with a consideration which had long since been

*From AMERICAN HUMOR by Constance Rourke, copyright 1931 by Harcourt, Brace & World; renewed 1959 by Alice D. Fore. Reprinted by permission of the publishers.

borne in upon the American mind by British criticisms. Culture was an obvious proof of leisure, of long establishment, of half a hundred desirable assurances that had been lacking in American life; it even seemed to resolve the vexing problem of manners. Culture was sought abroad as a tangible emblem. The resultant "pillage of the past" was to amount to monstrous proportions, and to include the play of many unworthy instincts—ostentation, boredom, a morbid inversion of personal desires; often, no doubt, it represented a natural response to the fine accumulations of time. Yet surely on the wide scale it was something more than these. Fumbling and fantastic, the restless habit seemed an effort to find an established tradition, with the solidity, assurance, and justification which traditions may bring. The American wish for establishment had often seemed a fundamental wish, with all the upheaval.

Many Americans continued to make the extravagant denials of *Innocents Abroad,* but the exodus was unbroken, and found an interpreter in Henry James. His talk of "dispossessed princes and wandering heirs" was not without a personal connotation. As a young man, considering Europe, he had wondered how he was to come into his "own." "The nostalgic poison had been distilled for him," he declared, speaking of himself. James became indeed, as Van Wyck Brooks has said, "an immortal symbol." Strangely enough in this connection, he was something more: an American artist who worked within native sequence.

Henry James has been pictured as a troubled evasionist without a country; and the charge has been turned to a militant charge against American civilization. Yet this theory can hardly account for the long engagement of a major talent. Such talent usually has only one great subject; the choice of that subject will be instinctive, resting upon innumerable elements of heritage and of intimate experience. The consciousness of the European relationship had been binding in America. Given favoring observation, some considerable artist was bound to use the international scene and to find its richest content.

But even a major talent will need the impetus which may come from other imaginative approaches. As formal literary expression of the time is scanned nothing arises to account for the scope and intention of James. He had none of those slightly inferior forerunners in his own medium by which the great writer is often heralded. He wrote as from a fresh impulse; yet the way for his achievement had been opened by a popular vanguard with whose efforts he had some contact. As a small boy he frequented Barnum's, where the Yankee farces were often performed, where the whole American legend was racily sketched, with the backwoodsman and the minstrel as occasional figures, and with melodrama well to the fore. *Our American Cousin* achieved its first great success when James was a lad of fifteen; the play created an immense volume of talk, and was continued for many years. During James's boyhood the streets of New York were alive with the color of the California adventure, with its outlining of the composite American character.

Somewhere James has spoken of the novelist's aptitude for judging the whole piece by a small bit of pattern.[1] Such hints as those abroad in New York during the '50's could go far with a sensitive young mind like his; and others existed to complement them, in the London magazines read before the fire in the New York house, in the visits of Thackeray there, in the glimpses of the great foreign world afforded by the constant voyaging of the family to Europe. James never lost the sense of romance with which his youthful apprehensions of Europe were tinged. He was to write of the European scene with warmth and luster and enchantment; even his dull passages have their inner glow. But he began on humble, even primitive ground in his consideration of the American character as this appeared within the European scene; and he kept throughout his life convictions which he must have drawn from the fund of a common native experience.

2

James was bent upon a purpose that had absorbed many American fabulists, that of drawing the large, the generic, American character. Deliberately, it seems, he abandoned the portrayal of local figures, though for this he had a singular genius: in regions familiar to him he caught the local speech, the manner, the inevitable effect of background. Barring the characters in *The Europeans* and *The Bostonians* and a scattering few elsewhere, his Americans are nomadic and rootless; even when they are seen on American soil they belong to no special locality; they are the composite type; the broad lineaments are unmistakable. He wrote of an American "confidence that broke down . . . a freedom that pulled up nowhere

... an idyllic ease that was somehow too ordered for a primitive social consciousness and too innocent for a developed." In drawing Roderick Hudson, with his "instinctive quickness of observation and his free appropriation of whatever might serve his purpose," James seemed to have in mind something more than a character: his young sculptor becomes a national type. "His appetite for novelty was insatiable, and for everything characteristically foreign, as it presented itself, he had an extravagant greeting; but in half an hour the novelty had faded, he had guessed the secret, he had plucked out the heart of the mystery, and was clamoring for a keener sensation. . . . The boy was living too fast . . . and giving alarming pledges of ennui in his later years. . . ."

James was candid, as the early fabulists had been candid. He wrote of Americans who treated Europe "collectively, as a vast painted and gilded holiday toy, serving its purpose on the spot, but to be relinquished, sacrificed, broken and cast away, at the dawn of any other convenience." Using the familiar symbolism of the comic name, he pictured the conquering Mrs. Headway, who by a gross energy and with impenetrable surfaces achieved an external European triumph.

He pictured Mr. Leavenworth, "a tall, expansive, bland gentleman, with a carefully brushed whisker and a spacious, fair, well-favored face, which seemed somehow to have more room in it than was occupied by a smile of superior benevolence, so that (with his smooth white forehead) it bore a resemblance to a large parlor with a very florid carpet but no pictures on the walls." Mr. Leavenworth was in fact the pretentious consummation of a dominating American idea. "You may be sure that I have employed a native architect for the large residential structure that I am erecting on the banks of the Ohio," he said to Roderick Hudson. "In a tasteful home, surrounded by the memorials of my wanderings, I hope to recover my moral tone. I ordered in Paris the complete appurtenances of a dining-room. Do you think you could do something for my library? It is to be filled with well selected authors, and I think a pure white image in this style"—he pointed to one of Roderick's statues—"standing out against the morocco and gilt, would have a noble effect. The subject I have already fixed upon. I desire an allegorical representation of Culture. Do you think now," Mr. Leavenworth inquired, "you could rise to the conception?"

These questing Americans—James showed some of them full of an eager pathos, others as indifferent and lost, moving about the world for lack of another occupation. He made an inclusion that went far beyond the efforts of any American before his time, except that of Hawthorne in *The Scarlet Letter.* He drew American women at full length. With the exception of Christopher Newman and Roderick Hudson and a few others the most significant of James's characters are women: it is they who engage in disastrous encounters abroad, they who embody diverse and contradictory American elements. Isabel Archer, Milly Theale, Mary Garland —their number could be extended: their close and delicate portraiture seemed James's greatest preoccupation. Some of his lesser feminine figures reveal hardy American habits; it is they who most often indulge in the monologue. "I don't apologize, Lord Lambeth," said Mrs. Westgate; "some Americans are always apologizing; you must have noticed that. We've the reputation of always boasting and 'blowing' and waving the American flag: but I must say that what strikes me is that we're perpetually making excuses and trying to smooth things over. The American flag has quite gone out of fashion; it's very carefully folded up, like a tablecloth the worse for wear. Why should we apologize? The English never apologize—do they? No, I must say *I* never apologize. You must take us as we come—with all our imperfections on our heads. Of course we haven't your country life and your old ruins and your great estates and all that. . . ." On she went at immense length, this pretty lady, then and later, "with a mild merciless monotony, a paucity of intonation, an impartial flatness that suggested a flowery mead scrupulously 'done over' by a steam roller that had reduced its texture to that of a drawing-room carpet."

The true heroines of James usually possess a bias of temperament which had appeared more than once in the fable of the contrast and casually elsewhere: Poe had stressed it. "Morella's erudition was profound." "I have spoken of the learning of Ligeia: it was immense—such as I have never known in women." The shadow is not deep in James's novels, but it exists. Mrs. Westgate's sister was little Bessie Alden, a great reader, who united native inquisitiveness with a sturdy integrity. There was Mary Garland, a prim and pretty bluestocking. The young women in *The Europeans*—the true Americans—appear against a background of high thinking; and those in *The Bostonians* form a galaxy absorbed in esoteric knowledge. When these women are not directly absorbed in books they are likely to fulfill the general intention by a definite leaning toward the arts: Isabel Archer walked blindly to her fate because of her belief in the fine accumulations of time. Occasionally James pictured the child of nature—fully feminine at last—as in Daisy Miller or Pandora Day, thus following another tradition; but in the main the women with whom he was most deeply engaged took the aloof, the conscious, the slightly studious part.

Portrait after portrait becomes clear in the great range of his novels and short stories. An entire gallery of characters is created to which Americans may well turn for knowledge and social experience and enlargement, or even for a sense of renewal. They are more than types: they are a whole society of typical individuals: they appear with narrow aggressions and an insular nobility, a careless honesty, a large and delicate purpose. Their ambitions are often blind, or have grown hard and unerring. This society of migratory Americans was a provincial society, transcending provincialism only by fine character. Race, history, even a sense of the future, is upon these people; they still remain singularly inclusive. They offer indeed a legible critique of the American character for those who care to read it; and in the end they reveal more than one unmistakable bias which had appeared in earlier years.

The wilderness and the farm had gone: only their faint traces were discernible in these narratives. James noted in Mr. Westgate a face of toil, a voice of leisure; he remarked a peculiar blankness on the faces of older women who may have belonged to a pioneer society. But for the most part the level has changed; these are people of leisure; they are distinctly urban. The range was wide, the innovation profound; the accomplishment of James, who began to write soon after the Civil War, seems little short of miraculous when set against the spare and simple portraiture of earlier years. Yet his illumination of the American character may have grown bright and deep because he possessed the momentum which a tradition may give. He was grounded in the Yankee fable; his basic apprehension of the American character was that which had been drawn there. He was acutely sensitive to foreign criticism, as a long line of popular writers had been before him.

"It was not in the least of American barbarism that she was afraid," he wrote of Lady Barberina. "Her dread was all of American civilization." The satirical recognition included the familiar foreign charge. In *Pandora's Box*[2] the German envoy was on his way "to explore a society abounding in comic aspects"—an American society comic to the European. Repeatedly James set the wickedness or subtlety or deceit of Europeans against American innocence. The contrast is clear in the small encounters of *Four Meetings;* it lies at the basis of *An International Episode;* it is dramatically posed, with all the implications of a wounding British scorn, in *The Modern Warning.* Even such fine characters as Kate Croy and Merton Densher reveal an ancestral blackness, against which is drawn the touching and exquisite nobility of Milly Theale, an American.

In later years James denied that the innocent Americans in *The Wings of the Dove* and *The Golden Bowl* were exhibited as Americans; yet the contrast remains. James never presented its opposite terms with imaginative force; and the pattern was repeated too often to be anything but the outgrowth of a profound conviction. He was captivated by the vision of American innocence. In *The Europeans* the American characters appear as the very perfection of a delicate and straitened purity—those indigenous Americans who were being contrasted with vagrant others born and bred in Europe. They were "charming," these true characters, as Felix said, "in a style of their own. How shall I describe it? It's primitive; it's patriarchal; it's the *ton* of the golden age." In one of his later prefaces James wrote with an almost hysterical emphasis of "the comparative *state of innocence* of my country folk."

Truly enough, this preoccupation may have been strengthened by influences outside the old view. The endowment of innocence for heroes and heroines alike had been present in the English novels of his period in a fanciful extreme, and it was not unnatural for the son of the elder Henry James to be concerned with moral and ethereal qualities. Truly enough too, his portrayals often reach far beyond simple effects of contrast and comprise a revelation of moral beauty transcending national considerations altogether; and the pattern was often broken by gross contradictions and incongruities. Yet innocence as drawn by Henry James remains rooted in an established idea. In *The American* he wrote the complete fable, with an altered ending.

3

Even the title was a fulfillment. Who ever heard of a significant English novel called *The Englishman* or an excellent French novel called *Le Français?* The simple and aggressive stress belonged to an imagination perennially engaged by the problem of the national type. The name Newman had significance, faintly partaking of that comic symbolism by which a hero in one of the Yankee fables was called Jedidiah Homebred.

At the opening of the story, as Newman strolled through the Salon Carré examining masterpieces, James declared that no one with an eye for types could have failed to perceive that he was an American. "Indeed such an observer might have made an ironic point of the almost ideal completeness with which he filled out the mold of race. . . . He had the flat jaw and firm, dry neck which are frequent in the American type. . . . Long, lean, and muscular, he suggested an intensity of unconscious resistance. . . . His usual attitude and carriage had a liberal looseness; but when, under a special intensity of inspiration, he straightened himself, he looked like a grenadier on parade." Newman was of the familiar build; he had the familiar consciousness of costume; in an ensuing scene he appeared in a blue satin cravat of too light a shade and with a shirt front obtrusively wide. But according to James it was the eye, of a clear cold gray, that told the final story: "an eye in which the unacquainted and the expert were singularly blended"—the innocent and the shrewd. "I can't make you out," said Mrs. Tristram, "whether you are very simple or very deep."

Newman's local origin was never given; though he stemmed from the Yankee, he was not of New England, certainly not of Boston. The Pacific Coast had been the scene of his financial successes; and these were fixed as occurring before 1868, that is, during the period of the gold rush. He might have been in San Francisco or Virginia City with Mark Twain; he had habits of the time and place. "He had sat with western humorists in circles around cast-iron stoves and had seen tall stories grow taller without toppling over, and his imagination had learnt the trick of building straight and high." Young Madame de Bellegarde said that if she had not known who Newman was she could have taken him for a duke—an American duke, the Duke of California. "The way you cover ground!" said Valentin de Bellegarde. "However,

being as you are a giant, you move naturally in seven league boots
. . . . You're a man of the world to a livelier tune than ours."

Fabulous stories were told about Newman. At the great ball
given by the Bellegardes he was presented to the Duchess, whose
nodding tiara and triple chins and vast expanse of bosom troubled
him, and who looked at him "with eyes that twinkled like a pair
of polished pin-heads in a cushion." "With her little circle of
admirers this remarkable woman reminded him of a Fat Lady at
a fair." "I've heard all sorts of extraordinary things about you," she
said, fixing her small unwinking gaze upon him. "*Voyons*, are they
true? . . . Oh, you've had your *légende*. You've had a career of the
most chequered, the most *bizarre*. What's that about your having
founded a city some ten years ago in the great West, a city which
contains today half a million inhabitants? Isn't it half a million,
messieurs? You're exclusive proprietor of the wonderful place and
are consequently fabulously rich, and you'd be richer still if you
didn't grant lands and houses free of rent to all newcomers who'll
pledge themselves to smoke cigars. At this game, in three years,
we're told, you're going to become President of all the Americas."

"He liked doing things that involved his paying for people," said
James; "the vulgar truth is he enjoyed 'treating' them. . . . Just as
it was a gratification to him to be nobly dressed, just so it was a
private satisfaction (for he kept the full flavor of it quite delicately
to himself) to see people occupied and amused at his pecuniary
expense and by his profuse interposition. To set a large body of
them in motion and transport them to a distance, to have special
conveyances, to charter railway-carriages and steamboats, harmo-
nized with his relish for bold processes and made hospitality the
potent thing it should be."

Newman preserved a negligent air in such enterprises just as he
casually gave an order for copies of half a dozen masterpieces to
Mademoiselle Noémie in order to provide money for her *dot*. But
he clearly saw the direction of Mademoiselle Noémie's purpose
when she announced to him that her paintings were daubs in the
hope that her candor might bring her a more considerable profit.
He passed over her declaration with his customary blankness,
dropping into some hidden cavern of his mind the revelation that
his taste had been at fault. "You've got something it worries me
to have missed," said Valentin. "It's not money, it's not even
brains, though evidently yours have been excellent for your pur-

pose. It's not your superfluous stature, though I should have rather liked to be a couple of inches taller. It's a sort of air you have of being imperturbably, being irremovably and indestructibly (that's the thing) at home in the world. When I was a boy my father assured me it was by just such an air that people recognized a Bellegarde. He called my attention to it. He didn't advise me to cultivate it; he said that as we grew up it always came of itself . . . . But you who, as I understand it, have made and sold articles of vulgar household use—you strike me—in a fashion of your own, as a man who stands about at his ease and looks straight over ever so many high walls. I seem to see you move everywhere like a big stockholder on his favorite railroad. You make me feel awfully my want of shares. And yet the world used to be supposed to be ours. What is it I miss?''

Newman's reply was resounding, and might have been taken out of many an American oration of the past. "It's the proud consciousness of honest toil, of having produced something yourself that somebody has been willing to pay for—since that's the definite measure.Since you speak of my washtubs—which were lovely —isn't it just they and their loveliness that make up my good conscience?''

"Oh, no; I've seen men who had gone beyond washtubs, who had made mountains of soap, in great bars; and they've left me perfectly cold."

"Then it's just the regular treat of being an American citizen," said Newman. "That sets a man right up."

The tone, as one knows Newman, was jocose, with an admixture of serious conviction. It was the comic belligerent tone that had spread through the assertive nationalism of the Yankee fables; and James seemed to enjoy the mixed quality. He glossed over nothing, writing with gusto of Newman's early preoccupation with money, which had also been dominant in Yankee swapping and bargaining. He admitted that his hero considered "what he had been placed in the world for was . . . simply to gouge a fortune, the bigger the better, out of its hard material. This idea completely filled his horizon and contented his imagination. Upon the uses of money, upon what one might do with a life into which one had succeeded in injecting the golden stream, he had up to the eve of his fortieth year very scantly reflected."

"I cared for money-making, but I have never cared so very

terribly about money," Newman told Madame de Cintré with expansive confidence, launching into self-revelation. As he sat in her drawing-room he stretched his legs; his questions had a simple ease. "Don't you find it rather lifeless here," he inquired, "so far from the street?" "Your house is tremendously old then?" he asked a little later. When Valentin had found the date, 1627, over the mantlepiece, Newman announced roundly, "Your house is of a very fine style of architecture." "Are you interested in questions of architecture?" asked Valentin. "Well, I took the trouble this summer to examine—as well as I can calculate—some four hundred and seventy churches. Do you call that interested?" "Perhaps you're interested in religion," answered his host. Newman considered for a moment. "Not actively." He spoke as though it were a railroad or a mine; and he seemed quickly to feel the apparent lack of nicety. To correct this he turned to Madame de Cintré and asked whether she was a Roman Catholic.

Satire invaded the portrait—a deep satire—but James loved Newman. Toward the end of his life he spoke of his young "infatuation" with his subject, and though by this he particularly meant an artistic absorption, his personal devotion was likewise plain. He revealed his hero as a man whom Madame de Cintré could love—that creature "tall, slim, imposing, gentle, half *grande dame* and half an angel; a mixture of 'type' and simplicity, of the eagle and the dove." It was Newman's goodness which drew her; but this alone would not have sufficed for the daughter of an old race if goodness had not been joined with an essential dignity.

But while Madame de Cintré and Valentin perceived the genuine stature of Newman others of his family remembered their prejudices. When Madame de Bellegarde first received Newman, knowing his wish to marry her daughter, she sat small and immovable. "You're an American," she said presently. "I've seen several Americans." "There are several in Paris," said Newman gaily. "Oh, really? It was in England I saw these, or somewhere else; not in Paris. I think it must have been in the Pyrenees many years ago. I'm told your ladies are very pretty. One of these ladies was very pretty—with such a wonderful complexion. She presented me with a note of introduction from some one—I forget whom—and she sent it with a note of her own. I kept her letter a long time afterwards, it was so strangely expressed, I used to know some of the phrases by heart. But I've forgotten them now—it's so many years ago. Since then I've seen no more Americans. I think my daughter-in-law has; she's a great gadabout; she sees every one."

Even the gentle Madame de Cintré furthered the critical note, perhaps from a mild notion that Newman would be amused. "I've been telling Madame de la Rochefidèle that you're an American," she said as he came up to her in her salon. "It interests her greatly. Her favorite uncle went over with the French troops to help you in your battles in the last century, and she has always, in consequence, wanted greatly to see one of your people. But she has never succeeded until tonight. You're the first—to her knowledge —that she has ever looked upon." Madame de la Rochefidèle lifted an antique eyeglass, looked at Newman from head to foot, and at last said something to which he listened with deference but could not understand, for Madame de la Rochefidèle had an aged and cadaverous face with a falling of the lower jaw that impeded her utterance. Madame de Cintré offered an interpretation. "Madame de la Rochefidèle says she's convinced that she must have seen Americans without knowing it." Newman considered that she might have seen many things without knowing it; and the French visitor, again speaking in an inarticulate guttural said that she wished that she *had* known it. This interchange was followed by the polite approach of a very elderly gentlemen who declared that almost the first person he had looked upon after coming into the world was an American, no less than the celebrated Doctor Franklin. But he too, in the circumstances, could hardly have known it.

The animus of James, who has so often been pictured as a happy expatriate, mounted as such episodes recurred. At the great reception given by the Bellegardes for Newman after the announcement of his engagement to Madame de Cintré, he was introduced to their friends by her elder brother. "If the Marquis was going about as a bear-leader," wrote James stormily, "the general impression was that the bear was a very fair imitation of humanity." James even made a comment on worldly society which might have derived from one of the early wise, wandering Yankees; its like had been heard in *Fashion*. "Every one gave Newman extreme attention: every one lighted up for him regardless, as he would have said, of expense: every one looked at him with that fraudulent intensity of good society which puts out its bountiful hand but keeps the fingers closed over the coin." Nearly fifty years later James could betray an enduring bitterness. "Great and gilded was the whole trap set, in fine, for his wary freshness and into which it would blunder upon its fate."

When the catastrophe came, when the Bellegardes broke their word and Claire was commanded to withdraw from her engagement, Newman was rejected and publicly humiliated because he was American: they found themselves unable to tolerate that circumstance in relation to their family. He was rejected on the score of manners—the old and vexing score. He should have known that to ask the old Marquise to parade through her own rooms on his arm the evening of the ball would be almost an effront. When the journey was accomplished and she said, "This is enough, sir," he might have seen the gulf widening before his eyes. His commercial connections were held against him; and James pointed the irony of the objection. The Bellegardes were shown as sordidly commercial; in shrewdness they far outdistanced Newman. He was beaten indeed because he was incapable of suspecting the treachery accumulating against him. At the end Newman was unable to maintain his purpose of revenge against the Bellegardes; he destroyed the scrap of evidence which would have proved their earlier inhuman crime. His act is not overstressed; a deep-lying harshness gave stringency to Newman's generous impulses. But the contrast is firmly kept.

With all the preordained emphasis these characters are rounded and complete. The integrity of Valentin was placed against the unscrupulous coldness of his older brother. Claire, with her lovely purity, lights the black picture created by the Marquise. If the balance seems to be tipped down by the inclusion of Mademoiselle Nioche and her deplorable father, there is always Mrs. Bread. As a great artist James had moved immeasurably beyond the simple limits of the original fable. A genuine tragedy was created whose elements were tangled deep in alienable differences. At the last Newman was unable to understand either the character or the decision of the woman he so deeply loved. Circling across the sea and the American continent, he returned again to Paris by an irresistible compulsion, and at twilight one evening, a gray time, walked to the convent of the Carmelite order in the Rue d'Enfer and gazed at the high blank wall which surrounded it. Within, his beloved was forever enclosed, engaged in rites which he could never understand, withdrawn for reasons which he could not fathom. He could never pass beyond that wall, in body or in spirit. The image was final, and became a dramatic metaphor: in the spelling of the old fable the outcome had changed from triumph to defeat. Defeat had become at last an essential part of the national portraiture.

4

Almost invariably the opening moods and even the later sequences of James's novels were those of comedy. He instinctively chose the open sunny level; the light handling of his early *Confidence*, uncomplicated by the international situation, shows what he could do in maintaining this when his materials permitted. He ran indeed through a wide gamut of humor, from that of the happy and easy view and a delicate satire to a broad caricature and irony. Social comedy appeared in Henry James. For the first time an American writer drew a society and infused his drawing with an acute sense of human disparities. Yet the aggregation of his novels does not spell comedy, but a kind of *tragédie Américaine*, which was in large part a tragedy of manners. "I have the instincts—have them deeply—if I haven't the forms of a high old civilization," Newman told Claire de Cintré; but the instincts, if he possessed them, were not enough. *Daisy Miller*, bringing down a storm of angry reproof upon James's head, was a classic instance which he multiplied with variations of subtlety and range.

Defeat for the American adventurer was new, at least in wide transcription. Triumph had hitherto been the appointed destiny in American portraiture, except for vagabonds and adventurers. Yet with all the tragic implications the ultimate ending of these latter-day fables was not that of tragedy. In the midst of his final encounters with the forces of opposition Newman gathered his energies; his spirits rose. When he confronted the Marquis de Bellegarde he "had a singular sensation; he felt his sense of wrong almost brim into gaity." He could laugh during the momentous interview with Mrs. Bread; at one moment in their plotting his face "lighted with the candor of childhood." The mood was unreasoning, beyond reason: it was a typical mood, that of resilience under opposition or criticism. Finally, after all the conflict, under his searching and baffled effort to understand inscrutable forces, this mood was resolved into something subtler and more enduring than resilience. When Newman stood before the wall that forever enclosed Claire de Cintré "the barren stillness of the place represented somehow his own release from ineffectual desire." Touching the nadir of despair and disillusionment, he was "disburdened"—free at last from those dark personalities by whom he had been cruelly wronged. He reached a moment of profound recognition, not perhaps of the inner character of the forces that worked against him —these he could never understand—but of his own final plight. He achieved that laden balance of mind and feeling from which an enduring philosophical comedy may spring. As one sees Newman beyond the end of the book he has become a far graver character, but for him something of humor might play quietly once more.

Again and again James pictured this low-keyed humor of defeat. For Isabel Archer more than one way of escape lay open; fronting these possibilities, she made the choice which meant renunçiation; and the outcome is not tragic, for all the wrench which it produces at the end, since James has revealed that free poise and nobility of her character which made renunciation inevitable and acceptance of her lot tolerable. Even *The Wings of the Dove* cannot be called tragedy. Milly Theale learned the worst there was to know of those to whom she was attached, their betrayal, their base purpose; yet with knowledge she still could keep a magnanimous love. James repeated this stress again in the recognition which finally lay between Kate Croy and Milton Denssher.[3] Each had plumbed a deep and even dangerous knowledge of the other; yet an indissoluble acceptance remained between them; and their final alliance had a touch of the secure upward swing which belongs to comedy.

In comedy reconcilement with life comes at the point when to the tragic sense only an inalienable difference or dissension with life appears. Recognition is essential for the play of a profound comedy; barriers must be down; perhaps defeat must lie at its base. Yet the outcome in these novels was in a sense the traditional outcome, for triumph was comprised in it; but the sphere had altered from outer circumstance to the realm of the mind and spirit; and triumph was no longer blind and heedless, but achieved by difficult and even desperate effort.

In this outcome James transcended the nationalistic altogether

—that obsession which had had so long a history. Yet in the aggregate of his novels he repeated a significant portion of the old fable. He showed that the American was in truth what the belligerent Yankee had always declared him to be, a wholly alien, disparate, even a new character. In the end the primary concern of James was with that character; and he kept a familiar touch of the fabulous in his narratives. "I had been plotting arch-romance without knowing it," he said of *The American;* and by romance he meant what Hawthorne had meant, life with a touch of the marvelous, an infusion which can be apprehended only imperfectly by the sense of fact. Romance appeared in the generality and scale which James gave to his characters and to his situations. Such titles as *The Wings of the Dove* and *The Golden Bowl* suggest a poetized conception completing the romantic character of the themes; and his handling is kept free from complicated circumstance. Poetry indeed overspread much of James's writing. Like that of the popular fabulists, it was packed with metaphor. "The morning was like a clap of hands." "She carried her three and thirty years as a light-wristed Hebe might have carried a brimming wine-cup." His figures could also be ironical; the romantic feeling is constantly enclosed by a close drawing. Recognition is fundamental in all of James's portraiture; yet a basic poetry of outline and expression remains clear, most of all in his later novels. Few writers have had so deep a sense of the poetry of character; and his poetical penetration was the rarer achievement because his approaches were not those of the primary emotions.

In commentary James once spoke of one of the women whom he had drawn as "unaware of life." Elsewhere he wondered "what it might distinguishably be in their own flourishing Order that could *keep* them, the passionless pilgrims, so unaware?" "Passionless" was surely not meant to include his major characters; yet even they could not be called passionate in the sense that the characters in *Wuthering Heights* are passionate; it is significant of his obsessions that elsewhere James could give the attribute "passionate" to a pilgrim in quest of the past. For the most part emotion in these Americans in his wide gallery is frustrated, buried, or lost. Instead, renunciation, tenderness, pity, are likely to be dominant among them. The finest of these feelings do not belong to the primary emotions; they are restrained or delicate or withdrawn. These characters indeed are of an established native mold; this diminution had prevailed elsewhere. In a fashion James himself revealed the same qualities; a profound tenderness suffuses the greatest of his writing, but not the compulsion of a deep and natural, simple emotion. He gains power by integrity, by a close intensity of view, often by intensity of the mind. His portrayals gain every possible concentration from the high art by which they are revealed. "Dramatize! dramatize!" he said again and again; and the dramatic quality belonged to his writings at every point, in the ready immediacy of the talk, in the swift juxtapositions, in swift and daring ellipses, particularly in his later novels. At one point he considered that the drama was his true form. "I feel at last as if I had found my *real* form, which I am capable of carrying far, and for which the pale little art of fiction, as I have practiced it, has been, for me, but a limited and restricted substitute." James failed in writing drama; nothing of true dramatic expression had appeared in American literature, and he was not to transcend its tendency. He necessarily failed, lacking a depth of simple emotion; the approach to the drama had been made before without completion, perhaps for the same reason. James returned to the novel, and kept the dramatic organization.

The highly conscious artist was uppermost in Henry James; and he joined in the traditional bias toward the inward view. Strangely enough, though he had no New England ancestry and was likely to be positive in his declarations to the contrary, he came closer than any of the earlier American writers to that introspective analysis which had belonged to the Puritan, closer even than Hawthorne. His scrutiny of motives, while delicate, was intense. He never used that direct revelation of elements in the stream of consciousness which had been ventured by Whitman and Hawthorne before him; yet his later novels are full of the unsaid and understated; they are full of complex moods and states of inner feeling revealed by the slightest and most ephemeral of notations. Whether or not James was subject to some untraceable Puritan influence, whether he touched popular sources, whether perhaps he gained greatly from the initial experiments of Hawthorne and Poe, his novels vastly amplified this new subject of the mind lying submerged beneath the scope of circumstance, which had long engaged the American imagination.

5

Nearly always the mark of that era in which an artist is young will in some way lie upon his work, however far he may advance into the future. Henry James bore the mark of that deeply experimental era which came to a culmination in the late '40's and early '50's. Like Poe, Hawthorne, Melville, Whitman, he performed that difficult and elliptical feat by which a writer both invades a province and occupies it. Like them he was in a sense a primary writer.

No American before him had made a full imaginative approach to living characters and the contemporary scene; the view hitherto had been mainly the retrospective view. He greatly extended the areas of native comedy; he all but created a new subject for the novel in his stress upon the inward view; he discovered the international scene, as Van Wyck Brooks has said, "for literature." There is irony in the fact that so wide and subtle an accomplishment should have been produced within a tradition that still bore the print of the pioneer. There is a further irony in the circumstance that the American character should first have been realized within the European scene. This remotnesss has been considered a flight and a loss; and truly enough to have perceived that character with equal amplitude against the native background would have meant an immense gain in imaginative understanding. Yet James's choice fulfilled the consciousness of a fundamental relationship; only the denial had been abortive.

The great experimental writer is like to betray signs of incompletion, to cover more than one era, to show hesitation as well as an unmistakable security. James showed some of these signs. They are apparent in the great division between his later and his earlier writing, and in the incalculable abysms of his later style. In a strange fashion after the middle of his career he showed a partial reversal of his sense of language, which took on an extreme gentility even while it attempted that colloquialism which had been part of the American tradition. He strove for elegance like a minor writer of the '30's who sought to prove that Americans too could enter the stately domain of English literature. He used quotations marks to set off such phrases as "detective story," and the attempted grace of his movements through the great morass of his words was often elephantine. In the final revisions of the earlier novels he often emasculated a vigorous speech. The result was a form of writing which was neither English nor American in character. Yet few experimental writers have maintained so fine an artistry or encompassed with that artistry so great a scope. His failures are minor failures within a great original accomplishment.

Howells was the only other measurable American writer of this time to employ the novelistic form; the concerns of Howells were largely regional; he was engaged by small portions of the American scene and of the American character; he never fused these into an unmistakable and moving whole. The real situation in *Silas Lapham* lay between the Yankee and the Bostonian, between Lapham and the Coreys, between Penelope and young Corey. Here were elements of social comedy or tragedy, which Howells pictured in one scene which remains a high scene in American humor, full of comedy indeed, full of pathos and hurt—the scene of the Coreys' dinner-party. But Howells evaded the full scope of the indicated differences, packing Lapham off to Vermont and Penelope and young Corey to South America. He made the same evasion in *The Lady of the Aroostook,* never showing Lydia in any prolonged contact with the superior Americans with whom her destinies were linked, never exploring the social situation beyond its superficial aspects, and again at the end sending his two major characters to far parts, where the manners and speech of the country girl need trouble nobody, and where Howells at any rate was not troubled by ensuing complications.

In spite of lapses in local observation, Howells had a striking aptitude for seizing essential elements in the native tradition: he knew the Yankee, the backwoodsman, the itinerant revivalist. His narratives are full of prime comic sketches, full of a racy contemporary and local speech. They reveal too that acute and expressive awareness with which the American constantly viewed himself, his fellow countrymen, his nation. His young men are always theorizing about America, and often have superior attitudes. "What a very American thing!" exclaims one of them when he heard Lydia saying "I want to know." "It's incredible," he continued. "Who in the world can she be?" The American quarrel with America, the product of a long self-consciousness, was beginning.

Howells had it in his power to draw social comedy of breadth and the first order, for disparities of background were included within his view; he was grounded within the comic tradition. He might have been the great artist to picture the American against the native scene, complementing the portrayals of James abroad. He had all the gifts except a passionate concern with his subject. Whether from lassitude or from a fundamental lack of imagination he never truly explored his materials; not one of his novels can be put beside *The Portrait of a Lady* or *The American.* He veered from one theme to another, from one locale to another. His novels were in the end not novels at all but an invaluable collection of minor notations on the American character.

Henry James stands alone in his time, not wholly to be accounted for, not in any immediate sense productive as an influence. He began writing in the '60's; his work was hardly a force among other writers for nearly half a century. In later years other American writers have followed him in using the international scene; yet his other great achievement, that of portraying the inner mind, cannot be said to have given any notable impetus to the American novel. It is abroad that the implications of his work have been pushed to their boundaries. Proust and Joyce, Dorothy Richardson and Virginia Woolf, may or may not have been influenced by James; but they have carried the whole stress of an American intention far beyond anything achieved by American writers, in their portrayal of the inner consciousness.

The fate of Henry James has been that of other primary writers within the American tradition. Each of these had stormed some battlement without a following sequence of writers. The prolific energies that create an entire literature were lacking in this long period, though a widely flung pattern had been created which had freshness and even magnificence.

NOTES

1 See "The Art of Fiction" (1884): "The power to guess the unseen from the seen, to trace the implication of things, to judge the whole piece by the pattern, the condition of feeling life in general so completely that you are well on your way to knowing any particular corner of it—this cluster of gifts may almost be said to constitute experience. . . ."—Ed.

2 A slip of the pen for *Pandora.*—Ed.

3 Clearly a slip of the pen for "Merton Densher."—Ed.

THE PORTRAIT
OF A LADY

1881

"The Portrait of a Lady"

ARNOLD KETTLE*

COMPARED with this the English novels which precede it, except perhaps those of Jane Austen, all seem a trifle crude. There is a habit of perfection here, a certainty and a poise, which is quite different from the merits and power of *Oliver Twist* or *Wuthering Heights* or even *Middlemarch*. The quality has something to do with the full consciousness of Henry James's art. Nothing in *The Portrait of a Lady* is unconscious, nothing there by chance, no ungathered wayward strands, no clumsiness. No novelist is so absorbed as James in what he himself might call his 'game.' But it is not an empty or superficial concern with 'form' that gives *The Portrait of a Lady* its quality. James's manner, his obsession with style, his intricate and passionate concern with presentation, do not spring from a narrow 'aesthetic' attitude to his art.

> "James had in his style and perhaps in the life which it reflected an idiosyncrasy so powerful, so overweening, that to many it seemed a stultifying vice, or at least an inexcusable heresy. . . . He enjoyed an excess of intelligence and he suffered, both in life and art, from an excessive effort to communicate it, to represent it in all its fullness. His style grew elaborate in the degree that he rendered shades and refinements of meaning and feeling not usually rendered at all. . . . His intention and all his labour was to represent dramatically intelligence at its most difficult, its most lucid, its most beautiful point. This is the sum of his idiosyncrasy."[1]

*"Henry James: *The Portrait of a Lady* (1880-81)." From AN INTRODUCTION TO THE ENGLISH NOVEL, vol. II; copyright 1951, by Hutchinson Publishing Group, Ltd. Reprinted by permission of author and the publisher.

[1]R. P. Blackmur, Introduction to H. James, *The Art of the Novel* (1934), p. xii.

The Portrait of a Lady is not one of James's 'difficult' novels; but Mr. Blackmur's remarks usefully remind us of the inadequacy of a merely formal approach to James's work. The extraordinary richness of texture of his novels makes such an approach tempting; but it will take us neither to James's triumphs nor to his failures.

The beauty of texture derives immediately from two qualities, which are ultimately inseparable. One is James's ability to make us know his characters more richly, though not necessarily more vividly, than we know the characters of other novelists; the other is the subtlety of his own standpoint. Without the latter quality the former would not, of course, be possible. You cannot control the responses of your reader unless you are in complete control of your material.

In *The Portrait of a Lady* there are—looking at the question from an analytical point of view—two kinds of characters: those whom we know from straightforward, though not unsubtle, description by the author and those who reveal themselves in the course of the book. The latter are, obviously, the important ones. The former—Mrs. Touchett, Henrietta Stackpole, the Countess Gemini, Pansy Osmond—are interesting primarily in their relationship to the chief characters, in their part in the pattern; we do not follow their existence out of their function in the book. But they are nevertheless not 'flat' characters. They come alive not as 'characters,' not as personified 'humours,' but as complete people (Pansy, perhaps, is the exception, but then is not the intention that we should see her as scarcely an independent being at all?) and if we do not follow them out of the part of the plot which concerns them it is because our interests are more involved elsewhere, not because they do not have a full existence of their own.

The way Henry James introduces his characters to us depends entirely on the kind of function they are to have in his story. The main characters are never described as they *are* (i.e. as the author knows them to be) but—by and large—as Isabel Archer sees them. We know them at first only by the first impression that they make. We get to know better what they are like in the way that, in life, we get to know people better through acquaintance. And just as in life we are seldom, if ever, quite certain what another person is like, so in a Henry James novel we are often pretty much at sea about particular characters for considerable portions of the book. In *The Portrait of a Lady* the person whom at first we inevitably know least about is Madame Merle. Henry James lets us know right from the start that there is something sinister about her; we are made quickly to feel that Isabel's reaction to her is less than adequate, but the precise nature of her character is not revealed until fairly far into the book.

It is not quite true to say that everything in *The Portrait of a Lady* is revealed through Isabel's consciousness. We know, from the start, certain things that Isabel does not know. We know, for instance—and twice Henry James explicitly reminds us of it— more about Ralph Touchett's feeling for Isabel than she herself perceives.

Indeed, there is a sense in which the novel is revealed to us through Ralph's consciousness, for his is the 'finest,' the fullest intelligence in the book and therefore he sees things—about Madame Merle, about Osmond, about Isabel herself—which Isabel does not see and inevitably such perceptions are transmitted to the reader. Again, we are offered important scenes—between Madame Merle and Osmond, between the Countess and Madame Merle—which reveal to us not the whole truth but enough of the truth about Madame Merle's stratagems to put us at an advantage over Isabel.

The truth is that Henry James's purpose in this novel is not to put Isabel between the reader and the situation (in the way that Strether's consciousness is used in *The Ambassadors*) but to reveal to the reader the full implications of Isabel's consciousness. For this to happen we must see Isabel not merely from the inside (i.e. know how she feels) but from the outside too. The method is, in fact, precisely the method of *Emma*, except that Jane Austen is rather more scrupulously consistent than Henry James. The scenes 'outside' Emma herself (like Jane Fairfax's visits to the post office) are brought to our knowledge by being related by a third party in the presence of Emma herself. Our only 'advantage' over Emma herself is provided by the words which Jane Austen uses to describe her. Henry James, as we have seen, takes greater liberties. Yet it is worth observing that the great scene at the centre of *The Portrait of a Lady* (Chapter XLII), in which Isabel takes stock of her situation, is of precisely the same *kind* as the scene in which (Vol. I, Chapter XVI) Emma takes stock of her dealings with Harriet.

Since James's purpose is to render the full implications of Isabel's situation it is necessary that we should know more than Isabel, should see her, that is to say, from the outside. The question remains: how *much* more should we know? And James's answer is: just as much as is necessary for a fully sympathetic understanding. Thus we are to know that Madame Merle has drawn Isabel into a trap, but we are not to know why. The full story is kept back, not because Henry James is interested in suspense in the melodramatic sense, but because if we were in on the secret the nature of Isabel's discovery of her situation could not be so effectively revealed. It is necessary to the novel that we should *share* Isabel's suspicions and her awakening. In order to give the precise weight (not just the logical weight but the intricate weight of feelings, standards, loyalties) to the issues involved in her final dilemma we must know not just what has happened to Isabel but the way it has happened.

It is from such a consideration that there will emerge one of Henry James's cardinal contributions to the art of the novel. With James the question "What happened?" carries the most subtle, the most exciting ramifications. To no previous novelist had the answer to such a question seemed so difficult, its implications so interminable. To a George Eliot the question is complicated enough: to understand what happened to Lydgate we must be made aware of innumerable issues, facets of character, moral choices, social pressures. And yet deep in George Eliot's novel is implicit the idea that if the reader only knows enough facts about the situation he will know the situation. It is the aim of Henry James to avoid the 'about' or, at least, to alter its status, to transform quantity into quality. His is the poet's ambition: to create an object about which we say not "It means. . . ." but "It is. . . ." (In this he is with Emily Brontë.) We cannot *understand* Isabel Archer, he implies, unless we feel as she feels. And it is, indeed, because he succeeds in this attempt that *The Portrait of a Lady* though not a greater novel than *Middlemarch* is a more moving one.

As a rule when Henry James describes a character (as opposed to allowing the person to be revealed in action) the description is of the kind we have noticed in *Emma* or *Middlemarch.*

"Mrs. Touchett was certainly a person of many oddities, of which her behaviour on returning to her husband's house after many months was a noticeable specimen. She had her own way of doing all that she did, and this is the simplest description of a character which, although by no means without liberal motions, rarely succeeded in giving an impression of suavity. Mrs. Touchett might do a great deal of good, but she never pleased. This way of her own, of which she was so fond, was not intrinsically offensive—it was just unmistakeably distinguished from the way of others. The edges of her conduct were so very clear-cut that for susceptible persons it sometimes had a knife-like effect. That hard fineness came out in her deportment during the first hours of her return from America, under circumstances in which it might have seemed that her first act would have been to exchange greetings with her husband and son. Mrs. Touchett, for reasons which she deemed excellent, always retired on such occasions into impenetrable seclusion, postponing the more sentimental ceremony until she had repaired the disorder of dress with a completeness which had the less reason to be of high importance as neither beauty nor vanity were concerned in it. She was a plain-faced old woman, without graces and without any great elegance, but with an extreme respect for her own motives. She was usually prepared to explain these—when the explanation was asked as a favour; and in such a case they proved totally different from those that had been attributed to her. She was virtually separated from her husband, but she appeared to perceive nothing irregular in the situation. It had become clear, at an early stage of their community, that they should never desire the same thing at the same moment, and this appearance had prompted her to rescue disagreement from the vulgar realm of accident. She did what she could to erect it into a law—a much more edifying aspect of it—by going to live in Florence, where she bought a house and established herself; and by leaving her husband to take care of the English branch of his bank. This arrangement greatly pleased her; it was so felicitously definite. It struck her husband in the same light, in a foggy square in London, where it was at times the most definite face he discerned; but he would have preferred that such unnatural things should have a greater vagueness. To agree to disagree had cost him an effort; he was ready to agree to almost anything but that, and saw no reason why either assent or dissent should be so terribly consistent.

Mrs. Touchett indulged in no regrets nor speculations, and usually came once a year to spend a month with her husband, a period during which she apparently took pains to convince him that she had adopted the right system. She was not fond of the English style of life, and had three or four reasons for it to which she currently alluded; they bore upon minor points of that ancient order, but for Mrs. Touchett they amply justified non-residence. She detested bread-sauce, which, as she said, looked like a poultice and tasted like soap; she objected to the consumption of beer by her maid-servants; and she affirmed that the British laundress (Mrs. Touchett was very particular about the appearance of her linen) was not a mistress of her art." (*Portrait of a Lady*, chap. III)

Here the description depends for its effect entirely on the quality of the author's wit, his organized intellectual comment, and the wit is of the sort (a penetrating delicacy of observation within an accepted social group) achieved by Jane Austen or George Eliot.

But some of the described characters in *The Portrait of a Lady* come poetically to life. This is the description of Isabel's first meeting with the Countess Gemini.

> "The Countess Gemini simply nodded without getting up; Isabel could see she was a woman of high fashion. She was thin and dark and not at all pretty, having features that suggested some tropical bird— a long beak-like nose, small, quickly-moving eyes and a mouth and chin that receded extremely. Her expression, however, thanks to various intensities of emphasis and wonder, of horror and joy, was not inhuman, and, as regards her appearance, it was plain she understood herself and made the most of her points. Her attire, voluminous and delicate, bristling with elegance, had the look of shimmering plumage, and her attitudes were as light and sudden as those of a creature who perched upon twigs. She had a great deal of manner; Isabel, who had never known anyone with so much manner, immediately classed her as the most affected of women. She remembered that Ralph had not recommended her as an acquaintance; but she was ready to acknowledge that to a casual view the Countess Gemini revealed no depths. Her demonstrations suggested the violent wavings of some flag of general truce—white silk with fluttering streamers." (chap. XXIV)

We are never to get to know the Countess very well, but already we see her with a peculiar vividness, the vividness evoked by poetic imagery. The bird image has a visual force so intense that it goes beyond surface illumination—"bristling with elegance" in its context contains a world of comment as well as vividness. So does the image of the flag of truce.

Henry James's predominant interest is, however, by no means in character. *The Portrait of a Lady,* he tells us in his Preface, has as its corner-stone "the conception of a certain young woman affronting her destiny." The interest, it is already indicated, is not primarily a psychological one, not a matter of mere personal analysis. And *The Portrait of a Lady* is indeed a novel of the widest scope and relevance. Though it is in the line of Jane Austen it has a quality which it is not misleading to call symbolic (already we have hinted at a link with what would appear at first to be a wholly different novel, *Wuthering Heights).* The Portrait of a Lady is a novel about destiny. Or, to use a concept rather more in tone with the language of the book itself, it is a novel about freedom. It would not be outrageous, though it might be misleading, to call it a nineteenth-century *Paradise Lost.*

Henry James is, of course, far too sophisticated an artist to offer us the 'subject' of his book on a platter. In his moral interest he avoids like the plague anything approaching the abstract.

> "I might envy," he writes in his Preface, "though I couldn't emulate, the imaginative writer so constituted as to see his fable first and to make out its agents afterwards: I could think so little of any fable that didn't need its agents positively to launch it; I could think so little of any situation that didn't depend for its interest on the nature of the persons situated, and thereby on their way of taking it."

And again, a little later:

> "There is, I think, no more nutritive or suggestive truth in this connexion than that of the perfect dependence of the 'moral' sense of a work of art on the amount of felt life concerned in producing it."[2]

James's novel is not a moral fable; but its moral interest is nevertheless central. Only the business of "launching," of presenting with all the necessary depth of "felt life," that "ado" which is the story of Isabel Archer, all this may easily distract our attention from the central theme. Indeed there was a time when James's novels apparently were regarded as "comedies of manners" (cf. Trollope) and even so superbly intelligent a reader as E. M. Forster seems to have missed the point of them almost completely.

The launching of *The Portrait of a Lady* is beautifully done. Gardencourt, the house in Albany, upper-class London: they are called up with magnificent certainty and solidity. So too are the people of the book: the Touchetts, Caspar Goodwood, Henrietta Stackpole, Lord Warburton, Isabel herself. If these characters are to contribute to a central pattern it will not be, it is clear, in the manner of anything approaching allegory. They are all too 'round,' too 'free' to be felt, for even a moment, simply to be 'standing for'

---

[2] I quote with some uneasiness from James's Preface (written, it will be recalled, some quarter of a century after the novel), not because I doubt the relevance or interest of his observations but because I am conscious of the difficulty of assimilating out of context sentences written in his most idiosyncratic, complex style.

anything. It is one of Henry James's achievements that he can convince us that his characters have a life outside the pages of his novel without ever leading us into the temptation of following them beyond his purpose. It is because everything in these early chapters of *The Portrait of a Lady* is realized with such fullness, such apparent lack of pointed emphasis, that we are slow to recognize the basic pattern of the novel, but it is also on this account that our imagination is so firmly engaged.

Before the end of the first chapter, however, a subsidiary theme has already been fairly fully stated and three of the main themes announced or, at any rate, indicated. The subsidiary theme is that generally referred to in Henry James's novels as the international situation—the relation of America to Europe. Graham Greene in a recent introduction to *The Portrait of a Lady* has tried to play down the importance of this theme. "It is true the innocent figure is nearly always American (Roderick Hudson, Newman, Isabel and Milly, Maggie Verver and her father), but the corrupted characters . . . are also American: Mme. Merle, Gilbert Osmond, Kate Croy, Merton Densher, Charlotte Stant. His characters are mainly American, simply because James himself was American."[3] In fact, of course, neither Kate Croy nor Densher is an American and one of the points about the other "corrupted" characters is that they are all expatriates, europeanized Americans, whom it is at least possible to see as corrupted by Europe.[4] The theme of the impact of European civilization on Americans—innocent or not—is not a main theme of *The Portrait of a Lady* but it is nevertheless there and we shall return to it later. And it is broached in the very first pages of the novel in the description of the Touchett *ménage* and in such details as the failure of Mr. Touchett to understand (or rather, his pretence at not understanding) Lord Warburton's jokes.

The main themes indicated in the first chapters are the importance of wealth, the difficulty of marriage and—fundamental to the other two—the problem of freedom or independence. In each case the theme appears to be merely a casual subject of conversation but in fact there is nothing casual there. The vital theme of freedom is introduced in the form of a joke—one of Mrs. Touchett's eccentric telegrams: " 'Changed hotel, very bad, impudent clerk,

[3]World Classics ed., p. ix.

[4]For a fuller discussion of this problem see *Henry James, the Major Phase* by F. O. Matthiessen and *Maule's Curse* by Yvor Winters.

address here. Taken sister's girl, died last year, go to Europe, two sisters, quite independent'." The telegram is discussed by Mr. Touchett and Ralph.

" 'There's one thing very clear in it,' said the old man; 'she has given the hotel-clerk a dressing.'

'I'm not sure even of that, since he has driven her from the field. We thought at first that the sister mentioned might be the sister of the clerk; but the subsequent mention of a niece seems to prove that the allusion is to one of my aunts. Then there was a question as to whose the two other sisters were; they are probably two of my late aunt's daughters. But who's "quite independent," and in what sense is the term used?—that point's not yet settled. Does the expression apply more particularly to the young lady my mother has adopted, or does it characterize her sisters equally?—and is it used in a moral or in a financial sense? Does it mean that they've been left well off, or that they wish to be under no obligations?—or does it simply mean that they're fond of their own way?' " (chap. I)

Ralph's frivolous speculations do in fact state the basic problems to be dealt with in the novel. The point is indeed not yet settled: it will take the whole book to settle it. And, even then, 'settle' is not the right word. One does not, Henry James would be quick to remind us, settle life.

The independence of Isabel is the quality about her most often emphasized. Mrs. Touchett has taken her up, but she is not, she assures Ralph "a candidate for adoption." " 'I'm very fond of my liberty'," (chap. II) she adds. From the very first the ambiguous quality of this independence is stressed. Isabel is attractive, interesting, 'fine' ("she carried within her a great fund of life, and her deepest enjoyment was to feel the continuity between the movements of her own soul and the agitations of the world" [chap. IV]); but she is also in many respects inexperienced, naïve. " 'It occurred to me,' Mrs. Touchett says, 'that it would be a kindness to take her about and introduce her to the world. She thinks she knows a great deal of it—like most American girls; but like most American girls she's ridiculously mistaken'." (chap. V) Henry James does not allow us, charming creature as she is, to idealize Isabel:

"Altogether, with her meagre knowledge, her inflated ideals, her confidence at once innocent and dogmatic, her temper at once exacting and indulgent, her mixture of curiosity and fastidiousness, of vivacity and indifference, her desire to look very well and to be if possible even better, her determination to see, to try, to know, her combination of the delicate desultory flame-like spirit and the eager and personal creature of conditions: she would be an easy victim of scientific criticism: if she were not intended to awaken on the reader's part an impulse more tender and more purely expectant." (chap. VI)

The Portrait of a Lady is the revelation of the inadequacy of Isabel's view of freedom. The revelation is so full, so concrete, that to abstract from it the main, insistent theme must inevitably weaken the impression of the book. But analysis involves such abstraction and we shall not respond fully to James's novel unless we are conscious of its theme. The theme in its earlier stages is fully expressed in the scene in which Caspar Goodwood for the second time asks Isabel to marry him (she has just refused Lord Warburton).

" 'I don't know,' she answered rather grandly. 'The world—with all these places so arranged and so touching each other—comes to strike one as rather small.'

'It's a sight too big for me!' Caspar exclaimed with a simplicity our young lady might have found touching if her face had not been set against concessions.

This attitude was part of a system, a theory, that she had lately embraced, and to be thorough she said after a moment: 'Don't think me unkind if I say it's just that—being out of your sight—that I like. If you were in the same place I should feel you were watching me, and I don't like that—I like my liberty too much. If there's a thing in the world I'm fond of,' she went on with a slight recurrence of grandeur, 'it's my personal independence.' But whatever there might be of the too superior in this speech moved Caspar Goodwood's admiration; there was nothing he winced at in the large air of it. He had never supposed she hadn't wings and the need of beautiful free movements —he wasn't, with his own long arms and strides, afraid of any force in her. Isabel's words, if they had been meant to shock him, failed of the mark and only made him smile with the sense that here was common ground. 'Who would wish less to curtail your liberty than I? What can give me greater pleasure than to see you perfectly independent—doing whatever you like? It's to make you independent that I want to marry you.'

'That's a beautiful sophism,' said the girl with a smile more beautiful still.

'An unmarried woman—a girl of your age—isn't independent. There are all sorts of things she can't do. She's hampered at every step.'

'That's as she looks at the question,' Isabel answered with much spirit. 'I'm not in my first youth—I can do what I choose—I belong quite to the independent class. I've neither father nor mother; I'm poor and of a serious disposition; I'm not pretty. I therefore am not bound to be timid and conventional; indeed I can't afford such luxuries. Besides, I try to judge things for myself; to judge wrong, I think, is more honourable than not to judge at all. I don't wish to be a mere sheep in the flock; I wish to choose my fate and know something of human affairs beyond what other people think it compatible with propriety to tell me.' She paused a moment, but not long enough for her companion to reply. He was apparently on the point of doing so when she went on: 'Let me say this to you, Mr. Goodwood. You're so kind as to speak of being afraid of my marrying. If you should hear a rumour that I'm on the point of doing so—girls are liable to have such things said about them—remember what I have told you about my love of liberty and venture to doubt it'." (chap. XVI)

The Portrait of a Lady is far from allegory yet one is permitted to feel, in the symbolic quality of the novel, that the characters, though unmistakably individuals, are more than individuals. Thus, in her rejection of Caspar Goodwood, Isabel is rejecting America, or at least that part of America that Goodwood represents, young, strong, go-ahead, uninhibited, hard. For Goodwood (as for Henrietta, who essentially shares his quality) the problem of freedom is simple and might be expressed in the words of Mr. Archibald Macleish's American Dream:

> *"America is promises*
> *For those that take them."*

Goodwood—and it would be wrong to see him as a wholly unsympathetic character—is prepared to take them with all that taking implies. To him and Henrietta (and they are, on one level, the most sensible, positive people in the book) Isabel's problem is not a problem at all. Freedom for them has the simple quality it possessed for the nineteenth-century liberal.

The rejection of Lord Warburton has, similarly, a symbolic quality—though, again, one must insist that this is not an allegory. Warburton is a liberal aristocrat. He embodies the aristocratic culture of Europe (that has so attracted Isabel at Gardencourt) and adds his own reforming ideas—a combination which Henry James, had he been the kind of aesthetic snob he is often held to be, might have found irresistible. Ralph Touchett sums up Warburton's social position magnificently:

> " '. . . He says I don't understand my time, I understand it certainly better than he, who can neither abolish himself as a nuisance nor maintain himself as an institution'." (chap. VII)

Isabel's rejection of Lord Warburton is not a light one. She feels very deeply the attraction of the aristocratic standards. But she feels also the limitations of Warburton and his sisters, the Misses Molyneux (it is worth comparing them with another 'county' family—the Marchants—in the wonderful *Princess Casamassima;* Henry James's attitude to the British aristocracy is by no means uncritical).

> " '. . . So long as I look at the Misses Molyneux they seem to me to answer a kind of ideal. Then Henrietta presents herself, and I'm straightway convinced by *her;* not so much in respect to herself as in respect to what masses behind her'." (chap. X) Ralph, too, (though he does not undervalue her) disposes of Henrietta:

> " 'Henrietta . . . does smell of the Future—it almost knocks one down!' " (chap. X)

Goodwood and Warburton rejected (almost like two temptations), Isabel is now 'free' to affront her destiny. But she is not free because she is poor. She has never, we are told early on, known anything about money, and it is typical of this novel that this fine, romantic indifference to wealth should be one of the basic factors in Isabel's tragedy.

Henry James's characters always have to be rich and the reason is not the obvious one. "I call people rich," says Ralph Touchett, "when they're able to meet the requirements of their imagination." (chap. XVIII) It is for this reason that he persuades his father to leave Isabel a fortune. She must be rich in order to be free of the material world. She must be free in order to 'live.'

It is Ralph's one supreme mistake in intelligence and it is the mistake that ruins Isabel. For it is her wealth that arouses Madame Merle's realization that she can use her and leads directly to the disastrous, tragic marriage with Osmond. And in the superb scene in which, sitting in the candlelight in the elegant, spiritually empty house in Rome, Isabel takes stock of her tragedy, she painfully reveals to herself the conclusion:

"But for her money, as she saw today, she would never have done it. And then her mind wandered off to poor Mr. Touchett, sleeping under English turf, the beneficient author of infinite woe! For this was the fantastic fact. At bottom her money had been a burden, had been on her mind, which was filled with the desire to transfer the weight of it to some other conscience, to some more prepared receptacle. What would lighten her own conscience more effectually than to make it over to the man with the best taste in the world? Unless she should have given it to a hospital there would have been nothing better she could do with it; and there was no charitable institution in which she had been as much interested as in Gilbert Osmond. He would use her fortune in a way that would make her think better of it and rub off a certain grossness attaching to the good luck of an unexpected inheritance. There had been nothing very delicate in inheriting seventy thousand pounds; the delicacy had been all in Mr. Touchett's leaving them to her. But to marry Gilbert Osmond and bring him such a portion—in that there would be delicacy for her as well. There would be less for him—that was true; but that was his affair, and if he loved her he wouldn't object to her being rich. Had he not had the courage to say he was glad she was rich?" (chap. XLII)

It is at the moment when Ralph is dying that the theme is finally stated in the form at once the most affecting and most morally profound.

"She raised her head and her clasped hands; she seemed for a moment to pray for him. 'Is it true—is it true?' she asked.

'True that you've been stupid? Oh no,' said Ralph with a sensible intention of wit.

'That you made me rich—that all I have is yours?'

He turned away his head, and for some time said nothing. Then, at last: 'Ah, don't speak of that—that was not happy.' Slowly he moved his face toward her again, and they once more saw each other.

'But for that—but for that——!' And he paused. 'I believe I ruined you,' he wailed.

She was full of the sense that he was beyond the reach of pain; he seemed already so little of this world. But even if she had not had it she would still have spoken, for nothing mattered now but the only knowledge that was not pure anguish—the knowledge that they were looking at the truth together. 'He married me for the money,' she said. She wished to say everything; she was afraid he might die before she had done so.

He gazed at her a little, and for the first time his fixed eyes lowered their lids. But he raised them in a moment, and then, 'He was greatly in love with you,' he answered.

'Yes, he was in love with me. But he wouldn't have married me if I had been poor. I don't hurt you in saying that. How can I? I only want you to understand. I always tried to keep you from understanding; but that's all over.'

'I always understood,' said Ralph.

'I thought you did, and I didn't like it. But now I like it.'

'You don't hurt me—you make me very happy.' And as Ralph said this there was an extraordinary gladness in his voice. She bent her head again, and pressed her lips to the back of his hand. 'I always understood,' he continued, 'though it was so strange—so pitiful. You wanted to look at life for yourself—but you were not allowed; you were punished for your wish. You were ground in the very mill of the conventional!'

'Oh yes, I've been punished,' Isabel sobbed." (chap. LIV)

The necessity here of stating in its dreadful simplicity the agonizing truth so that the relationship of the two may be purified and deepened shows an intuition the very opposite of sentimental.

Isabel, then, imagining herself free, has in fact delivered herself into bondage. And the bondage has come about not casually but out of the very force and fortune of her own aspirations to freedom. She has sought life and because she has sought it in this way she has found death.

Freedom, to Isabel and to Ralph (for he has been as much concerned in the issue as she), has been an idealized freedom. They have sought to be free not through a recognition of, but by an escape from, necessity. And in so doing they have delivered Isabel over to an exploitation as crude and more corrupting than the exploitation that would have been her fate if Mrs. Touchett had never visited Albany.

" 'Do you still like Serena Merle?' " is Mrs. Touchett's last question of Isabel.

" 'Not as I once did. But it doesn't matter, for she's going to America.'

'To America? She must have done something very bad.'

'Yes—very bad.'

'May I ask what it is?'

'She made a convenience of me.'

'Ah,' cried Mrs. Touchett, 'so she did of me! She does of every-one.' " (chap. LIV)

The Portrait of a Lady is one of the most profound expressions in literature of the illusion that freedom is an abstract quality inherent in the individual soul.

It is interesting to compare James's book with another great novel written not very long before, *Madame Bovary*, the story of another woman "ground in the very mill of the conventional." It is true that Emma Bovary is, unlike Isabel Archer, not in the least 'fine,' that she fails to escape from her petty-bourgeois social *milieu* and that she is quite incapable of the exalted moral discipline to which Isabel is dedicated, yet we will learn something of James's novel, I think, from a glance at Flaubert's. What is shocking in *Madame Bovary* is the appalling passivity of Flaubert's characters, their inability to fight in any effective way the bourgeois world which Flaubert detests and which relentlessly warps and destroys all fineness in them. The strength of the novel lies in the very ruthlessness of its exposure of romantic attitudes; but therein also lies its weakness, the sense we get of something less than the human capacity for heroism, the uneasy suspicions of a *roman à thèse*. *The Portrait of a Lady* gives, as a matter of fact, no more positive response to its revelation of bourgeois values than *Madame Bovary*, yet we do experience a sense of human resilience and dignity. The interesting question is how far this sense—embodied in the 'fineness' of Isabel herself—is merely romantic and illusory.

The issue can perhaps be put in this way: is not the accumulated effect of the novel to present human destiny as inexorably one of suffering and despair? There are a number of tendencies making for this effect. In the first place there is the insistent use of dramatic irony in the construction of the book. Chapter after chapter in the early reaches of the novel is designed to emphasize the fatality facing Isabel's aspirations. The fifth chapter tells us she has come to Europe to find happiness; the sixth that she likes unexpectedness ("I shall not have success (in Europe) if they're too stupidly conventional. I'm not in the least stupidly conventional"). The seventh chapter ends with the following exchange:

> " 'I always want to know the things one shouldn't do.'
> 'So as to do them?' asked her aunt.
> 'So as to choose,' said Isabel."

The eighth draws to a close with

> " 'I shall never make anyone a martyr.'
> 'You'll never be one, I hope.'
> 'I hope not. . . .' "

This is all, it may be argued, simply Henry James at work, extracting from every situation its maximum of point. But the art, it seems to me, is in a subtle sense self-betraying. What is achieved is a kind of inevitability, a sense of Isabel's never standing a chance, which amounts not to objective irony but to the creation of something like an external destiny. Is not martyrdom becoming, in a sense at once insidious and—with all the associations and overtones one may care to give the word—romantic? Is there not to be here a breath—a very sophisticated and infinitely worldly breath—of the emotional and moral inadequacy involved in George Eliot's vision of those latter-day Saint Theresas?

Our final judgement must depend on the climax—the famous ending—of the book. It is from this ultimate impression that we shall have to decide whether James indeed plays fair with Isabel and us, whether he reveals in full profundity and (in the least cold sense of the word) objectivity a tragic situation or whether there is a certain sleight of hand, the putting across not of life but of something which merely for the moment passes for life. But before we consider this final climax it is worth noting what would seem an odd weakness in the novel. Is it not a little strange that of all the essential parts of Isabel's story which are revealed to us the section of her life most pointedly avoided is that immediately before her decision to marry Osmond? She has met him, got to know him somewhat; she then goes away for a year, travelling in Europe and the Middle East with Madame Merle. When she comes back to Florence she has decided to marry Osmond. This is, from the novelist's point of view, the most difficult moment in the book. How to convince us that a young woman like Isabel would in fact marry a man like Osmond? And it is a moment which, despite the revealing conversation with Ralph (which does indeed tell us something) is, I suggest, not satisfactorily got over. And the point is that if Isabel's marriage to Osmond is in any sense a fraud perpetrated upon us for his own ends by the author, the book is greatly weakened.

At the end of the novel Isabel, after Ralph's death and another encounter with Caspar Goodwood, returns to Rome. Is her return to Osmond irrevocable, an acceptance now and for ever of her 'destiny,' or is it tentative, no ending, the situation unresolved? Mr. F. O. Matthiessen, arguing in the latter sense, has a most interesting observation:

> "The end of Isabel's career is not yet in sight. That fact raises a critical issue about James's way of rounding off his narratives. He was keenly aware of what his method involved. As he wrote in his notebook, upon concluding his detailed project: 'With strong handling it seems to me that it may all be very true, very powerful, very touching. The obvious criticism of course will be that it is not finished—that it has not seen the heroine to the end of her situation—that I have left her *en l'air.* This is both true and false. The *whole* of anything is never told; you can only take what groups together. What I have done has that unity—it groups together. It is complete in itself—and the rest may be taken up or not, later'."[5]

James's own evidence is of course conclusive as to his intention, but it is not necessarily relevant as to what is in fact achieved; and it seems to me that, although the ending of *The Portrait of a Lady* does not completely and irrevocably round off the story—the possibility of Isabel's later reconsidering her decision is not excluded —yet the dominant impression is undoubtedly that of the deliberate rejection of 'life' (as offered by Caspar Goodwood) in favour of death, as represented by the situation in Rome. The scene with Goodwood is indeed very remarkable with its candid, if tortured, facing of a sexual implication which James is apt to sheer off. On the whole the effect of this scene, though one understands completely the quality of Isabel's reaction, is further to weight the scales against a return to Rome. Even if Goodwood himself is impossible, the vitality that he conveys is a force to be reckoned with and Isabel's rejection of this vitality involves more clearly than ever the sense that she is turning her face to the wall.

Isabel's return to Rome is certainly not a mere surrender to the conventional force of the marriage vow. The issue as to whether or not she should leave her husband is twice quite frankly broached by Henrietta, as well as by Goodwood. Isabel's first reply to Henrietta is significant:

[5] *Henry James, The Major Phase* (1946), p. 151.

" 'I don't know what great unhappiness might bring me to; but it seems to me I shall always be ashamed. One must accept one's deeds. I married him before all the world; I was perfectly free; it was impossible to do anything more deliberate. One can't change that way,' Isabel repeated." (chap. XLVII)

Later, when she discovers how little free she had in fact been, it is her obligation towards Pansy that becomes the most important factor. But always there is the sense of some deep inward consideration that makes the particular issues—the character of Osmond, her own mistakes, the needs of Pansy, the importunity of Goodwood—irrelevant. The recurring image in the last pages is of a sea or torrent in which Isabel is immersed. Goodwood becomes identified with the torrent. Her temptation is to give herself up to it.[6] When she breaks loose from him and the image she is once more 'free,' free and in darkness. The lights now are the lights of Gardencourt and now she knows where to turn. "There was a very straight path." (chap. LV)

It seems to me inescapable that what Isabel finally chooses is something represented by a high cold word like duty or resignation, the duty of an empty vow, the resignation of the defeated, and that in making her choice she is paying a final sacrificial tribute to her own ruined conception of freedom. For Henry James, though he sees the tragedy implicit in the Victorian ruling-class view of freedom, is himself so deeply involved in that illusion that he cannot escape from it. His books are tragedies precisely because their subject is the smashing of the bourgeois illusion of freedom in the consciousness of characters who are unable to conceive of freedom in any other way. His 'innocent' persons have therefore always the characters of victims; they are at the mercy of the vulgar and the corrupt, and the more finely conscious they become of their situation the more unable are they to cope with it in positive terms. Hence the contradiction of a Fleda Vetch[7] whose superior consciousness (and conscience) leads her in effect to reject life in favour of death. This is a favourite, almost an archetypal situation, in James's novels. It achieves its most striking expression in *The Portrait of a Lady* and *The Wings of the Dove* in which another rich American girl meets, even more powerfully

[6]It is at such a moment that one sees the force of Stephen Spender's linking of James with Conrad's "in the destructive element immerse" in an otherwise not very helpful book (*The Destructive Element*, 1937).

[7]In *The Spoils of Poynton*.

and more exquisitely, the fate of Isabel Archer.

For James in his supreme concern for 'living' (Milly Theale in *The Wings of the Dove*, Strether in *The Ambassadors* have, like Isabel, this immense, magnificent desire to 'live') ultimately, in effect, turns his back on life. This is not unconnected, I think, with the fact that his characters never do anything like work. This description of Madame Merle is not untypical of a day in the life of a Henry James figure:

> "When Madame Merle was neither writing, nor painting, nor touching the piano, she was usually employed upon wonderful tasks of rich embroidery, cushions, curtains, decorations for the chimney-piece; an art in which her bold, free invention was as noted as the agility of her needle. She was never idle, for when engaged in none of the ways I have mentioned she was either reading (she appeared to Isabel to read 'everything important'), or walking out, or playing patience with the cards, or talking with her fellow inmates." (chap. XIX)

The contemplation of such a way of life is likely, after all, to lead to idealism, for the necessities behind such an existence are by no means obvious. It is a superficial criticism to accuse James of snobbery or even of being limited by his social environment (what artist is not?). But there can be no doubt that what the bourgeois world did for James was to turn him into a moral idealist chasing a chimera of ideal conduct divorced from social reality.

It is not that his sense of social reality is in any way weak. On the contrary his picture of his world has, it has already been emphasized, a magnificent solidity, a concrete richness of the subtlest power. Nor is he in any easy, obvious sense taken in by that world (note his attitude to Warburton, his description of American-French society in Chapter XX and his total contempt for Osmond and his values); his picture of European bourgeois life is in its objective aspect as realistic as that of Balzac or Flaubert or Proust. No, if we are to isolate in James's novels the quality that is ultimately their limitation, it is to the core of his point of view, his philosophy, that we are led. The limiting factor in *The Portrait of a Lady* is the failure of James in the last analysis to dissociate himself from Isabel's errors of understanding.

One of the central recurring themes of James's novels is the desire to 'live,' to achieve a fullness of consciousness which permits the richest yet most exquisite response to the vibrations of life. And yet with this need to live is associated almost invariably the sense of death. Living, he seems to be saying again and again, involves martyrdom. The pleasure he finds in the contemplation and description of living at its most beautiful, most exalted point is subtly increased if the living creature is faced with death. Ralph Touchett is not alone among the dying swans of James's books: he is one of a line culminating in Strether (who discovers how to live too late) and in the fabulous Milly Theale. The attraction of this subject to James seems to me most significant. "Very true . . . very powerful . . . very touching . . ." one can almost hear him breathing out the words. It is a kind of apotheosis of his vision of life. And it is intimately, inextricably, linked up with his philosophic idealism. His 'good' characters, in their unswerving effort to live finely, turn out to be in the full implication of the phrase, too good for this world. Their sensibility becomes an end in itself, not a response to the actual issues of life. The freedom they seek turns out to be an idealized freedom; its ends, therefore, can only end, in a desire not merely to be free *in* this world but to be free *of* this world.

The popularity of James's novels among our intelligentsia today is significant too. It includes, I feel certain, not merely a genuine admiration for his extraordinary qualities, but also a powerful element of self-indulgence. It is not only pleasanter but easier to involve oneself in an idealized sensibility, a conscience[8] removed into realms outside the common and often crude basis of actual living. Many besides Isabel Archer imagine that they can buy themselves out of the crudities through the means of a high-grade consciousness and a few thousand pounds. And Henry James, albeit unconsciously, offers a subtle encouragement. He expresses the fate of Isabel Archer but expresses it in a way that suggests that it has, if not inevitability, at least a kind of glory to it. So that when Isabel takes her decision to return to Rome the dominant sense is not of the waste and degradation of a splendid spirit, but of a kind of inverted triumph. Better death than a surrender of the illusion which the novel has so richly and magnificently and tragically illuminated.

[8]It is interesting to speculate whether Conrad, when he referred to James as "the historian of fine consciences" was using the word in its English sense or with the French implication of 'consciousness.'

The Portrait of a Lady: "The Eternal Mystery of Things"

LYALL H. POWERS*

THE DENOUEMENT OF *The Portrait of a Lady*, like that of another great American novel—*The Adventures of Huckleberry Finn*—has provided scholars and critics with some uneasiness. It seems not to untie enough. James anticipated this reaction to his "wine and water novel"; in his notebooks he wrote (March 18, 1878): "The obvious criticism of course will be that it is not finished —that I have not seen the heroine to the end of her situation— that I have left her *en l'air.*" The answer he then provided to this criticism appears not to have proved wholly satisfactory. "The *whole* of anything is never told; you can only take what groups together. What I have done has that unity—it groups together. It is complete in itself—and the rest may be taken up or not, later."[1] Since Howells's attempt in his review of the novel in 1882 to accept "what seems a fragment instead of a whole,"[2] probably the best words on the subject are those few devoted to it by Dorothy Van Ghent: *"The Portrait . . .* is deeply informed with the tragic view of life: that tragic view whose essence is contained in the words, 'He who loses his life shall find it.' . . ."[3]

*Copyright c 1959, by The Regents of the University of California. Reprinted from NINETEENTH-CENTURY FICTION, XIV, 143-155 by permission of The Regents.

[1] *The Notebooks of Henry James*, ed. Matthiessen and Murdock (New York, 1955), p. 18.
[2] *The Century*, XXV (November, 1882), 26.
[3] *The English Novel: Form and Function* (Rinehart, 1953), p. 212; cf. p. 215: "The knowledge

Several of James's critics have approximated Mrs. Van Ghent's accuracy in touching on the heart of the novel,[4] but none, nevertheless, finds its form complete; the conclusion is always found unsatisfactory, or it is misunderstood. Carl Van Doren sees in Isabel "the type of youth advancing toward knowledge of life . . . innocence . . . flowering under the sun of experience. . . ," yet he avers that "The conclusion, on various grounds, does not satisfy, but it consistently enough rounds out Isabel's chronicle." Arnold Kettle makes the fruitful suggestion that "It would not be outrageous, though it might be misleading, to call [*The Portrait*] a nineteenth-century *Paradise Lost.*" He does not follow this lead, however, and simply confesses that

> It seems to me inescapable that what Isabel finally chooses is something . . . like duty or resignation, the duty of an empty vow, the resignation of the defeated, and that in making her choice she is paying a final sacrificial tribute to her own ruined conception of freedom.[5]

The recent comment of Quentin Anderson is likewise both typical and enlightening; in *The American Henry James* he says of Isabel Archer that "just as in the case of Milly Theale and Densher, Ralph's love will be her real inheritance," and adds, "the novel closes at the moment when Isabel has her foot on the threshold of the adult world."[6] Nevertheless, Anderson cannot accept without qualification James's feeling about the completeness of the novel: "the book clearly seems more rounded off to him than it can to the uninitiated reader."[7]

Here I would disagree with Anderson in particular and with the other critics of *The Portrait* generally. It seems to me that one need not be initiated in Anderson's sense to perceive in the novel that unity and completeness which James himself claimed for it.

she has acquired has been tragic knowledge, but her story does not stop there, as it would if it were a tragedy—it goes on out of the pages of the book, to Rome, where we cannot follow it; for the knowledge has been the means to 'life,' and having learned to live, she must 'live long,' as she says. It is only the process of the learning that the portrait frame itself holds."

[4]See Oscar Cargill, *"The Portrait of a Lady:* A Critical Reappraisal," *Modern Fiction Studies,* III (Spring, 1957), 11-32, and especially 24 ff., for a good summary of the critical reaction. I consider Cargill's interpretation briefly below, n. 19.

[5]*The American Novel* (rev. ed.; New York, 1940), pp. 173, 174; and *An Introduction to the English Novel* (2 vol.; London, 1953), II, 19, 31.

[6](New Brunswick, N.J., 1957), p. 190.

[7]*Ibid.,* p. 189.

The form of the novel *is* complete and, once identified, familiar and indeed satisfactory.

I

The form of the novel is, of course, essentially the pattern traced by the career of Isabel Archer, the career which begins within the sheltered confines of Gardencourt and leads her via Rome to Gardencourt again. Isabel's career is defined quite strictly by the polarity set up in the novel between Ralph Touchett and Gilbert Osmond; and we must be clearly aware of this polarity in order properly to appreciate the heroine's career. Of course the opposition between Ralph and Osmond is unmistakable, but the novel encourages us to pay close attention to the nature of this opposition. Osmond's attitude in suing for Isabel's love is exactly repeated by Ralph. In chapter xxix, Osmond "leaned forward, a hand on each knee; for some moments he bent his eyes on the floor. '. . . I'm in love with you.' "[8] In chapter xxxiv Isabel is involved in a similar situation with Ralph, who "straightened himself, then leaned forward, resting a hand on each knee. He fixed his eyes on the ground . . ." (IV, 69). His confession of love differs from Osmond's; " 'I love you, but I love without hope' " (IV, 72). The two are thus closely compared as suitors for Isabel. The distinction between them, however, is clearly drawn in such passages as this, toward the end of chapter xxiv:

> [Osmond] had consulted his taste in everything . . . that was what made him so different from everyone else. Ralph had something of this same quality, this appearance of thinking that life was a matter of connoisseurship; but in Ralph it was an anomaly, a kind of humorous excrescence, whereas in Mr. Osmond it was the keynote, and every . . . thing was in harmony with it (III, 377).

At the outset of chapter xlv the opposition is defined with simple clarity: "[Osmond] wished her to have no freedom of mind, and he knew perfectly well that Ralph was an apostle of freedom" (IV, 245).

Ralph is indeed an apostle of freedom, but for Isabel he is much more than that: for her he is virtually the author of her freedom. The bequest of £70,000 is, of course, the material sign of that

[8] *The Novels and Tales*, New York Edition, IV, 17. Subsequent references to the novel will be given in the text by volume and page number only.

freedom; the burden of that gift is exactly the burden of her free-dom. In a sense, Ralph is responsible for the Isabel whose fortunes we follow through the novel: it was he who made her "sufficient to have stood though free to fall." Throughout, Ralph does his best to extend his benevolent influence over Isabel; his difficulty in this attempt arises from his awareness that he must interfere but little if her freedom is to have any real meaning. Part of the dramatic effectiveness of the novel derives, in fact, from the depiction of Ralph's failure and decline as he is faced with Osmond's success. The opening of chapter xxviii, for instance, where Warburton is mounting to the Opera box shared by Osmond and Isabel, is typical: "He took his way to the upper regions and on the staircase met Ralph Touchett slowly descending, his hat at the inclination of ennui, his hands where they usually were" (IV, 1-2). This decline is similarly suggested early in chapter xxxiv, where Ralph pleads against Osmond; the note of descent and the imagery of falling are unmistakably present.[9] And finally, of course, the fact of Ralph's constant physical decline and ultimate death serves to emphasize his apparent loss, which is Osmond's gain. But here we reach the familiar paradox of the novel's end: Ralph's unfortunate death is singularly fortunate for Isabel in that it saves her from abject servitude to the evil incarnate which is Gilbert Osmond.

I suppose that it will be generally admitted that Osmond is James's most completely evil character. His principal fault is his towering egotism, so significantly described by Isabel in the impor-tant chapter xlii: " 'He took himself so seriously, it was something appalling. Under all his culture, his cleverness, his amenity, under his good-nature, his facility, his knowledge of life, his egotism lay hidden like a serpent in a bank of flowers' " (IV, 196). Osmond is surely the chief of that tribe of emotional cannibals who stalk through James's fiction.[10] The force of the evil of this crew is typically represented or expressed by those conventions and insti-tutions whose nature is dehumanizing. In *The Portrait* this repre-sentative function is filled principally by the institutions of the

[9]See IV, 69-70: "I had amused myself with planning out a high destiny for you. . . . You were not to come down so easily and so soon." Isabel replies, "Come down, you say?" "Well, that renders my sense of what has happened to you. You seemed to me to be soaring far up in the blue—to be, sailing in the bright light, over the heads of men. Suddenly someone tosses up a faded rosebud—a missile that should never have reached you—and straight you drop to the ground. It hurts me . . . hurts me as if I had fallen myself."

[10]See Osborn Andreas, *Henry James and the Expanding Horizon* (Seattle, 1948), chapter i and *passim*.

Roman Catholic church. Perhaps Osmond has confessed enough in his early exchange with Isabel:

> "You say you don't know me, but when you do you'll discover what a worship I have for propriety."
>
> "You're not conventional?" Isabel gravely asked.
>
> "I like the way you utter that word! No, I'm not conventional: I'm convention itself . . ." (IV, 21).

But in order to impress the point, James has Osmond surrounded with the marks of the conventional, of addiction to the institutionalized. The vaulted ante-chamber of his villa is "as high as a chapel" (III, 334); he confesses to Isabel that he has " 'envied the Pope of Rome—for the consideration he enjoys' " (III, 382); and on her reminding him " 'You ought indeed to be a Pope!' " Osmond admits " 'Ah, I should have enjoyed that!' " Isabel returns again to the question " 'You'd like to be the Pope?' " and Osmond —" 'I should love it' " (III, 427). It is in St. Peter's that Osmond notably resumes his pursuit of Isabel: "He now approached with all the forms—he appeared to have multiplied them on this occasion to suit the place" (III, 425). And, the pursuit having succeeded, Osmond and Isabel take up residence "in a high house in the very heart of Rome" (IV, 100). Closely associated with all this is the pathetic figure of little Pansy, the convent flower. The convent, a familiar figure in James's writing (we recall its role in *The American* and its influence upon Mme. de Mauves, an adult Pansy Osmond), gives here "the impression of a well-appointed prison" (IV, 374); and the kind remark of the nun, Mme. Catherine, to Pansy "seemed to represent the surrender of a personality, the authority of the Church" (IV, 382).

Finally, Osmond is completed by his association with Mme. Merle, who is as much his tool of sin, his implement of evil, as Hester Prynne was Roger Chillingworth's. Just as Osmond is "convention itself," so is Mme. Merle not merely worldly but "the great round world itself!" (III, 362). "She's complete" (III, 252). "She's perfect. She has no faults" (III, 332). Her function as Osmond's cat's-paw is emphasized in her final outburst at her master—the striking exchange on the subject of her treatment of Isabel:

> "It was precisely my deviltry that stupified her. I couldn't help it; I was full of something bad. . . . You've dried up my soul. . . . You've made

me as bad as yourself. . . . Your wife was afraid this morning, but in me it was really you she feared."[11]

It is to this perfect deviltry that Isabel in all her freedom has wedded herself. It is to this deviltry that Ralph has directed all his force of opposition. And it is to this deviltry that Isabel returns after the death of Ralph.

II

In turning again to Isabel Archer, the pattern of whose career gives the novel its form, we recall that we first see her as an innocent young woman freshly unaware of the great wide world and its lurking evils. She is perhaps recognizable to us, as she was to Grace Norton, as patterned to some extent on Minny Temple,[12] whose "moral spontaneity" delighted James.[13] Her career begins within the sheltered confines of the edenic Gardencourt, and, appropriately enough, the first nine chapters of *The Portrait* are devoted in great part to establishing the fact of Isabel's virtually prelapsarian innocence. Coupled with this innocence is Isabel's strong desire for independence, for freedom. Her early exchange with Mrs. Touchett at the close of chapter vii is typical:

"I always want to know the things one shouldn't do."
"So as to do them?" asked her aunt.
"So as to choose," said Isabel (III, 93).

It is this urgent desire for freedom that causes Isabel to reject the proposals of Warburton and Goodwood: her situation with the former "might contain oppressive, might contain narrowing elements" (III, 155-156), and with the latter might "deprive her of the sense of freedom. . . . The idea of diminished liberty was particularly disagreeable to her" (III, 162). Ralph's gift of £70,000 pro-

[11]III, 334-336. The nature of Osmond's influence—taking away her innocence—is interestingly expressed by Serena Merle in her words, " 'The matter is that I would give my right hand to be able to weep, and that I can't.' " Osmond asks, " 'What good would it do you to weep?' " Serena replies, " 'It would make me feel as I felt before I knew you' " (III, 334). One is here reminded of Blake's "A tear is an intellectual thing."

[12]James admitted to Grace Norton in December, 1880, "I had her [Minny] in my mind and there is in the heroine a considerable infusion of my impression of her remarkable nature." Quoted in Leon Edel's introduction, *The Portrait of a Lady*, Riverside Editions, p. xiv; the date of the unpublished letter is given in Cargill, "*The Portrait of a Lady:* A Critical Reappraisal," p. 12.

[13]See *The Letters of Henry James*, ed. Lubbock (New York, 1920), I, 26.

vides Isabel with the onerous freedom she sought. That it was indeed as onerous as true freedom must always be is a principal theme in the novel.

It is early suggested that, despite the protestations of her wish to be free to make her own choices, Isabel was in fact reluctant to accept this responsibility in full. On Ralph's early suggestion to her that she wishes to " 'drain the cup of experience,' " Isabel exclaims, " 'No, I don't want to touch the cup of experience. It's a poisoned drink! I only want to see for myself' " (III, 312). And at the crucial moment of Osmond's profession of love—" 'Oh don't say that please,' she answered with an intensity that expressed the dread of having, in this case too, to choose and decide" (IV, 18). This reluctance to accept the responsibility of freedom is an important flaw in Isabel's character. For as she is freed from Gardencourt and moves into the world to begin the experience she at once desires and dreads, it is the burden of her freedom that makes her the easy prey of Gilbert Osmond:

> And she had loved him, she had so anxiously and yet so ardently given herself—a good deal for what she found in him, but a good deal also for what she brought him and what might enrich the gift. . . . *but for the money*, as she saw to-day, she would never have done it. And then her mind wandered off to poor Mr. Touchett . . . the beneficent author of infinite woe! For this was the fantastic fact. At bottom *her money had been a burden*, had been on her mind, which was filled with the desire to transfer the weight of it to some other conscience, to some more prepared receptacle (IV, 192-193; my italics).

Thus she makes her great donation to the "charitable institution" which she conceives Osmond to be—the donation of her money, her freedom, herself. But there is another aspect to Isabel's weakness: she was herself touched with that evil so eminently incarnate in Osmond—the evil of emotional cannibalism. Her coming to him "with charged hands" was the equivalent of purchasing him—as she herself recognizes: "She could not have done otherwise. The finest—in the sense of being the subtlest—manly organism she had ever known had become her property . . ." (IV, 194). Poor Isabel had bought the mansion of a love—and been possessed by it.

In becoming Mrs. Osmond, Isabel has entered into an intimate relationship with the serpent in the bank of flowers; her experience of the evil of the world is given her most fully. The innocent young woman of the Gardencourt phase is notably altered by her union with Osmond. The effect of his influence on Isabel is visible from the moment of her first visit to his villa; even then her fresh, spontaneous nature begins to curb itself—"She was very careful therefore as to what she said, as to what she noticed or failed to notice; more careful than she had ever been before" (III, 379). But especially after her marriage, the alteration in Isabel is striking; virtually all of the characters notice and comment on the phenomenon. The most perceptive observation is, of course, Ralph's; he is prepared to find her changed, masked, but even the confirmation of his expectations is startling—"Ralph, in all this, recognised the hand of the master; for he knew that Isabel had no faculty for producing studied impressions" (IV, 142). He ponders the change:

> Poor human-hearted Isabel, what perversity had bitten her? Her light step drew a mass of drapery behind it; her intelligent head sustained a majesty of ornament. The free, keen girl had become quite another person; what he saw was the fine lady who was supposed to represent something. What did Isabel represent? Ralph asked himself; he could only answer by saying that she represented Gilbert Osmond. "Good heavens, what a function!" he then woefully exclaimed. He was lost in wonder at the mystery of things (IV, 143-144).

It seems, indeed, that everyone but poor Isabel recognizes the evil influence of Osmond upon her. Isabel's problem, the complication which sustains the novel to its end, is the conflict within herself between what she conceives of as her duty to her husband, and what she feels there is of truth in the sentiments of her friends about Osmond—and about Mme. Merle.

> Isabel had had three years to think over Mrs. Touchett's theory that Madame Merle had made Gilbert Osmond's marriage. . . . Madame Merle might have made Gilbert Osmond's marriage, but she certainly had not made Isabel Archer's. That was the work of—Isabel scarcely knew what: of nature, providence, fortune, of the eternal mystery of things (IV, 158).

And it is Isabel's attempt and final success at seeing into this eternal mystery that constitutes her problem.

In order to save herself in her condition, Isabel—like us all—must identify the evil that is to be faced, must be aware of what knowledge her experience has brought her.[14] The task is made

---

[14]See Mark Schorer's perceptive comment in *"Women in Love," The Achievement of D.*

difficult, as I say, by her conception of the duty[15] she owes her husband—himself the chief representative of evil in her world.

> Isabel was trying as much as possible to take her husband's view. She succeeded after a fashion, but she fell short of the point I mention. After all she couldn't rise to it; something held her and made this impossible. . . . There was a vague doubt that interposed—a sense that she was not quite sure (IV, 177-178).[16]

The "sense that she was not quite sure"—and perhaps the occasional reappearance of the failing Ralph—enables Isabel finally to recognize the evil in her world. The *anagnorisis* in this drama is long drawn out. It certainly begins no later than chapter xlii—following Isabel's intrusion on Osmond "sitting while Madame Merle stood"—where Isabel received that "start that accompanies unexpected recognition" (IV, 186). Her long reverie concludes, almost as it began, with Isabel "gazing at a remembered vision—that of her husband and Madame Merle unconsciously and familiarly associated" (IV, 205). Her eyes are further opened on Mme. Merle's return from Naples to learn the success of Warburton's suit for Pansy; Isabel's frightened question " 'What have you to do with me?' " is arrestingly answered by Serena Merle's terrible " 'Everything!' " (IV, 327). Thus, the Countess Gemini's disclosure of Pansy's progenitors is almost completely superfluous.

Isabel's reluctance to admit the identity of the evil she must face accounts for the drawing out of the *peripeteia*. Her first move, surely, is her offer at the close of chapter xliii to aid Rosier's cause

H. Lawrence, ed. F. J. Hoffman and H. T. Moore (Norman, Okla., 1953), p. 164: "we can recognize the inevitability of her [Isabel's] renunciation of the right to ignorance once her education in corruption is completed, and she gains her moral freedom. . . ."

[15]The nice problem of the recognition of one's *proper* duty is a common theme in James's novels, at least in those of the 'eighties: it is Verena Tarrant's, Hyacinth Robinson's, and Nick Dormer's quite as much as Isabel's.

[16]It is to be noted that one of Isabel's reasons for refusing to leave Osmond—" 'One must accept one's deeds. I married him before all the world' " (IV, 284)—is very evidence of the persistent evil influence of her husband. As late as chap. li Isabel reasons thus: "What he thought of her she knew, what he was capable of saying to her she had felt; yet they were married, for all that, and marriage meant that a woman should cleave to the man with whom, uttering tremendous vows, she had stood at the altar" (IV, 361). We recognize here an echo of Osmond's words to her of a few pages earlier: " 'I'm not aware that we're divorced or separated; for me we're indissolubly united. . . . You don't like to be reminded of that, I know; but I'm perfectly willing. . . . Because I think we should accept the consequences of our actions, and what I value most in life is the honour of a thing!' " (IV, 356). In other words, marriage with Osmond is simply another of those dehumanizing institutions so dear to him, another "surrender of personality, the authority of the Church."

with Pansy: " 'I'll do what I can for you. I'm afraid it won't be much, but what I can I'll do' " (IV, 222). A further step in this direction is Isabel's words of comfort to Pansy, returned to the convent for freshening—" 'I won't desert you,' " and " 'Yes—I'll come back' " (IV, 386). But these marks of change in Isabel, of her opposition to Osmond, are but fuller evidence of that conflicting stream that had been present in her from the outset, that "vague doubt that interposed." Indeed, with our first information that Isabel has married comes Mme. Merle's assertion that Isabel takes the opposite line to Osmond " 'in everything.' " " 'They think quite differently' " (IV, 93). It is clear, however, that Isabel is unable to take any important positive *action* in opposition to Osmond until the imminence of Ralph Touchett's death obliges her to choose between continued passivity and overt action.

Thus one can say that Ralph's death is quite literally responsible for Isabel's breaking her association with the evil which Osmond is and represents. It is perhaps permissible to say that in this Ralph assumes a Christ-like role.[17] Quentin Anderson wisely points out, in *The American Henry James*, that "as in the case of Milly Theale and Densher, Ralph's love will be her real inheritance" (p. 190).[18] Ralph's love for Isabel serves the same function, ultimately, as Milly's for Densher: the means of salvation.

The effect of Isabel's choice to return to Gardencourt against Osmond's wishes—her first *act* of positive opposition—is clearly represented in the novel in terms of a rebirth theme. The opening of chapter liii, describing her journey from Rome ("the place

[17]Indeed, Ralph's role throughout the novel has been rather Christ-like—"Ralph's little visit was a lamp in the darkness. . . . He made her feel the good of the world" (IV, 203). " 'You won't lose me—you'll keep me. Keep me in your heart,' " he says finally to Isabel (IV, 413).

[18]It is surprising that Ernest Sandeen, in *"The Wings of the Dove* and *The Portrait of a Lady:* A Study of James's Later Phase," PMLA, LXIX (December, 1954), 1060-1075, so completely overlooks the similarity between Ralph and Milly—"in *Wings* there is no character to correspond to Ralph Touchett in *Portrait"*(p. 1061)—especially when his essay makes such observations as this: "Because the image from which Isabel Archer emerged was marked by disease and early death, it is an interesting circumstance that not Isabel but Ralph Touchett is afflicted with this disease of consumption and dies of it near the end of the story" (pp. 1062-1063). And the later comment, "Milly is not provided with a patron-guardian who is also a sacrificial victim" (p. 1065), seems to overlook the point that Milly is herself the patron-guardian to Densher and for his sake is the sacrificial victim. Sandeen's remark that Milly is a "profoundly tragic figure" (p. 1065) might be amended to read that Milly is as tragic as Christ—or as Ralph Touchett. Sandeen seems not to have noticed that the Ralph-Isabel relationship is essentially similar to the Milly-Merton one; and that finally one might say of Ralph to Isabel, "His memory's your love. You *want* no other."

where people suffered" [IV, 328]), suggests passage through a kind of Wasteland—"strange-looking, dimly-lighted, pathless lands, in which there was no change of seasons, but only, as it seemed, a perpetual dreariness of winter" (IV, 390). Then occurs the statement of the death theme: "She had moments indeed in her journey from Rome which were almost as good as being dead."[19] But there is with this the definite promise of rebirth; first, in such statements as this:

> She saw herself, in the distant years, still in the attitude of a woman who had her life to live. . . . Deep in her soul—deeper than any appetite for renunciation—was the sense that life would be her business for a long time to come. . . . It was a proof of strength—it was a proof she should someday be happy again" (IV, 392).

And second, the rebirth theme is struck in the peculiar references to Gardencourt—the scene of Isabel's state of innocence, of pre-experience—which suggest that Isabel is returning to her original innocence: "Gardencourt had been her starting point, and to those muffled chambers it was at least a temporary solution to return" (IV, 391). This recalls her earlier thought: "There seemed to Isabel in these days something sacred in Gardencourt . . ." (IV, 296). It is clear, however, that Isabel's exodus from Gardencourt was as final as that of Adam and Eve from the Garden of Eden. If she returns to Gardencourt it will not be to regain her original innocence. Isabel's thoughts of the sacredness of Gardencourt conclude, "No chapter of the past was more perfectly irrecoverable." To confirm this fact, the opening of chapter liv relates that "Isabel's arrival at Gardencourt on this second occasion was even quieter than it had been on the first . . . Mrs. Osmond was a stranger . . ." (IV, 403). But that her return does mark the gaining of a new innocence—does indicate the completion of her salvation through Ralph's death—this is my thesis.

III

Isabel as we last see her has not regained her prelapsarian innocence, but rather has achieved that higher innocence, that superior goodness, which comes to the fallen who are saved. The pattern here is the familiar one of the paradox of the fortunate fall. Isabel's

---

[19] IV, 391; cf. Anderson, pp. 190-191.

knowledge of evil, her fall into the evil embrace of Gilbert Osmond, is the equivalent of the *felix culpa* over which the Easter *exultet* rejoices.[20] The result of her spiritual rebirth is seen in her determination to return and confront the evil of the world, to work at the redemption of that evil, to do in short whatever work the spiritually regenerate necessarily undertake here below. It is for this purpose that she is determined to return to Osmond, not, I submit, for those other possible reasons which, singly or combined, must always seem insufficient to the reader of *The Portrait*. That she is returning simply to maintain the institution of her marriage with Osmond we cannot accept, for as we have seen, that institution is itself an evil. ("Shall we continue in sin that grace may abound?") The more plausible reason, that she returns to keep her promise to Pansy, is significantly treated near the end of chapter liii, in the conversation between Isabel and Henrietta:

> "I don't see why you promised little Miss Osmond to go back."
> "I'm not sure I myself see now," Isabel replied. "But I did then."
> "If you've forgotten your reason perhaps you won't return."
> Isabel waited a moment. "Perhaps I shall find another" (IV, 397-398).

The *other* reason she surely finds at Ralph's death. The final objection, raised by Henrietta's last words to Goodwood (" 'Look here, Mr. Goodwood,' she said; 'just you wait!' "), that Isabel may yet change her mind, has been sufficiently well answered in James's *Notebooks*—if not in the closing lines of the novel itself. The note for the end of the novel reads, "the last line of the story: a characteristic characterization of Isabel." The editors comment that:

> the final speech by Henrietta . . . is to be 'characteristic' of her rather than of Isabel. James' note thus makes it clear that he intended from the time of his first draft to have this speech be indicative of Henrietta's unquenchable optimism rather than what it has sometimes been interpreted to be, a sure forecast of Isabel's future action.[21]

---

[20] "O certe necessarium Adae peccatum [et nostrum] quod Christi morte deletum est! O felix culpa, quae talem ac tantum meruit habere redemptorem!" Cited in A. O. Lovejoy, "Milton and the Paradox of the Fortunate Fall," *Essays in the History of Ideas* (Baltimore, 1948), p. 285; see also pp. 286—287, and p. 287 n. 26.

[21] *Notebooks*, pp. 18, 19. In his excellent reappraisal of *The Portrait*, Cargill makes an interesting case for Isabel's return to the protection of her virginal life with Osmond—the final experience with Goodwood being the deciding factor. His point is a good one, but I cannot accept it as a completely satisfactory explanation of the novel's conclusion; it does not sufficiently account for the nobility of Isabel's character as seen in the closing action

Finally, there seems to be a clear forecast of what Isabel's return to Osmond will bring. Isabel's successful confrontation of Osmond's principal aide on their concurrent visits to Pansy at the convent is prophetic, it seems to me. Mme. Merle has been exposed, and she knows it.

> Isabel saw it all as distinctly as if it had been reflected in a large clear glass. It might have been a great moment for her, for it might have been a moment of triumph. That Madame Merle had lost her pluck and saw before her the phantasm of exposure—this in itself was a revenge, this in itself was almost *the promise of a brighter day* (IV, 378-379; my italics).

It is on the threshold of just such a brighter day that we leave Isabel. The journey on which she sets out is familiar: "She had not known where to turn; but she knew now. There was a very straight path" (IV, 436). Indeed, one might almost suppose that Caspar Goodwood had recognized it as he utters his final speech: "Oh, she started—." It is as though Isabel had heard the words 'of the Archangel Michael:

> *thou has attaind the summe*
> *Of wisdom . . .*
> *only add*
> *Deeds to thy knowledge answerable . . .*
> *then wilt thou not be loath*
> *To leave this Paradise, but shalt possess*
> *A Paradise within thee happier farre.*

As I suggested at the outset, then, *The Portrait of a Lady* has indeed the unity which James claimed for it. The career of Isabel Archer has the completeness of form of the familiar pattern of redemption, of the fortunate fall. As the novel ends we recognize her arrival; we know to what she has attained; there are really no further questions to ask. The straight path before her is known to us all.

of the book, nor does it seem adequately to take into account the pattern of the whole development of the novel.

THE BOSTONIANS

1886

"The Bostonians"

LIONEL TRILLING*

The Bostonians is one of a pair of novels, the other being *The Princess Casamassima*, which, in the family of Henry James's works, have a special connection with each other, a particular isolate relationship, as of twins. They were published in the same year, 1886, their previous serial appearances in magazines having been in part concurrent, and although *The Bostonians* was in point of fact the earlier conceived and the first written, they almost seem to have been composed simultaneously, in a single act of creation. They are set apart from James's other novels by having in common a quick responsiveness to the details of the outer world, an explicit awareness of history, of the grosser movements of society and civilization. They share a curious knowledge of the little groups of queer people who, in small dark rooms, agitate the foolish questions which will eventually be decided on the broad field of the future. Very likely it was because James was conscious of these characteristics of the two books—and, we feel, was pleased with them as the evidence of the enlargement of his social intelligence —that he had especially high hopes that the two novels would be happily received by the public.

The disappointment of these hopes is well known. With the exception of his later defeat in the theater, no check given to James's ambition was so disastrous. The English press treated *The*

Princess Casamassima with an almost absolute contempt, and if it was more indulgent with *The Bostonians,* this was only because it found some satisfaction in an American's account of the eccentricity of American manners. The American reviewers were outraged by *The Bostonians;* their more lenient response to *The Princess Casamassima* was in part dictated by their settled opinion of the English social system, which the book might be thought to satirize. Both novels were called queer and foolish, and their failure caused a serious decline in their author's reputation and market.

When, in April of 1883, James had written out in his notebook the full scenario of *The Bostonians,* he had summarized his intention by saying, "I wished to write a very *American* tale."[1] It is possible to say of those of James's novels that are set in America —*The Bostonians* is the last until *The Ivory Tower* of some twenty years later—that they have a tone different from the novels which are set in Europe. I regard with suspicion my natural impulse to say this is a specifically "American" tone, for I should not know how to explain with any confidence what that is. Yet it seems to me worth observing that, as against the heavy chiaroscuro which in *The Princess Casamassima* is appropriate to the rich clotted past of civilization as that novel evokes it, *The Bostonians* seems suffused by "the dry American light," and that it is marked by a comicality which has rather more kinship with American than with British humor, or with wit of any transatlantic kind. It is said of Miss Birdseye that "she was heroic, she was sublime, the whole moral history of Boston was reflected in her displaced spectacles"; it is said of Dr. Mary Prance that "it is true that if she had been a boy, she would have borne some relation to a girl," and also that "she was determined that she wouldn't be a patient, and it seemed that the only way not to be one was to be a doctor"—humor is latent in all James's writing, implicit in the nature of his prose, but I can bring to mind no other of his novels in which it breaks so gaily out of latency and implicitness into the memorable free overtness of such sentences as these and of scenes analogous to these sentences.

As a representation of the American actuality, *The Bostonians* is in every way remarkable, and its originality is striking. James's Boston, Cambridge, and Cape Cod are superbly rendered, and these localities may still be known—for they have changed less than most American places—through his descriptions of them. No American writer before James had so fully realized the contemporary, physical scene of moral action and social existence. Nor had the nature of the American social existence ever been so brilliantly suggested. Manners have changed since James wrote, but not the peculiar tenuity of the fabric of American social life. The London of *The Princess Casamassima* is no doubt the city of dreadful loneliness, and the barriers of class which it represents are real enough, yet the story sees to it that people at opposite social poles from each other shall meet and become involved with each other. It is thus perfectly in the tradition of the English novel, which characteristically likes the social mixture to be thick and variously composed, and this is a literary preference which corresponds, at whatever distance, to an actuality of English life. But in the America of *The Bostonians*, as in the America that Tocqueville had observed some forty years before, society is but little organized to allow for variousness and complexity, and the social atoms seem to have a centrifugal tendency. Basil Ransom lives in New York with no other companion than his little variety actress. He makes every effort to avoid the company of his cousin, Mrs. Luna, and she, a lady of family and means, seems to have no social circle at all. Mrs. Burrage is by way of being a New York "hostess," but the guests at the party which she gives for Verena Tarrant seem all to have met each other for the first time. It is of the essence of Olive Chancellor's nature that she cannot endure social intercourse; a speech to a crowd is her notion of human communication, and she cannot laugh. Verena Tarrant has presumably never had a friend until Olive Chancellor institutes their ambiguous alliance. Dr. Prance lives in virtual solitude. Miss Birdseye, having devoted a long life to humanity, becomes herself an object of devotion, but rather as if she were everyone's old school, or some dear outworn ideal. The character of Miss Birdseye scandalized Boston because it was thought to be a portrait of Elizabeth Peabody, Hawthorne's famous reforming sister-in-law, and William James—who had, in any case, a poor opinion of *The Bostonians* —undertook to rebuke his brother for his failure of taste. (Henry replied in a letter, a masterpiece of justifiable ambiguity, which has become the classic statement of the relation of the novelist's imagination to real persons.) Even with the most extravagant notions of the Boston sensibility, it is difficult to understand what the ground of the offense was supposed to be, for if Miss Birdseye is indeed a portrait of Miss Peabody, it is the tenderest and most endearing imaginable. And perhaps that is what constituted the offense—for the law recognizes a certain wrong for which the novelist may be liable; it is called "invasion of privacy," and we may suppose that Boston was disturbed because James had committed this wrong, not in the mere legal meaning of the term, but in a way far more disturbing: it was not Miss Peabody's privacy that he had invaded but rather the privacy of his readers. He had forced them into intimacy with a person whom they daily greeted, he had made her available to their understanding and to their conscious love, had terribly implied that the actual woman might be the object of the same emotions that they inevitably felt toward the image of her in the novel.

The Bostonians and *The Princess Casamassima* seem to be set apart from the rest of James's canon by the public and political matter with which they deal. But their representation of large, overt, opposed forces and principles does not, in point of fact, mark their inspiration as of an essentially different kind from that of James's other novels. It may be said of James—with, of course, some risk of excessive simplification—that virtually all his fiction represents the conflict of two principles, of which one is radical, the other conservative. The two principles are constant, although circumstances change their particular manifestations and the relative values which they are judged to have. They may be thought of as energy and inertia; or spirit and matter; or spirit and letter; or force and form; or creation and possession; or Libido and Thanatos. In their simpler manifestations the first term of the grandiose duality is generally regarded with unqualified sympathy and is identified with the ideality of youth, or with truth, or with art, or with America; the second term is regarded with hostility and represented as being one with age, or convention, or philistinism, or decadent Europe. But James's mind is nothing if not "dialectical"—the values assigned to each of the two opposing principles are not permitted to be fixed and constant. Daisy Miller's crude innocent defiance of European conventions is as right as rain, but *Madame de Mauves* suggests that only a small change in circumstance can make American innocence a downright malevolence. Art as against the philistine morality may not always be in the right—creation may corrupt itself into its opposite, possession, as in *The Author of Beltraffio*. Life may be seen to express itself in death and through death. And in *The Birthplace* James seems to be saying that truth can exist only in and through the life of institutions, or that it can be communicated only through sadly inadequate approximations of truth.

The nature of the terms of James's dialectic suggests why his fiction is always momentous. And it is quite within the scope of his genius to infer the political macrocosm from the personal microcosm, to write large and public the disorders of the personal life and to suppose, as he did in *The Bostonians* and *The Princess Casamassima*, that it is the most natural thing in the world that they should

> *Divert and crack, rend and deracinate*
> *The unity and married calm of states. . . .*

If we compare the two political movements which James undertook to represent, the revolutionary anarchism of *The Princess Casamassima* will perhaps on first inspection seem to promise more as a theme for a novel than the militant feminism of *The Bostonians*. In a struggle for general social justice there is a natural force and dignity; and in a violent revolutionary intention there is the immediate possibility of high tragedy. But the doctrinaire demand for the equality of the sexes may well seem to promise but a wry and constricted story, a tale of mere eccentricity. The movement for female equality which became endemic in America and in the Protestant countries of Europe in the nineteenth century was predominantly social and legal in its program and even had —although not always—an outright anti-erotic bias which exposed it to the imputation of crankishness and morbidity. It would seem to be susceptible only of comic treatment, and the comedy it seems to propose is not of an attractive kind—it cannot, we know, have anything of the ancient bold freedom of *Lysistrata* or *The Thesmophoriazusae*, in which the women of Athens, in their very act of subverting the natural order of things, affirm the natural erotic community between men and women.

There is indeed some unpleasantness in the comedy of *The Bostonians*, yet exactly by risking this, by daring to seize on the qualities of the women's-rights movement which were "unnatural" and morbid, James possessed himself of a subject which was even larger in its significance than that of *The Princess Casamas-*

sima. A movement of social revolution may question the culture in which it exists, or it may not—indeed we can say of social revolutions that they do not in fact question cultures as much as they seem to do and say they do. But a movement of sexual revolution is to be understood as a question which a culture puts to itself, and right down to its very roots. It is a question about what it means to be a man and what it means to be a woman— about the quality of being which people wish to have. James was interested in the thin vagaries of the female movement of reform only as they suggested a conflict between men and women that went far deeper than any quarrel over rights and equalities. And the conflict that he perceived was not the battle of the sexes which Meredith and Shaw delighted in, a fine formality of marching and countermarching and intricate maneuver on a commodious plain, chosen by mutual consent, the point of the engagement being to demonstrate that women have as bright a spiritedness, as firm a resolution, and as particular an intention of sexuality as men. The opposing forces met on the field as if by appointment, they were animated by the sense of adventure, and defeat brought nothing much worse than honorable captivity on parole—no one in the least believes that John Tanner regrets his surrender to Ann Whitfield. The conflict which James described was very different from this. It was the bitter total war of the sexes which Strindberg conceived and which reached its fullest ideological and artistic expression in the works of D. H. Lawrence.

Tocqueville, whose great book figures in *The Bostonians* because it is the favorite reading of the hero of the novel, had noted the beginnings of sexual disorientation of America; and in James's own time, American observers who were not bound by convention, men so unlike as Walt Whitman and Henry Adams, were aware that something had gone wrong with the sexual life of the nation. "The men hate the women, and the women hate the men," Whitman had said. Adams spoke of American men as having sacrificed their sexuality to business and the machine, and as having induced in American women an indifference even to maternity. And James, when he had set down his intention of "writing a very *American* tale," went on to say, "I asked myself what was the most salient and peculiar point of our social life, the answer was: the situation of women, the decline of the sentiment of sex. . . ."

No more than Tocqueville or Henry Adams or D. H. Lawrence did James understand the sexual situation as an isolated fact, however momentous. For him, as for them, it was the sign of a general diversion of the culture from its course of nature. He makes this plain by his choice of a hero for *The Bostonians.* It was of course essential to his plan that his hero be an outlander, alien to the culture of Boston, and James at first thought that he should be a young man from the West. But a Western hero, he soon saw, was not possible. It must have occurred to him, for one thing, that in the West progressive social and political ideas had established themselves with relative ease, feminism in particular having made far greater advances than in the East, so that he would scarcely be setting up a counterprinciple to Boston. And then the assumptions about a Western hero were inevitably that he was emancipated from tradition, optimistic, concerned with practice rather than with theory, and likely to be impatient of intellectual refinements, and, of course, that he was materially successful. Such a hero might indeed be used to make a cultural-sexual point—in 1906 the western hero of William Vaughn Moody's *The Great Divide* was to rape the New England heroine for her own good; the audiences of Broadway were delighted with this show of benevolent violence which, as the play made clear, was symbolic of the energies of modern business enterprise and quite disposed of the decadent finickiness of the New England conscience. James had no desire for such an effect. He understood quite as well as Lawrence that the true masculine principle could not be affirmed by a hero who was energetic and successful in the material business of the modern world. In the dramatic nature of the case the spokesman for masculinity should be able to lay claim to none but personal powers; and he will be the better suited to his role if, like Basil Ransom, he has witnessed and participated in the defeat of his cultural tradition, if he has suffered the ruin of his fortunes, and is a stranger in the land of his conquerors.

By choosing a Southerner for his hero, James gained an immediate and immeasurable advantage. By this one stroke he set his story beyond any danger of seeming to be a mere bicker between morbid women and stupid men, the subject of dull, ill-natured jokes. When he involved the feminist movement with even a late adumbration of the immense struggle between North and South, he made it plain that his story had to do with a cultural crisis. Nor could this crisis, if properly understood, seem particular to America, for North and South, as James understands them, represent the two opposing elements in that elaborate politics of culture which, all over the civilized world, has been the great essential subject of the literature of the nineteenth and twentieth centuries.

The South had never had a vigorous intellectual life, and of the systematic apologists for its customs and manners as against the customs and manners of an ever more powerful industrial capitalism, only a very few had been men of real intellectual authority. Yet with the strange previsionary courage which led him, in *The Princess Casamassima*, to imagine types of political character unknown to his own time but familiar to ours, James conceived Basil Ransom as if he were the leading, ideal intelligence of the group of gifted men who, a half-century later, were to rise in the South and to muster in its defense whatever force may be available to an intelligent romantic conservatism. Rejecting much of the sentimental legend of the South, admitting the Southern faults and falsities the more easily because they believed that no civilization can be anything but imperfect, the Southern Agrarians yet said that the South stood for a kind of realism which the North, with its abstract intellectuality, was forgetting to its cost. Like their imagined proto-martyr Ransom, they asserted a distrust of theory, an attachment to tradition, and above all, the tragic awareness of the intractability of the human circumstance.

But Basil Ransom is more daring than any of his intellectual descendants of the South. He has the courage of the collateral British line of romantic conservatives—he is akin to Yeats, Lawrence, and Eliot in that he experiences his cultural fears in the most personal way possible, translating them into sexual fear, the apprehension of the loss of manhood. "The whole generation is womanised," he says, "the masculine tone is passing out of the world; it's a feminine, a nervous, hysterical, chattering, canting age, an age of hollow phrases and false delicacy and exaggerated solicitudes and coddled sensibilities, which, if we don't soon look out, will usher in the reign of mediocrity, of the feeblest and flattest and the most pretentious that has even been. The masculine character, the ability to dare and endure, to know and yet not to fear reality, to look the world in the face and take it for what it is— a very queer and partly very base mixture—this is what I want to preserve, or rather, as I may say, to recover; and I must say that

I don't in the least care what becomes of you ladies while I make the attempt."

And the fear of the loss of manhood, which we are familiar with in Yeats, in Lawrence, and in *The Waste Land*, is given reason for its existence everywhere in *The Bostonians.* The book is full of malign, archaic influences; it is suffused with primitive fear. It is not for nothing that Olive Chancellor's sister is named Mrs. Luna —with her shallow, possessive sexuality, which has the effect of conjuring away all masculine potency, she might as well have been named Mrs. Hecate. The very name of Olive Chancellor might suggest a deteriorated Minerva, presiding in homosexual chastity over the Athens of the New World. The meeting of Olive's colleagues is referred to as a rendezvous of witches on the Brocken, a characterization which is supported throughout the book by James's rather unpleasant sense of the threatening sordidness of almost all women except those in their first youth. Verena Tarrant is conceived as a sort of Iphigenia in Tauris, forced to preside as the priestess of the sacrifice of male captives. Basil Ransom is explicit in his feeling that when he is with Olive Chancellor he is not "safe." And indeed his position is at all times a precarious one. We have the impression that he is the only man in Boston, among hordes of doctrinaire Bacchae, and certainly he is the only man in the book—Verena's poor young suitor, Burrage, lives under the shadow of his mother; Dr. Tarrant is a kind of shaman, gloomily doing sexual service of some dim, grim, shameful kind to deprived Boston ladies; and Matthias Pardon, the newspaper man, is represented as the castrate priest of the huge idol of publicity, which, in the dialectic of the book, stands in hateful opposition to the life of emotion and true sexuality. Perhaps the novel's crucial scene is that which takes place in Memorial Hall at Harvard, when Ransom finds it necessary to enforce upon Verena's imagination the pathos of the fate of the young men who had died in the recent war. These young men had been his enemies, but he feels bound to them by the ties of the sex they have in common, and the danger of battle had never been so great as the sexual danger of his present civil situation.

There is one biographical circumstance of the writing of *The Bostonians* which ought to be mentioned in any account of the novel. I have no doubt it bears in an important way upon the personal problems of Henry James's own life which are implied, we must inevitably suppose, by Ransom's fears. But the investigation of these problems lies outside my competence and my purpose, and I mention the circumstance only for reasons that are purely literary, only, that is, because an awareness of it is likely to make for a warmer understanding of the book.

In 1881 James visited his country and his family for the first time since 1876, the year in which he made his decision to establish his home in England. From the beginning the visit was not a happy one. James disliked Boston, where he lived to be near his parents in Cambridge, and he was bored and restless. In January he went to stay with Henry Adams in Washington, and there, on the thirtieth of the month, he received the telegram announcing his mother's serious illness which was intended to prepare him for her death.

It was James's first familial loss and it shocked and saddened him deeply. Yet it also, as he writes of it in his notebook, moved him to a kind of joy. He had always known that he loved his mother, but not until he saw her in her shroud did he know how tender his love was. Mrs. James had been a quiet woman, with none of the spiritual quality of her husband, the elder Henry James. But her son wrote of her, "She was our life, she was the house, she was the keystone of the arch. She held us all together, and without her we are scattered reeds. She was patience, she was wisdom, she was exquisite maternity." And as his impassioned memorial of her draws to its close, he says, "It was the perfect mother's life—the life of a perfect wife. To bring her children into the world—to expend herself for years, for their happiness and welfare—then, when they had reached a full maturity and were absorbed in the world and their own interests—to lay herself down in her ebbing strength and yield up her pure soul to the celestial power that had given her this divine commission." Perhaps nothing that Henry James ever wrote approaches this passage in the explicit cognizance it takes of the biological nature of moral fact.

James stayed with his father and his sister Alice until May, when, at his father's insistence, he returned to England and his work. But in December came the news of his father's imminent death. The elder Henry James, it was said, had no wish to survive his wife; in his last illness he refused food and gently faded away. The younger Henry arrived too late to see his father for the last time, too late even for the funeral. William James's famous letter of farewell to their "sacred old Father" also arrived too late, but Henry took it to Cambridge cemetery and read it aloud over the grave, sure, as he wrote to William, that "somewhere out of the depths of the still bright winter air" the father heard.

His mother was the strength that is not power as the world knows power, the strength of conservation, the unseen, unregarded, seemingly unexerted force that holds things to their center. She had lived the ancient elemental course of life, which is without theory or formulation, too certain of itself and too much at one with itself even to aspire. His father, according to his particular lights, had had the masculine power, "the ability to dare and endure, to know and yet not to fear reality." During his sad visit to his parental land in 1883, the last for twenty years, when the parental family had come to an end, Henry James wrote out the scenario of *The Bostonians*, which is a story of the parental house divided against itself, of the keystone falling from the arch, of the sacred mothers refusing their commission and the sacred father endangered.

NOTES

1 The tense of the predicate verb cannot pass without notice. James was not to compose the book until two years later, but when once he had completed the scenario, he felt that the main work was behind him, so natural to him was the act of writing, so little uncertainty intervened for him between the intention and the act. Yet no one who has read both the scenario and the novel can fail to see how much was conceived in the actual writing that could never have been conceived in the scenario, however "divine" James thought "the principle of the scenario" to be.

THE PRINCESS
CASAMASSIMA

1886

"The Princess Casamassima"

LIONEL TRILLING*

In 1888, on the second of January, which in any year is likely to be a sad day, Henry James wrote to his friend William Dean Howells that his reputation had been dreadfully injured by his last two novels. The desire for his productions, he said, had been reduced to zero, editors no longer asked for his work, they even seemed ashamed to publish the stories they had already bought. But James was never without courage. "However, I don't despair," he wrote, "for I think I am now really in better form than I ever have been in my life and I propose yet to do many things." And then, no doubt with the irony all writers use when they dare to speak of future recognition, but also, surely, with the necessary faith, he concludes the matter: "Very likely too, some day, all my buried prose will kick off its various tombstones at once."

And so it happened. The "some day" has arrived and we have been hearing the clatter of marble as James's buried prose kicks off its monuments in a general resurrection. On all sides James is being given the serious and joyous interest he longed for in his lifetime.

One element of our interest must be the question of how some of James's prose ever came to be buried at all. It is not hard to understand why certain of James's books did not catch the contemporary fancy. But the two books on which James placed the blame for his diminishing popularity were *The Bostonians* and *The Princess Casamassima,* and of all James's novels these are the two

*From THE LIBERAL IMAGINATION by Lionel Trilling. Copyright 1948, by The Macmillan Company. Reprinted by permission of the publisher.

which are most likely to make an immediate appeal to the reader of today. That they should not have delighted their contemporary public, but on the contrary should have turned it against James, makes a lively problem in the history of taste.[1]

In the masterpieces of his late years James became a difficult writer. This is the fact and nothing is gained for James by denying it. He himself knew that these late works were difficult; he wished them to be dealt with as if they were difficult. When a young man from Texas—it was Mr. Stark Young—inquired indirectly of James how he should go about reading his novels, James did not feel that this diffidence was provincial but happily drew up lists which would lead the admirable young man from the easy to the hard. But the hostility with which *The Bostonians* and *The Princess Casamassima* were received cannot be explained by any difficulty either of manner or intention, for in these books there is none. The prose, although personally characteristic, is perfectly in the tradition of the nineteenth-century novel. It is warm, fluent, and on the whole rather less elaborate and virtuose than Dickens' prose. The motives of the characters are clear and direct—certainly they are far from the elaborate punctilio of the late masterpieces. And the charge that is sometimes made against the later work, that it exists in a social vacuum, clearly does not pertain here. In these novels James is at the point in his career at which society, in the largest and even the grossest sense, is offering itself to his mind with great force. He understands society as crowds and police, as a field of justice and injustice, reform and revolution. The social texture of his work is grainy and knotted with practicality and detail. And more: his social observation is of a kind that we must find startlingly prescient when we consider that it was made some sixty years ago.

It is just this prescience, of course, that explains the resistance of James's contemporaries. What James saw he saw truly, but it was not what the readers of his time were themselves equipped to see. That we now are able to share his vision required the passage of six decades and the events which brought them to climax. Henry James in the eighties understood what we have painfully learned from our grim glossary of wars and concentration camps, after having seen the state and human nature laid open to our horrified inspection. "But I have the imagination of disaster—and see life as ferocious and sinister": James wrote this to A. C. Benson in 1896, and what so bland a young man as Benson made of the statement, what anyone then was likely to make of it, is hard to guess. But nowadays we know that such an imagination is one of the keys to truth.

It was, then, "the imagination of disaster" that cut James off from his contemporaries and it is what recommends him to us now. We know something about the profound disturbance of the sexual life which seems to go along with hypertrophy of the will and how this excess of will seems to be a response to certain maladjustments in society and to direct itself back upon them; D. H. Lawrence taught us much about this, but Lawrence himself never attempted a more daring conjunction of the sexual and the political life than Henry James succeeds with in *The Bostonians.* We know much about misery and downtroddenness and of what happens when strong and gifted personalities are put at a hopeless disadvantage, and about the possibilities of extreme violence, and about the sense of guilt and unreality which may come to members of the upper classes and the strange complex efforts they make to find innocence and reality, and about the conflict between the claims of art and of social duty—these are among the themes which make the pattern of *The Princess Casamassima.* It is a novel which has at its very center the assumption that Europe has reached the full of its ripeness and is passing over into rottenness, that the peculiarly beautiful light it gives forth is in part the reflection of a glorious past and in part the phosphorescence of a present decay, that it may meet its end by violence and that this is not wholly unjust, although never before has the old sinful continent made so proud and pathetic an assault upon our affections.

II

The Princess Casamassima belongs to a great line of novels which runs through the nineteenth century as, one might say, the very backbone of its fiction. These novels, which are defined as a group by the character and circumstance of their heroes, include Stendhal's *The Red and the Black,* Balzac's *Père Goriot* and *Lost Illusions,* Dickens' *Great Expectations,* Flaubert's *Sentimental Education;* only a very slight extension of the definition is needed to allow the inclusion of Tolstoi's *War and Peace* and Dostoevski's *The Idiot.*

The defining hero may be known as the Young Man from the Provinces. He need not come from the provinces in literal fact, his social class may constitute his province. But a provincial birth and rearing suggest the simplicity and the high hopes he begins with —he starts with a great demand upon life and a great wonder about its complexity and promise. He may be of good family but he must be poor. He is intelligent, or at least aware, but not at all shrewd in worldly matters. He must have acquired a certain amount of education, should have learned something about life from books, although not the truth.

The hero of *The Princess Casamassima* conforms very exactly to type. The province from which Hyacinth Robinson comes is a city slum. "He sprang up at me out of the London pavement," says James in the preface to the novel in the New York Edition. In 1883, the first year of his long residence in England, James was in the habit of prowling the streets, and they yielded him the image "of some individual sensitive nature or fine mind, some small obscure creature whose education should have been almost wholly derived from them, capable of profiting by all the civilization, all the accumulation to which they testify, yet condemned to see things only from outside—in mere quickened consideration, mere wistfulness and envy and despair."

Thus equipped with poverty, pride, and intelligence, the Young Man from the Provinces stands outside life and seeks to enter. This modern hero is connected with the tales of the folk. Usually his motive is the legendary one of setting out to seek his fortune, which is what the folktale says when it means that hero is seeking himself. He is really the third and youngest son of the woodcutter, the one to whom all our sympathies go, the gentle and misunderstood one, the bravest of all. He is likely to be in some doubt about his parentage; his father the woodcutter is not really his father. Our hero has, whether he says so or not, the common belief of children that there is some mystery about his birth; his real parents, if the truth were known, are of great and even royal estate. Julien Sorel of *The Red and the Black* is the third and youngest son of an actual woodcutter, but he is the spiritual son of Napoleon. In our day the hero of *The Great Gatsby* is not really the son of Mr. Gatz; he is said to have sprung "from his Platonic conception of himself," to be, indeed, "the son of God." And James's Hyacinth Robinson, although fostered by a poor dressmaker and a shabby fiddler, has an English lord for his real father.

It is the fate of the Young Man to move from an obscure position into one of considerable eminence in Paris or London or St. Petersburg, to touch the life of the rulers of the earth. His situation is as chancy as that of any questing knight of medieval romance. He is confronted by situations whose meanings are dark to him, in which his choice seems always decisive. He understands everything to be a "test." Parsifal at the castle of the Fisher King is not more uncertain about the right thing to do than the Young Man from the Provinces picking his perilous way through the irrationalities of the society into which he has been transported. That the Young Man be introduced into great houses and involved with large affairs is essential to his story, which must not be confused with the cognate story of the Sensitive Young Man. The provincial hero must indeed be sensitive, and in proportion to the brassiness of the world; he may even be an artist; but it is not his part merely to be puzzled and hurt; he is not the hero of *The Way of All Flesh* or *Of Human Bondage* or *Mooncalf.* Unlike the merely sensitive hero, he is concerned to know how the political and social world are run and enjoyed; he wants a share of power and pleasure and in consequence he takes real risks, often of his life. The "swarming facts" that James tells us Hyacinth is to confront are "freedom and ease, knowledge and power, money, opportunity, and satiety."

The story of the Young Man from the Provinces is thus a strange one, for it has its roots both in legend and in the very heart of the modern actuality. From it we have learned most of what we know about modern society, about class and its strange rituals, about power and influence and about money, the hard fluent fact in which modern society has its being. Yet through the massed social fact there runs the thread of legendary romance, even of downright magic. We note, for example, that it seems necessary for the novelist to deal in transformation. Some great and powerful hand must reach down into the world of seemingly chanceless routine and pick up the hero and set him down in his complex and dangerous fate. Pip meets Magwitch on the marsh, a felon-godfather; Pierre Bezuhov unexpectedly inherits the fortune that permits this uncouth young man to make his tour of Russian society; powerful unseen forces play around the proud head of Julien Sorel to make possible his astonishing upward career; Rastignac, simply by being one of the boarders at the Maison Vauquer which also shelters the great Vautrin, moves to the very center of Parisian intrigue; James Gatz rows out to a millionaire's yacht, a boy in dungarees, and becomes Jay Gatsby, an Oxford man, a military hero.

Such transformations represent, with only slight exaggeration, the literal fact that was to be observed very day. From the late years of the eighteenth century through the early years of the twentieth, the social structure of the West was peculiarly fitted—one might say designed—for changes in fortune that were magical and romantic. The upper-class ethos was strong enough to make it remarkable that a young man should cross the borders, yet weak enough to permit the crossing in exceptional cases. A shiftless boy from Geneva, a starveling and a lackey, becomes the admiration of the French aristocracy and is permitted by Europe to manipulate its assumptions in every department of life: Jean Jacques Rousseau is the father of all the Young Men from the Provinces, including the one from Corsica.

The Young Man's story represents an actuality, yet we may be sure that James took special delight in its ineluctable legendary element. James was certainly the least primitive of artists, yet he was always aware of his connection with the primitive. He set great store by the illusion of probability and verisimilitude, but he knew that he dealt always with illusion; he was proud of the devices of his magic. Like any primitive storyteller, he wished to hold the reader against his will, to *enchant,* as we say. He loved what he called "the story as story"; he delighted to work, by means of the unusual, the extravagant, the melodramatic, and the supernatural, upon what he called "the blessed faculty of wonder"; and he understood primitive story to be the root of the modern novelist's art. F. O. Matthiessen speaks of the fairytale quality of *The Wings of the Dove;* so sophisticated a work as *The Ambassadors* can be read as one of those tales in which the hero finds that nothing is what it seems and that the only guide through the world must be the goodness of his heart.

Like any great artist of story, like Shakespeare or Balzac or Dickens or Dostoevski, James crowds probability rather closer than we nowadays like. It is not that he gives us unlikely events but that he sometimes thickens the number of interesting events beyond our ordinary expectation. If this, in James or in any storyteller, leads to a straining of our sense of verisimilitude, there is always the defense to be made that the special job of literature is, as Marianne Moore puts it, the creation of "imaginary gardens with real toads in them." The reader who detects that the garden is imaginary should not be led by his discovery to a wrong view of the reality of the toads. In settling questions of reality and truth in fiction, it must be remembered that, although the novel in certain of its forms resembles the accumulative and classificatory sciences, which are the sciences most people are most at home with, in certain other of its forms the novel approximates the sciences of experiment. And an experiment is very like an imaginary garden which is laid out for the express purpose of supporting a real toad of fact. The apparatus of the researcher's bench is not nature itself but an artificial and extravagant contrivance, much like a novelist's plot, which is devised to force or foster a fact into being. This seems to have been James's own view of the part that is played in his novels by what he calls "romance." He seems to have had an analogy with experiment very clearly in mind when he tells us that romance is "experience liberated, so to speak; experience disengaged, disembroiled, disencumbered, exempt from the conditions that usually attach to it." Again and again he speaks of the contrivance of a novel in ways which will make it seem like illegitimate flummery to the reader who is committed only to the premises of the naturalistic novel, but which the intelligent scientist will understand perfectly.

Certainly *The Princess Casamassima* would seem to need some such defense as this, for it takes us, we are likely to feel, very far along the road to romance, some will think to the very point of impossibility. It asks us to accept a poor young man whose birth is darkly secret, his father being a dissipated but authentic English lord, his mother a French courtesan-seamstress who murders the father; a beautiful American-Italian princess who descends in the social scale to help "the people"; a general mingling of the very poor with persons of exalted birth; and then a dim mysterious leader of the revolution, never seen by the reader, the machinations of an underground group of conspirators, an oath taken to carry out an assassination at some unspecified future day, the day arriving, the hour of the killing set, the instructions and the pistol given.

Confronted by paraphernalia like this, even those who admire the book are likely to agree with Rebecca West when, in her exuberant little study of James, she tells us that it is "able" and "meticulous" but at the same time "distraught" and "wild," that the "loveliness" in it comes from a transmutation of its "perversities"; she speaks of it as a "mad dream" and teases its vast unlikelihood, finding it one of the big jokes in literature that it was James, who so prided himself on his lack of naïveté, who should have brought back to fiction the high implausibility of the old novels which relied for their effects on dark and stormy nights, Hindu servants, mysterious strangers, and bloody swords wiped on richly embroidered handkerchiefs.

Miss West was writing in 1916, when the English naturalistic novel, with its low view of possibility, was in full pride. Our notion of political possibility was still to be changed by a small group of quarrelsome conspiratorial intellectuals taking over the control of Russia. Even a loyal Fabian at that time could consider it one of the perversities of *The Princess Casamassima* that two of its lower-class characters should say of a third that he had the potentiality of becoming Prime Minister of England; today Paul Muniment sits in the Cabinet and is on the way to Downing Street. In the thirties the book was much admired by those who read it in the light of knowledge of our own radical movements; it then used to be said that although James had dreamed up an impossible revolutionary group he had nonetheless managed to derive from it some notable insights into the temper of radicalism; these admirers grasped the toad of fact and felt that it was all the more remarkably there because the garden is so patently imaginary.

Yet an understanding of James's use of "romance"—and there is "romance" in Hyacinth's story—must not preclude our understanding of the striking literary accuracy of *The Princess Casamassima*. James himself helped to throw us off the scent when in his preface to the novel he told us that he made no research into Hyacinth's subterranean politics. He justified this by saying that "the value I wished most to render and the effect I wished most to produce were precisely those of our not knowing, of society's not knowing, but only guessing and suspecting and trying to ignore, what 'goes on' irreconcilably, subversively, beneath the vast smug surface." And he concludes the preface with the most beautifully arrogant and truest thing a novelist ever said about his craft: "What it all came back to was, no doubt, something like *this* wisdom—that if you haven't, for fiction, the root of the matter in you, haven't the sense of life and the penetrating imagination, you are a fool in the very presence of the revealed and assured; but that if you *are* so armed, you are not really helpless, not without your resource, even before mysteries abysmal." If, to learn about the radical movement of his time, James really did no more than consult his penetrating imagination—which no doubt was nourished like any other on conversation and the daily newspaper— then we must say that in no other novelist did the root of the matter go so deep and so wide. For the truth is that there is not a political event of *The Princess Casamassima*, not a detail of oath or mystery or danger, which is not confirmed by multitudinous records.

III

We are inclined to flatter our own troubles with the belief that the late nineteenth century was a peaceful time. But James knew its actual violence. England was, to be sure, rather less violent than the Continent, but the history of England in the eighties was one of profound social unrest often intensified to disorder. In March of 1886, the year in which *The Princess Casamassima* appeared in book form, James wrote to his brother William of a riot in his street, of ladies' carriages being stopped and the "occupants hustled, rifled, slapped, and kissed." He does not think that the rioters were unemployed workingmen, more likely that they were "the great army of roughs and thieves." But he says that there is "immense destitution" and that "everyone is getting poorer—from causes which, I fear, will continue." In the same year he wrote to Charles Eliot Norton that the state of the British upper class seems to be "in many ways very much the same rotten and *collapsible* one of the French aristocracy before the revolution."

James envisaged revolution, and not merely as a convenience for his fiction. But he imagined a kind of revolution with which we are no longer familiar. It was not a Marxian revolution. There is no upsurge of an angry proletariat led by a disciplined party which plans to head a new strong state. Such a revolution has its conservative aspect—it seeks to save certain elements of bourgeois culture for its own use, for example, science and the means of production and even some social agencies. The revolutionary theory of *The Princess Casamassima* has little in common with this. There is no organized mass movement; there is no disciplined party but only a strong conspiratorial center. There are no plans for taking over the state and almost no ideas about the society of the future. The conspiratorial center plans only for destruction, chiefly personal terrorism. But James is not naïvely representing a radical Graustark; he is giving a very accurate account of anarchism.

In 1872, at its meeting in The Hague, the First International voted the expulsion of the anarchists. Karl Marx had at last won his long battle with Bakunin. From that point on, "scientific socialism" was to dominate revolutionary thought. Anarchism ceased to be a main current of political theory. But anarchism continued as a force to be reckoned with, especially in the Latin countries, and it produced a revolutionary type of great courage and sometimes of appealing interest. Even in decline the theory and action of anarchism dominated the imagination of Europe.

It is not possible here to give a discriminating account of anarchism in all its aspects; to distinguish between the mutation which verges on nihilism and that which is called communist-anarchism, or between its representatives, Sergei Nechayev, who had the character of a police spy, and Kropotkin or the late Carlo Tresca, who were known for their personal sweetness; or to resolve the contradiction between the violence of its theory and action and the gentle world toward which these are directed. It will have to be enough to say that anarchism holds that the natural goodness of man is absolute and that society corrupts it, and that the guide to anarchist action is the desire to destroy society in general and not merely a particular social form.

When, therefore, Hyacinth Robinson is torn between his desire for social justice and his fear lest the civilization of Europe be destroyed, he is dealing reasonably with anarchist belief. "The unchaining of what is today called the evil passions and the destruction of what is called public order" was the consummation of Bakunin's aim which he defended by saying that "the desire for destruction is at the same time a creative desire." It was not only the state but all social forms that were to be demolished according to the doctrine of *amorphism;* any social form held the seeds of the state's rebirth and must therefore be extirpated. Intellectual disciplines were social forms like any other. At least in its early days anarchism expressed hostility toward science. Toward the arts the hostility was less, for the early leaders were often trained in the humanities and their inspiration was largely literary; in the nineties there was a strong alliance between the French artists and the anarchist groups. But in the logic of the situation art was bound to come under the anarchist fire. Art is inevitably associated with civil peace and social order and indeed with the ruling classes. Then too any large intense movement of moral-political action is likely to be jealous of art and to feel that it is in competition with the full awareness of human suffering. Bakunin on several occasions spoke of it as of no account when the cause of human happiness was considered. Lenin expressed something of the same sort when, after having listened with delight to a sonata by Beethoven, he said that he could not listen to music too often. "It affects your nerves, makes you want to say stupid, nice things, and stroke the heads of people who could create such beauty while living in this vile hell. And you mustn't stroke anyone's head—you might get your hand bitten off." And similarly the Princess of James's novel feels that her taste is but the evidence of her immoral aristocratic existence and that art is a frivolous distraction from revolution.

The nature of the radicals in *The Princess Casamassima* may, to the modern reader, seem a distortion of fact. The people who meet at the Sun and Moon to mutter their wrongs over their beer are not revolutionists and scarcely radicals; most of them are nothing more than dull malcontents. Yet they represent with complete accuracy the political development of a large part of the working class of England at the beginning of the eighties. The first great movement of English trade unionism had created an aristocracy of labor largely cut off from the mass of the workers, and the next great movement had not yet begun; the political expression of men such as met at the Sun and Moon was likely to be as fumbling as James represents it.

James has chosen the occupation of these men with great discrimination. There are no factory workers among them; at that time anarchism did not attract factory workers so much as the members of the skilled and relatively sedentary trades: tailors, shoemakers, weavers, cabinetmakers, and ornamental-metal workers. Hyacinth's craft of bookbinding was no doubt chosen because James knew something about it and because, being at once a fine and a mechanic art, it perfectly suited Hyacinth's fate, but it is to the point that bookbinders were largely drawn to anarchism.

When Paul Muniment tells Hyacinth that the club of the Sun and Moon is a "place you have always overestimated," he speaks with the authority of one who has connections more momentous. The anarchists, although of course they wished to influence the masses and could on occasion move them to concerted action, did not greatly value democratic or quasi-democratic mass organizations. Bakunin believed that "for the international organization of all Europe one hundred revolutionists, strongly and seriously bound together, are sufficient." The typical anarchist organization was hierarchical and secret. When in 1867 Bakunin drew up plans of organization, he instituted three "orders": a public group to be known as the International Alliance of Social Democracy; then above this and not known to it the Order of National Brothers; above this and not known to it the Order of International Brothers, very few in number. James's Muniment, we may suppose, is a National Brother.

For the indoctrination of his compact body of revolutionists, Bakunin, in collaboration with the amazing Sergei Nechayev, compiled *The Revolutionary Catechism*. This vade mecum might be taken as a guidebook to *The Princess Casamassima*. It instructs the revolutionist that he may be called to live in the great world and to penetrate into any class of society: the aristocracy, the church, the army, the diplomatic corps. It tells how one goes about compromising the wealthy in order to command their wealth, just as the Princess is compromised. There are instructions on how to deal with people who, like James's Captain Sholto, are drawn to the movement by questionable motives; on how little one is to trust the women of the upper classes who may be seeking sensation or salvation—the Princess calls it reality—through revolutionary action. It is a ruthless little book: eventually Bakunin himself complains that nothing—no private letter, no wife, no daughter— is safe from the conspiratorial zeal of his co-author Nechayev.

The situation in which Hyacinth involves himself, his pledge to commit an assassination upon demand of the secret leadership, is not the extreme fancy of a cloistered novelist, but a classic anarchist situation. Anarchism could arouse mass action, as in the riots at Lyon in 1882, but typically it showed its power by acts of terror committed by courageous individuals glad to make personal war against society. Bakunin canonized for anarchism the Russian bandit Stenka Razin; Balzac's Vautrin and Stendhal's Valbayre (of

Lamiel) are prototypes of anarchist heroes. Always ethical as well as instrumental in its theory, anarchism conceived assassination not only as a way of advertising its doctrine and weakening the enemey's morale, but also as punishment or revenge or warning. Of the many assassinations or attempts at assassination that fill the annals of the late years of the century, not all were anarchist, but those that were not were influenced by anarchist example. In 1878 there were two attempts on the life of the Kaiser, one on the King of Spain, one on the King of Italy; in 1880 another attempt on the King of Spain; in 1881 Alexander II of Russia was killed after many attempts; in 1882 the Phoenix Park murders were committed, Lord Frederick Cavendish, Secretary for Ireland, and Undersecretary Thomas Burke being killed by extreme Irish nationalists; in 1883 there were several dynamite conspiracies in Great Britain and in 1885 there was an explosion in the House of Commons; in 1883 there was an anarchist plot to blow up, all at once, the Emperor Wilhelm, the Crown Prince, Bismarck, and Moltke. These are but a few of the terroristic events of which James would have been aware in the years just before he began *The Princess Casamassima*, and later years brought many more.

Anarchism never established itself very firmly in England as it did in Russia, France, and Italy. In these countries it penetrated to the upper classes. The actions of the Princess are not unique for an aristocrat of her time, nor is she fabricating when she speaks of her acquaintance with revolutionists of a kind more advanced than Hyacinth is likely to know. In Italy she would have met on terms of social equality such notable anarchists as Count Carlo Cafiero and the physician Enrico Malatesta, who was the son of a wealthy family. Kropotkin was a descendant of the Ruriks and, as the novels of James's friend Turgenev testify, extreme radicalism was not uncommon among the Russian aristocracy. In France in the eighties and still more markedly in the nineties there were artistic, intellectual, and even aristocratic groups which were closely involved with the anarchists.

The great revolutionary of *The Princess Casamassima* is Hoffendahl, whom we never see although we feel his real existence. Hoffendahl is, in the effect he has upon others, not unlike what is told of Bakunin himself in his greatest days, when he could enthrall with his passion even those who could not understand the language he spoke in. But it is possible that James also had the famous Johann Most in mind. Most figured in the London press in 1881 when he was tried because his newspaper, *Freiheit*, exulted in the assassination of the Czar. He was found guilty of libel and inciting to murder and sentenced to sixteen months at hard labor. The jury that convicted him recommended mercy on the ground that he was a foreigner and "might be suffering violent wrong." The jury was right—most had suffered in the prisons of Germany after a bitter youth. It is not clear whether he, like James's Hoffendahl, had had occasion to stand firm under police torture, but there can be no doubt of his capacity to do so. After having served his jail sentence, he emigrated to America, and it has been said of him that terrorist activities in this country centered about him. He was implicated in the Haymarket Affair and imprisoned for having incited the assassin of President McKinley; Emma Goldman and Alexander Berkman were his disciples, and they speak of him in language such as Hyacinth uses of Hoffendahl. It is worth noting that Most was a bookbinder by trade.

In short, when we consider the solid accuracy of James's political detail at every point, we find that we must give up the notion that James could move only in the thin air of moral abstraction. A writer has said of *The Princess Casamassima* that it is "a capital example of James's impotence in matters sociological." The very opposite is so. Quite apart from its moral and aesthetic authority, *The Princes Casamassima* is a brilliantly precise representation of social actuality.

IV

In his preface to *The Princess* in the New York Edition, James tells us of a certain autobiographical element that went into the creation of Hyacinth Robinson. "To find his possible adventures interesting," James says, "I had only to conceive his watching the same public show, the same innumerable appearances I had myself watched and of his watching very much as I had watched."

This, at first glance, does not suggest a very intense connection between author and hero. But at least it assures us that at some point the novel is touched by the author's fantasy about himself. It is one of the necessities of successful modern story that the author shall have somewhere entrusted his personal fantasy to the tale; but it may be taken as very nearly a rule that the more the author disguises the personal nature of his fantasy, the greater its force will be. Perhaps he is best off if he is not wholly aware that he is writing about himself at all: his fantasy, like an actual dream, is powerful in the degree that its "meaning" is hidden.

If Hyacinth does indeed express James's personal fantasy, we are led to believe that the fantasy has reference to a familial situation. James puts an insistent emphasis upon his hero's small stature. Hyacinth's mere size is decisive in the story. It exempts him from certain adult situations; for example, where Paul Muniment overcomes the class barrier to treat the Princess as a woman, taking so full an account of her sexual existence and his own that we expect him to make a demand upon her. Hyacinth is detached from the sexual possibility and disclaims it. The intention is not to show him as unmanly but as too young to make the claims of maturity; he is the child of the book, always the very youngest person. And this child-man lives in a novel full of parental figures. Hyacinth has no less than three sets of parents: Lord Frederick and Florentine, Miss Pynsent and Mr. Vetch, Eustache Poupin and Madame Poupin, and this is not to mention the French-revolutionary grandfather and the arch-conspirator Hoffendahl; and even Millicent Henning appears, for one memorable Sunday, in a maternal role. The decisive parental pair are, of course, the actual parents, Lord Frederick and Florentine, who represent—some will feel too schematically—the forces which are in conflict in Hyacinth. Undertaking to kill the Duke as a step in the destruction of the ruling class, Hyacinth is in effect plotting the murder of his own father; and one reason that he comes to loathe the pledged deed is his belief that, by repeating poor Florentine's action, he will be bringing his mother to life in all her pitiful shame.

It is as a child that Hyacinth dies; that is, he dies of the withdrawal of love. James contrives with consummate skill the lonely circumstance of Hyacinth's death. Nothing can equal for delicacy of ironic pathos the incidents of the last part of the book, in which Hyacinth, who has his own death warrant in his pocket, the letter ordering the assassination, looks to his adult friends for a reason of love which will explain why he does not have to serve it on himself, or how, if he must serve it, he can believe in the value of his deed. But the grown-up people have occupations from which he is excluded and they cannot believe in his seriousness. Paul

Muniment and the Princess push him aside, not unkindly, only condescendingly, only as one tells a nice boy that there are certain things he cannot understand, such things as power and love and justification.

The adult world last represents itself to Hyacinth in the great scene of lust in the department store. To make its point the crueler, James has previously contrived for Hyacinth a wonderful Sunday of church and park with Millicent Henning;[2] Millicent enfolds Hyacinth in an undemanding, protective love that is not fine or delicate but for that reason so much the more useful; but when in his last hunt for connection Hyacinth seeks out Millicent in her shop, he sees her standing "still as a lay-figure" under Captain Sholto's gaze, exhibiting "the long grand lines" of her body under pretense of "modeling" a dress. And as Hyacinth sees the Captain's eyes "travel up and down the front of Millicent's person," he knows that he has been betrayed.

So much manipulation of the theme of parent and child, so much interest in lost protective love, suggests that the connection of Hyacinth and his author may be more intense than at first appears. And there is one consideration that reinforces the guess that this fantasy of a child and his family has a particular and very personal relation to James in his own family situation. The matter which is at issue in *The Princess Casamassima*, the dispute between art and moral action, the controversy between the glorious unregenerate past and the regenerate future, was not of merely general interest to Henry James, nor, indeed, to any of the notable members of the James family. Ralph Barton Perry in his *Thought and Character of William James* finds the question so real and troubling in William's life that he devotes a chapter to it. William, to whom the antithesis often represented itself as between Europe-art and America-action, settled in favor of America and action. Henry settled, it would seem, the other way—certainly in favor of art. But whether Henry's option necessarily involved, as William believed, a decision in favor of the past, a love of the past for, as people like to say, the past's sake, may be thought of as the essential matter of dispute between William and Henry.

The dispute was at the very heart of their relationship. They had the matter out over the years. But in the having-out William was the aggressor, and it is impossible to suppose that his statement of the case did not cause Henry pain. William came to suspect that the preoccupation with art was very close to immorality. He was perhaps not so wrong as the clichés in defense of art would make him out to be; his real error lay in his not knowing what art, as a thing to contemplate or as a thing to make, implied for his brother. His suspicion extended to Henry's work. He was by no means without sympathy for it, but he thought that Henry's great gifts were being put at the service of the finicking and refined; he was impatient of what was not robust in the same way he was. Henry, we may be sure, would never have wanted a diminution of the brotherly frankness that could tell him that *The Bostonians* might have been very fine if it had been only a hundred pages long; but the remark and others of similar sort could only have left his heart a little sore.

When, then, we find Henry James creating for his Hyacinth a situation in which he must choose between political action and the fruits of the creative spirit of Europe, we cannot but see that he has placed at the center of his novel a matter whose interest is of the most personal kind. Its personal, its familial, nature is emphasized by Alice James's share in the dispute, for she and William were at one aginst their brother in aggressively holding a low view of England, and William's activism finds a loud and even a shrill echo in Alice, whose passionate radicalism was, as Henry said of her, "her most distinguishing feature." But far more important is the father's relation to the family difference. The authority of the elder Henry James could be fairly claimed by both his sons, for he was brilliantly contradictory on the moral status of art. If William could come to think of art as constituting a principle which was antagonistic to the principle of life, his father had said so before him. And Henry could find abundant support for his own position in his father's frequent use of the artist as one who, because he seeks to create and not to possess, most closely approximates in mankind the attributes of divinity.

The Princess Casamassima may, then, be thought of as an intensely autobiographical book, not in the sense of being the author's personal record but in the sense of being his personal act. For we may imagine that James, beautifully in control of his novel, dominant in it as almost no decent person can be in a family situation, is continuing the old dispute on his own terms and even taking a revenge. Our imagination of the "revenge" does not require that we attribute a debasing malice to James—quite to the contrary, indeed, for the revenge is gentle and innocent and noble. It consists, this revenge, only in arranging things in such a way that Paul Muniment and the Princess shall stand for James's brother and sister and then so to contrive events to show that, at the very moment when this brilliant pair think they are closest to the conspiratorial arcanum, the real thing, the true center, they are in actual fact furthest from it.[3] Paul and the Princess believe themselves to be in the confidence of *Them*, the People Higher Up, the International Brothers, or whatever, when really they are held in suspicion in these very quarters. They condescend to Hyacinth for his frivolous concern with art, but Hyacinth, unknown to them, has received his letter of fatal commission; he has the death warrant in his pocket, another's and his own; despite his having given clear signs of lukewarmness to the cause, he is trusted by the secret powers where his friends are not. In his last days Hyacinth has become aware of his desire no longer to bind books but to write them: the novel can be thought of as Henry James's demonstrative message, to the world in general, to his brother and sister in particular, that the artist quite as much as any man of action carries his ultimate commitment and his death warrant in his pocket. "Life's nothing." Henry James wrote to a young friend, "—unless heroic and sacrificial."

James even goes so far as to imply that the man of art may be close to the secret center of things when the man of action is quite apart from it. Yet Hyacinth cannot carry out the orders of the people who trust him. Nor of course can he betray them—the pistol which, in the book's last dry words, "would certainly have served much better for the Duke," Hyacinth turns upon himself. A vulgar and facile progressivism can find this to be a proof of James's "impotence in matters sociological"—"the problem remains unsolved." Yet it would seem that a true knowledge of society comprehends the reality of the social forces it presumes to study and is aware of contradictions and consequences; it knows that sometimes society offers an opposition of motives in which the antagonists are in such a balance of authority and appeal that a man who so wholly perceives them as to embody them in his very being cannot choose between them and is therefore destroyed. This is known as tragedy.

V

We must not misunderstand the nature of Hyacinth's tragic fate. Hyacinth dies sacrificially, but not as a sacrificial lamb, wholly innocent; he dies as a human hero who has incurred a certain amount of guilt.

The possibility of misunderstanding Hyacinth's situation arises from our modern belief that the artist is one of the types of social innocence. Our competitive, acquisitive society ritualistically condemns what it practices—with us money gives status, yet we consider a high regard for money a debasing thing and we set a large value on disinterested activity. Hence our cult of the scientist and the physician, who are presumed to be free of the acquisitive impulses. The middle class, so far as it is liberal, admires from varying distances the motives and even the aims of revolutionists: it cannot imagine that revolutionists have anything to "gain" as the middle class itself understands gain. And although sometimes our culture says that the artist is a subversive idler, it is nowadays just as likely to say that he is to be admired for his innocence, for his activity is conceived as having no end beyond itself except possibly some benign social purpose, such as "teaching people to understand each other."

But James did not see art as, in this sense, innocent. We touch again on autobiography, for on this point there is a significant connection between James's own life and Hyacinth's.

In Chapter XXV of *A Small Boy and Others,* his first autobiographic volume, James tells how he was initiated into a knowledge of style in the Galerie d'Apollon of the Louvre. As James represents the event, the varieties of style in that gallery assailed him so intensely that their impact quite transcended aesthetic experience. For they seemed to speak to him not visually at all but in some "complicated sound" and as a "deafening chorus"; they gave him what he calls "a general sense of glory." About this sense of glory he is quite explicit. "The glory meant ever so many things at once, not only beauty and art and supreme design, but history and fame and power, the world in fine raised to the richest and noblest expression."

Hazlitt said that "the language of poetry naturally falls in with the language of power," and goes on to develop an elaborate comparison between the processes of the imagination and the processes of autocratic rule. He is not merely indulging in a flight of fancy or a fashion of speaking; no stancher radical democrat ever lived than Hazlitt and no greater lover of imaginative litera-ture, yet he believed that poetry has an affinity with political power in its autocratic and aristocratic form and that it is not a friend of the democratic virtues. We are likely not to want to agree with Hazlitt; we prefer to speak of art as if it lived in a white bungalow with a garden, had a wife and two children, and were harmless and quiet and cooperative. But James is of Hazlitt's opinion; his first great revelation of art came as an analogy with the triumphs of the world; art spoke to him of the imperious will, with the music of an army with banners. Perhaps it is to the point that James's final act of imagination, as he lay dying, was to call his secretary and give her as his last dictation what purported to be an autobiograph-ical memoir by Napoleon Bonaparte.

But so great an aggression must carry some retribution with it, and as James goes on with the episode of the Galerie d'Apollon, he speaks of the experience as having the effect not only of a "love-philtre" but also of a "fear-philtre." Aggression brings guilt and then fear. And James concludes the episode with the account of a nightmare in which the Galerie figures; he calls it "the most appalling and yet most admirable" nightmare of his life. He dreamed that he was defending himself from an intruder, trying to keep the door shut against a terrible invading form; then suddenly there came "the great thought that I, in my appalled state, was more appalling than the awful agent, creature or presence"; where-upon he opened the door and, surpassing the invader for "straight aggression and dire intention," pursued him down a long corridor in a great storm of lighting and thunder; the corridor was seen to be the Galerie d'Apollon. We do not have to presume very far to find the meaning in the dream, for James gives us all that we might want; he tells us that the dream was important to him, that, having experienced art as "history and fame and power," his arrogation seemed a guilty one and represented itself as great fear which he overcame by an inspiration of straight aggression and dire inten-tion and triumphed in the very place where he had had his imperi-ous fantasy. An admirable nightmare indeed. One needs to be a genius to counter-attack nightmare; perhaps this is the definition of genius.

When James came to compose Hyacinth's momentous letter

from Venice, the implications of the analogue of art with power
had developed and became clearer and more objective. Hyacinth
has had his experience of the glories of Europe, and when he writes
to the Princess his view of human misery is matched by a view of
the world "raised to the richest and noblest expression." He understands no less clearly than before "the despotisms, the cruelties, the exclusions, the monopolies and the rapacities of the past."
But now he recognizes that "the fabric of civilization as we know
it" is inextricably bound up with this injustice; the monuments of
art and learning and taste have been reared upon coercive power.
Yet never before has he had the full vision of what the human spirit
can accomplish to make the world "less impracticable and life
more tolerable." He finds that he is ready to fight for art—and
what art suggests of glorious life—against the low and even hostile
estimate which his revolutionary friends have made of it, and this
involves of course some reconciliation with established coercive
power.

It is easy enough, by certain assumptions, to condemn Hyacinth
and even to call him names. But first we must see what his position
really means and what heroism there is in it. Hyacinth recognizes
what very few people wish to admit, that civilization has a price,
and a high one. Civilizations differ from one another as much in
what they give up as in what they acquire; but all civilizations are
alike in that they renounce something for something else. We do
right to protest this in any given case that comes under our notice
and we do right to get as much as possible for as little as possible;
but we can never get everything for nothing. Nor, indeed, do we
really imagine that we can. Thus, to stay within the present context, every known theory of popular revolution gives up the vision
of the world "raised to the richest and noblest expression." To
achieve the ideal of widespread security, popular revolutionary
theory condemns the ideal of adventurous experience. It tries to
avoid doing this explicitly and it even, although seldom convincingly, denies that it does it at all. But all the instincts or necessities
of radical democracy are against the superbness and arbitrariness
which often mark great spirits. It is sometimes said in the interests
of an ideal or abstract completeness that the choice need not be
made, that security can be imagined to go with richness and nobility of expression. But we have not seen it in the past and nobody
really strives to imagine it in the future. Hyacinth's choice is made

under the pressure of the counterchoice made by Paul and the Princess; their "general rectification" implies a civilization from which the idea of life raised to the richest and noblest expression will quite vanish.

There have been critics who said that Hyacinth is a snob and the surrogate of James's snobbery. But if Hyacinth is a snob, he is of the company of Rabelais, Shakespeare, Scott, Dickens, Balzac, and Lawrence, men who saw the lordliness and establishment of the aristocrat and the gentleman as the proper condition for the spirit of man, and who, most of them, demanded it for themselves, as poor Hyacinth never does, for "it was not so much that he wished to enjoy as that he wished to know; his desire was not to be pampered but to be initiated." His snobbery is no other than that of John Stuart Mill when he discovered that a grand and spacious room could have so enlarging an effect upon his mind; when Hyacinth at Medley had his first experience of a great old house, he admired nothing so much as the ability of a thing to grow old without loss but rather with gain of dignity and interest; "the spectacle of long duration unassociated with some sordid infirmity or poverty was new to him; for he had lived with people among whom old age meant, for the most part, a grudged and degraded survival." Hyacinth has Yeats's awareness of the dream that a great house embodies, that here the fountain of life "overflows without ambitious pains,"

> And mounts more dizzy high the more it rains
> As though to choose whatever shape it wills
> And never stoop to a mechanical
> Or servile shape, at others' beck and call.

But no less than Yeats he has the knowledge that the rich man who builds the house and the architect and artists who plan and decorate it are "bitter and violent men" and that the great houses "but take our greatness with our violence" and our "greatness with our bitterness."[4]

By the time Hyacinth's story draws to its end, his mind is in a perfect equilibrium, not of irresolution but of awareness. His sense of the social horror of the world is not diminished by his newer sense of the glory of the world. On the contrary, just as his pledge of his life to the revolutionary cause had in effect freed him to understand human glory, so the sense of the glory quickens his

TRILLING : *"The Princess Casamassima"* 125

response to human misery—never, indeed, is he so sensitive to the
sordid life of the mass of mankind as after he has had the revelation of art. And just as he is in an equilibrium of awareness, he is
also in an equilibrium of guilt. He has learned something of what
may lie behind abstract ideals, the envy, the impulse to revenge
and to dominance. He is the less inclined to forgive what he sees
because, as we must remember, the triumph of the revolution
presents itself to him as a certainty and the act of revolution as an
ecstasy. There is for him as little doubt of the revolution's success
as there is of the fact that his mother had murdered his father. And
when he thinks of revolution, it is as a tremendous tide, a colossal
force; he is tempted to surrender to it as an escape from his
isolation—one would be lifted by it "higher on the sun-touched
billows than one could ever be by a lonely effort of one's own."
But if the revolutionary passion thus has its guilt, Hyacinth's passion for life at its richest and noblest is no less guilty. It leads him
to consent to the established coercive power of the world, and this
can never be innocent. One cannot "accept" the suffering of others, no matter for what ideal, no matter if one's own suffering be
also accepted, without incurring guilt. It is the guilt in which every
civilization is implicated.

Hyacinth's death, then, is not his way of escaping from irresolution. It is truly a sacrifice, an act of heroism. He is a hero of
civilization because he dares do more than civilization does: embodying two ideals at once, he takes upon himself, in full consciousness, the guilt of each. He acknowledges both his parents.
By his death he instructs us in the nature of civilized life and by
his consciousness he transcends it.

VI

Suppose that truth be the expression, not of intellect, nor even,
as we sometimes now think, of will, but of love. It is an outmoded
idea, and yet if it has still any force at all it will carry us toward
an understanding of the truth of *The Princess Casamassima*. To be
sure, the legend of James does not associate him with love; indeed,
it is a fact symptomatic of the condition of American letters that
Sherwood Anderson, a writer who himself spoke much of love,
was able to say of James that he was the novelist of "those who
hate." Yet as we read *The Princess Casamassima* it is possible to

ask whether any novel was ever written which, dealing with decisive moral action and ultimate issues, makes its perceptions and
its judgments with so much loving-kindness.

Since James wrote, we have had an increasing number of novels
which ask us to take cognizance of those whom we call the underprivileged. These novels are of course addressed to those of us who
have the money and the leisure to buy books and read them and
the security to assail our minds with accounts of the miseries of
our fellow men; on the whole, the poor do not read about the poor.
And in so far as the middle class has been satisfied and gratified
by the moral implications of most of these books, it is not likely
to admire Henry James's treatment of the poor. For James represents the poor as if they had dignity and intelligence in the same
degree as people of the reading class. More, he assumes this and
feels no need to insist that it is so. This is a grace of spirit that we
are so little likely to understand that we may resent it. Few of our
novelists are able to write about the poor so as to make them
something more than the pitied objects of our facile sociological
minds. The literature of our liberal democracy pets and dandles its
underprivileged characters, and, quite as if it had the right to do
so, forgives them what faults they may have. But James is sure that
in such people, who are numerous, there are the usual human
gradations of understanding, interest, and goodness. Even if my
conjecture about the family connection of the novel be wholly
mistaken, it will at least suggest what is unmistakably true, that
James could write about a workingman quite as if he were as large,
willful, and complex as the author of *The Principles of Psychology.*
At the same time that everything in the story of *The Princess
Casamassima* is based on social difference, everything is also based
on the equality of the members of the human family. People at the
furthest extremes of class are easily brought into relation because
they are all contained in the novelist's affection. In that context it
is natural for the Princess and Lady Aurora Langrish to make each
other's acquaintance by the side of Rosy Muniment's bed and to
contend for the notice of Paul. That James should create poor
people so proud and intelligent as to make it impossible for anyone, even the reader who has paid for the privilege, to condescend
to them, so proud and intelligent indeed that it is not wholly easy
for them to be "good," is, one ventures to guess, an unexpressed,
a never-to-be-expressed reason for finding him "impotent in mat-

ters sociological." We who are liberal and progressive know that the poor are our equals in every sense except that of being equal to us.

But James's special moral quality, his power of love, is not wholly comprised by his impulse to make an equal distribution of dignity among his characters. It goes beyond this to create his unique moral realism, his particular gift of human understanding. If in his later novels James, as many say he did, carried awareness of human complication to the point of virtuosity, he surely does not do so here, and yet his knowledge of complication is here very considerable. But this knowledge is not an analytical one, or not in the usual sense in which that word is taken, which implies a cool dissection. If we imagine a father of many children who truly loves them all, we may suppose that he will see very vividly their differences from one another, for he has no wish to impose upon them a similarity which would be himself; and he will be quite willing to see their faults, for his affection leaves him free to love them, not because they are faultless but because they are they; yet while he sees their faults he will be able, from long connection and because there is no reason to avoid the truth, to perceive the many reasons for their actions. The discriminations and modifications of such a man would be enormous, yet the moral realism they would constitute would not arise from an analytical intelligence as we usually conceive it but from love.

The nature of James's moral realism may most easily be exemplified by his dealings with the character of Rosy Muniment. Rosy is in many ways similar to Jennie Wren, the dolls' dressmaker of *Our Mutual Friend;* both are crippled, courageous, quaint, sharp-tongued, and dominating, and both are admired by the characters among whom they have their existence. Dickens unconsciously recognizes the cruelty that lies hidden in Jennie, but consciously he makes nothing more than a brusque joke of her habit of threatening people's eyes with her needle. He allows himself to be deceived and is willing to deceive us. But James manipulates our feelings about Rosy into a perfect ambivalence. He forces us to admire her courage, pride, and intellect and seems to forbid us to take account of her cruelty because she directs it against able-bodied or aristocratic people. Only at the end does he permit us the release of our ambivalence—the revelation that Hyacinth doesn't like Rosy and that we don't have to is an emotional relief and a moral enlightenment. But although we by the author's express permission are free to dislike Rosy, the author does not avail himself of the same privilege. In the family of the novel Rosy's status has not changed.

Moral realism is the informing spirit of *The Princess Casamassima* and it yields a kind of social and political knowledge which is hard to come by. It is at work in the creation of the character of Millicent Henning, whose strength, affectionateness, and warm sensuality move James to the series of remarkable prose arias in her praise which punctuate the book; yet while he admires her, he knows the particular corruptions which our civilization is working upon her, for he is aware not only of her desire to pull down what is above her but also of her desire to imitate and conform to it and to despise what she herself is. Millicent is proud of doing nothing with her hands, she despises Hyacinth because he is so poor in spirit as to consent to *make* things and get dirty in the process, and she values herself because she does nothing less genteel than exhibit what others have made; and in one of the most pregnant scenes of the book James involves her in the peculiarly corrupt and feeble sexuality which is associated in our culture with exhibiting and looking at luxurious objects.

But it is in the creation of Paul Muniment and the Princess that James's moral realism shows itself in fullest power. If we seek an explanation of why *The Princess Casamassima* was not understood in its own day, we find it in the fact that the significance of this remarkable pair could scarcely have emerged for the reader of 1886. But we of today can say that they and their relationship constitute one of the most masterly comments on modern life that has ever been made.

In Paul Muniment a genuine idealism coexists with a secret desire for personal power. It is one of the brilliances of the novel that his ambition is never made explicit. Rosy's remark about her brother, "What my brother really cares for—well, one of these days, when you know you'll tell me," is perhaps as close as his secret ever comes to statement. It is conveyed to us by his tone, as a decisive element of his charm, for Paul radiates what the sociologists, borrowing the name from theology, call *charisma*, the charm of power, the gift of leadership. His natural passion for power must never become explicit, for it is one of the beliefs of our culture that power invalidates moral purpose. The ambiguity of

Paul Muniment has been called into being by the nature of modern politics in so far as they are moral and idealistic. For idealism has not changed the nature of leadership, but it has forced the leader to change his nature, requiring him to present himself as a harmless and self-abnegating man. It is easy enough to speak of this ambiguity as a form of hypocrisy, yet the opposition between morality and power from which it springs is perfectly well conceived. But even if well conceived, it is endlessly difficult to execute and it produces its own particular confusions, falsifications, and even lies. The moral realist sees it as the source of characteristically modern ironies, such as the liberal exhausting the scrupulosity which made him deprecate all power and becoming extravagantly tolerant of what he had once denounced, or the idealist who takes license from his ideals for the unrestrained exercise of power.

The Princess, as some will remember, is the Christina Light of James's earlier novel, *Roderick Hudson,* and she considers, as Madame Grandoni says of her, "that in the darkest hour of her life, she sold herself for a title and a fortune. She regards her doing so as such a terrible piece of frivolity that she can never for the rest of her days be serious enough to make up for it." Seriousness has become her ruling passion, and in the great sad comedy of the story it is her fatal sin, for seriousness is not exempt from the tendency of ruling passions to lead to error. And yet it has an aspect of heroism, this hunt of hers for reality, for a strong and final basis of life. "Then it's real, it's solid!" she exclaims when Hyacinth tells her that he has seen Hoffendahl and has penetrated to the revolutionary holy of holies. It is her quest for reality that leads her to the poor, to the very poorest poor she can find, and that brings a light of joy to her eye at any news of suffering or deprivation, which must surely be, if anything is, an irrefrangible reality. As death and danger are—her interest in Hyacinth is made the more intense by his pledged death, and she herself eventually wants to undertake the mortal mission. A perfect drunkard of reality, she is ever drawn to look for stronger and stronger drams.

Inevitably, of course, the great irony of her fate is that the more passionately she seeks reality and the happier she becomes in her belief that she is close to it, the further removed she is. Inevitably she must turn away from Hyacinth because she reads his moral seriousness as frivolousness; and inevitably she is led to Paul who, as she thinks, affirms her in a morality which is as real and serious as anything can be, an absolute morality which gives her permission to devaluate and even destroy all that she has known of human good because it has been connected with her own frivolous, self-betraying past. She cannot but mistake the nature of reality, for she believes it is a thing, a position, a finality, a bedrock. She is, in short, the very embodiment of the modern will which masks itself in virtue, making itself appear harmless, the will that hates itself and finds its manifestations guilty and is able to exist only if it operates in the name of virtue, that despises the variety and modulations of the human story and longs for an absolute humanity, which is but another way of saying a nothingness. In her alliance with Paul she constitutes a striking symbol of that powerful part of modern culture that exists by means of its claim to political innocence and by its false seriousness—the political awareness that is not aware, the social consciousness which hates full consciousness, the moral earnestness which is moral luxury.

The fatal ambiguity of the Princess and Paul is a prime condition of Hyacinth Robinson's tragedy. If we comprehend the complex totality that James has thus conceived, we understand that the novel is an incomparable representation of the spiritual circumstances of our civilization. I venture to call it incomparable because, although other writers have provided abundant substantiation of James's insight, no one has, like him, told us the truth in a single luminous act of creation. If we ask by what magic James was able to do what he did, the answer is to be found in what I have identified as the source of James's moral realism. For the novelist can tell the truth about Paul and the Princess only if, while he represents them in their ambiguity and error, he also allows them to exist in their pride and beauty: the moral realism that shows the ambiguity and error cannot refrain from showing the pride and beauty. Its power to tell the truth arises from its power of love. James had the imagination of disaster and that is why he is immediately relevant to us; but together with the imagination of disaster he had what the imagination of disaster often destroys and in our time is daily destroying, the imagination of love.

NOTES

1 Whoever wishes to know what the courage of the artist must sometimes be could do no better than to read the British reviews of *The Bostonians* and *The Princess Casassima.* In a single year James brought out two major works; he thought they were his best to date and expected great things of them; he was told by the reviewers that they were not really novels at all; he was scorned and sneered at and condescended to and dismissed. In adjacent columns the ephemeral novels of the day were treated with gentle respect. The American press rivaled the British in the vehemence with which it condemned *The Bostonians,* but it was more tolerant of *The Princess Casamassima.*

2 The reviewer for *The Athenaeum* remarked it was "an odd feature of the book that nearly all the action, or nearly all of which the date is indicated, takes place on Sundays." The observation was worth making, for it suggests how certain elements of the book's atmosphere are achieved: what better setting for loneliness and doubt than Sunday in a great city? And since the action of the book must depend on the working schedule of the working-class characters, who, moreover, live at considerable distance from one another, what more natural than that they should meet on Sundays? But the reviewer thinks that "possibly a London week-day suggests a life too strenuous to be lived by the aimless beings whom Mr. James depicts." The "aimless beings" note was one that was struck by most of the more-or-less liberal reviewers.

3 When I say that Paul and the Princess "stand for" William and Alice, I do not mean that they are portraits of William and Alice. It is true that, in the conditioning context of the novel, Paul suggests certain equivalences with William James: in his brisk masculinity, his intelligence, his downright common sense and practicality, most of all in his relation to Hyacinth. What we may most legitimately guess to be a representation is the *ratio* of the characters —Paul:Hyacinth :: William:Henry. The Princess has Alice's radical ideas; she is called "the most remarkable woman in Europe," which in effect is what Henry James said Alice would have been if the full exercise of her will and intellect had not been checked by her illness. But such equivalence is not portraiture and the novel is not a family *roman à clef.* And yet the matter of portraiture cannot be so easily settled, for it has been noticed by those who are acquainted with the life and character of Alice James that there are many points of similarity between her and Rosy Muniment. Their opinions are, to be sure, at opposite poles, for Rosy is a staunch Tory and a dreadful snob, but the very patness of the opposition may reasonably be thought significant. In mind and pride of mind, in outspokenness, in will and the license given to will by illness, there is similarity between the sister of Paul and the sister of William and Henry. There is no reason why anyone interested in Henry James should

not be aware of this, provided that it not be taken as the negation of Henry's expressed love for Alice and William—provided, too, that it be taken as an aspect of his particular moral imagination, a matter which is discussed later.

4 "Ancestral Houses" in *Collected Poems*. The whole poem may be read as a most illuminating companion-piece to *The Princess Casamassima*.

"*The Princess Casamassima:*
Violence and Decorum"

FREDERICK J. HOFFMAN*

The problems of violence and decorum can best be seen in the light of two stages of the human and social economy: first, the relationship of human passion to social and moral forms (the question of "manners" is of great pertinence); and, second, the interaction of human acts with ideologies. One can imagine two antithetic poles: at the one extreme "manners," at the other ideological systems. In nineteenth century literature, these two radically opposed forms of the human mind moved more and more closely together, until they came within range of each other. The result was to challenge the novelist in a curious way: he had in all conscience to produce a "novel of manners of violence"; that is, he had to account for violence in a literary form that was not prepared to accommodate it.

I do not mean to say that violence is in itself necessarily alien to manners, but rather that the pace, volume, and quality of impact of violence changed steadily. It became more impersonal, less available to the ministrations of ordinary decorum. The novelist of manners needed to assume that the relationships of his characters with one another and with social structures were credible (not necessarily "realistic," but acceptable on the level of the imagination). The increase in pace and rhythm of violence diminished the

*From *The Mortal No: Death and the Modern Imagintion* by Frederick J. Hoffman. Copyright 1964. Reprinted by permission of the publishers, Princeton University Press, and the author.

possibility of credible human relationships. Distortions of the human and social patterns increasingly troubled the best nineteenth century novelists. In some cases, these distortions were ingeniously maneuvered into fictional designs that accounted for them and yet somehow ended in a personal revelation, tragic, ironic, or pathetic. But the effort became more and more arduous, the results less and less certain.

To return to the initial subject of this chapter: Stendhal portrays his heroes performing willed acts of revolt against, or exploitations of, the existing order; but these heroes also live in a society that either is not easily maneuverable in terms of individual heroics or is indifferent to them. For the Beyliste, energy is exhausted in private wars, cloak and dagger intrigues, futile stratagems in *opéra-bouffe* little states. He lives amid the ruins of Napoleonic energy. It is not that there are no opportunities for vigorous acts, but that they do not lead to satisfactorily "heroic" results. As a result, the Stendhal novel invariably yields to comedy and irony. Intelligence, virtue, skill, manners are never really soberly exercised or observed. Fabrice of *La Chartreuse de Parme* (1839) is continually engaged in activities the futility or absurdity of which drains him of his seriousness. He is, of course, at center, "un homme sérieux"; but he does not live in a serious time, or at least the kind of man he is cannot really act seriously within it.

There is another strain in nineteenth century literature, which is worth at least a brief mention; it leads to a reversal of manners and such terms as nobility and virtue belong to the commonplace, to men and women at the bottom of the economic and moral ladders. This hierarchic reversion, quite thoroughgoing and devastating, is a development parallel to the technological enhancement of violence. Ultimately it led to the Marxist dialectic, which is fundamentally secular and proletarian, and it forced a reversal of social and literary evaluations. It led also to the type of novel that uses the masses as hero, in which virtues are gleaned from commonplace acts or are rescued from the ruins of nobility, or are quite inversively judged in terms of the distortions of former heroism. Zola's *L'Assommoir* (1877) and his *Germinal* (1885) are obviously the most remarkable nineteenth century examples of this type.

Germinal is an especially fascinating example of the genre. The ancestor of the proletarian or "strike" novel of the twentieth century, it is a consequence of research energy, and of a simple and even a crude "block structure."[1] Unlike either Stendhal or James, Zola had no set of manners to use as a basis of his examination of social forces. Though the middle class was central to the cohesiveness of Second Empire society, the established manners of that class were there primarily to be abused and ridiculed; and Zola did not possess Stendhal's subtlety in the manipulating of social strategies.

He had therefore to work in terms of a balancing and counterbalancing of forces and appetites; these terms need almost to be taken literally. What makes *Germinal* interesting is that, in the absence of a respected set of manners, Zola "imported" ideologies as forms of order, definition, and even decorum. Zola visualized a social pattern of progress toward a new society and a "new man." *Germinal* is an examination of the several forms by which social forces and human appetites may be balanced. In a genuine sense, Zola tried to improvise manners to accommodate forces, while James attempted to bring forces within the patterns of convention and decorum, to assimilate violence formally and to preserve the "grand design" of manners with which he examined the intricacies of human moral exchange.

In the sense of its being constructed out of basic materials, *Germinal* is an important antecedent of the twentieth century novel of social change. There is much improvisation, much quick adjustment to the immediate exigency, and the kind of alert characterization of environment and action that suggests a novelist's working "on the run," keeping pace with events and formulating their meaning as he describes them. The novel is both "scientific" and tendentious. Fortunately neither characteristic is strong here, though they are both responsible for causing damage to other Zola works. Instead, we are confronted with powerful forces driven by powerful appetites; and the novelist plays the two against each other, usually with considerable success.

There are a number of pertinently suggestive scenes: Souvarine's destruction of the mines *(Germinal)*, Stevie's destruction (his having been literally blown to bits), the growing dominance of the abstractly materialistic symbol of the silver mine (Conrad's *Nostromo*, 1904), a variety of suicides in the novels of Dostoevsky and Turgenev, the suicide of Hyacinth Robinson (James's *The Princess*

Casamassima, 1886). The truth is that violence and its ideologies gradually succeeded in pulling the novel of manners entirely out of focus; it is replaced by the novel of violence, whose angle of vision is consistently distorted, whose author first yields to the distortion and ends by creating an art from its terms. Looking at the extreme poles of this development, one may put at one the half-comic analytics of Julien Sorel's courtship of Mathilde de la Mole (it is an ironic use of "classical" literary mannerisms), and at the other, Picasso's *Guernica* painting. There are many literary expressions of that painting's techniques (war novels, portrayals of concentration camp experiences), but Picasso's work has the grace and power of distortion to suggest itself as a basic text of modern violence.

The novel of manners died hard, in a sense is not dead at all, but is certainly diminished. Our concern with it here is not to describe its decline, but to examine its attempts to come to terms with violence. Everyone involved in this history begins with a disturbed social conscience: the novelist is sensitive to the weakening of the aristocracy, the "upper class," knows about the sporadically successful explosions of revolutionary enthusiasm. He tries to bring the facts of violence within the range of manners. His successes are always only partial; the discourse of manners becomes less and less competent to discuss violence.

Manners are at first a source of protection against violence, an attempt to contain it within social forms. To be serious about manners is to argue a moral preference for older forms but at the same time a conscientious attempt to examine them for weaknesses. The novelist asks himself: Why do they no longer account for *all* human exigencies? Why do they no longer serve to motivate all moral decisions? Why is the *direction* of social motivations changing, even reversing itself? This reversal occurs in every aspect of nineteenth century life: the shift from Hegel to Marx, the continuous failure of efforts to establish societies of "rational harmony," the shift of rhetoric from the drawing-room to the street barricades, the resistance shown by revolutionary characters to efforts to represent them as comic or absurd figures, the steady move toward the secularization of thought and life.

Henry James tried, in *The Princess Casamassima* (1886), to attend directly to these matters, more than that to contain them within the "novel of manners." "Experience, as I see it," he said in his Preface, "is our apprehension and our measure of what happens to us as social creatures. . . ."[2] His original idea was to find a hero who is somehow linked to both extremes of society, whose act of violence would therefore be an act against himself or "his own." James combined this device of a social suicide with a personal suicide; in doing so, he preserved his most cherished moral expression, that of the hero's renouncing an end or purpose to preserve the decorum of means. But he had also to "give way" in this novel to the force of violent circumstance. That is, in order to have Hyacinth "renounce" his purpose, he must have him turn the violence against himself. So there is blood after all; there is an explosion. And this suicide is different from all other deaths in James's fiction. It is, for example, the second suicide with which the Princess is associated; but Roderick Hudson's death (if indeed it is a suicide) is a romantic gesture of despair, to which no superficial social motive is attached.

Hyacinth Robinson dies of the violence of forces to which he has attached himself, for idealistic and for hereditary reasons. His mother had killed his aristocratic father for motives that are halfway class resentment, halfway partake of the full intensity of the *crime passionnel.* Neither motive suffices to force Hyacinth to repeat the violence. He remains dedicated to both extremes of the social scale; but he cannot so divide his loyalties and still escape some kind of violence. Many significant deaths in nineteenth century fiction have ideological motives of one degree or another of intensity: Julien Sorel, whose ideological struggles fail him because of an essential weakness in society, who cannot therefore avenge himself against either society or passion; Nezhdanov, of Turgenev's *Virgin Soil* (1877), who like Hyacinth finds it impossible to clarify or strengthen his loyalty to either class of society, and who must therefore die by his own hand (that is, his hand is maneuvered ideologically into the commission of suicide); Kirillov, of Dostoevsky's *The Devils* (1871), who wills his suicide in the interest of proclaiming a secular defiance of God; Decoud, of Conrad's *Nostromo,* who commits suicide because he cannot stand isolation, but fundamentally because he is possessed of no ideology that will enable him to endure it.

The force of Robinson's predicament is revealed to him early. At a very early age he is taken by Miss Pynsent to the "huge dark tomb" of Newgate prison to see his dying mother for the only time of his life. She is on the edge of death, wasted and old, and Hyacinth is overcome by distaste. She whines repeatedly, "Il a honte de moi—il a honte, Dieu le pardonne!" (v, 53) Eventually Hyacinth agrees to an embrace, but the experience stuns him into a moody silence: ". . . he sat looking out of the window in silence till they reentered Lomax Place" (v, 56).

The full force of this scene is revealed only gradually: Hyacinth looks at death in a prison hospital; he defines himself in terms of the scene, as a member of the disinherited, disenchanted, "illegitimate" class. He is a "bastard" and "of the left." There are many reasons why he will not be able to forget these origins. A child of bad fortune, he will grow to something resembling manhood (though in one sense he simply moves from one mother to the next), and the taint of his illegitimacy combines with the political fact of his mother's French ancestry.

It is not surprising that the major effects of *The Princess Casamassima* should be achieved through a succession of mises-en-scène, but it is unusual that one of them should be the London streets: The "feeling and smell of the carboniferous London damp; the way the winter fog blurred and suffused the whole place . . ." (v, 82). In fact, James's novel is in this respect a "manners" version of Dostoevsky's use of St. Petersburg. But for James the street scene communicates a social disturbance; it is not a projection of Robinson's conscience, as St. Petersburg is of Raskolnikov's. Instead, the details of London stand in clear distinction from the décor of the Princess' town and country homes. The Jamesian line goes all the way down, from the drawing-room to the slum and prison.

From London streets James selects social and socialist types. He is not interested in making them doctrinally precise and would regard ideological niceties as unnecessary distractions. Eustache Poupin is characterized as "an aggressive socialist," all "humanitary and idealistic" (v, 93). Socialist slogans come easily to him and he is accustomed to violence, but ultimately the slogans do not triumph over personal commitments; Poupin and Robinson are in the same corner at the end, and the old man despairs over the criminal necessities that emerge from his political training.

The pivotal word for the Poupins, as it is for the Princess, is *they*. The word has directly opposite meanings: "they" are the aristocrats and owners to Poupin, anarchists and socialists to the Princess. But "they," in Poupin's phraseology, "was a comprehensive allusion to everyone in the world but the people—though who, exactly, in their length and breadth, the people were was less definitely established." (v, 107) Here James touches lightly upon an aspect of the clash between ideology and manners: the difficulty in ascertaining the human condition within a frame of ideological reference.

Hyacinth is alone to resolve the ambiguity. Both of the "they's" ultimately define themselves to him: the people have a democratic energy; the aristocracy seems to him largely necessary to art. But this is an "old-fashioned" realization. It does not prevent Hyacinth's suicide, as its kind did not prevent the destruction of churches in the Spanish Civil War. The disparity between the two extremes is too obvious and is forced too passionately for art or the love of tradition to forestall disaster. In this sense, there is a direct line of descent from Robinson's suicide to Picasso's *Guernica;* both are the consequence of violent distortions of what Hannah Arendt has called "the miracle of being."[3]

But M. Poupin has after all a great respect for "conscientious craftsmanship," and in the business of book-binding there is a chance that art may survive. Robinson thinks at one time that he will go beyond binding books, to writing one, but this is a slender line of resolve, as against the crude power of print in doctrinary pamphlets and leftist newspapers. *The Princess* is nevertheless one of a few James novels in which a commercial enterprise is not only respected but admired. Most of James's Americans produce obscure and vulgar "things" which they sell in huge quantities, as a result of which they are able to travel to Europe to see and even to buy "real things." It is ironic that Hyacinth, when once he knows the Princess, can think of nothing better to do for her than to give her books beautiful bindings; the tribute merely bores her. Since the craft of book-binding is halfway a trade and halfway an art, it is very appropriate that it should provide Robinson a livelihood. The Princess' scorn of his gift is an expression of her apparently uncompromising rejection of the Prince's world of *bibelots* and *objets d'art.*

The closest James came to an accurate representation of a leftist functionary is the figure of Paul Muniment: ". . . he probably indeed had a large easy brain quite as some people had big strong fists . . ." (v, 114). Muniment does represent the bureaucacy of violence, the orderly and efficient leftist stance which made Hyacinth think of "a rank of bristling bayonets . . ." (v, 119). He is the only character of the novel, in fact, who seems consistently and casually impersonal. There are slogans and there are personal idealisms which yield a harvest of abstractions; but only in Muniment do the ideological lines seem to harden into an *abstract* person. Everyone else is in at least some respect vagrantly human and "inefficiently" humane. It is true that Paul seems at times to love his crippled sister, but she is proved in the end to be an unattractive person, on precisely the same level—the ideological —on which he is proved to be less than personally real. Rosy Muniment's illness is hopeless, and she should therefore expect sympathy, but her bright cheerful indulgence is willful.

The only person among Hyacinth Robinson's generation who is miraculously free of ideological encumbrances is Millicent Henning, a middle-class professional woman by virtue of a hard, sure determination, who had come as far as her type could. She had absolutely no sense of the "masses," except that she "simply loathed them, for being so dirty . . ." (v, 163). Millicent is significantly the only person who offers Hyacinth sexual love; but she is entirely and arbitrarily amoral, and when he seeks her out before his suicide, hoping to escape into her arms, she has already taken up the mediocre playboy, Captain Sholto. Sex is scarcely ever an important resort for James's heroes, but here he brings to it a value that it does not elsewhere have—the value that Winston and Julia found in it, in Orwell's *1984*. But Millicent is a shameless and unsentimental Philistine, whose most "artistic" ambition is for "a front garden with rockwork . . ." (v, 164). She is a heroine of another revolution, the unideological one of middleclass raisings —as distinguished from Communist or Fascist "risings."

In a very real sense, *The Princess Casamassima* is a novel of manners that criticizes manners. It does more than offer a genteel satire of aberrant or ridiculous types within a social structure; James honestly tries to come to grips with the evil that has come to threaten society. In the end he is a conservative, for he could be no other; and Hyacinth's long letter to the Princess from Venice is written more by his creator than by him. The center of James's criticism is the Princess herself. Women are always the focus of his moral criticism. The Princess "sins" at both extremes of the social spectrum. When she marries the Prince, at the urging of her mother (*Roderick Hudson*, 1876), she denies everything she might independently have believed to be valuable; and she forces the death of Roderick Hudson, an artist. There is something dreadfully serious about James's interest in monuments, the arts, scenes, which Christina Light has defied and defiled in her marriage.

The punishment is boredom. The Princess' weariness over the dull Prince and his world is James's symbol of nineteenth-century *acedia*. At one extreme we have the Princess living in a world of precious and dull objects (Hyacinth, in his first visit to the Princess, sinks into "a seat covered with rose-coloured brocade and of which the legs and frame appeared of pure gold") (v, 284). At the other extreme, resentment of the world's harsh inequities variously seeks articulation. The Princess suffers the illusion (it is the form taken by her sense of atonement) that "they" at the other extreme are more "exciting," more purposeful, more courageous and noble. As James says of her, she belongs to the class who "could be put on a tolerable footing only by a revolution" (v, 293). She wants to avenge herself upon the Prince's class because she has also been exploited by it.[4]

She does not succeed in doing much more than merely demean herself, and in being one of the instruments (Miss Pynsent and Mr. Vetch are the others) of the education of Hyacinth, which leads to his suicide. As the Princess descends, she moves from one kind of décor to another, and ends in a "vulgar little house" in Madeira Crescent. James's description of the place is rich in the several ironies at his disposal. His interest in the relation of scene to human motive is nowhere more clearly relevant. It was obviously, he says, "her theory that the right way to acquaint one's self with the sensations of the wretched was to suffer the anguish of exasperated taste . . ." (vi, 182). It is not the place that is important, but her reasons for choosing it. She is not the repentant sinner choosing a life of remorse, but a would-be conspirator. And she is left at the end with the realization that neither charm nor conviction interests the conspiratorial group at the "mysterious, revolutionary center." As Paul Muniment tells her, the movement is interested only in her (or the Prince's) money; it is her sole "value."

The Princess Casamassima is a strangely rich, varied, and confused book. The superficial line of meaning is clear enough: Hyacinth, a bastard product of the aristocracy and proletariat, has first to confirm himself in his role of proletarian "questing knight"; then, because of his having seen other worlds, his education progresses antithetically to his resolve. He must therefore, as a noble young man, fulfill his pledge, which is to help destroy the nobility. That is, he must acquit himself honorably and to do so requires the use of violence against a world of manners. But he can no longer serve this role, and must therefore set himself up as the "nobility" he will destroy.

The suicide is James's way of resolving the tensions caused by a conflict of violence and manners. It is a neat, a "clever" device; but the wonder is if James truly means it. For, in terms of the novel of manners, of the aesthetic maneuvering of moral conventions, the suicide restricts and limits violence, sets it aside and leaves its major concerns unresolved and inoperative. In a sense, the novel of manners retreats from the implications of violence, while at the same time it tries to "personalize" it, to remove it to the introspective singularity of a man who (by birth, degrees of education, consciousness) is both, and inextricably, assailant and victim.

But, as the character of the conspirators is mysterious beyond necessity, the progression of events leading to Hyacinth's suicide is arbitrary and unconvincing. At best, it testifies to a few simple truths: that James was aware of imbalances in society that were too serious to be ignored; that he knew of the sporadic explosions of violence, the social earthquakes of 1848, 1871, and others;[5] finally, that he could not give up the one principle that dominated both his life and his fiction: that the moral conflicts could and would be represented in the relationships of consciousnesses to each other, no matter how violent these conflicts might be.

James sacrificed his "son" to preserve this principle, to give it a fund of "grace" from which it might subsequently draw. *The Princess Casamassima* is substantially different from other James novels. For one time, evil (which is alway present in one form or another in the other novels) is here for a while externalized, brought out into the open, dissociated at times from the systole and diastole of the human conscience, made "a public thing." But it does not long remain so extrusive. James "accommodates himself" to the violence, which is a natural consequence of moral extroversion. With the Princess and a minor functionary of the "movement" looking on, the "thing" that was Hyacinth Robinson becomes mute testimony of a violence finally captured and turned against itself: "Hyacinth lay there as if asleep, but there was a horrible thing, a mess of blood, on the counterpane, in his side, in his heart" (vi, 430).

The "horrible thing" that testifies to the suicide of Hyacinth nevertheless is still "of a piece." Brutality spent, the idea of an intelligence superintending the moral conventions is saved. Partly this is because the violence is still triggered by a personality, against another or against itself. We do not know what dark plots have initiated or will survive Hyacinth's act. Julien Sorel and Hyacinth Robinson have comparable instruments of destruction at their disposal. Not long before their time, men of violence hacked at each other with swords, or tortured each other with primitive (though sometimes very ingenious) instruments. Both James and Stendhal are concerned to "personalize" ideological tensions; both succeed only partially in doing so.

However inadequately explained the suicide of Hyacinth is, as an act of violence it differs radically from Sorel's attack upon Mme. Rênal. Both sources of the tensions that cause the suicide are impersonal. They have to do with class differences, with classes formulating them, with leaders announcing the necessity of acts. *The Princess Casamassima* is not a novel of "class warfare," but it is one of a few nineteenth century novels which identify the possibilities of such warfare and try to range the classes against one another.

The major conflict in the "great tradition" of nineteenth century fiction is that between manners and ideologies. The latter term undergoes important changes; the most important of these is the change from an implicit set of beliefs to one that is forcefully, creatively explicit. An explicit ideology begins as a theory of history, and it proceeds in the direction of "proving" the future in terms of a "proven" past. This kind of ideology generates several types of personality that are marginal to it. One of the most interesting of these is the skeptic. Others are the opportunist, the "bushwacking" secret agent; the *isolé* whose moral conscience is almost entirely engaged in coming to terms with itself outside of or beyond established society (Africa and Asia, "dark" or "mysterious" continents both serve as the locale of such retreats); and finally, the victim *per se*, who suffers violence after having achieved only a rudimentary sense of the "bad, bad" world.

The Princess Casamassima portrays violence within the social forms which ordinarily contain it. But its hero is in this case sacrificed so that the forms may continue. The novel appeared before major disasters occurred or were even contemplated. Conrad is already (in *The Secret Agent*) on his way to the world of senseless and irrational explosions. There is a neat and just symmetry in the instruments of destruction used by Stendhal's Julien Sorel and James's Robinson; they are far less horrifying, for example, than Emma Bovary's poison. They argue, in other words, an intimacy with both motive and object. Violence in this sense is still "manners," or it is an act of passionate intensity directed both against them and in deference to them. Hyacinth Robinson's act is a great testimony to the nineteenth century novelist's attempt to accommodate himself to deep and intense disruptions of the moral and social economies. James could not look forward to the time when such an attempt might prove entirely meaningless. For him, meaning needed forms and the special literary conventions according to which men and women were recognizably related.

NOTES

1 F. W. J. Hemmings describes the problem very appropriately as follows: "The form of *L'Assommoir*. . . could be illustrated by a curved line rising to a zenith and then sinking again; but *Germinal* has more than one dimension: it has to be described in terms of cubic capacity, of the balance of weights and counterweights. . . ." (*Emile Zola*, Oxford, Clarendon Press, 1953, p. 179).

2 *The Princess Casamassima*, New York, Scribner's, 1908, Vol. 5, p. vii. Other references, acknowledged in the text, are to this edition.

3 *The Origins of Totalitarianism* (1951), New York, Meridian Books, 1958, p. 469.

4 It must be admitted that most of the Princess' motives for her acts come from her hatred and scorn of the Prince and his world, and especially from her resentment over having been "caught" in a form of *mariage de convenance*. In this sense, she is James's instrument for dramatizing his sense of distress, even horror, over the decline of the aristocracy, and its venality and mediocrity. The

energy of the Princess' attachment to "the cause" is not easy to analyze; the least one may say of it, however, is that it is *not* motivated by any ideological interest in history.

5 For a detailed examination of these matters, see W. H. Tilley's *The Background of the Princess Casamassima*, Gainesville, University of Florida Monographs, number 5, fall 1960.

THE TRAGIC MUSE

1890

"The Tragic Muse"

LYALL H. POWERS*

Of all James's major novels, *The Tragic Muse* has least attracted the attention of critics and scholars. Perhaps they have been too willing to take at face value James's apparent admission, in the Preface, that the novel is at best a qualified success—that its structure is marred and the expression of its themes therefore blurred. Yet the novel occupies a place of crucial significance in James's career: it marks the moment of transition between two modes of literary expression and it addresses itself to problems that were most urgently plaguing James at that time of his life. Furthermore, a sympathetic and attentive reading of the novel will permit us to recognize that *The Tragic Muse* is considerably more successful artistically than James's rather coy remarks in his Preface might lead us to expect; those remarks, after all, are concerned with problems of composition rather than with the features of the finished work.

James had called *The Bostonians* (1886) and *The Princess Casamassima* (1886) "my two best things."[1] They were intended to inaugurate his new period as a successful professional man of letters. They were fashioned to an appreciable extent in the mode of French literary Naturalism, which—especially under the pen of Emile Zola—was succeeding very well in the world of letters south of the Channel. James's expectations were high, yet these two novels suffered a sorry fate. "They have reduced the desire, and the demand, for my productions to zero,"[2] he lamented to Howells

*Part of this essay, in slightly different form, appeared in *PMLA*, LXXIII (June 1958), 270-274; it is reprinted with the permission of the Modern Language Association.

at the beginning of 1888. It might have been expected, then, that James would seriously reconsider the line he had taken in following Zola's lead, and try a new tack. He did not do so—at least not immediately. His next novel, published in the *Atlantic Monthly* during 1889-1890, was *The Tragic Muse*, and it indicates quite clearly the persistence of Naturalist influence.

That persistence in the chosen line may have been due simply to a kind of inertia; but there is strong evidence to suggest that James had not yet done with fictional experiment in the Naturalist mode—not, at least, to his own satisfaction. Certainly *The Tragic Muse* was associated in his mind with the two earlier novels, for its inception dates from June of 1884 at the latest: a sketch of the subject was entered in his Notebooks under that date. And it can be convincingly argued that the very failure of the two novels of 1886 ("from which I expected so much and derived so little") was responsible for his persisting in the line he had taken. The idea for the novel had, in any case, been simmering in his mind for some time before it was brought to a boil in 1888, when he began to set it out.

The Tragic Muse reflects another preoccupation of James's, in addition to Naturalistic fiction—his interest in the theater. When Edward Compton invited him, in December of 1888, to prepare a dramatized version of *The American* for theatrical production, James was delighted to comply. From the beginning he had been interested in the theater, and he had seized an earlier opportunity to dramatize his novella *Daisy Miller*. Although it was not produced, that disappointment did not prevent his accepting Compton's offer. He seems to have regarded it, indeed, as a compensatory opportunity; furthermore, writing for the theater was a means of reaching a large group of the public immediately. It was also a means of gathering abundant financial rewards—if one was successful. At the time of writing *The Tragic Muse*, then, James was full of thoughts about the theater, its exciting possibilities as well as its threatening dangers. Much of his fiction of those few years is full of material of the theater. The very title of *The Tragic Muse* is indicative of that fact, but in addition, James's narrative manner generally tends to be more dramatic: there is much use of dramatic entrances and exits, of *coups de théâtre* and *scènes à faire;* the stories depend more heavily on dialogue (largely uncommented); and there is a much higher incidence of theatrical metaphor in the fiction of this period at the end of the eighties. One might almost say that James's "dramatic years" had their beginning in that fiction, and especially in *The Tragic Muse*. That novel is, then, something of a transitional work: it points ahead toward the dramatic experiment of the first half of the nineties while it unmistakably carries on the Naturalist experiment of the eighties.

The Tragic Muse, one of James's largest novels, is apparently a combination of two stories—the "political case" and the "theatrical case," as James called them in his Preface. The former of these concerns Nick Dormer, son of a political family, who successfully campaigns for a seat in the British House of Commons. He is urged on by his mother and by the memory of his father, Sir Nicholas, to whom he had given his pledge to carry on the political tradition of the family. He is encouraged and promised material support in this pursuit by the substantial Mr. Carteret, an old friend of his father; he is further encouraged by his rich and attractive cousin, the widow Julia Dallow. Continued political success will mean marriage with the politically ambitious and influential Julia, which in turn will mean a home for his mother and unmarriageable sister Grace—in one of Julia's houses; and consequent to that marriage, a generous settlement from the very rich and politically powerful Carteret. The difficulty in all this, which renders Nick's political victory rather Pyrrhic, is the fact that Nick Dormer is—as he says —"two men": one enjoys the flurry of campaigning and the flush of political victory, while the other yearns for the quiet privacy of the painter's studio. One man is the responsible public servant, the other the "irresponsible" private dévoté of art. While most of Nick's family and friends appeal to the public man in him, the private or inner man heeds the encouragement of Gabriel Nash, a friend of Nick's during his time at Oxford and apparently something of an aesthete, and the quieter support of his sister Biddy Dormer—a dabbler in sculpture. Quite obviously, the drama results from the conflict between the public political Nick and the private artistic Nick. The former enjoys the initial triumph, but soon the latter makes his demands felt: thus, his fiancee, Julia, breaks their engagement, and Nick resigns his seat as M. P. and turns to follow his penchant for painting. The conclusion of the novel brings him and Julia—and painting!—all together again. But the end is somewhat ambiguous: one seems to be left in doubt about the final victor.

The theatrical case deals with the career of Miriam Rooth, daughter of a woman with aristocratic pretensions and of an artistic Jewish *brocanteur*. She first appears, in her vulgarly genteel poverty, as a burning aspirant to the stage and momentarily under the wing—protective but skeptical—of Gabriel Nash. She is introduced to Peter Sherringham, brother of Julia Dallow, who is a rising young diplomat and an amateur of the theater. He in turn introduces Miriam to the semi-retired Mme Carré, once one of the glories of the French stage, and becomes her sponsor. He also falls at least half way in love with her. Although Miriam's beginnings are rough and rude, her success is rapid and she becomes the darling of the London theater—the English Rachel. At an early stage of her success Miriam sits to Nick Dormer for her portrait as The Tragic Muse. She finally refuses Sherringham's offer of marriage, for his conditions are that she leave the theater and confine herself to private life as a diplomat's wife. She marries Basil Dashwood, a fellow actor. Her career will present other difficulties to overcome, but her continued success seems to be assured.

These two "cases" are developed for the reader largely in accord with the Naturalist mode as James had adapted it from Zola. In particular he makes use of some of Zola's principles as expressed in "Le Roman experimental."

The Tragic Muse is a full-scale example, the third of this period, of the Jamesian "experimental novel." It is concerned, indeed, with a double experiment. We have Nick Dormer, bred up in a richly political atmosphere and with traditionally political antecedents, introduced to environmental influences which push him in two opposed directions—into the House of Commons and into the artist's studio. We also have Miriam Rooth, the progeny of an artistic Jew and of a daughter of the house of Neville-Nugent, determined by heredity to the life of art, but with a tinge of the commercial and mercenary always present.

The political strain in Nick Dormer's blood is made abundantly clear, and the presence of his father, the earlier Nicholas, is only less pervasive in this novel than that of Mrs. Newsome in *The Ambassadors*. Like Hyacinth Robinson, Nick is acutely conscious of his ancestry and the force with which it weighs upon him. He enumerates to his old friend Gabriel Nash the items that comprise that force: "every thing, every one that belongs to me, that touches me near or far; my family, my blood, my heredity, my traditions, my promises, my circumstances, my prejudices; my little past— such as it is; my great future—such as it has been supposed it may be." And later in the novel he reiterates to Julia Dallow the "tremendous force" of his "hereditary talent" for politics: "Innumerable vows and pledges repose upon my head. I'm inextricably committed and dedicated. I was brought up in the temple like the infant Samuel; my father was a high-priest and I am a child of the Lord." This is the force, of heredity and of part of his environment, which Nick feels is propelling him relentlessly into the House of Commons.

But there is a strong suggestion that he has, like Hyacinth Robinson, a mixed heredity. Two statements by Lady Agnes about her son are revealing. In upbraiding Nick for neglecting his political duty she refers to an inveterate (and "irresponsible") interest in painting: "he had had from his earliest childhood the nastiest hankerings after a vulgar little daubing trash-talking life." Yet when his sister Grace deplores his taking up painting—because he will never do things people will like—Lady Agnes is quick to affirm that "as it happened, her children did have a good deal of artistic taste: Grace was the only one who was totally deficient in it. Biddy was very clever." We might put no particular credence in this defensive statement of Lady Agnes' except for her happy reference to Biddy: Biddy does confirm the suggestion, with her dabbling at sculpture, that the artistic flair has been inherited from some antecedent black sheep.

This apparent mixture of influences accounts for Nick's confusion, his perplexity in the face of the antagonistic attractions in the environment warring for his soul. He tries to explain the difficulty to his mother, that he is two men, "two quite distinct human beings, who have scarcely a point in common." Julia Dallow comes to recognize the duality which Nick describes, charging him (in unintentional irony) with really being everything he pretends not to be. Finally Nick laments to Gabriel, "I don't know *what* I am—heaven help me!"

The hereditary strains are realized for Nick in the contacts he makes in his customary milieu. First, his immediate family, excluding Biddy, clearly "stand for" the political strain; likewise the solid presence of Mr. Carteret at Beauclere, who never fails to remind Nick of his political heredity—that he is his father's son; and then the figure of Julia Dallow, who virtually symbolizes the attraction of the political life for Nick—"you're the incarnation of politics" Nick pointedly tells her.[3] But on the other hand his environment presents him with the inspirational Gabriel Nash (firmly on the side of Art and in favor of Nick's chucking politics for painting), and with the compassionate Biddy. Nash assures Nick that he has artistic ability and ought to pursue his artistic penchant. And then, of course, Nick's interest in Miriam Rooth —the tragic muse and a kind of goddess of art—brings him again into close connection with another realization of that side of his heredity.

Miriam Rooth's case is almost as fully treated as Nick's: her heredity is frequently emphasized. Biddy's comment on Miriam's papa is: "A Jewish stockbroker, a dealer in curiosities, what an odd person to marry—for a person who was well born!" The "well born" person, Mrs. Rooth, claims to be a Neville-Nugent of Castle Nugent; and Gabriel Nash assures us:

> That's the high lineage of [Miriam's] mama. I seem to have heard it mentioned that Rudolf Roth was very versatile and, like most of his species, not unacquainted with the practice of music. He had been employed to teach the harmonium to Miss Neville-Nugent and she had profited by his lessons. If his daughter's like him—and she's not like her mother—he was darkly and dangerously handsome. So I venture rapidly to reconstruct the situation.

Nash's rapid reconstruction points out that Miriam also had a mixed hereditary complement, and incidentally that the paternal contribution to her strain was itself mixed. (And notice also, by the way, that Miriam's case exemplifies the theory of hereditary "crossing"—whereby the son inherits the mother's characteristics and the daughter the father's—which Zola accepted from Lucas' *Traité de l'hérédité naturelle*.) Peter Sherringham's observations on Miriam's progenitors increase the novel's emphasis on these determining forces. He thinks it odd that the histrionic Miriam should have sprung from Mrs. Rooth's loins, "till he reflected that the evolution was after all natural: the figurative impulse in the mother had become conscious, and therefore higher, through

POWERS : *"The Tragic Muse"* 155

finding an aim, which was beauty, in the daughter." He agrees with both Gabriel and Nick, however, that Miriam most favors her father: "the Hebraic Mr Rooth, with his love of old pots and Christian altar-cloths, had supplied in the girl's composition the aesthetic element, the sense of colour and form."

Miriam's genetic background is, then, quite fully enough presented, so that we can hardly ignore its apparent bearing on her actions in the novel, its determining role in the "experiment." What is odd, however, is that at first glance it would seem that Miriam's environmental experience consists chiefly of the realization of the artistic strain in her character. She certainly has not a completely smooth row to hoe, but the chief obstacle she has to overcome seems to be the roughness of her own genius—not some opposed influence pulling her away from artistic pursuits. While Nash professes skepticism about Miriam's ability and even her potentiality, he nevertheless introduces her to Mme Carré. La Carré is also at first quite dubious about Miriam's promise, yet she too is largely instrumental in propelling the girl toward her goal. And finally the interest of Sherringham in things theatrical and his personal attention to Miriam—including some substantial material favors—are likewise apparently the means of adding impetus to her drive to become the English Rachel.

But Peter Sheringham's role is somewhat complex: his assistance to Miriam depends on selfish motives—he is interested in the woman rather than in the actress—and therefore comes really to represent an antagonistic force in Miriam's environment. Mrs. Rooth regards him as an admirable match for Miriam, a match that would mean her leaving the stage, as Peter ultimately demands in asking for Miriam's love. There is the strong suggestion that she is seriously attracted to Peter and even that, could she have been entirely sure of his intention, she might have accepted his offer of marriage. In response to her mother's confident assertion that Peter has already proposed a dozen times—

> "Proposed what to me?" Miriam rang out. "I've told you *that* neither a dozen times nor once, because I've never understood. He has made wonderful speeches, but has never been serious."
> . . . .
> ". . . He's in love with me, *je le veux bien;* he's so poisoned—as Mr Dormer vividly puts it—as to require a strong antidote; but he has

never spoken to me as if he really expected me to listen to him, and he's the more of a gentleman from that fact. He knows we haven't a square foot of common ground—that a grasshopper can't set up a house with a fish. So he has taken care to say to me only more than he can possibly mean. That makes it stand just for nothing."

Miriam's situation, then, has been as difficult as Nick's, and the appearance of smooth progress to her goal has been illusory. Her struggle is quite discernible, after all, in such touches as her brushing away her tears as she informs her mother of Peter's imminent departure. But her acceptance of that departure amounts, finally, to her recognizing the right road for her. The place of marriage in her life dedicated to art is sardonically sketched out by Nash: "She ought to marry the prompter or the box keeper." He continues his portrait of her proper husband—imagines him writing her advertisements, adding up her profits, carrying her shawl, and spending his days in her rouge-pot. She marries Basil Dashwood. In accepting (or taking) him Miriam is simply (given her temper, her hereditary complement) allowing her dominant passion to be directed into its proper channels—the theater.

Nick Dormer has also been involved perceptibly in Miriam's problem, and his own in a way parallels hers: the Nick-Julia connection strongly resembles the Miriam-Peter. Like Miriam, Nick has been driven by a dominant passion—the passion for doing his duty. And Nick's passion is guided, like Verena Tarrant's, by forces of his environment into channels which, according to values expressed by the novel, are the wrong ones. His dilemma results from his failure to recognize the true path of duty; and there is a strong suggestion that Nick is all the while really aware of his error and is engaged in an attempt at self-deception. The motif of sporting imagery frequently associated with Nick's political activity serves to imply that that activity was a caprice on his part, a game undertaken for the fun of it. ("He had risen to the fray as he had risen to matches at school," etc.)[4] Two voices, however, admonish him that he has not really been playing the game, "one of them fitfully audible in the depths of his own spirit and the other ... [that of] Gabriel Nash." Yet he persists in the imitation, feeling that he must do his duty as it is clearly understood by his mother and sister, by Julia Dallow, by Mr. Carteret, and by the spirit of his father. His successful pursuit of his duty culminates, symbolically as well as realistically, in his engagement to Julia—the incarnation of politics.

No sooner has he succeeded in this one pursuit than he feels, like Hyacinth Robinson after a similar success, an acute distaste for "the beastly cause." And he blurts out in awful honesty to Julia that he has imperiled his immortal soul, that he has been hypocritical, dishonest with himself as well as with others. For the moment, however, he seems willing to stand by his wretched success. But his situation is immediately complicated again (and again we are reminded of *The Princess Casamassima*) by his subsequent success in the other cause, his almost abandoned art. Nash's visit to his studio convinces Nick that his painting is successful: Nick "found himself imputing value to his visitor—attributing to him . . . the dignity of judgment, the authority of knowledge. Nash was an ambiguous character but an excellent touchstone." This occurrence opens his eyes, he now sees his proper road and, like Verena Tarrant, is ready to follow the true dictates of his nature—or at least to let himself be propelled in that direction, for he is still somewhat confused about his duty (and he *must* attend to his duty —for that is his dominant passion). Nash sets him straight on that, too; and by stealing his thunder.

> "Don't you recognize in any degree the grand idea of duty?"
>
> "If I don't grasp it with a certain firmness I'm a deadly failure, for I was quite brought up on it," Nick said.
>
> "Then you're indeed the wretchedest failure I know. Life *is* ugly after all."
>
> "But what do you call right? What's your cannon of certainty there?"
>
> "The conscience that's in us—that charming conversible infinite thing, the intensest thing we know. . . . One must do one's best to find out the right, and your criminality appears to be that you've not taken the commonest trouble."

Fortunately, Julia herself cancels the vow Nick has made to her, so that he can be saved from Hyacinth Robinson's fate and can follow straight to his goal—beset with doubts and confronted with obstacles, to be sure, but essentially unwavering. Both Nick and Miriam, then, were determined to meet the ends they do: in both cases they followed an hereditary impulse. The environmental representatives of their mixed hereditary strains so contrived, in the ensuing struggle of the elements, to make clear to Nick and

Miriam the right direction of their most profound passion and their best self-realization.

The experiment of *The Tragic Muse* winds up with Peter Sherringham marrying, to everyone's relief, Biddy Dormer. Miriam's marriage to Dashwood is really little more than a symbolic expression of her being wedded to the theater: so far as the satisfaction of her essential passion is concerned, nothing is altered. And Nick Dormer's finally returning to Julia to paint her portrait indicates to the careful reader that, in spite of Nash's dire prophecy, Nick has remained faithful to his true path of duty—to remain the celibate artist. The complex experiment is done, and the conclusion to be drawn therefrom is a familiar Jamesian lesson: it is the lesson of the master.

It hardly needs to be pointed out that, as with Verena Tarrant of *The Bostonians* and Hyacinth Robinson of *The Princess Casamassima*, Nick and Miriam are by no means merely passive objects swept on by the hereditary and environmental forces in their respective situations; in each instance it is the character's *consciousness* of the forces within and around that determines his lot. Discovery of the dominant passion—for love, say, in Verena, and for doing one's duty, in Nick—and the ability to choose the best avenue for the satisfaction of that passion, those are of principal importance in the three novels of the eighties. But James has emphasized the influential roles of heredity and environment in *The Tragic Muse* and its two predecessors: they determine what his hero's consciousness can do and they set the limits within which the character's choice is free to work.

It is important further to note that the concerns of that consciousness, in Miriam and in Nick alike, are the demands of art and the urging of the artistic sensibility. And James's professed fear of his novel's division, its threatening to break into two parts —his political case and his theatrical case—we can see was ill founded. At bottom the two cases are one, are parallel or complementary: both address themselves to the problem of how to lead a fruitful artistic life in a difficult and largely unsympathetic world; both seek an answer to the question "how can one be an artist?"

James had once again adapted the Naturalistic mode, this time to give dramatic expression to a problem that had vexed him "from far back." For that problem is the central theme of the novel:

To "do something about art"—art, that is, as a human complication and a social stumbling-block—must have been for me early a good deal of a nursed intention, the conflict between art and "the world" striking me thus betimes as one of the half-dozen great primary motives.[5]

If it was an old problem for James, it must nevertheless have presented itself to him with particular urgency at that moment of his career. One can see in the development he gave it in *The Tragic Muse* a peculiar relevance to his position as he faced a crucial turning point in his life. That crucial moment involved the apparent failure of the two novels which preceded *The Tragic Muse*, but more urgently the proposed venture into the theater—a not completely disinterested wooing of the not entirely chaste theatrical muse. It would seem that the relation of Nick to Miriam in the novel is a metaphoric equivalent of James's personal situation vis-à-vis Compton's offer of a career as dramaturge. James had always considered writing for the theater to be "the most cherished of all [his] projects"; but now, in the eighties, that project had a mercenary edge to it—he was interested in the quick and abundant returns possible to the successful playwright. He had decided to devote the time usually spent on the novel to "pot-boiling" for the stage. Here would be a solution to his financial problems;[6] here also would be the opportunity to reach a large audience professionally. James must, however, have suffered something like a twinge of conscience in contemplating this venture with its faint aroma of prostitution. (It will not do, of course, to attempt to brush aside this consideration by claiming that James the professional always wrote for money: he did, but not as his principal aim.)[7] This troublesome aspect of his situation is clearly represented in the relation of Nick to Miriam as a model for his canvas: she functions to some extent as Nick's muse, but he is troubled by an ambiguous quality in her—the mixture of the aesthetic and the mercenary.

Nick is pleased to paint Miriam as "The Tragic Muse" but does not complete a second painting of her. Indeed he is never unequivocally at ease with her as a model, and the bothersome quality is expressed in terms of her racial characteristics: as he works at her portrait Nick is "troubled about his sitter's nose, which was somehow Jewish without the convex arch." He is impressed by her resemblance to her father, the Jewish stockbroker, and entertains the notion that her mother is probably Jewish too:

> He found himself seeing the immemorial Jewess in her hold up a candle in a crammed back shop. . . . it had never occurred to him before that she was a grand-daughter of Israel save on the general theory, so stoutly held by several clever people, that few of us are not under suspicion. The late Rudolf Roth had at least been, and his daughter was visibly her father's child; so that, flanked by such a pair, good Semitic presumptions sufficiently crowned the mother.

It is Miriam's Jewishness that bothers Nick as he paints her, a quality associated in his mind with her father, himself an odd mixture of the aesthetic and the commercial. These are the salient terms of the metaphor (as I would call it) which James employs to help express Nick's doubts about his own artistic pursuits, and which reflects James's own doubts about his projected pursuits in the theater.

Now this is certainly not to suggest that Miriam is herself mercenary, an artist devoted to the commercial reward. It is just that something of that quality expresses itself to Nick. Indeed it is a fear—the commercial threat—which Miriam herself has good reason to entertain: she laments freely in the novel those popular successes which threaten to prevent her from trying her talents in a variety of roles and so coming to master her demanding art. So much the better for the metaphoric aspect of the novel as it was developed under James's pen: Miriam does represent the dramatic art with all its annoyance of glaring publicity, its need to satisfy the many-headed monster, its susceptibility to the influence of the shekel. And as Nick, the private artist who struggles throughout the novel to learn to be true to himself, contemplates this ambiguous representative figure, he cannot but be troubled.

If Nick has some misgivings about this muse, he needs some more satisfactory source of inspiration to rely on—some ultimate authority for his activity about which he finally need have no doubts. That authority would be some divine representative of the pure spirit of art who would inspire him not to specific acts of creation but, more generally, to lead the artist's life and do the artist's work in whatever form came to hand. For Nick that divine authority appears in the form of the appropriately named Gabriel Nash. Indeed it is Gabriel's annunciation that first made him aware of the artistic burden he bore. Gabriel is a fascinating character in the novel: he is unusual, capricious, marvellous. After encouraging Nick to forsake all for art he returns to chastize Nick mildly for pursuing his painting so industriously. He seems suspicious of any *doing* at all: what one *does* is of little moment, but what one *is* matters supremely. Nash's point seems to be simply that *being* is the important consideration, for what one does will follow from that safely; whereas attention to what one *does* can lead to dishonesty, hypocrisy—one can *do* without being. And in being an artist (whatever one does) one *participates* in the eternal Being of Art. Nash is himself apparently the manifestation of that timeless essence: "I shall never grow old," he tells Nick, "for I shall only *be*, more and more . . . I daresay I'm indestructible, immortal." It is significant that this exchange (jocular in tone but surely of profound seriousness for James and reader alike), on the occasion of Nick's painting Gabriel's portrait, is introduced by a description of the subject's discomfiture at being fixed on canvas: "it was new to him to be himself interpreted. . . . From being outside the universe he was suddenly brought into it, and . . . reduced to [the position] of humble ingredient and contributor." The chapter concludes with other significant allusions to Nash's relation to temporality—"punctuality was not important for a man who felt that he had the command of all time," and "Nick now recalled with a certain fanciful awe the special accent with which [Nash] had ranked himself among imperishable things." After sitting to Nick for his portrait Nash disappears from his life; and similarly the portrait itself gradually fades away to nothing but a blur resembling the roughest preliminary sketch. Nick explains this phenomenon to Biddy by saying that "Nash has melted back into the elements—he's part of the great air of the world."

It is apparent that Gabriel Nash serves as the temporal manifestation of the eternal essence in which Nick as artist participates. James has used him as the symbol of the undying spirit of art. And we can see that in this metaphoric expression James embodied his own problem and its potential solution at the moment when he was bidding farewell to the novel and hail to the theater. It expresses his fear that he might suffer seriously as an artist by his theatrical "pot-boiling" but also his trust that an exalted and ultimate inspiration would see him through—would enable him to continue to *be* the faithful artist regardless of the kind of thing he might undertake to *do*.

Some doubt about Nick's success at the end of the novel remains, and that dubiousness casts a grim light on my rather sanguine reading of *The Tragic Muse* as an expression of hope. Gabriel Nash's dire prophecy that Nick would succumb to Julia's attraction at last seems near to being fulfilled:

> She'll get you down to one of the country houses, and it will all go off charmingly—with sketching in the morning, on days you can't hunt, and anything you like in the afternoon, and fifteen courses in the evening. . . . You'll go about with her and do all her friends, all the bishops and ambassadors, and you'll eat your cake and have it, and everyone, beginning with your wife, will forget there's anything queer about you, and everything will be for the best in the best of worlds. . . . That's the sort of thing women do for a man—the sort of thing they invent when they're exceptionally good and clever.

For Nick does accept Julia's invitation to go down for Christmas and while there sketches "the whole company"; worse yet, he finally does a rather successful portrait of Julia. But at this point we may recognize an ambiguous note in Gabriel's utterance: like all prophecies, it has its ambiguity, is both a warning and a forecast, and contains both an indication of the means to success as well as the caution against failure.

The key indication is the painting of the portrait. The novel develops a minor motif which might be called "the law of the portrait": to put it simply, this law is that the effect of painting someone's portrait is to assure his disappearance from the artist's life. Nick paints Miriam; she marries another and removes herself from his orbit. He later paints Nash, who also disappears from his life. Nick indeed seems subconsciously aware of this mysterious law: upon his original engagement to Julia he refuses her request to sit to him for her portrait, and with the startling and apparently inexplicable "Never, never, never!" Miriam's refusal to sit again to Nick makes explicit reference to the law:

> ". . . You'll find other models. Paint Gabriel Nash."
>
> "Gabriel Nash—as a substitute for you?"
>
> "It will be a good way to get rid of him. Paint Mrs Dallow too," Miriam went on . . . , "paint Mrs Dallow if you wish to eradicate the last possibility of a throb."
>
> "The last possibility? Do you mean in her or in me?"
>
> "Oh in you. I don't know anything about 'her.'"
>
> "But that wouldn't be the effect," he argued with the same supervening candour. "I believe that if she were to sit to me the usual law would be reversed."

"The usual law?"

"Which you cited a while since and of which I recognised the general truth. In the case you speak of," he said, "I should probably make a shocking picture."

"And fall in love with her again? Then for God's sake risk the daub." Miriam laughed out as she floated away to her victoria.

The penultimate paragraph of the novel refers, not to "a shocking picture," but rather to "the noble portrait of a lady" which attracted general attention at a recent exhibition. We may safely assume, surely, that the usual law was not reversed after all, and that Nick Dormer remains the devoted, irresponsible, and unworldly artist, celebrating the cult of Gabriel Nash—the great religion of Art.

The Tragic Muse occupies a position of peculiar importance in the Jamesian canon: it offers the fullest fictional development of certain recurrent themes pertaining to the life of art and the artist, and it permits the clearest understanding of the close relationship between James's stories of artists and his stories of man in general. The aesthetic attitude expressed in the novel by Gabriel Nash is rehearsed in numerous short stories, the majority of which were written and published during the last decade and a half of the nineteenth century. And many of these tales are concerned with the opposition between artistic *being* and *doing* as Gabriel Nash expressed it in *The Tragic Muse.* Typically, the faithfully dedicated artist recognizes his need of patient leisure and "irresponsible spaces" for contemplation and careful *couvage* in order for his artistic conception to develop and flower; but he is faced always with the importunate demands of the world that he look to his obligation of doing his duty, of producing something "to show." And if he does produce—publish books, paint pictures, carve statues which society can handle and heft, visit and view—then he will have succeeded in the impercipient eyes of the world. Yet in doing his "duty" as the world expects, he runs the grave risk of misdirecting his energies and being unfaithful to his art; he risks rendering all to Caesar.

This theme appears as early as "The Madonna of the Future" (1873) and in several of the stories of the nineties. It is effectively expressed in "The Next Time" (1895), where the hero Ralph Limbert is in the strange position of being incapable of producing a pot-boiler with vulgar appeal: he cannot "make a sow's ear out of a silk purse"[8]—he *cannot do* what he *is not*. He remains a failure in the eyes of the world while his sister-in-law, Jane Highmore (who never spoke "of the literary motive as if it were distinguishable from the pecuniary") succeeds wonderfully. James's opinion of that success emerges sharply in such passages as this:

> Between our hostess [Mrs Highmore] and Ray Limbert flourished the happiest relation, the only cloud on which was that her husband eyed him rather askance. When he was called clever this personage wanted to know what he had to "show"; it was certain that he showed nothing that could compare with Jane Highmore. Mr. Highmore took his stand on accomplished work and, turning up his coat-tails, warmed his rear with a good conscience at the neat bookcase in which the generations of triplets were chronologically arranged.

Now Mr. Highmore obviously has a good deal in common with Mrs. Coventry of "The Madonna of the Future," who was anxious for the painter Theobald's *show* to begin: for both, what matters is what shows; they care nothing for one's attempt to *be* the faithful artist. They are thus related to George Gravener and Miss Anvoy of "The Coxon Fund" (1894) as regards their attitude to the artist Frank Saltram: "But what is there, after all, at his age, to show?" The same idea echoes in the words of Mrs. Warren Hope of "The Abasement of the Northmores" (1900), who wonders about her husband's career—"what was there, at fifty-seven, as the vulgar said, to 'show' for it all but his wasted genius, his ruined health and his paltry pension?" To these can be added Morgan Mallow, the successful mediocrity of "The Tree of Knowledge" (1900), as he faces his son, returned from an "irresponsible" artistic sojourn in Paris:

> [Morgan] had come down on him for having, after so long, nothing to show, and hoped that on his next return this deficiency would be repaired. *The* thing, the Master complacently set forth was—for any artist, however inferior to himself—at least to "do" something. "What can you do? That's all I ask." *He* had certainly done enough, and there was no mistake about what he had to show. Lance had tears in his eyes. . . . It wasn't so easy to continue humbugging—as from son to parent—after feeling one's self despised for not grovelling in mediocrity.

James attempts to enlist our sympathetic response to the faithful artists by means of religious imagery associated with them and their activity—frequently it is a sort of angelic motif. Theobald of "The Madonna of the Future" is spoken of by his model, Serafina, in this way: "I'm sure *nostro signore* has the heart of an angel and the face of a saint." The work of Ralph Limbert persists, in spite of his efforts at vulgarization, in "addressing itself to the angels." In "The Death of the Lion" (1894), Miss Fanny Hurter, who is one of the very few capable of properly appreciating the work of Neil Paraday, has "the face of an angel"; and the narrator of the story, another of the appreciative few, expresses his awakening dedication to Paraday's work as "the sense of an angel's having swept down and clasped me to his bosom." The characterization of Frank Saltram in "The Coxon Fund" relies largely on the imagery of temples, altars, and the kingdom of light.

And this all finds a strong parallel in *The Tragic Muse*, where the attitude of Miriam and Nick to their art and their place of artistic activity is frequently expressed with the aid of religious imagery, and where the significantly named Gabriel Nash plays an important role.[9] Not only does he impress on Nick the importance of *being* the artist and of trusting his essential artist-self and its promptings—"that charming conversible infinite thing, the intensest thing we know"—he also scorns the world's insistence on doing something to show: "having something to show's such a poor business. It's a kind of confession of failure."

This attitude of James's is reminiscent of Emerson's comment that " 'Tis not important how the hero does this or this, but what he is. What he is will appear in every gesture and syllable."[10] But the idea was apparently given James by his father; the autobiographical *Notes of a Son and Brother* records this reminiscence of his father's advice: "What we were to do . . . was just to *be* something, something unconnected with specific doing, something free and uncommitted, something finer in short than being *that*, whatever it was, might consist of."[11]

A representative passage from the writings of James's father will also indicate the connection between the artist and the ordinary man in James's fiction, for the connection made by father and son is essentially the same. In *Moralism and Christianity* Henry James, Sr. wrote:

But now observe that when I speak of the aesthetic man or Artist, I do not mean the man of any specific function, as the poet, painter, or musician. I mean the man of whatsoever function, who in fulfillment of it obeys his own inspiration or taste, uncontrolled either by his physical necessities or his social obligations. He alone is the Artist, whatever be his manifest vocation, whose action obeys his own internal taste or attraction, uncontrolled by necessity or duty. The action may perfectly consist both with necessity and duty . . . but these must not be its animating principles, or he sinks at once from the Artist into the artisan.[12]

And we recall again Nash's urging Nick simply to *be*, to recognize his *duty to himself.*

This antinomy of being and doing in the stories of artists, and especially in *The Tragic Muse*, is closely related to the central oppositions in James's other fiction, most obviously in the international stories—here the opposition is between "America" and "Europe." The dilemma of the innocent American is that he is confronted, in Europe, by a world which relies on what shows— correct manners and conventional behavior. The particular evil of that world and its code of manners is that it permits the grossest hypocrisy: what one smoothly does is no necessary reflection of what one really is. The naive American has no artifice to enable him to appear other than he really is—which was, we recall, the ironic dilemma of Ralph Limbert in "The Next Time." One horrible alternative open to the American is to adopt the manners he sees, with no assurance that they will faithfully represent *him*. In that case he will cease to be what he spontaneously *is* and try to do things according to the way of the world. The classical example of that choice is Gilbert Osmond of *The Portrait of a Lady*, the polished veneer on a personal void, who blandly confesses "I'm not conventional: I'm convention itself." The painful solution is to come to terms with that world without losing fidelity to one's self, to accept only those features of conventional behavior which honestly represent what one is—and to avoid being "ground in the very mill of the conventional."

James's stories of artists simply examine the same problem in those particular terms most appropriate to the life of the artist. In attempting to achieve a workable compromise with "the world," the artist must still remain faithful to his essential nature as artist —"the intensest thing we know." Clearly this is the problem which both Nick Dormer and Miriam Rooth share: their problem is one, although their artistic mediums are apparently quite opposed. And each must cherish his "silk purse." So the "theatrical case" and the "political case" of *The Tragic Muse*, as James calls them, are really closely united in their treatment of the problem of the conflict of "art and 'the world' "; and can be seen, finally, to be typically Jamesian in their profoundest concerns.

NOTES

1 Quoted in Virginia Harlow, *Thomas Sergeant Perry* (Durham, N. C., 1950), p. 316.
2 *The Letters of Henry James*, ed. Lubbock, 2 vols. (New York, 1920), I, 135.
3 See *The Tragic Muse* (New York Edition), VIII, 75. Cf. Nick's earlier thoughts of Julia (VII, 263-264): "Miss Dallow . . . had suddenly become a larger fact in his consciousness than his having turned actively political. She was indeed his being so. . . . She had made the business infinitely prettier, . . . converting it into a kind of heroic 'function,' the form of sport most dangerous."
4 *Tragic Muse*, VII, 261: "his boyishness could still take pleasure in an inconsiderate show of agility. . . . he could do these things because it was amusing and slightly dangerous, like playing football or ascending an Alp, pastimes for which nature had conferred on him an aptitude not so very different from a due volubility on platforms." Cf. VII, 263: "he appreciated the coincidence of the hit and the hurrah, the hurrah and the hit"; cf. VIII, 75, etc.
5 *The Art of the Novel*, ed. Blackmur (New York, 1953), p. 79.
6 See *The Selected Letters of Henry James*, ed. Edel (New York, 1955), p. III: Mr. Edel writes "There is no doubt that he was impressed by the substantial royalties derived by playwrights from a successful box-office. Dependent as he still was then upon his literary earnings, he had also experienced some anxiety over the continued limited sale of his books and his increasing difficulties in placing his longer works in the magazines. It seemed to him that an immediate solution was to confine himself to the writing of short stories—*à la Maupassant*, he wrote in his notebooks—and to devote the time he would normally have given his longer fictions to 'pot-boiling' for the theatre. His was a calculated siege of the theatre. He promised himself that he would persist even if at first he encountered defeat."
7 It may be objected that this is an erroneous interpretation of James's situation; as who should say: "as a professional writer he always wrote for money." But to reason, as some have, in this manner is to share in the confusion of Mrs.

Jane Highmore ("The Next Time"), who never spoke of the literary motive as if it were distinguishable from the pecuniary. James clearly felt that there was a distinction to be made between the two motives.

8 Cf. *The Notebooks of Henry James*, ed. Matthiessen and Murdock (New York, 1955), pp. 181, 200; and Edel, *Selected Letters*, p. 112. James originally used the term to refer to his own failure in the theater, in a letter to his brother William, January 9, 1895, after the failure of "Guy Domville" (see *Letters*, ed. Lubbock, I, 229).

9 I have treated these ideas in greater detail in two essays: "Mr. James's Aesthetic Mr. Nash—Again," *Nineteenth-Century Fiction*, XIII (March 1959), 341-349, and "Henry James's Antinomies," *University of Toronto Quarterly*, XXXI (January 1962), 125-135. It will be readily seen that the attitude of Gabriel Nash bears some resemblance to that expressed in the works of Walter Pater, and especially in the conclusion to his *Renaissance* and in *Marius the Epicurean*. The similarity between James and Pater (noted by Stuart P. Sherman, F. O. Matthiessen, and Giorgio Melchiori) has been responsible, I suppose, for more recent attempts to identify Nash with Oscar Wilde, apostle of Pater. But a careful examination of "The Author of 'Beltraffio' " as well as of *The Tragic Muse* indicates that James is not aiming finally at the position of the aesthetes, at formulating a prescription for the 'art of life.' Even less is he attempting to satirize them in the person of Gabriel Nash. It is apparent that at the outset of the novel Nick Dormer is embarrassed about his association with Nash (and, indeed, his attraction to him), and therefore tries to avoid introducing him to his sister Biddy Dormer. The reason for the embarrassment is obviously that Nick is full of his sense of "duty"—to the political career his family and friends have planned for him. It is equally obvious that the triumph of "art" in the novel is due to a great extent to the influence of Nash on Nick. No, James is concerned rather with the problem of how to live the artist's life in a world fundamentally inimical (as he felt) to such an existence. James's position is close to that of Croce as expressed in his *Aesthetics*, and even closer to that adopted by the Bloomsbury Group under the influence of the ideas of G. E. Moore as expressed in *Principia Ethica*. (But cf. note 12, below.)

10 "Society and Solitude," *The Complete Works*, ed. Edward Waldo Emerson (Boston and New York, 1883-1893), VII, 184.

11 *Henry James: Autobiography*, ed. Dupee (New York, 1956), p. 268.

12 Quoted in Frederick H. Young, *The Philosophy of Henry James, Sr.* (New York, 1951), p. 185.

WHAT MAISIE KNEW

1897

What Maisie Knew: The Evolution of a "Moral Sense"

JAMES W. GARGANO*

Henry James's *What Maisie Knew* presents from a complex point of view the initiation of a young girl into a world of vortical activities and emotions. The novel, moreover, as an example of James's celebrated "dramatic" method, contains ambiguities resulting from the special techniques (not to speak of stylistic eccentricities) he developed from 1896 to 1901, the period of *The Awkward Age* and *The Sacred Fount.* It is not surprising, therefore, to find critics in radical disagreement as to what Maisie learns from the disruptions, reunions, and chance encounters that nourish her consciousness. Does she, as Beach maintains,[1] learn nothing, or does she, as Dupee declares, "know at last . . . that she is in fact an instrument of badness among [her parents and stepparents] and a not unwilling one so long as she goes along with them in her desire for support and affection?"[2] Are we to adopt the ambiguous view of Pelham Edgar who, after insisting that the novel traces the development of Maisie's moral sense, confesses that "as we close the book we are in the same predicament as Mrs. Wix, and ask ourselves what, after all, did Maisie really know?"[3]

[1] Joseph Warren Beach, *The Method of Henry James* (Philadelphia, 1954), p. 239.
[2] F. W. Dupee, *Henry James* (New York, 1951), p. 192.
[3] Pelham Edgar, *Henry James: Man and Author* (Boston and New York, 1927), p. 127.

Or is Canby right in assuming that in *Maisie* James, as a rather headstrong virtuoso, was concerned with "stage effects, not character and personality?"[4]

Of the most recent studies of the novel, those of Bewley and F. R. Leavis are discerning and occasionally analytical.[5] Unfortunately, the controversy between the writers turns on the question of *Maisie's* kinship to *The Turn of the Screw*. Yet, when they specifically discuss *Maisie*, they are, characteristically, almost completely at odds: Bewley finds in Mrs. Wix's desire to keep Maisie an "erotic" interest in Sir Claude, while Leavis assails this view as the "oddest of ... perversities."[6] The disputants also differ as to why Maisie finally chooses to return to England with Mrs. Wix, and more importantly they put forth conflicting opinions concerning the "tone" of the novel. Both writers agree, however, that Maisie herself is untainted by the evil that festers around her. Not until 1956 was it suggested (perhaps on the basis of Bewley's attempt to relate the novel to *The Turn of the Screw?*) that Maisie herself is so vitiated by the evil of her "protectors" that she seeks to resolve her dilemma by offering to become Sir Claude's mistress.[7] If it can be substantiated, this interpretation of Maisie's character would further contribute to the element of "horror" Bewley discovers in *What Maisie Knew*.

In spite of the disparity of critical opinion concerning *Maisie*, the novel has not been examined with the care that it merits. Generally, it has been praised, patronized, and explained in a few discursive paragraphs or pages. In attempting to determine what Maisie knows at the end of the novel, I shall examine the book's internal logic of episode and authorial commentary in the hope of capturing its staged revelations. For despite obscurities, *What Maisie Knew* does possess an order and a lucidity in the precisely articulated preparatory scenes that consummate in the superficially ambiguous final chapters. In this study my aim has not been to promote another doctrinaire thesis, but to show, with a measure of documentation that critics of *Maisie* have avoided, the sure and

[4]Henry S. Canby, *Turn West, Turn East* (Boston, 1951), p. 216.

[5]Marius Bewley, *The Complex Fate* (London, 1952), pp. 96-144. This book contains two "interpolations" by F. R. Leavis.

[6]*Ibid.*, p. 128.

[7]Harris W. Wilson, "What Did Maisie Know?" *College English*, XVII (Feb., 1956), 279-281.

deliberate architectonics through which James reveals his theme.

James's preface to *Maisie* emphasizes three aspects of the novel that should help direct the reader to its meaning. First of all, by describing his youthful heroine as endowed with "an expanding consciousness," he establishes the novel's concern with the theme of growth. Second, he insists that Maisie must "for the satisfaction of the mind" be "saved";[8] this comment, enforced by his allusions to the child's moral insights and by his observations on the moral value of two scenes, declares James's intention to deal affirmatively with Maisie's development. Finally, James's reference to "our own commentary [which] constantly attends and amplifies,"[9] calls attention to the authority of his interpolations—some of them surprisingly explicit—which explore and occasionally fix the significance of Maisie's thoughts and actions. I do not mean to imply that James mechanically glosses the difficulties of the dramatic scenes in set passages of exegesis. Instead, the wealth of authorial explanation is in a sense made integral by the basic technique of the novel—a central intelligence not altogether capable (as Strether is finally capable in *The Ambassadors*) of assessing and conceptualizing the value of her experiences. James, then, in his own words compensates for Maisie's limitations by "going so 'behind' the facts of her spectacle as to exaggerate the activity of her relation to them" without violating the unique sense of the child's response to those facts.[10]

Unless his preface is deliberately misleading, James puts on record how in a general way he intended *Maisie* to be read. I believe that his hints can be taken as serious guides to the meaning of the novel. In confessing this, I admit impatience with the sophistical arrogance that denies a writer, especially one with James's critical acumen, any authority to explain his own creations.

That the heroine's consciousness expands to self-understanding and moral awareness is proved both by her increasingly sensitive response to the events in which she plays a part and by James's comments on her development. The first important scene which shows the direction of Maisie's initiation occurs early and announces with singular clarity the motif of moral growth. At the outset of the novel, Maisie is caught in the continuing hostilities

[8] *The Novels and Tales of Henry James* (New York edition), XI, vi-vii.
[9] *Ibid.*, p. x.
[10] *Ibid.*, p. x.

between her divorced parents, with each of whom she spends, in turn, six months of the year. Condemned to carry insults from one parent to another, she achieves her first "expansion" when she refuses to report their abusive messages and thus thwarts their plans to make her a "centre of hatred." Almost too pointedly, James interprets her feigned stupidity as a "great date in her small still life: the complete vision, private but final, of the strange office she filled. It was literally a moral revolution and accomplished in the depths of her nature" (p. 15). Clearly then, Maisie acquires "vision," undergoes a profound spiritual alteration, and, by frustrating her mother and father's perverted sport, functions as a force for good. This scene alone, it seems to me, undermines Beach's argument that Maisie learns nothing from her experiences. Since James is here speaking *in propria persona*, the reader must accept the passage as incontrovertible evidence that Maisie is launched under fair auspices.

A favorable start, however, does not insure a safe arrival at distant ports. As Maisie grows older she must confront, with pathetically little assistance, the enigma of her situation. Her mother's marriage to Sir Claude and her father's marriage to Miss Overmore (now known as Mrs. Beale) require from her a subtle allocation of loyalty that taxes her youthful ingenuity. To add to the confusion, her stepparents are soon involved in a "relationship" strongly condemned by Mrs. Wix, Maisie's comical but sturdily moral governess. Moreover, her mother's second marriage is followed by a series of "attachments" to Mr. Perriam, Lord Eric, and the Captain, while her father's denigration of conventional codes culminates in his being the paid lover of the Countess. But Maisie, in addition to being exposed to the sordid intricacies of her guardians' amours, is often present at uninhibited adult discussions of them. Nevertheless, her innocence remains surprisingly unsmirched in the immediate proximity of pitch.

And yet, as James shows in *The Awkward Age*, a close cousin to *Maisie*, innocence is not necessarily defiled by knowledge. Aggie's antiseptic education is a ludicrously inept preparation for life in a world with little resemblance to Eden, while Nanda's exposure leads to knowledge, growth, and self-sufficiency. Maisie, like Nanda, is "a sort of drain-pipe with everything flowing through," and like Nanda too she remains uncontaminated. Less squeamish than many of his readers and critics, James did not subscribe to the Duchess's formula for creating in Aggie the perfect child, a paragon who should be nurtured "privately, carefully, and with what she was *not* to learn—till the proper time—looked after quite as much as the rest."[11]

That Maisie's exposure to infection does not lead to paralysis, statsis, or corruption is apparent if the novel's basically simple focus, by no means simply achieved by the artist, is recognized: no matter how devious the adult intrigues, the center of interest always remains fixed in the child's acquisitive sensibility. In his preface, James himself warns against taking the Faranges and their associates as his subjects, for they are lacking in inherent interest because they are "figures of too short a radiation"; they can only be invested with meaning by "the child's own importance, spreading and contagiously acting."[12] Beach's quaint derogation of Maisie's role seems to me to limit the novel's radiation and to reduce it to sparkling but empty virtuosity: "Maisie herself has really no story. She is hardly more than an observer eagerly following from her side-box the enthralling spectacle of the stage."[13] Far from being shunted to a side-box, the girl is constantly on stage in the midst of actions too urgent to be dismissed as mere spectacle.

There are at least four scenes (in addition to the episode describing her moral revolution) which dramatize Maisie's journey toward knowledge and maturity. The first scene occurs when Sir Claude, about to turn Maisie over to Mrs. Beale, asks her if she dreads seeing her father. In this situation, in which she might easily have condemned her father, she colors with "an odd unexpected shame at placing in an inferior light . . . so very near a relative as Mr. Farange" (p. 119). As interpreter of her increasing sensitivity, James characterizes her emotion as "more mature than any she had yet known." He further indicates that at this moment Sir Claude, who is capable of fine discrimination, "caught his first glimpse of her sense of responsibility" (p. 120).

In other words, the child does not assume the facile irreverence that her stepfather too casually expects. Instead, with an unusual exhibition of propriety and force of character, she compels Sir Claude to take her conduct seriously. Once again she resists the adult tendency to make her a counter in an irresponsible game of

[11] *The Novels and Tales of Henry James* (New York edition), IX, 53.
[12] *Ibid.*, p. xiii.
[13] Beach, p. 239

hate. Her self-conscious integrity attests that her moral revolution has not proved abortive. Indeed, it has the subsidiary effect of modifying the cynicism and obtuseness of her adult associates; like Morgan Moreen in "The Pupil," she contributes significantly to the education and refinement of those who should be enlightening her.

Of course I am not suggesting that Maisie can translate her reactions into abstract concepts; after all, though almost inordinately impressionable and discerning, she often lacks the maturity to understand what, in fact, is happening to her. As she unconsciously stores up sensations and insights, she is naturally less concerned with what she learns than with the wonder of the phenomena she observes; moreover, as the preface warns, the experiences "that she understands darken off into others that she rather tormentedly misses."[14] The imaginative collaborator whom James assumes as his reader must then, with the author's assistance, supply the normative terms that describe her progress. The reader will not be disturbed, however, when after what seems a startling stretch of intelligence and feeling, Maisie lapses into childish naïveté. To expect an arbitrarily consistent development of all her faculties is to treat her as if she were a geometrical proof and not a child. Her mistakes, which are many and sometimes amusing, make her in James's words "the ironic centre," but they do not nullify her slowly expanding vision.

A second incident showing the deepening of Maisie's nature is that in which her unbelievably stupid father takes her to the splendid house of the Countess. Here the girl's quick perceptions detect behind her father's attentions a desire to give his projected abandonment of her the best of appearances. The scene is triumphantly Jamesean in its rich and ingratiating evocation of Maisie's diversity, complexity, and not incongruous innocence. The child's aesthetic sense is vividly awakened; the daughter experiences filial palpitations and responsibilities; the imperiled little identity maturely considers her own interests; and her groping moral nature —never given a harsh prominence—slowly builds up to a vision of the ugly implications of what she has been exposed to. The gradual progression of the scene toward éclaircissement subtly illuminates James's moral intention, for though Maisie is child enough to feel enjoyment in the presence of the Countess's expen-

[14] Op. cit., p. x.

sive possessions, she "all in a moment"—her knowledge invariably comes in flashes—admits her father's degradation in allying himself with someone whom "neither her mother, nor Mrs. Beale, nor Mrs. Wix, nor Sir Claude, nor the Captain, nor even Mr. Perriam and Lord Eric could possibly have liked" (p. 196). It might not be too extravagant to say that Maisie enters the house a child and leaves it precociously wise, for her initial pleasure in discovering herself in the enchanted world of the Arabian Nights is dissipated by the recognition of "something in the countess that falsified everything" (p. 196). That she betrays, at the end of the scene, a juvenile delight in the money lavished on her by the Countess does not detract from James's moral purport; on the contrary, it is evidence that his moral sense does not interfere with the aesthetic rigor which demands that he be true to the child's nature.

Certainly a child who undergoes a moral revolution, learns responsibility, and rejects a revolting father is making rather wholesome progress. James never intimates that she is crushed or arrested by her experiences or that she is acquiring the calculated immorality to attempt to become her stepfather's mistress. In scene after scene, Maisie's accumulated insight is brought into play, but never more tenderly than when, with the Captain in Kensington Park, she desperately urges her companion to be loyal to her mother. With the "small demonic foresight" James attributes to her in the preface, she envisions her mother's potential disaster.

> "Good-bye." Maisie kept his hand long enough to add: "I like you too." And then supremely: "You do love her?"
> "My dear child—!" The captain wanted words.
> "Then don't do it only for just a little."
> "A little?"
> "Like all the others."
> "All the other?"—he stood staring.
> She pulled away her hand. "Do it always!" (p. 155).

Although a rigid moralist may condemn her encouragement of an illicit affair, she "supremely" reveals a deep passion for loyalty and an understanding of the moral consequences of promiscuity. Her sense of responsibility, whose birth Sir Claude witnessed, has by now confronted those bitter realities not easily resolved by resort to simple moral fiat. Maisie's allegiance is obviously not to a re-

strictive code; unlike other James characters, notably Winterbourne, Mrs. Newsome, and Mrs. Pocock, she is emancipated
from—or has never made—the narrow commitment that prevents
humane action. Perhaps, to act with responsible freedom is necessarily to transgress. Certainly, however, Maisie's earnest, even
embarrassing approval of the Captain's love can seem immoral
only to those who subscribe to the unbending dogmas of Woollett.

The scene with the Captain, in spite of its immediate impact—
James saw in it, on rereading, an "effect of associated magic"—is
in a sense completed by the perfectly wrought episode dealing
with Maisie's last meeting with her mother at Folkestone. The
child, with almost motherly solicitude, tried to "adopt her ladyship's practical interests and show her ladyship how perfectly she
understood them" (p. 222). Unfortunately, the battered but still
arrogant parent is outraged at having the Captain—now "the biggest cad in London"—recommended to her. Maisie matches her
mother's angry explosion, but even anger is accompanied by a
terrible prevision of tragedy:

> in the midst of her surge of passion—of which in fact it was a part—
> there rose in her a fear, a pain, a vision ominous, precocious, of what
> it might mean for her mother's fate to have forfeited such loyalty as
> that. There was literally an instant in which Maisie fully saw—saw
> madness and desolation, saw ruin and darkness and death (p. 225).

Such a dark vision—perhaps the key word in the novel is "vision"—proves that the child has traveled a surprisingly straight
course from the moment she decided not to feed her parents'
mutual hatred. Without Mrs. Wix's moral sense—which, though
by no means contemptible, assesses human action by doctrinal
requirements—Maisie wrests from the urgency of each of her
predicaments a moral vision or a moral imperative.

Despite its inclusiveness, nevertheless, Maisie's vision is not
complete until she has focused a true image of Sir Claude. For all
her maturity, she would like to find in him not only a father-
substitute but the Prince Charming who, through the largess of
treats, outings, and affection, instills romance into her life; their
activities release her from the constricting classroom into the
glamorous world of parks, restaurants, and foreign travel. His
constant avowals of love and loyalty and his easygoing acceptance
of her precocity, charm her into a state of devotion. Yet, James

compels her to learn, a lesson terrible to a child, that her fairy-tale hero is incapable of ideal behavior in the real world. Her childhood dies with the death of her delusion. Maisie's most impressive act —the real measure of what she knows—is her precipitation of the situation which divests Sir Claude of his specious attractions and exposes his obsessively compromising nature.

Maisie does not, however, suddenly begin to judge Sir Claude at the end of the novel. From the beginning of their association, she occasionally observes in him a shiftiness with which she (like Mrs. Wix) attempts to compromise. For example, when he asks if she might help him hide Mrs. Beale from Mrs. Wix's vigilance, she is described as gaining a "first glimpse of something in him that she wouldn't have expected" (p. 85). At another point, fear of leaving Mrs. Wix drives her to tears, but she "couldn't have told you if she had been crying at the image of their separation or at that of Sir Claude's untruth" (p. 118). Still, she delusively believes that Sir Claude has been saved when, submitting to Mrs. Wix's moral pressure, he flees with her to Boulogne. When the governess joins them, Sir Claude seems momentarily to have "embraced his fine chance" and risen to ideal action. But Sir Claude proves himself a most unheroic hero when, accepting the first pretext, he announces his decision to return to England. In the ensuing debate with Mrs. Wix, he confesses his fear of Mrs. Beale and ultimately counters righteous arguments with a princely manner whose "excess of light" draws "depraved concession" from Mrs. Wix. Though Maisie fails to support her governess's high-flying morality, she astutely notices with "slight oppression . . . that [Sir Claude] had unmistakeably once more dodged" (p. 264).

Sir Claude's defection is the prelude to a series of events that round out Maisie's education: Mrs. Wix's desperate attempt to infuse a moral sense into her charge, Mrs. Beale's dramatic appearance in Boulogne, and Sir Claude's return, as a "different" man, into a situation likely to prove explosive. James's technical daring keeps the action moving, with imaginative brilliance and poise, through surprises, ironies, and charged, elliptical dialogue. Apart from its thematic function, the cluster of scenes displays a mastery of dramatic nuance, spectacle, and timing rarely equalled in James's work. Finally, however, the scenes mass the important characters in Boulogne and prepare for the showdown leading to Maisie's disenchantment with her hero.

Since the three events have a cumulative value, it is necessary to indicate their importance. In Mrs. Wix's intense campaign to indoctrinate Maisie, the child performs like a dull student indeed. Her egregious "stupidity" has persuaded many critics that, even after all her opportunities for "accumulations," she knows next to nothing. These critics forget, however, that Maisie confronts Mrs. Wix's query as to whether she "really and truly" has any moral sense with clever dissimulation:

> Maisie was aware that her answer, though it brought her down to heels, was vague even to imbecility, and this was the first time she had appeared to practice with Mrs. Wix an intellectual inaptitude to meet her—the infirmity to which she had owed so much success with papa and mamma. The appearance did her injustice (p. 279).

In addition to her feigned ignorance, Maisie gives the appearance of childishness because she has no ready-made Sunday-school code to mouth with impressive facility. Almost pragmatically but most sensitively, she picks her way through the disorder and complexity of a world that Mrs. Wix interprets in simple Biblical terms. Yet though the pupil does not, like her tutor, know the answers in the back of the book, she is not without values. Indeed, her life with depraved parents has ironically served to teach her "one of the sacred lessons of home" that "there were things papa called mamma and mamma called papa a low sneak for doing and for not doing" (p. 260). In a sense Maisie is a more searching practical moralist than the literal-minded instructor whose formidable moral stance continually awes her. Moreover, through all of her disingenuous sallies, Maisie is motivated by the ideal of loyalty to Sir Claude—an ideal that Mrs. Wix cannot sustain.

Mrs. Beale's appearance in Boulogne demonstrates that Mrs. Wix's moral sense can be rather easily trifled with. When Maisie's stepmother breathlessly courts the governess's support, Mrs. Wix is so taken in by the extravagant display of kindness that she practically agrees to accept the woman she had earlier reviled. No wonder Maisie "became on the spot quite as interested in Mrs. Wix's moral sense as Mrs. Wix could possibly be in hers" (p. 301). Yet, strangely, in spite of James's persistently ironical view of Mrs. Wix, most critics continue to accept her as the moral norm of the novel, forgetting that she is often actuated by materialistic considerations. Though it would be foolish to deny Mrs. Wix a measure of comic grandeur—her heroic speeches are always slightly preposterous—she is too high-pitched, narrow, and unsophisticated to embody James's sense of moral vision. On the whole, she has an old-fashioned, grandmotherly rectitude, but she is no vessel of wisdom. Her light is bright enough for the nursery, but it is no radiance. Her own complaint (perhaps her most touching utterance) that Maisie's affairs have led her into moral quicksands is a gauge of her limitations: " 'I ask myself where I am; and . . . say to myself that I'm too far, too far, from where I started.' " (p. 282). I cannot agree with Bewley's contention that Mrs. Wix is the only adult in the novel "capable of being educated into fineness,"[15] for "fineness," with its suggestion of sensitive discrimination, is just what Mrs. Wix will never achieve. Though she can, at times, burst into grotesque displays of moral energy, she rather resembles Mrs. Micawber—as Mrs. Beale cruelly points out—in her decision to "never, never, never desert Miss Farange" (p. 126). To the end she remains, in spite of her nagging and doctrinaire morality, "peculiarly and soothingly safe; safer than anyone in the world" (p. 26). It is indeed most characteristic of her that even after Maisie's sacrifice of Sir Claude she still wonders what the child really knows.

Mrs. Beale's descent upon Maisie and Mrs. Wix is for her the climactic event in a long struggle for security and power. The one-time governess, whom both Maisie and Sir Claude confess they fear, has designedly achieved status through her marriage to Maisie's father. Then, having quickly calculated that with Farange she is on a sinking ship, she attaches herself to the susceptible Sir Claude. The acute Maisie, reacting with childlike ambivalence, recognizes her stepmother's combination of beauty and strength: "it took [Mrs. Beale] but a short time to give her little friend an impression of positive power—an impression that seemed to begin like a long bright day. This was a perception on Maisie's part that neither mamma, nor Sir Claude, nor Mrs. Wix . . . had exactly kindled" (p. 124). This "power" is, in the Boulogne scenes, hurled with tremendous force against Mrs. Wix's long-standing moral "prejudice" concerning Mrs. Beale's sinister influence on Sir Claude. Almost completely ignoring Maisie, who is only a pawn in her game, she wrings important concessions from her former enemy, but her masterful diplomatic coup gives Maisie a vivid

[15]Bewley, p. 101.

sense of a cold-blooded, intriguing nature: she lost "herself in the meanings that, dimly as yet and disconnectedly, but with a vividness that fed apprehension, she could begin to read into her stepmother's independent move" (p. 300). It is precisely the maneuver which subverts Mrs. Wix's opposition that begins to enlighten Maisie and to prepare her to reject her stepmother.

Sir Claude's return to Boulogne after the grand entrance of Mrs. Beale affords a picture of the indecisive man awaiting the moment of decision. Unlike the energetic and even dazzling Mrs. Beale, he dreads the consequences that his sexual passions and moral shiftlessness have logically created. He torments himself with the necessity of accepting Mrs. Beale (as he had earlier accepted Maisie's mother) as a terrible fate. Obviously, he is morally and psychologically capsized in a world where even hesitant action leads to commitment. His single free and seemingly responsible deed, his escape with Maisie to Boulogne, was a noisy and scared retreat and not the "miracle" she had supposed. For all Mrs. Wix's rhetorical excesses, she accurately characterizes him as a soul lost by his slavery to passion. Even with his doom upon him, he continues to dodge, protesting to Maisie that since his return to France he has not seen his mistress. It is the beginning of Maisie's disenchantment that "there settled on her, in the light of his beautiful smiling eyes, the faintest purest coldest conviction that he wasn't telling the truth" (p. 319). When desperately he asks Maisie to sacrifice Mrs. Wix, the child, with an ineluctable vision of his equivocal character, forces her life to its crisis by proposing escape from both Mrs. Beale and Mrs. Wix. Sir Claude's refusal to act enables Maisie to see the halfheartedness of his conversion and the inveteracy of his evasive, devious behavior.

Unmistakably, Maisie's proposal to Sir Claude and his reaction to it have all the ingredients of a climactic scene. Nevertheless, it must be granted that James presents the scene in a maddeningly elusive manner. In attempting to realize every emotional nuance of the charged situation, he resorts—to use favorite words of his —to audacious "jumps" and "leaps" that make less for precise accounting of motive than for dramatic tension. Emotional intensity is achieved by short questions, exclamations, and broken sentences; the insistence on Maisie's "whiteness" and "fright" and on Sir Claude's "whiteness" and "fright," and the recurrence of words like "temptation" and "weakness" give an impression of agitated rather than minutely discriminated feelings. In short, the passage is affective and connotative; it is a tense dramatization and not a clarification. In a sense it is incomplete, and needs the illumination later shed on it by Sir Claude.

I do not believe that the "obscurity" of the scene in terms of meaning (not as drama) is intended to disguise a naked appeal by Maisie to Sir Claude's sexual passion. Rather, the incident is the consummation of the novel's design in that the child rises above Sir Claude (and thus loses her hero) and above Mrs. Wix, who before her final heroics shows that she too can compromise. Maisie's fear of herself, which can be misread as a fear of her rising sexual feelings, stems from her need to create an exigency which will prove or expose Sir Claude. Such a crisis will complete her vision, for her stepfather's reaction to it will, for all time, clear the troubled moral atmosphere. In asking no less than heroism from him she becomes herself heroic. And like other innocent heroines of James, she is doomed to ask too much. No wonder James says that she experienced "something still deeper than a moral sense" (p. 354).

My reading of this difficult and crucial passage is supported by Sir Claude's answer to Mrs. Wix's accusation that he had destroyed the child's moral sense. In a spirit of revolt against the narrowness and tyranny of her views, he refuses to be "treated as a little boy" (for Mrs. Wix has a sort of moral arrogance) and finely declares:

> "I've not killed anything," he said; "on the contrary I think I've produced life. I don't know what to call it—I haven't even known how decently to deal with it, to approach it; but whatever it is, it's the most beautiful thing I've ever met—it's exquisite, it's sacred" (p. 354).

I maintain that Sir Claude cannot be referring to an intended seduction. No amount of ingenuity concerning James's "obliquity" or "ambiguity" can evade the apparent significance of this speech.

The sum of Maisie's knowledge is not like the answer to a problem in addition, for in the Jamesean sense she knows "everything." But to be less oracular, Maisie reaches maturity when, by requiring her idol to satisfy her most strenuous spiritual demands, she refuses to accept life as a compromise. She has learned that Sir Claude's self-deceptive hopes to "square" people—to work out

with them convenient arrangements involving no moral decision
—never actualize. Before taking her stand at the end of the novel,
she had been abandoned by a father whose mistress "falsified
everything" and by a mother whose promiscuity may end in "ruin
and darkness and death." When on the high ground of principle
she provokes the situation which betrays Sir Claude's temporizing
nature, Maisie surrenders her last childish fantasy. That her expanding consciousness has brought her a ripeness, a kind of perfection, is shown by Sir Claude's final panegyric:

> [Sir Claude speaks] with a relish as intense now as if some lovely work
> of art or of nature had suddenly been set down among them. He was
> rapidly recovering himself on this basis of fine appreciation. "She
> made her condition—with such a sense of what it should be! She made
> the only right one" (p. 356).

Ironically, the deflated hero, the man who prefers to be lost with
Mrs. Beale rather than "saved" with Mrs. Wix and Maisie, is the
most sensitive appreciator of his stepdaughter. (Mrs. Wix only
dimly perceives what she has gained.) Yet, though he can fully
evaluate his loss, the logic of events has stripped him of all illusions
about his own character. Even when he pronounces Maisie to be
free and laughingly proclaims her too good for himself and Mrs.
Beale, he accepts his own inescapable indecision as the queer law
of his life. In the end, I am sure, this constantly frightened playboy
is more afraid of Maisie's simple but intense heroism (as Vanderbank is of Nanda's in *The Awkward Age*) than he is of Mrs. Beale's
sexual power. When Maisie looks back from the steamer and fails
to see him on the "balcony," she must know that he knows his
doom.

THE AWKWARD AGE

1899

"The Pragmatism of
Henry James"

JOSEPH J. FIREBAUGH*

In his search for perfect integration of form and content, Henry James had to be an artist primarily; but this does not mean that he was a thinker secondarily. Indeed, James was thinking most precisely when he was acting as a creative artist. Ideas were most meaningful to him then, when he was viewing them from several points of vantage, seeking their relevance to human lives. A reading of the "Notebooks" shows how paltry—in comparison to their subsequent development—James's original ideas were. To find out what James's real thoughts were—as opposed to his partially expressed, half-formed views—we have to go not to letters or notebooks, but rather to the work of art itself. James himself has spoken of "the vanity of the *a priori* test of what an *idée-mère* may have to give."[1] His ideas grew so luxuriantly in the very process of creation, that to conclude, concerning any given work, that he accomplished only what he set out to accomplish, that he expressed only the thought which he set out to express, would be to deny the very evidence before our eyes. That evidence is the completed work of art.

Let us take, for instance, "The Awkward Age," which begins as a statement of a rather slight social problem, and ends as a brilliant novel which implies a total view of human relationships and a

*From *The Virginia Quarterly Review*, xxvii, 419-435. Copyright 1951, by *The Virginia Quarterly Review*, The University of Virginia, and reprinted with their permission and the author's.

theory of truth. How slender the problem was to begin with, and how richly it developed under James's creative hand, must be a perpetual excitement to students of the human imagination. Even more exciting, because it is usually ignored, is the theory of human life which James here implies.

"The Awkward Age" is a problem novel, and the problem originally posed does little to invalidate the somewhat harsh judgment that Herbert J. Muller passed on "writers like Henry James who have brewed genteel little tempests in exquisite teapots." Here, in part, is the first statement of the problem in a notebook entry for March 4, 1895:

> The idea of the little London girl who grows up to "sit with" the free-talking modern young mother—reaches 17, 18, etc.—comes out—and, not marrying, has to "be there"—and, though the conversation is supposed to be expurgated for her, inevitably hears, overhears, guesses, follows, takes in, becomes acquainted with, horrors. A real little subject, this, I think—a real little situation for a short tale—if circumstance and setting is really given it.

The entire statement hardly runs to 350 words, and the "real little subject" gives only a few hints of its later subtleties. At this point, the idea gives no appearance of being more important than a fashionable mother's drawing-room distress that her daughter has "come out" all too soon.

Now such a trivial problem arouses no strong feeling in modern society, whatever it may have done in James's own circle. Its sheer artificiality to a world whose daughters have always been "out," more or less, and doing their own bit to keep the conversation untidy, this unreality, by modern standards, can hardly be exaggerated. Anyone seeing this as James's only concern would never read the book—would regard it as a "genteel little tempest"; or he would read it for its technical brilliance alone. Doubtless few enough persons do read the book today, but publishers recently thought enough of its salability to bring out a new edition. If any of the new audience, which this edition presumably represents, is reading the book merely as a novel of manners or as a technical *tour de force*, that reader is missing the entire point of the novel.

It seems probable that James felt real concern over the problem itself. His use of the word "horrors" suggests as much. When he made the entry in his notebook, he was writing as a member of a certain sort of social group, which might be expected to be concerned with that problem, in its most superficial aspects as well, no doubt, as in its more immediately important ones. When James began to write the novel, to cast it, to see its implications for the individual characters, then, too, he began to express, unavoidably, the ultimate philosophical problem which the "real little situation" posed. But to see how this was all accomplished, we need to turn to Mrs. Brookenham and her little circle of leisured friends. A woman in her early forties, Mrs. Edward Brookenham, a person of fashion in spite of her husband's not too adequate means, is the presiding spirit of a highly compact circle of very intelligent and cultivated friends. Their amusement is their friendship. About the relationships within the group and peripheral to it, they talk endlessly, freely, and subtly. It is good talk. James does more than give us occasional specimens: nearly the whole novel is written in dialogue which coruscates as brightly as it needs to in order to show us that, if there is such a thing as conversation, it was to be found at that "temple of analysis," Mrs. Brookenham's home in Buckingham Crescent.

The leading members of the circle are two eligible bachelors: Vanderbank, a government official of no great means but of great social charm; and Mitchett, known as "Mitchy," an extremely wealthy man whose father was in trade; Mitchy is an ugly, humorous, clever, outspoken, charming person. This is the nucleus.

Others, more or less peripheral, are the Duchess, an Englishwoman, who has lived on the continent for years, and who has now brought her niece, Aggie, aged sixteen or seventeen, back to England to seek for her a fortunate marriage. There is Lord Petherton, who, we gradually learn, is the Duchess's lover, who has almost no income of his own, and who is supported almost entirely by his friend Mitchy.

Aggie has been reared in perfect innocence. The Duchess has kept the girl carefully insulated from her own free life. She is, as a result, still, in all respects but her years, a child. Her reading is scrutinized carefully. English history, for instance, she knows only through bowdlerized children's books. Petherton himself, something of a *roué*, treats her as a mere child.

Without particularly intending it, Mrs. Brookenham has achieved a different result with her daughter Nanda. She has tried to postpone her "coming out," both because of the difficulty of editing conversations for the ears of a *jeune fille*, and because she dislikes admitting that she has a daughter as old as Nanda. But Nanda is two years older than Aggie, no one has spoken for her hand, and so she can be put off no longer. She is admitted to the drawing room.

Nanda, however, has already had advantages of social intercourse—advantages which the Duchess views as utterly unsuitable. She has formed a friendship with Tishy Grendon, an unhappily married women, whose sister, Carrie Donner, is a divorcée. Nanda is not the innocent that Aggie is. At Tishy's first, as later at her mother's, she meets other members of the circle: Mr. Cashmore, who is courting Carrie Donner; and his wife, Lady Fanny Cashmore, who is the rather stupid but beautiful sister of Lord Petherton, and who keeps the little group in suspense by not running away with any of the men who would be willing to have her.

There are only two other characters in the circle: Edward Brookenham, as the husband—often present, but, like a fire extinguisher, only occasionally useful (the image is James's)—of Mrs. Brook, as she is called; and Harold, Nanda's youthful brother, who is having no trouble becoming quite popular, despite a penchant for borrowing five-pound notes from his mother's guests. Before the novel ends, Harold is believed to be the real reason why Lady Fanny doesn't run off with one of her suitors.

Into this decidedly "fast" modern set, is introduced, as the novel begins, an elderly gentleman "of the old school," Mr. Longdon, who has not been a participant in a London season for thirty years. His connection with the Brookenhams is a sentimental one: once in love with Mrs. Brookenham's mother, Lady Julia, he retired from society shortly after she rejected him, and has lived for most of his life with a widowed sister.

At a dinner party to which Mrs. Brookenham invites him, he is "rather frightened" by the changes in society that he perceives—by the freedom, for instance, with which nicknames are employed, and at the tone of the conversation. This much he confesses to Vanderbank, whom he becomes acquainted with there—it turns out that Mr. Longdon was in love with *his* mother too, before the day of Lady Julia—and who is, of all Mrs. Brook's set, most like Mr. Longdon in having certain old-fashioned standards. His tone is as free as anyone's; but his standards about the education of young women are as rigid as those of the Duchess—or of Mr. Longdon himself.

When Mr. Longdon finally meets Nanda, who, not having "come out" as yet, of course has not been at her mother's dinner party, he is again shocked. For, despite a great deal of freedom of manner which, "exposed" as she has been, she has inevitably picked up, she has a striking physical resemblance to her grandmother, Lady Julia, with whom Mr. Longdon was long ago in love. The scene in which Nanda enters the novel is one of James's most exquisite portrayals of the modern, knowledgeable *jeune fille.* Her resemblance to Lady Julia holds Mr. Longdon's interest long enough for him to become gradually aware of Nanda's great personal worth. With the Duchess and Vanderbank he feels that as a young girl, she is terribly "exposed" to an atmosphere not at all suitable; and he agrees with the Duchess that she should be married as soon as possible, so that her position as a young married woman will justify her actual state of knowledge. He and Nanda become good friends. She is constantly shocking him by the extent of her awareness—by, for instance, her knowledge that the Duchess and Lord Petherton are by tacit agreement always asked to the same week-ends.

To get Nanda out of this sophisticated circle seems to Longdon the immediate necessity: by her marriage, if possible. He discovers that she is deeply in love with Vanderbank, who is also fond of Nanda, but who hasn't the money to marry a girl who will bring no dowry. Because he himself likes Vanderbank, he decides to offer him a substantial sum of money if he will marry Nanda; in this he is abetted by the Duchess, who suspects that Mrs. Brook wants Vanderbank for herself, and knows that Mrs. Brook wants the wealthy Mitchy for Nanda. The Duchess, however, wants Mitchy for her Aggie. The scene in which Longdon puts the matter to Vanderbank, James later regarded as one of his "positively most artful passages." Vanderbank is grateful for the offer, and asks time for consideration. Faced with a delay, Mr. Longdon at once invites Nanda for an extended stay at Beccles, his country place.

During this long stay—which lasts for five months—Mitchy and Vanderbank come for a week-end. Nanda, though she is being thought of by others as a piece in a game, has become a person in her own right, really as a consequence of her exposure. She has guessed at Mr. Longdon's offer to Vanderbank. (Vanderbank, though he had pledged secrecy to Longdon, had broken his pledge nearly at once by telling both Mrs. Brook and Mitchy. Though themselves pledged to secrecy, they may have dropped hints which the intelligent Nanda could not have ignored.) During this week-end Nanda gives Vanderbank ample opportunity to propose, and he does not do so. The admirable Mitchy, who is in love with Nanda, who does not however love him, she manages to advise to marry the perfectly sweet little Aggie. Mitchy, seeing thus that he has no chance with Nanda, and hoping that his removal from the scene may help Nanda with Vanderbank, decides to take Nanda's suggestion. Thus the scheme of the Duchess is accomplished, with the help of Longdon, the English gentleman, and Nanda, the *jeune fille* who is so little of a *jeune fille*. Mrs. Brook is defeated in the hope she had entertained that Mitchy and Nanda would marry.

Mrs. Brook is able to take her revenge. Knowing that Longdon hates her, and realizing his desire to keep Nanda away from her house; desiring, moreover, Vanderbank for herself, and feeling, no doubt, jealousy of her charming daughter—though much of this is left to inference—she demands that Nanda return to Buckingham Crescent. This she does in the climactic scene: certainly the most brilliant scene in the novel, of which James later justifiably boasted:

> Were I minded to use in this connexion a "loud" word . . . I should speak of the composition of [these chapters], with all the pieces of the game on the table together and each unconfusedly and contributively placed, as triumphantly scientific.[2]

All the important characters are assembled in Tishy Grendon's drawing room, after a dinner party she has given for the recently married Mitchy and Aggie.

Something, however, has happened to Aggie, and it is demonstrated at this party. She has "come out" farther than the Duchess could possibly have wished. Before, an entirely innocent girl, she is now conducting an outrageous flirtation with Lord Petherton, her husband's best friend and her aunt's lover. On this occasion, the flirtation takes the form of a struggle over a French novel, Vanderbank's property, which he has loaned to Mrs. Brook, and which Nanda has chanced earlier to bring to Tishy's. Using this episode, Mrs. Brook asks Nanda directly if she has read the "hideous" book. She admits it, saying, however, that "One hardly knows now, I think, what is and what isn't."

Vanderbank thus knows how much Nanda knows. Mrs. Brook understands him well enough to know that he will now never propose. She has saved him for herself, she supposes, by withdrawing Nanda from Mr. Longdon's and by revealing to Vanderbank the extent of Nanda's awareness. But the consequence of her act is that Vanderbank now nearly stops calling. With Mitchy on the continent traveling with Aggie, the tightly knit group, which has been her life, has ended.

The novel ends with three great scenes: Nanda pleading with Vanderbank not so completely to desert her mother; promising Mitchy to try to help rescue his vagrant wife Aggie; and pleading with Longdon to forgive Vanderbank's failure ever to give him a final answer to his generous proposal. She agrees to come and live permanently with the elderly Mr. Longdon, whom she promises never to desert, and whose heiress she will be. Thus, a confirmed old maid of twenty, she retires to the country with her elderly friend.

II

Such a summary cannot begin to indicate all the complexities, either of relationship or motivation, which exist in the novel; nor all of the inferences which might be made by "the acute observer we are constantly taking for granted." The fable clearly poses to such an observer an ethical problem which it then regards in several lights. Despite all its ambiguity, it appears to me to offer James's answer to the problem. How this is done, exactly, remains to be demonstrated.

In its simplest terms the problem is the one represented by the fable of the fall of the good man—the conflict of knowledge *vs.* innocence, good *vs.* evil, or, to use more civilized terminology, realities *vs.* conventions. James was aware as he was writing his novel of the breadth of these problems, but in writing *about* his novel, he avoids stating that breadth. He comes closest to exact statement in his "Preface," in which he writes:

Putting vividly before one the perfect system on which the awkward age is handled in most other European societies, it threw into relief the inveterate English trick of the so morally well-meant and so intelligently helpless compromise. . . . Nanda's retarded, but eventually none the less real, incorporation means virtually Nanda's exposure. It means this, that is, *and many things besides* [my italics]—means them for Nanda herself and, with a various intensity, for the other participants in the action; but what it particularly means, surely, is the failure of successful arrangement and the very moral, sharply pointed, of the fruits of compromise. It is compromise that has suffered her to be in question at all, and that has condemned the freedom of the circle to be self-conscious, compunctious, on the whole much more timid than brave.[3]

Even here he is ambiguous, no doubt deliberately so. For, in the novel, while it is clear that Mrs. Brook and others are attempting a compromise about Nanda, it is equally clear that on a profounder level, society is attempting a compromise in its treatment of the young. Its difficulty with this convention is symptomatic of a deeply underlying conflict and of an actual hypocrisy.

The Duchess, for instance, in her absolute determination to keep awareness from Aggie until she is safely married, is compromising between what human life really is, generally, what her life is specifically, and what life can be made, by social convention, to appear to be. Aggie stands for innocence preserved by convention. Nanda, her antithesis, for knowledge, for reality. Mr. Longdon's thoughts beautifully sum up their respective positions and their symbolic attributes:

> Both the girls struck him as lambs with the great shambles of life in their future, but while one, with its neck in a pink ribbon, had no consciousness but that of being fed from the hand with the small sweet biscuit of unobjectionable knowledge, the other struggled with instincts and forebodings, with the suspicion of its doom and the far-borne scent, in the flowery fields, of blood.

Nanda sees Aggie as perfect. She tells Mitchy: "Now the beauty of Aggie is that she knows nothing—but absolutely, utterly: not the least little tittle of anything. . . . Ah, say what you will it *is* the way we ought to be."

Nanda longs, that is, for an innocence which she knows perfectly well she can never attain because she has never fully had it; it is the longing of all men, weary of the burden of awareness, for some prelapsarian state of innocence. She has previously told Vanderbank, "Girls understand now. It has got to be faced. . . ."

And after this brief lapse in facing it, she tells Mitchy: "You're so good that nothing shocks you. . . . There's a kind of delicacy you haven't got . . . not *the* kind." And by *the* kind she means the kind that Vanderbank has, that the Duchess has, that Longdon most sincerely possesses—a delicacy of social convention, true enough in Longdon to his real self, less true in Vanderbank, not at all true in the Duchess. Nanda, because of her "exposure," does not have *the* kind either. Like Mitchy, she is so good that nothing shocks her. When her mother calls the French novel which is in dispute at Tishy Grendon's "too hideous," Nanda, who has read it, "seemed to wonder. 'Is it?' she murmured."

One of James's deepest ironies is that Nanda, who is so "in question" because of her "exposure" is so much better than Aggie, who is not "in question" at all. This is because Nanda has had the opportunity to develop much more fully as a person. She is so fully an individual that she is quite able to take events into her own hands and to face facts as they are. Once she tells Mr. Longdon:

> "One's just what one *is*—isn't one? I don't mean so much," she went on, "in one's character or temper—for they have, haven't they? to be what's called 'properly controlled'—as in one's mind and what one sees and feels and the sort of thing one notices. . . . Granny wasn't the kind of girl she *couldn't* be—and so neither am I."

In "coming out" so completely after her marriage, so completely as to shock even this sophisticated set, who might have realized what they were preparing her for, Aggie has to be explained to the bewildered, unhappy Mitchy by Nanda, who understands her better than anyone:

> "Aggie's only trying to find out—"
>
> "Yes—what?" he asked, waiting.
>
> "Why, what sort of a person she is. How can she ever have known? It was carefully, elaborately, hidden from her—kept so obscure that she could make out nothing. She isn't now like *me.*"
>
> He wonderingly attended. "Like you?"
>
> "Why, I get the benefit of the fact that there was never a time when I didn't know *something* or other and that I became more and more aware, as I grew older, of a hundred little chinks of daylight."

This is her advantage—that in her gradually increasing awareness, she has become an individual. Whatever her mother's mixed motives in not keeping her as successfully isolated as the Duchess has kept Aggie, the result for Nanda has been that she has grown up. Aggie is still a child, using the new freedom of marriage for experimentation. Nanda has an integrity which Aggie has not attained, a certain wholeness of personality. The ironical truth is that the sophisticated but conventional Duchess has reared a moral monster, by the completeness of her compromise; the equally sophisticated but less conventional Mrs. Brookenham, by a compromise that is less complete, has permitted Nanda to become an actual person.

The disadvantage for Nanda, and thus the ultimate irony of her situation, rests in the compromise of Vanderbank. His fault is that he on the one hand accepts the freedom of conversation in Mrs. Brook's circle, and enjoys his relationships there as the peak of mature, civilized social behavior; but his attitude towards the rearing of young girls is that of the Duchess exactly: they should not be exposed. His compromise is really that implied in the "double standard"; and it is fundamentally hypocritical. Through being honestly herself Nanda loses him; but one feels that, even granting the depth of her passion for Vanderbank, his is the real loss. For he hasn't, despite his intelligence, the frame of mind, morally, which would enable him to appreciate Nanda's great integrity. Nanda knows both how much she has lost—a man of charm and intelligence and poise—and how little—a man of *"the* kind" of delicacy—a delicacy more sensitive to appearance than to fact.

It is the Duchess who states the case most succinctly, in the scene in which she is persuading Mr. Longdon of the necessity of arranging an immediate marriage for Nanda:

> "If Nanda doesn't get a husband early in the business—"
> "Well?" said Mr. Longdon, as she appeared to pause with the weight of her idea.
> "Why, she won't get one late—she won't get one at all. One, I mean, of the kind she'll take. She'll have been in it too long for *their* taste."
> . . . "Been in what?"
> . . . "Why, in the *mal' aria* they themselves have made for her."

There it is: the hypocrisy, the social compromise, the basic dishonesty of wanting one sort of life for oneself, and another for one's mate. The Duchess, Vanderbank, and Mrs. Brook, thought that they had solved their problem, but they hadn't, as events proved. Nanda had; but her gain as an individual seeking honesty was her loss as a human being seeking love. This is the tragedy of the novel.

Mr. Longdon, too, solves the problem, and despite the shock to his standards which Nanda at first represented, comes to realize through her a new integration. A courtly old gentleman, perhaps the most sympathetically presented character in the book, Longdon's social intercourse has all been with a much more proper earlier generation—the generation of the forties and fifties. He is not represented as brilliant. Most of Mrs. Brook's circle are cleverer than he. When he makes a successful joke, it seems by accident. To Nanda, he admits: "Yes—I'm rather slow; but I generally end by finding out. And I've got, thank Heaven, . . . quite prejudices enough."

After their first meeting, Nanda concludes that Mr. Longdon does not really like her; and he never denies that at that time her guess was correct: there has been, after all, so much difference between her manner and that of Mr. Longdon's lost love whom Nanda so strongly resembles. But, as he becomes acquainted with her, he comes to like her. Nanda sums it up: "Liking me has been for him a painful, gradual process. I think he does now. . . . He accepts me at last as different—he's trying with me on that basis. He has ended by understanding that when he talks to me of Granny I can't even imagine her." And she continues: "I shall never change—I shall always be just the same. The same old-mannered, modern, slangy hack. . . . What I am I must remain. I haven't what's called a principle of growth . . . I'm about as good as I can be—and about as bad. If Mr. Longdon can't make me different, nobody can."

If Nanda does not have "what's called a principle of growth," Mr. Longdon, though so many years her elder, does. "It had always wound up, indeed, their talk, with some assumption of the growth of his actual understanding." Nanda could tell her mother: "I'm little by little changing him—gradually showing him that, as I couldn't possibly have been different, and as also, of course, one can't keep giving up; the only way is for him not to mind and to take me just as I am. That, don't you see? is what he would never have expected to do."

When the end of the action is reached, that is exactly what Mr. Longdon is prepared to do. Nanda has broken down in tears at the realization of her final loss of Vanderbank. (As this scene shows, the charge that James did not know how to deal with human passion is simply false. He can portray it, and he understands it: Mitchy has said, earlier, to Mr. Longdon: "Any passion so great, so complete . . . is—satisfied or unsatisfied—a life.") In the quiet that follows Nanda's tears, she and Mr. Longdon make plans for her final removal to Beccles, and she explains to him:

> "Your taking me as I am. It *is*, you know, for a girl—extraordinary."
> "Oh, I know what it is!" he exclaimed with an odd weariness in his tenderness.
> But she continued, with the shadow of her scruple, to explain. "We're many of us, we're most of us—as you long ago saw and showed you felt—extraordinary now. We can't help it. It isn't really our fault. There's so much else that's extraordinary that if we're in it all so much *we* must naturally be." It was all obviously clearer to her than it had ever been, and her sense of it found renewed expression; so that she might have been, as she wound up, a very much older person than her friend. "Everything's different from what it used to be."
> "Yes, everything," he returned with an air of final indoctrination. "That's what he [Vanderbank] ought to have recognized."
> "As *you* have?" Nanda was once more—and completely now— enthroned in high justice. "Oh, he's more old-fashioned than you."
> "Much more," said Mr. Longdon with a queer face.
> "He tried," the girl went on, "he did his best. But he couldn't. And he's so right—for himself."

"For himself"—that is one of the key phrases of the book. All of the characters, both sympathetic and unsympathetic, are trying to be true to themselves—or to find out what they, themselves, are. Even the unsympathetically drawn Mrs. Brookenham has her view of sincerity. But to be right for oneself is not enough: Longdon, who may stand for James himself, grows when he learns to accept what is right for others.

As a character, Mrs. Brookenham was to James one of his most satisfactory creations. But she is distinctly the evil principle of the novel. The most attractive characters—Mitchy, Nanda, and Mr. Longdon—in ascending order—are those whose delicacy, finally, is not a delicacy of mere conventionalism. Mitchy and Nanda have none of it. Mr. Longdon, through Nanda, develops in toler- ance—tolerance not of Mrs. Brook's sort, which is basically con- ventional—but a tolerance of other human beings, and of their struggles with evil. Indignant as Longdon is that Vanderbank should plead for his good graces through Nanda, it is just suggested that the plea will ultimately be granted.

"The Awkward Age" is really a study of what happens when people treat others as means rather than as ends. The Duchess and Mrs. Brook, the evil beings of the novel, scheme constantly, and with some success. Even the good Nanda does it, with Mitchy, and Longdon, with Vanderbank. None of their schemes meets with real success. The only success is that of Nanda, who has been true to herself, and of Longdon, who has grown in realization of the value of other selves. Ironically, the most successful—the Duchess, who gets Mitchy and his fortune for Aggie, and Mrs. Brook, who succeeds in preventing the marriage of Vanderbank and Nanda—have been actually the least successful. The marriage is unhappy, and Mrs. Brook's circle is broken. The defeated— Nanda and Longdon—have successfully maintained their integrity, have even reintegrated themselves under the blows and strains of human events.

Pragmatism, in attempting to discover the value of an idea by examining its effects in human life, is a method almost designed for the reader of fiction, whatever his acknowledged beliefs. And Henry James virtually acknowledged pragmatism. When his brother's book of that title appeared in 1907, James wrote him with more than brotherly enthusiasm: "I was lost in the wonder of the extent to which all my life I have (like M. Jourdain) unconsciously pragmatised. You are immensely and universally right." Two years later, after "The Meaning of Truth" had appeared, he wrote with similar conviction, in a letter to his brother:

> You surely make philosophy more interesting and living than anyone has *ever* made it before, and by a real creative and undemolishable making; whereby all you write plays into *my* poor "creative" consciousness and artistic vision and pretension with the most extraordinary suggestiveness and force of application and inspiration. Thank the powers—that is thank *yours!*—for a relevant and assimilable and *referable* philosophy, which is related to the rest of one's intellectual life otherwise and more conveniently than a fowl is related to a fish. In short, dearest William, the effect of these collected papers of your present volume—which I read all individually before—seems to me exquisitely and adorably cumulative and, so to speak, consecrating; so that I, for my part, feel Pragmatic invulnerability constituted.

Such letters serve only to verify what "The Awkward Age" itself quite clearly implies and asserts to the attentive reader.

The critical emphasis upon James as a craftsman, which seems to have started as early as the first competent reviews of the novel, and which was indeed inevitable in view of the fact that James was writing this book dramatistically, almost entirely in dialogue, and providing only stage directions for the ten long "occasions" or acts of his novel; an emphasis which James himself continued in his own critical discussion of the book in the "Preface" prepared for the New York edition of his works; and which was continued by such critics as Lubbock, who, though treating the novel respectfully, saw it as a technical *tour de force*, and F. O. Matthiessen, who spoke rather unfairly of its "strained virtuosity": this critical emphasis on technique has ignored the idea which was so integral to it. This idea is quite different from the view that would make of James an excessively fastidious old man, perturbed over the decay of manners. That he was as perturbed as Mr. Longdon is no doubt true. Like Mr. Longdon, however, he saw that the truth for one age is not the truth for another, and that, in the process of accepting a new truth, the individual need not sacrifice his integrity. Henry James expressed fictionally in "The Awkward Age" what his brother William James was expressing in the pragmatic philosophy: the discovery of truth in the market place of human life: truth as process rather than truth as absolute: truth for men, not Truth for Man. To misunderstand this fact about "The Awkward Age" is simply to misunderstand Henry James.

Of course, to separate the idea from the work of art, as we have done it here, is to do a certain violence to the work. James himself felt that in this book one could "see the grave distinction between substance and form in a really wrought work of art signally break down," and he held "it impossible to say, before 'The Awkward Age,' where one of these elements ends and the other begins." Edith Wharton had found that for James "every great novel must first of all be based on a profound sense of moral values and then constructed with a classical unity and economy of means." In view, however, of the concentration in late years on this "classical unity and economy of means," upon James the technician, it seems now necessary to emphasize James the moralist—in "The Awkward Age," the pragmatic moralist. Fusion of form and content is after all a two-term relationship. In studying the art of

Henry James the second of these terms cannot, without hypocrisy, be ignored.

NOTES

1 Preface to vol. IX of the New York Edition. See *The Art of the Novel*, ed. Blackmur (New York, 1947), p. 101.

2 *Art of the Novel*, p. 117.

3 *Art of the Novel*, pp. 103, 105.

THE SACRED FOUNT

1901

"The Sacred Fount"

LEON EDEL*

Half a century has elapsed since Henry James wrote *The Sacred Fount,* and criticism, on the whole, still tends to regard it in a mood of weary bafflement. Over none of his novels have the critical waves melted so helplessly into their own shimmering foam. When the book appeared in 1901, the few reviewers who attempted to read it either masked their bewilderment in derision or candidly admitted they could not understand. Henry James had "out-Jamesed" himself; he was "intent on making nothing out of nothing"; he had written a "brilliantly stupid piece of work." And so it has been, with one or two rare exceptions, in the ensuing decades. In a work as recent as the brief sketch of the novelist by Michael Swan, *The Sacred Fount* is still "that strange and baffling book." And Mr. Swan's curious account of it reveals just how baffled he is.

Criticism of the book has run to strange extremes: from coyness to elaborate speculation. When he read it, William Dean Howells, a staunch defender of Henry James and a devoted friend, announced he had "mastered the secret" of the novel but "wouldn't for the present divulge it." That was in 1903 and the "secret" remained undivulged when Howells died seventeen years later. In 1936 Wilson Follett, in an article couched in the sensational terms of journalism rather than the more sober evaluative terms of criticism, described the book as "Henry James's Portrait of Henry James." The novelist, he wrote in the *New York Times Book*

*"An Introductory Essay," copyright 1953, by Leon Edel. From THE SACRED FOUNT, ed. Edel, Grove Press, Inc. Reprinted by permission of the author and the publisher.

Review, had been "leering" at his critics for many years, in "one of the most stupendous parodies ever concocted . . . it is Henry James deliberately turning a searchlight on Henry James." The novel, he said, was a parody, a parable, an allegory, a lampoon on his own fictional methods. It is difficult to reconcile our knowledge of Henry James with this gratuitous flight of fancy. James could turn the light (but never the searchlight!) of irony on himself on occasions, as in "Pandora," where he makes fun of "Daisy Miller." But he took the art of fiction too seriously ever to burlesque or parody his own practice of it. He believed in the novelist as an historian, and accordingly a realist, and all his fiction was addressed to the demonstration of this fundamental truth. He once chided Anthony Trollope for an aside in a novel that fiction was, after all, "making believe." Henry James's point in *The Sacred Fount* is not, as Follett argued, that "life" destroys the artist's "make-believe, " but that the "make-believe" has a reality of its own. This James often said. His short story "The Real Thing" is his best fictional statement of it.

Rebecca West wittily showed her impatience with *The Sacred Fount* when she described it as "a small, mean story" that "worries one like a rat nibbling at the wainscot." And her description of the book has often been quoted, how "a week-end visitor spends more intellectual force than Kant can have used on *The Critique of Pure Reason,* in an unsuccessful attempt to discover whether there exists between certain of his fellow-guests a relationship not more interesting among these vacuous people than it is among sparrows."[1]

But, as Miss West would be perhaps the first to recognize, *The Sacred Fount* was the work of a serious artist, and however much vacuity she might find in it, there was also a great deal of applied art. And Edmund Wilson, some fifteen years after Miss West, set himself in his essay on Henry James's "ambiguity" to unraveling the meaning of the art.[2] He saw promptly the significance of the narrator and the relationship between this work and *the Turn of the Screw.* Unfortunately he did not pursue his inquiry further. In fact he quite suddenly dropped it with a baffled: *"The Sacred Fount* is mystifying, even maddening." No greater tribute could have

---

[1] *Henry James,* London, 1916. (Ed.)
[2] "The Ambiguity of Henry James," 1934; reprinted in *The Triple Thinkers,* Oxford Unversity Press, 1948. (Ed.)

been paid to James, who had boasted he worked for "mystification." Wilson observed that "if anyone got to the bottom of it, he would throw a good deal of light on James."

A significant attempt at a critical examination of the book was made by R. P. Blackmur in the *Kenyon Review* in 1942. His essay showed a closer and more sensitive reading of the text than any critic had hitherto vouchsafed it. He recognized it as a viable work of fiction, closer to Joyce and Proust, Virginia Woolf and Franz Kafka, than to nineteenth-century fiction. And he established the important relationship between the method in the ghostly tales— the process of "mystification," of evoking a fairy-tale fascination in the reader—and the method of this novel. In his essay, criticism is no longer baffled, even if it does not attempt a full explication. It is at least performing its function of attempting to see into a work and to catch its dominant mood. Similarly in 1947, in England, Edward Sackville West gave the book the close reading it deserves.[3] He was enchanted. He found it a "supreme exercise in the spirit of poetic analysis," a "profound inquiry" into human relationships. As an artistic *tour de force*, he wrote, "the book is extraordinarily perfect."

When criticism throws up its hands in bewilderment over a work of art or waivers between such extremes, it is reasonable to inquire whether the work in question is really art. Has there been a failure in communication or a failure in perception—or both? The precise question—particularly at this moment when the work is being reprinted—is the extent to which criticism now, after fifty years, can illuminate and assess an admittedly intricate novel written by a master of the craft of fiction, who, therefore, whatever his lapses, presumably knew what he was about.

Our method will be quite simply to begin with the text, as all criticism worthy of the name must begin, to determine what a close reading may yield. This done, we shall seek further light by relating this work to other works of James and to other Jamesian modes of representation. Finally, since no work is created in a void but is the projection of a given mind at a given time (and we might add in a given place), we will seek the illumination of biography. It will be shown that any one of these approaches to *The Sacred Fount* can clarify the work and that by using all three we may arrive at the richest understanding.

[3] See *Inclinations,* London, 1949, pp. 42-71. (Ed.)

2. PALACE OF THOUGHT, HOUSE OF CARDS

The Sacred Fount is a first person narrative. The narrator, instead of telling us something about himself in the traditional manner of such self-revelatory fiction, plunges us at once into the story itself. Indeed, we must determine for ourselves, whether he is (as we suspect) a man. It is clear from the outset, therefore, that we have a very difficult problem in this book: the reader may not remain passive and receive from the narrator the whole story. He must actively deduce from the things said to him by the narrator, and from the things said to the narrator by other characters, what sort of a person the narrator himself is. This is where criticism can stumble. To read the book inattentively is to take everything on the narrator's terms.

The narrator, never named or identified, and never described physically to us, takes a train from Paddington Station to Newmarch where he is to join a house party for the week-end. He shares a compartment with two acquaintances who are also bound for Newmarch: Gilbert Long, a man the narrator has always found to be depressingly dull, and Mrs. Brissenden, who seems much younger and prettier than she had appeared before.

Thus in a few paragraphs the stage is set. We discover the narrator to be a man addicted to close and subtle observation, inordinately curious, and constantly piecing together the evidence presented to him by his eyes and ears. He is deeply puzzled by the strange transformation in Mrs. Brissenden. "How could a woman who had been plain so long become pretty so late?" How could she have acquired this second youth?

We learn from a conversation between Long and the narrator that she had married Guy Brissenden, a man many years younger than herself. "What was it they called it?—a case of child-stealing. Everyone made jokes. Briss isn't yet thirty." But Mrs. Brissenden, who is now over forty, looks twenty-five. It is Gilbert Long who makes the remark about "child-stealing"; he concludes that Mrs. Brissenden has simply ceased to grow older. The narrator is hardly satisfied. Moreover he is puzzled by something else: Long, too, is changed. He discusses this with Mrs. Brissenden at the first opportunity.

Long had always been a "heavy Adonis," banal and quite unfriendly. Now he is not only amiable but shows signs of alertness and intelligence. Mrs. Brissenden confirms to the narrator his view that Long somehow is different. She suggests that "a very clever woman has for some time past . . ." but the eager narrator, with that exasperating habit certain of James's characters have of butting in, finishes the sentence for her ". . . taken a particular interest in him?" Mrs. Briss toys with the idea that this woman has given him "steadily, more and more intellect." She thinks a certain Lady John is the source of Long's new wit, and Lady John is also due at Newmarch.

At their destination, on this August day, the narrator sees Guy Brissenden and is struck by the way he has aged. Gradually therefore the central theme of the book has been unfolded for us: Mrs. Brissenden seems to be draining Guy Briss of his youth in her process of growing younger and more beautiful. The narrator promptly translates this equation into a question: whose sacred fount is Long therefore draining to acquire his greater mental capacities? He sees this as a challenging puzzle: the solution is to look for a lady once clever, now dull. If we examine the equations, we arrive at this generalization: women exercise a two-fold influence on men; they can sometimes deprive men of their manhood, wither their very being, and grow young in the process. Or they can endow men with superior intelligence and insight. Otherwise stated, physical relations with women can be perilous to men; but the Platonic relationship of the mind can be a life-giving force to men, and depleting to women.

It is this vampire theme which preoccupies the narrator during the remaining day and a half at Newmarch. He discovers soon enough that Lady John is hardly a great fountain of wit and intelligence. She is thoroughly down-to-earth, a hat "askew on the bust of Virgil." Later the narrator speaks of her as having a "vision as closed as Obert's was open." Ford Obert, R. A., is an artist encountered at the week-end party. He sees *into* life and people since he has the "painter-sense deeply applied."

Something he says focuses the narrator's attention on another woman, May Server, as a possible source for Long's mental rejuvenation. He had painted her portrait when she was a creature of great beauty and calm. Now her beauty is fading and she is a restless flirt, flitting from man to man at the party in a pathetic effort to recover something that she has lost. We learn, too, that she is a woman depleted apparently not only of her calm and her fugitive beauty: she has lost her three children.

As the narrator becomes increasingly absorbed in his speculation, he is disturbed by the thought that he is invading other
people's privacy. Ford Obert offers reassurance. When the narrator wonders whether he should "nose about for a relation that a
lady has her reasons for keeping secret," Obert replies this is
harmless and "positively honorable" so long as the investigator
sticks to "psychologic evidence." He observes that "resting on
psychologic signs alone, it's a high application of the intelligence.
What's ignoble, " he adds, "is the detective and the keyhole."

The narrator indeed pursues his researches as a "high application of the intelligence." He studies the persons present at Newmarch; he wanders through the rooms and in the grounds; his
observation is merciless; he watches for signs, listens for stray
remarks; he is a detective of the intelligence, terribly proud of his
ratiocinative capacity and his insights. Yet doubts begin to arise.
Isn't he the victim of a "ridiculous obsession?" He admits to agita-
tion and anxiety. Early in the book he refers to "the common fault
of minds for which the vision of life is an obsession" to seek "a law
that would fit certain given facts." He warns himself against the
grouping of such facts "into a larger mystery . . . than the facts as
observed, yet warranted."

Later "the curiosity to which I had so freely surrendered myself
began to strike me as wanting in taste." Nevertheless there remained Obert's reminder about the detective and the keyhole; and
so while the narrator has occasional qualms—"the amusing question was stamped for me as none of my business"—he continues
his fascinating cerebration. He reads what he can in the relationships—and into them, perhaps—until he is brought up short: "I
remember feeling seriously warned," he says to himself during
dinner on the second evening, "not to yield further to my idle
habit of reading into mere human things an interest so much
deeper than mere human things were in general prepared to supply." And as he watches May Server's pathetic struggle—or what
seems to him to be such—he says: "It would have been almost as
embarrassing to have had to tell them how little experience I had
had in fact as to have had to tell them how much I had had in
fancy. . . ."

He is extraordinarily vain over his powers of observation and
insight. "*I* alone was magnificently and absurdly aware—everyone

else was benightedly out of it. . . ." Lady John bluntly warns him against this belief in his omniscience. "Give up . . . the attempt to be providence. . . . A real providence *knows;* whereas you . . . have to find out." Her warning falls on deaf ears. *"I,* in my supernatural acuteness, " he again remarks at another point of his self-laudation, and goes on to speak of "my plunges of insight" and the "joy of the intellectual mastery of things unamenable, that joy of determining, almost of creating results!"

Almost creating results! Then he does think himself a providence! For he goes on to boast of "my relish of the way I was keeping things together" and "my accumulations of lucidity" which are "such as to defy all leakage." He describes himself—as the end of his Newmarch week-end approaches—as having created a veritable "palace of thought." And there is a sense of exaltation at twilight of the second day that the novelist works up into one of his soaring moods that evoke the "spirit of the place." What follows is the anti-climax: the palace of thought seems to become, by a few swift strokes, a collapsing house of cards.

Mrs. Brissenden, apparently stirred up by the narrator's continuing "researches," asks to see him late in the evening. They have a long talk—a big final scene. The narrator unrolls his speculations, with great subtlety, stating some of them as hard fact, only to find that Mrs. Brissenden is no longer helpful. Was Gilbert Long really more intelligent and witty than he had been? "There's really nothing in him at all," says Mrs. Brissenden. Was there anything going on between Mrs. Server and Long? Between Long and Lady John? "Of course you could always imagine—which is precisely what is the matter with you," Mrs. Brissenden observes at one point as she deflates the narrator's theories. Long was, apparently, having an affair with Lady John, not with May Server, and May in turn had been making up to Guy. As for the vampire situation between Mr. and Mrs. Briss, the narrator is too much of a gentleman to allude to that.

"You see too much," she says at one point. At others she tells him: "You talk too much." Again: "You're abused by a fine fancy." And still again: "You build up houses of cards." And: "You overestimate the penetration of others."

And finally, point-blank: "I think you're crazy."

The narrator must protect himself. He decides Mrs. Brissenden is "suffering and stammering and lying"—trying to cover up her own strange conduct, perhaps not only her "eating poor Briss" but possible infidelities, perhaps her own interest in Long. "I was there to save my priceless pearl of an inquiry and to harden, to that end, my heart." Mrs. Brissenden has shaken and continues to shake him. She tells him "people have such a notion of what you embroider on things that they're rather afraid to commit themselves or to lead you on." In other words, the very testimony he has accumulated becomes questionable.

"You're costing me a perfect palace of thought," he mourns. There's nothing he can do. She opposes to his speculations what seems like blunt reality at every turn, and yet reality seems impossible to him beside the beauty of the imagined and the imaginative, which, to him, are just as real.

"I *should* certainly never again, on the spot, quite hang together, even though it wasn't really that I hadn't three times her method. What I too fatally lacked was her tone." With these words James ends his novel. Nothing has been solved; nothing is settled. We have had an hypothesis, a series of assumptions and speculations. There have been precious few facts to go on. The reader can only take the narrator at his word; and *his* word has been based largely upon appearance. As for the reality——!

3. MASK OF DEATH, MASK OF LIFE

That indeed is what this book is about: appearance and reality. It is written over the face of it, visible to every reader providing he can remind himself at each stage that the story belongs exclusively to the ingenious narrator. When the unnamed and undescribed narrator tells us that he alone "was magnificently and absurdly aware," we must remember that this is what *he* thinks. He may indeed be; and again he may be as "crazy" as Mrs. Brissenden suggests he is. When he speaks of "my accumulations of lucidity" we must by the same token remember that someone else may not find these accumulations lucid at all. In this light, Mrs. Brissenden's charge "you build up houses of cards" has as much value as the narrator's remark about "my plunges of insight." We are asked by Henry James to determine the credibility of the witness, but we are not given enough evidence to arrive at an answer. It was this, we suspect, that Edmund Wilson found "maddening." What we do have is more than ample evidence of the narrator's hungry, subtle imagination, his curiosity, his feeling for people, his sense of place and mood, his fine artistic being, his artistic vanity. We are ready to believe that such a mind enjoys "the intellectual mastery" of which it boasts. We also can believe that it experiences that "joy of determining, almost of creating results."

The results are created for us. Yet what we end up with is a fantasy, a series of hypotheses, an atmosphere, a tone, a surfeit of analysis. Mrs. Server's three lost children are among the few concrete facts vouchsafed us along with the description of the beauties of Newmarch. One important scene, however, does permit us to search a little further.

It occurs in the fourth chapter, on the morning of the second day. The narrator asks Mrs. Server to come with him to examine certain pictures in one of the rooms at Newmarch. When they arrive in the great saloon they find that Ford Obert and Gilbert Long are already there. The narrator looks at Mrs. Server closely. She strikes him as "all pale pinks and blues and pearly whites and candid eyes—an old dead pastel under glass." Since they are looking at pastels, this seems to be an attempt to identify her with the inanimate works of art on the walls. Gilbert Long, hitherto dumb, but now in possession of the wit he has—in the narrator's view—derived from another's fount, is expatiating on the pictures and seems, in Obert's view, to be an "unexpected demon of a critic." This noted, we find on glancing again at the text that Obert never says so. The narrator has planted that idea with us. It was what Obert's eyes "most seemed to throw over to me." It is the narrator who is reading the evidence. Once again we must take it on his say-so. Obert's eyes alone have spoken, and we have no guarantee that they might not have been saying something else. And Obert never confirms the interpretation. Indeed he is unaware of it.

Contemplating the picture under discussion, Mrs. Server wonders "what in the world does it mean?" We wonder as well. It is that of a young man in black, the dress of another era, with a "pale, lean, livid face" and a stare "from eyes without eyebrows, like that of some whitened old-world[4] clown." In his hand he holds an object that "strikes the spectator at first simply as some obscure,

[4]This is one of Henry James's rare lapses and a revelation of his sense of his new-world identity. He is writing a novel set in the old world, and is probably thinking of the clowns seen as a boy in the Cirque d'Hiver and the Cirque d'Été; but he speaks as if from a distance, as if he were in the New World and were recalling something from the Old World.

some ambiguous work of art." On a second glance this is seen by the narrator to be a "representation of a human face, modelled and colored, in wax, in enamelled metal, in some substance not human. The object thus appears a complete mask, such as might have been fantastically fitted and worn."

Mrs. Server suggests the picture might be called "The Mask of Death." "Why so?" the narrator queries. "Isn't it much rather the Mask of Life? It's the man's own face that's Death. The other one, blooming and beautiful——"

"Ah, but with an awful grimace!" Mrs. Server rejoins.

The narrator ignores the interruption and continues blandly: "The other one, blooming and beautiful, is Life, and he's going to put it on; unless indeed he has just taken it off."

"He's dreadful, he's awful—that's what I mean," says Mrs. Server.

The narrator pursues the matter, insisting the artificial face is "extremely studied and, when you carefully look at it, charmingly pretty. I don't see the grimace."

"I don't see anything else!" Mrs. Server replies.

When Obert is asked about the picture he says nothing; he escapes by paying Mrs. Server a compliment instead. There is no return anywhere else in the book to the pastel and we are left to make what we can of this episode. It cannot be regarded as a scene accidentally thrown in by Henry James. It is clearly not a momentary conceit that welled up in his fancy. By the time he wrote this book Henry James had been a master of his craft for a quarter of a century; he had reached that state of mastery in which every incident, every name, every scene was calculated not to "pad" the story but to advance its movement or light up character or situation.

Yet the introduction of the pastel of a man with a mask does seem a piece of such obvious and hackneyed symbolism as to be almost unworthy of the subtle mind of the novelist. We say this and promptly catch ourselves up: for is this not still another instance in which the description is furnished by the narrator? It is *he* who tells us what's in the picture and who promptly draws our attention to the fact that the face is Death and that it is the mask that is really alive. This is not challenged by Mrs. Server, and we must take it as given: indeed we have no alternative. There ensues, however, a sharp difference between Mrs. Server and the narrator about the aspect of the mask. *Blooming, beautiful, charmingly pretty*—this is his description to which we must oppose Mrs. Server's, *dreadful, awful* and *awful grimace.* And the entire episode is all the more striking for the fact that but two pages earlier Mrs. Server herself has been seen by the narrator not as a person alive but as one "all Greuze tints . . . an old dead pastel under glass."

What has been underlined here for us if not the very theme of the book? We are again confronted with appearance and reality: and the difference of opinion over which aspect is Life and which Death, which Beauty and which a mere grimace, is a measure of how a palace of thought can also be a house of cards.

4. RAGE OF WONDERMENT

What world are we in when we have wandered into that strange week-end at Newmarch and found ourselves at the mercy of the narrator, limited to his vision of everything, limited to his view of his own creative sense and of his own "magnificence"? He resembles very much the governess of *The Turn of the Screw* who face to face with her ghosts insists in telling us: "I was wonderful." There is a passage in *The Sacred Fount* which is filled with extraordinary echoes of the ghostly tale. The governess in *The Turn of the Screw* describes how, walking at Bly at the end of a June day, in the long English twilight, she is haunted by the thought that she will meet, at some turn of the path, the handsome man whom she saw but twice in Harley Street, and who is her employer. "What arrested me on the spot—and with a shock much greater than any vision had allowed for—was the sense that my imagination had, in a flash, turned real. He did stand there!—but high up, beyond the lawn and at the very top of the tower. . . ." Then she becomes aware of her mistake. So in *The Sacred Fount,* in the twilight of the August day at Newmarch, the narrator goes for a walk. He has no such adventure as the governess. He meets no ghosts, he sees only the twilight, the trees, the rooks, but he encounters May Server . . .

> I scarce know what odd consciousness I had of roaming at close of day in the grounds of some castle of enchantment. I had positively encountered nothing to compare with this since the days of fairy-tales and of the childish imagination of the impossible. *Then* I used to circle round enchanted castles, for then I moved in a world in which the strange

"came true." It was the coming true that was the proof of the enchantment, which, moreover, was naturally never so great as when such
coming was, to such a degree and by the most romantic stroke of all,
the fruit of one's own wizardry. I was positively—so had the wheel
revolved—proud of my work. . . . Yet I recall how I even then knew
on the spot that there was something supreme I should have failed to
bring unless I had happened suddenly to become aware of the very
presence of the haunting principle, as it were, of my thought. This was
the light in which Mrs. Server, walking alone now, apparently, in the
grey wood and pausing at sight of me, showed herself in her clear dress
at the end of a vista. It was exactly as if she had been there by the
operation of my intelligence, or even by that—in a still happier way
—of my feeling.

Decidedly at dusk, in the works of Henry James, one could dream,
and the dreams seemed to come true. "We were in a beautiful old
picture, we were in a beautiful old tale. . . ." The question was:
where did the dream end and the reality begin? *The Sacred Fount*
and *The Turn of the Screw* were not isolated works which posed
this problem. They were two works in a chain of fiction that began
in 1897 and extended past the turn of the century, each concerned
with fathoming a surrounding world or reducing a series of "facts,"
a certain amount of data, to a reasonable order. The works follow
in an extraordinarily logical progression, and seem to move
through the stages from childhood to maturity. *What Maisie Knew*
of 1897 is concerned with a "light vessel of consciousness," and the
question of what exactly Maisie did know carries over to what did
the governess know in *The Turn of the Screw* (1898). The governess
also is trying to piece together a mystifying situation. What did the
little telegraph girl *In the Cage* (1898) piece together from her angle
of vision and out of the evidence presented to her by the laconic
texts of other people's telegrams? And what did Nanda, emerging
from late adolescence, know and discover in *The Awkward Age*
(1899)? And finally, what did the narrator really fathom in *The
Sacred Fount?* James himself pointed to the similarities between
What Maisie Knew and *In the Cage:* "The rage of wonderment
attributed in our tale to the young woman employed at Cocker's
differs little in essence from the speculative thread on which the
pearls of Maisie's experience . . . pearls of so strange an iridescence
—are mostly strung."[5] *In the Cage,* James agrees, does endow his

[5] Preface to vol. XI of New York Edition (containing *What Maisie Knew* and "In the

little heroine with a great deal of "divination." And he warns in his preface, in words akin to the narrator's in *The Sacred Fount,* of "the danger . . . of imparting to too many others, right and left, the critical impulse and the acuter vision. . . ."[6]

It is *The Turn of the Screw* which, of this entire group, invites closest comparison with *The Sacred Fount.* Newmarch and Bly are country residences; and in both places, as Edmund Wilson discerned, there are "the same passages of a strange and sad beauty, the same furtive happenings in an atmosphere of clarity and brightness, the same dubious central figure, the same almost inscrutable ambiguity." Mr. Wilson goes on to see, with great clarity, James's theory of the omniscient narrator. Both the story of the governess and that of the preoccupied observer in *The Sacred Fount* contain, he writes, "two separate stories to be kept distinct: a romance which the narrator is spinning and a reality which we are supposed to divine from what he tells us about what actually happens." This is the heart of James's method. Fully grasped, it would have obviated the long-spun controversy over the ghostly tale. But Mr. Wilson does not seem to take advantage of his insight. He goes on to say: "The truth is, I believe, that Henry James was not clear about the book in his own mind." This seems highly doubtful. An author who planned his works as carefully as Henry James and endowed his narrators with special and consistent "points of view," not only knew what he was about, but was actually constructing a puzzle, a maze, a labyrinth, with diabolical ingenuity. He is constantly on guard against making any slips likely to disturb his plan of composition. There seems to be no slips in *The Sacred Fount.* Whatever ambiguity there is, has been willed by James. (We speak of course of the conscious part of his work and not the subterranean unconscious part, which is another question entirely.) The novelist's goal is above all his "mystification." He will not unravel the mystery for us; he is stubbornly determined to leave that to his reader.

In *The Turn of the Screw* James achieved his mystification in a way which readers usually overlook. There are, so to speak, three narrators in this story. The first is the individual, perhaps James himself, who begins by telling us "The story had held us, round the Cage"); see *The Art of Fiction*, ed. Blackmur (New York, 1947), p. 156. The second word of the quotation should be "range." (Ed.)

⁶*Art of the Novel*, p. 155: "danger . . . of imputing [sic] to too many others [etc.]. . . ." (Ed.)

fire. . . ." This unidentified First Narrator goes on to mention a second personage, Douglas. Douglas now briefly takes over the narrative: he tells of a ghost story with a special "turn of the screw." It is in an old manuscript; and Douglas then describes the writer of the manuscript, the governess. He is, in a sense, a Second Narrator—but not in reality; his account, in turn, is being quoted, or summarized, by the First Narrator. Then it is Douglas who begins to read the story, and the Third and most important Narrator—the governess, takes over. The story we finally are given is hers. Douglas and the First Narrator disappear.

Readers usually forget this extremely elaborate setting provided for us by the author—a setting by which he withdraws and places between himself and his audience a series of narrators. Each narrator provides a certain set of "facts" which are not evaluated for us. The question at issue is the credibility of the principal witness. And James's attitude is one of complete *neutrality.* So neutral is he that he leaves a wide imaginative margin for the reader who, if he is not careful, will be adding material from his own mind to the story. This is what most readers of *The Turn of the Screw* have done. The same trap is set for readers of *The Sacred Fount.*

5. BLISS AND BALE

In Henry James's essay "The Art of Fiction" he observes that "the deepest quality" of a work of art will always be the "quality of mind of the person who produced it." This means, what must be obvious to us all (as it was to the novelist), that in the last resort, try as he may, the author cannot cut the umbilical cord that attaches him to the work he has created. He may be able to provide a multitude of narrators but his is the hand that performs the magic, his the mind that nourishes the minds of the narrators. He provides the tone, the voice, the elements of the story, the lucidity and the imagination. In other words, the critic can attempt to probe the "quality of mind" that informed the work, even a work as artfully vague as *The Sacred Fount.*

The idea of depletion is a common one among many men who think of sex as a depleting force. Henry James seems to have held some such view. Yet in his case there was a much deeper view of the relations between men and women, going back to the primary scene of his own childhood. In his own family, his mother appeared as a woman of strength compared with his father who expressed his feelings with much greater openness than the mother. Henry James seems to have believed all his life that it was his mother's strength which sustained the father. The father, who had lost a leg when he was a boy, struck him as a vacillating and rather ineffectual figure, as indeed he often was, in spite of his great nobility of character and his vigorous life as an intellectual. The weight of these contradictions, both paternal and maternal, weighed upon the young Henry James and played an important part in his insistence, later, on his own autonomy and sovereignty: in his fear of involvements of any kind with men and women. It was safest to stand firmly on his own feet.

There is ample evidence of this in his work. A striking statement of it is to be found in the opening pages of *The Portrait of a Lady* where he describes the Touchett parents as seen by their son Ralph: "His father, as he had often said to himself, was the more motherly; his mother, on the other hand, was paternal, and even, according to the slang of the day, gubernatorial." Henry James might have been writing of his own parents. In his recollections of his boyhood he has very little to say about his mother so that everything that he does say takes on great significance. And the sketch he gives of her is that of a woman depleted, like May Server, through devotion to her husband and children. "The only thing I might well have questioned . . ." he muses, "was the possibility on the part of a selflessness so consistently and unabatedly active, of its having anything ever left *acutely* to offer."

This was his first view of the operation of the "sacred fount" by which a process of nourishment and depletion was carried out; and he saw it all around him, in "strong" female relatives and in a grandmother who survived her husband by many years; and later, in middle life, in the spectacle of his own father who lost all will to live after the death of the mother. In Henry James's mind—and in his fiction—love was a force capable of depleting and destroying. Women could influence men, change them for good or bad, and what resulted usually was a stultifying dependency. The significant relationship was what a woman of feeling and perception could impart to a man, what a maternal, all-serving figure could do for a man's mind. It is no accident that in discussing the woman who parted with her wit in *The Sacred Fount* the narrator invokes Egeria—"We shall find the right woman—our friend's mystic

Egeria." Egeria was one of the nymphs in Rome from whom King Numa, the successor to Romulus, received instruction; he met her in a grove which had a kind of sacred fount, a spring gushing from a dark recess and from which the Vestal Virgins drew water for their rites. Ovid has told how Egeria, disconsolate when Numa died, melted into tears and became a fountain herself, attaining definitive form as a source.

In James's works men sometimes draw their mental strength from women but can also be physically destroyed by them. James's first short story, published anonymously, was that of a Balzacian heroine who plots with a boatman to destroy her lame husband. The young Henry James was sufficiently attracted to Mérimée's *La Vénus d'Ille* to have translated it. It tells how a statue of Venus comes alive, not beneficently, like Pygmalion's statue, but to crush and kill a man who had placed his engagement ring on the statue's finger. The hero of one of James's early stories, "Osborne's Revenge," sees the heroine as a woman who "drained honest men's hearts to the last drop, and bloomed white upon the monstrous diet." This story is one of his earliest experiments in appearance and reality; for while the heroine gives this impression of being a vampire, she turns out to be wholly innocent of the charge. The heroine of another early blood-and-thunder tale, "De Grey: A Romance," fights the family curse which dooms De Grey heirs to early death and only succeeds in reversing it ". . . she blindly, senselessly, remorselessly drained the life from his being. As she bloomed and prospered, he drooped and languished. While she was living for him, he was dying for her." It was a case of bliss and bale. James was twenty-five when his cousin Minny Temple died. Minny, to whom he was deeply attached, promptly was converted into a May Server figure in a letter written by Henry to his brother William: "Among the sad reflections that her death provokes for me, there is none sadder than this view of the gradual change and reversal of our relations: I slowly crawling from weakness and inaction and suffering into strength and health and hope: she sinking out of brightness and youth into decline and death. It's almost as if she had passed away—as far as I am concerned—from having served her purpose, that of standing well within the world, inviting and inviting me onward by all the bright intensity of her example. . . ."[7] This is strangely like the narrator's musing in *The Sacred*

[7] Letter of Feb. 13, 1870. Quoted in Edel, *Henry James: the Untried Years* (Philadelphia and New York, 1953), p. 326. (Ed.)

Fount as to what would happen to Mrs. Brissenden if her fount, Guy, her husband, were to die. "She would have loved his youth, and have made it her own, in death as in life, and he would have quitted the world, in truth, only the more effectually to leave it to her."

When James was thirty-four the fantasy still haunted him. In "Longstaff's Marriage," as in "De Grey," one or the other of the lovers must die; their attraction for each other means depletion or extinction. And in this story it is the woman who dies—like Minny—and the man who survives. Finally, at fifty-seven, James gave the fantasy its most elaborate statement in *The Sacred Fount*.

Henry James himself regarded *The Sacred Fount* as a trifle, a *jeu d'esprit* intended as a short story but which he found had grown to 20,000 words. When this happened to the novelist, his usual procedure was to go through with his work no matter where it would lead him, on the professional theory that having expended so much labor he must get some return for it. He always made it a rule to finish any work once it was started. Not to finish would be a waste of effort, a sign of failure in ingenuity. James accordingly tossed off another 60,000 words of this "fine flight . . . into the high fantastic" with his characteristic vigor. His professional sense was sound. He collected $3,500 in advances on royalties from the American and English publishers and, having thus cleared his desk and earned his money, he set to work on *The Ambassadors*. That novel, as a matter of fact, has in it an interesting carry-over from *The Sacred Fount*—for what is Lambert Strether doing but once more being the sensitive observer seeking to fathom a relationship, that between Madame de Vionnet and Chad? Madame de Vionnet is again a May Server, at whose sacred fount Chad has acquired poise and a measure of polish. It is she who is left depleted at the end.

In an unpublished letter to the Duchess of Sutherland the novelist spoke of his book as a "profitless labyrinth" and as "fantastic and insubstantial: I mean to serve, in future, to make up for it, nothing but boiled mutton and potatoes." In another unpublished letter, to Mrs. Humphry Ward,[8] he offered more details. Mrs.

[8] I am indebted to Miss Dorothy Ward for this letter and to Mr. Donald Brien for the letter to the Duchess of Sutherland.

Ward, as a fellow novelist, was entitled, he felt, to a fuller answer to her puzzled inquiry after reading the book. Closely read, the answer provides us with an important clue to Henry James's intention. After asserting that the book wasn't "worth discussing" and dismissing it as "the merest of *jeux d'esprit*"and "a small fantasticality" and also as "a consistent joke," he nevertheless adds: "Let me say for it, however, that it has, I assure you, and applied quite rigorously and constructively, I believe, its own little law of composition." And he adds "As I give but the phantasmagoric I have, for clearness, to make it *evidential.* . . ."

The key words for us are *own little law of composition, phantasmagoric,* and *evidential.* For *phantasmagoric* is that which is appearance, and *evidential* is that which deals with reality. And we have seen how Henry James adhered consistently to his "law of composition," that of keeping the story entirely within the eyeview and the mind of the narrator. We might translate James's sentence as follows: "As I give but the appearance of things, I have, for clearness, to make them offer such evidence as they can. . . ."

We return now to our point of departure. Is this elaborately written book an independent work of art or must it be set down as a failure, even if it stemmed from a great master of fiction? Its theme is tenuous, it is a flight into fantasy, it is slight indeed when set into the long shelf of Henry James's substantial fictions. Yet it is, taken as a technical performance, a masterpiece of the storyteller's art. Having predicated a situation, Henry James does create a vivid little drama of shadow and substance; on artistic ground there is much to commend the work. The narrative is tight, the action confined to a brief compass of time, and after the prelude, the unity of place is carefully observed. We are conscious of the lapse of the hours, of movement from bright sunlight to sunset and twilight; we stroll on lawn and terrace; and only the characters involved in the action are presented to us. We are told nothing more than is necessary to keep the story going, and the drama is built wholly out of the tensions of human relationships. Above all there is the striking compositional method that reminds one of those experimental films in which the camera eye is ours, but is also the eye of the person in the film. This process of self-revelation, exercised by an omniscient narrator, leaves us with two levels of reading: the narrative itself, and the evidence in it which we must appraise in order to evaluate the credibility of the narrator. As a "high application of the intelligence" *The Sacred Fount* is to be cherished and studied. It deserves its honored little place on the Jamesian shelf. And it deserves better of its critics.

"Henry James's Subjective Adventurer: 'The Sacred Fount' "

TONY TANNER*

'**B**UT if nothing was more impossible than the fact, nothing was more intense than the vision.' These words from *In the Cage* succinctly point to a profound problem to which James addressed himself in some of his later fiction—the problem of the relationship between vision and fact. The heroine of the story is a poor telegraphist whose position is, for James, a very suggestive one. She works at the very hub of society, reading clues, deciphering hints, thriving on suggestions, and at the same time she is for ever excluded from an active recognized part in that society. Her dreams, her theories, her ever-expanding speculations are her compensation, even her vocation: they are made possible by her curious situation of being at once intimate with and alienated from the arcana of high society. For her the opportunity to see and speculate constitutes a privilege more valuable than her own humdrum life spent with her fiancé, the lower-class Mr. Mudge. The essential difference between her and Mr. Mudge—her essential rarity—is brought out in a passage concerning their visit to Bournemouth. They both visit the band-stand, the noisy centre of the town life, but their appetites and interests differ.

> She preferred to sit at the far end, away from the band and the crowd; as to which she had frequent differences with her friend, who re-

*From ESSAYS AND STUDIES, 1963, New Series, volume xvi (ed. S. Gorley Putt), published for The English Association by John Murray. Copyright 1963, by The English Association. Reprinted by permission of the author.

minded her often that they could have only in the thick of it the sense of the money they were getting back. That had little effect on her, for she got back her money by seeing many things, the things of the past year, fall together and connect themselves, undergo the happy relegation that transforms melancholy and misery, passion and effort, into experience and knowledge.

Mr. Mudge leads a purely physical existence—he voices the claims of the creature who wishes to join the herd. The heroine prefers to remain away from it all—considering her money well spent if she can be left to her work of imaginative reconstruction, allowing the mind to find order and connection where it will, endowing the arbitrary with a sense of sequence, redeeming life from chaos, making facts serve the need of vision.

In the Cage is minor—but important. For here in miniature James has submitted the habit of speculation to a comic exaggeration and at the same time asserted its purpose and value. As a person the telegraphist must go away with Mr. Mudge to Chalk Farm—but as a principle she represents for James the function and predicament of the artist. The price she has to pay is exclusion from participation—indeed it is the very condition of her work: the profit is, however, large—the imaginative transformation of the world. The action of the story is, wrote James, 'simply the girl's "subjective" adventure': she is one of those few people for whom consciousness in itself is 'a romance', one of those rare and privileged people who are gifted with 'the critical impulse and the acuter vision'. James became increasingly interested in what he equivocally called 'the morbid imagination', 'that rash, that idle faculty [which] continues to abound in questions, and to supply answers to as many of them as possible'[1]—and his most profound examination of this faculty is *The Sacred Fount*, written in 1901 just before he embarked on his last major phase.

The theme of the book is not so esoteric as some critics have made out: it fits in with one of James's recurring preoccupations. Briefly: the narrator tells of a week-end visit to a country house called Newmarch. On the train going down he notes that a man —Gilbert Long—whom he once considered dull and stupid, now seems bright and intelligent. He also notes that a lady—Grace Brissenden—whom he knows to be old, seems in fact to be grow-

---

[1]Preface to vol. xi of the New York Edition. See *The Art of the Novel,* ed. Blackmur (New York, 1947), pp. 155, 157.

ing younger and more vivacious with the years. On later meeting her husband—Briss—he fancies him to be old and exhausted. On the strength of these impressions the narrator starts to construct a theory—a theory which is at first helped by equivocal hints from other people. The theory is based on the idea of the depletion and appropriation of human energy—particularly between the sexes. The 'sacred fount' of the life force is 'like the greedy man's description of the turkey as an "awkward" dinner dish. It may be sometimes too much for a single share, but it's not enough to go round.' Thus in any marriage one person will be a taker, the other a giver. ' "One of the pair," I said, "has to pay for the other".' A conversation with Mrs. Brissenden brings this out more clearly. She speaks first:

> 'One of them always gets more out of it than the other. One of them —you know the saying—gives the lips, the other gives the cheek.'
> 'It's the deepest of all truths. Yet the cheek profits too,' I more prudently argued.
> 'It profits most. It takes and keeps and uses all the lips give.'

It is those characters in James who 'take and keep and use' the sacred life energy of another person who are the real villains— whether one cares to think of Olive Chancellor trying to draw Verena Tarrant into her freezing orbit, or Gilbert Osmond exploiting Isabel Archer for his sterile ends, or the more minor cruelty exercised by Lady Beldonald in *The Beldonald Holbein* or the 'atrocity of art' with which Mrs. Grantham takes her revenge on the innocent Lady Gwyther in *The Two Faces*, the general fault common to all is that they batten on other people, use them, manipulate them, exploit them, make them over for their own ends, instead of reverencing their unique and independent jet of life. The narrator's theory, then, is related to a central Jamesian concern, and in the light of this theory he is sure that just as Briss seems to be 'paying' for his wife, so some lady must be paying for the unbelievably enhanced and energized Gilbert Long. His improvement is such that she must be paying a great deal—she must be almost drained of her own spirit and wit. So he sets about looking for 'the right idiot'—right, that is, for his theory. One could almost put it this way—he is trying to find warrant for writing a James novel.

Newmarch is no ordinary country house. It is 'a place of charm

so special as to create rather a bond among its guests'. It is sometimes discussed in theatrical terms—'an ample stage'—and it is
clearly more emblematic than real: 'life became a mere arrested
ramble or stimulated lounge, and we profited to the full by the
noble freedom of Newmarch, that over-arching ease which in
nothing was so marked as in the tolerance of talk. The air of the
place itself, in such conditions, left one's powers with a sense of
play; if one wanted something to play at one simply played at
being there.' It is a sort of ideal world in which people are released
from all material contingencies and provided with a setting which
most encourages and permits them to indulge their talent for
forming relationships. 'Was *any* temporary collocation, in a house
so encouraging to sociability, out of the range of nature?' It has all
the appearance of being James's version of paradise, a sort of
Platonic idea of 'society'. Certainly all the challenges which James
found in society are here in an extreme form. The atmosphere of
the house is one of 'clear dimness and rich gleams' and in this
ambiguous brilliant dusk the relationship between appearances
and reality is almost preternaturally difficult to infer and establish.
Every room leads to another room—there are 'great chains' of
rooms—and everybody seems a possible screen for somebody else
until the whole place seems to be composed of nothing but screens,
and every spoken thing seems a mask for an unspoken gesture of
sinister portent. The consensus of gracious forms at some times
seems to be an expression of mankind's finest social instincts; and
at other times it seems a prolonged massive charade of non-expres-
sive and concealing postures. At times the atmosphere of the
house is distinctly oppressive, as when the narrator walks out into
the garden and finds the air 'a sudden corrective to the grossness
of our lustres and the thickness of our medium, our general heavy
humanity'. More remarkable is the narrator's meditation in the
garden. 'We were all so fine and formal, and the ladies in particular
at once so little and so much clothed, so beflounced yet so
denuded, that the summer stars called to us in vain. We had
ignored them in our crystal cage, among our tinkling lamps; no
more free really to alight than if we had been dashing in a locked
railway-train across a lovely land.' That society might be abysmal,
that it might be a condemnation and a sentence, a suffocating and
weary imprisonment, that there might be terror as well as beauty
in 'conditions so highly organized'—these pessimistic feelings are

part of the late James's ambivalent attitude towards society. New-march is the social world, and the narrator goes back into it to continue his quest: but while, as a house, it is not so horrifying as Atreus's palace in *Agamemnon*, or the guilt-saturated mansion of *Rosmersholm*, it is a place more of darkness than light and there is a hint of something mephitic in the thick social air.

In its populated gloom the one thing necessary is some guiding light, and since society has come to ignore the stars and preferred the inadequate substitute of its 'tinkling lamps' the narrator's quest is really for some sort of better illumination—in every sense of that word. When he speaks of 'raking the gloom for lights' he reveals himself in his most suggestive stance. All his ideas and fancies are spoken of in terms of light: 'a blaze of suggestion', 'the flame of my fancy', 'sparks were what we wanted' and so on. His theory acts as 'a torch in the darkness': as he says—'I start, for my part, at any rate, quite in the dark—or in a darkness—lighted, at best, by what you have called the torch of my analogy.' In this book, as in many others by James, the importance of eyesight is stressed continu-ally. From the start the narrator 'watches with curiosity', he is always attracted by the prospect of there being 'something for me to see'. He always wants 'a glimpse'—a word to which he often recurs and which, as with the girl in the cage, seems to indicate a preferred mode of seeing. For glimpses stimulate the imagination as a revealed panorama seen in absolute clarity would not. Typi-cally he refers to the 'general, amiable consensus of blindness' around him in such a way as to dignify and sanctify his dedication to the holy task of 'the very act of seeing'. He likes to 'watch and watch' and lives in a separate 'world of observation' to such an extent that he attracts the accusation—'You see too much'. His defence is that 'one couldn't know anything without seeing all'—but in this case 'seeing', unlike the faculty exercised by early Jamesian protagonists, but like that of the girl in the cage, is a source of visions. 'Observation breeds ideas' as he puts it, and he elsewhere talks of 'the momentum already acquired by the act of observation'. His 'extraordinary interest in my fellow-creatures' stimulates his eyes, and seen glimpses promote imagined specula-tions. And speculation—this is the main point—is a source of illumination.

It is also important to note that speculation is also allied to 'creation'. 'To see all this was at the time, I remember, to be

inhumanly amused as if one had found one could create something. I had created nothing but a clue or two to the larger comprehension I still needed, yet I positively found myself overtaken by
a mild artistic glow.' More than that, at one crucial point the lady
Mrs. Server, whom he suspects to be his missing character and
with whom he is possibly infatuated, seems to appear at the dictates of his imagination. 'It was exactly as if she had been there
by the operation of my intelligence. . . .' At the time of this meeting
Newmarch has become like some 'castle of enchantment,' and the
narrator is reminded of the 'days of fairy-tales and of the childish
imagination of the impossible'. 'In those days,' he goes on 'I moved
in a world in which the strange "came true".' By extension he feels
there is now a touch of 'wizardry' in his own imaginative version
of the world. 'I had thought it all out, and to have thought it was,
wonderfully, to have brought it.' Thus when Mrs. Server finally
appears in 'the thin suffusion of twilight' there is something
vaguely hallucinatory and conjured about her presence. We feel
that this encounter might be an overspill from the 'wealth' of his
imagination into the world of fact. That the imagination might be
capable of evoking its own necessary mirages is an aspect of the
book to be remembered.

But at this point we should more clearly establish what is the
motivating force behind the narrator's strenuous activity—what
drives him to his compulsive watching, his endless envisioning?
What does he mean when he speaks of being 'on the scent
of something ultimate'? A key statement occurs early in the
book.

> I was just conscious, vaguely, of being on the track of a law, a law that
> would fit, that would strike me as governing the delicate phenomena
> —delicate though so marked—that my imagination found itself play-
> ing with. A part of the amusement they yielded came, I dare say, from
> my exaggerating them—grouping them into a larger mystery (and
> thereby a larger 'law') than the facts, as observed, yet warranted; but
> that is the common fault of minds for which the vision of life is an
> obsession.

He talks about wanting 'absolute certainty' and claims a right 'to
judge of what other people did'. He also refers to 'the sense of a
discovery to be made' and his 'sense of reality'—and we may be
sure that he means the reality that lies muffled and obliterated

under the thick pile of appearances. He wants to get at the underlying pattern, to tease out deeper meanings. He claims that 'the
more things I fitted together the larger sense, every way, they
made'—for him only those things which cohere can signify; the
random, the contingent, the unrelated cannot yield up a meaning.
It is in making things 'hook up', in finding a theory which will
embrace the glimpsed facts, that he finds 'the joy of the intellectual
mastery of things unamenable, that joy of determining, almost of
creating results'. Like the girl in the cage he represents an activity
rather than an involved character. 'I alone was magnificently and
absurdly aware—everyone else was benightedly out of it.' He is
one of the privileged and perhaps cursed few who care to be
conscious, who seek for the higher awareness, who catechize and
interrogate the surfaces of the world in an effort to find a core of
meaning.

Yet though he is after an explaining law, he is also desirous of
constructing a picture. That is to say he also wants to *add* something to the world—in particular those symmetries and harmonies
which are alien to its gratuitous configurations. 'Things in the real
had a way of not balancing; it was all an affair, this fine symmetry,
of artificial proportion.' The desire to account for things leads on
to the instinct to alter them or add to them in the interests of an
ideal of 'composition'. The narrator continually discusses his ambition in the terms of painting and he explicitly compares his
chosen task to that of the painter Obert: 'I only talk as you paint.'
He talks of 'fresh accession' enriching 'the picture' and often alludes to 'my gallery'. He views chance collocations with a painter's
eye and at moments his desire for composition supersedes his need
for elucidation. So, referring back to his avowed search for a law,
we see that he wants to establish *both* the laws which explain
actual human events, *and* the laws which govern the act of artistic
creation. The idea which relates these two sets of laws is that of
'analogy': the ideally composed artistic world can shed illuminating light on the fractured imperfect physical world. 'Our world is
brazen: the poet only delivers a golden'. Thus Sir Philip Sidney,
and without exploring the neoplatonic implications we can see
that James is continuing a long aesthetic debate, the question of
the relationship between the brazen and golden worlds, between
vision and fact.

The narrator certainly epitomizes the artistic instinct for James.

The initial line of his inquiry—is Gilbert Long having an affair which is in some way nourishing him with unexpected energy at the expense of some unknown suffering woman?—extends to the whole question of discerning or imposing a principle of order in or on the world. He talks about his theory very much as many critics have talked about a work of art; 'that special beauty of my scheme through which the whole depended so on each part and each part guaranteed the whole.' He wants and works to elicit a golden world from the brazen world—not however a world where people are better than in our world but a world in which their lives have more logic and shape. And as he talks about his golden world he continually implies that it is fragile, insubstantial, but precious. He refers to his constructed theory, his composed picture, as 'a great glittering crystal palace', 'a palace of thought', 'the kingdom of thought I had won'—though Mrs. Brissenden who most nearly understands him and most grievously threatens him refers to his speculations as 'houses of cards'. He makes his 'flight into luminous ether' and in those rarefied territories of the imagination he constructs a delicate artefact which orders and ordains the lower empiric world. But the risk is great. Having made his brilliant construction he concedes—'but there was no objective test to which I had yet exposed my theory.' Random scraps of information and alternative points of view continually threaten his 'whole airy structure'. He is often made to 'tremble for the impunity of my creation' and he comes to object to the possibility of verifying his vision. He does not wish 'to expose to the world, to defend against the world, to share with the world, that now so complex tangle of hypotheses that I have had for convenience to speak of as my theory.' He is in the position of the alienated artist, cherishing his product, and nervously guarding it against what Yeats called 'the brutality, the ill-breeding, the barbarism of truth.' (And Yeats himself constructed 'A Vision' as 'a last act of defence against the chaos of the world.') His highly organized vision becomes self-sealing and so far from explaining the life around him it becomes a consolation to be set over against that life, a preferable extension of creation. If the facts do not fit the theory—why, so much the worse for the facts. That at least is the feeling.

The relation of the narrator's art to reality is, then, a curious one. He starts his theory from a 'recognized fact'—the change in Gilbert Long—but from then on facts seem to become more of a menace and less to be desired. He says quite early to Ford Obert: 'If I had a material clue I should feel ashamed: the fact would be a deterrent.' The 'affluence' of his vision is based on 'amazingly little evidence.' In fact the less of one seems to mean more of the other. 'It would have been almost as embarrassing to have to tell them how little experience I had had in fact as to have had to tell them how much I had had in fancy.' This clearly relates him to the girl in the cage. One 'straw' picked up from the world of facts yields him a rich harvest of imagined 'possibilities.' And in the interests of his theory he sometimes reads what does not happen into the actual, and sometimes misses things which actually happen. When a recalcitrant indigestible fact seems imminent it induces intense nervousness in the narrator. 'Things *had*, from step to step, to hang together'—that is the ambition, the need: but at crucial moments they seem, worryingly enough, 'to hang a little apart.' The slightest hint can set his fantastic imagination to work —the swish of a skirt, the stoop of a back—for to him the world is seething with *suggestiveness:* but the crisis comes when he is confronted with a *fact* which not only cannot be assimilated and dissolved in the 'solution' of his theory, but which also threatens to demolish his imaginative superstructure. This is what happens at the end. His whole theory has come to depend on Mrs. Server's being the poor woman who is 'paying' for Long: but Mrs. Brissenden comes to assure him that Long is in fact having an affair with Lady John, a talkative, energetic, self-possessed woman who will not fit the requirements of his theory at all. There is something hard, ruthless and dominating about Mrs. Brissenden and she is referred to in terms of brass—and it is her brass which shatters the pure crystal of his theory. Her harsh assurance as to the *facts* leaves his vision completely dismantled—'a pile of ruins'. It is possible that she is lying, or working for her own ends; but her very presence, and what she comes to stand for, are inimical to his careful 'embroidery' work, his artistic instinct, his search for a hidden logic. For she embraces a random, unpredictable world: she disdains his imaginative efforts to describe and prescribe for the real world. 'Things are not . . . gouged out to *your* tune.' If his theory fails, his vision vanishes, and art, as it were, loses out to life.

In this book James has subjected the activities of the 'morbid imagination' to their most damaging criticisms. He allows certain key questions to be raised concerning the narrator's habit of speculation. Is this activity necessary, is it pernicious? Should he stop, can he stop? Is he neurotic, even mad? Is he so obsessed with Mrs. Server that he sees the world in a distorted manner? These are the sort of questions which James allows to be raised around the narrator. He himself sometimes feels that his curiosity is 'wanting in taste' and at certain contented moments at Newmarch he feels that there is no 'application' for 'a transcendent intelligence' and that 'we existed . . . to be really what we looked'. At other moments his 'estimate of the value of perception' undergoes a sudden reversal. He suddenly 'wished to unthink every thought with which I had been occupied for twenty-four hours'. Certainly he thinks it a bad thing to communicate his visions to other people, for that would make them 'begin to vibrate, to crack and split, from within'. If imagination and speculation are a curse, then it is one which he feels he must bear alone. More than once he proclaims his readiness to 'give up everything' and at times he envies in other people 'the state of exemption from intense obsessions' and desires to 'break off sharp' from his own. But he cannot remain detached and indifferent, he cannot make himself impervious to suggestion. His imaginative speculation seems to work autonomously, independent of his social-physical presence.

The comments of other characters add to our ambivalent assessment of the narrator. Gilbert Long says he has got Briss 'on the brain' and will not join him in his speculations. The artist Obert after following him for a while drops out—'It isn't any of one's business, is it?' Lady John accuses him of having 'the imagination of atrocity', of trying to be a 'providence' and she adds her witty warning: 'You can't be a providence and not be a bore.' Many complain of his constant questioning and his habit of trying to involve them in his meditative speculations, but it is Mrs. Brissenden who voices the most damning sequence of charges. 'You see too much'—'You talk too much'—'You're abused by a fine fancy' —'I think you're crazy.' Obviously she is his fiercest opponent, she and all she stands for, but since the narrator himself refers to his 'private madness' James clearly intends to allow the idea of the abnormality if not the insanity of art to lie like a vein through the novel. It is—we might say—the verdict of the practical world, the people who make themselves at home amongst the surface facts.

Does he inquire too curiously? 'The state of my conscience was that I knew too much—that no one had really any business to know what I knew.' But what kind of knowledge is it that disdains facts and winces at proferred information? We may call it imaginative penetration, the attempt to ensnare the essence by speculation, the registering of nuances and possibilities and suggestions which afford faint intimations of a profounder level of reality. But of course all this labour might be misdirected. It might have its origins in inward disorder, the unhealthy hypertrophy of the speculative faculty: it might spring from unacknowledged passions gone sour. It can interfere with fruitful living in the empirical world—'the lap of the actual'—and it might constitute a menace, an intrusion for less 'conscious' people. It might lead to a valuation of art over life, or an impotent solipsism. It might take a man out of the world in a number of ways. These are some of the risks for the subjective adventurer—what are the gains? Are we to dismiss the narrator as 'crazy' along with Mrs. Brissenden, or does James make him stand for a set of attitudes and activities that he valued, valued despite the attendant risks? Valued, perhaps, because those very risks make the activity heroic?

If 'art is our flounderings shown' as Colonel Voyt suggests in *The Story in It*, then the narrator's attempt to chart the tangled relations of the people around him has at least the value of drawing up a tentative map for a troubled sea. Even if the flounderings are due to the ineradicable predatory instincts of men and women— still it is better to have a pattern of pursuit and carnage than no pattern at all. Any light is at least a minor triumph against the darkness. But as the narrator comes to realize, 'the condition of light . . . was the sacrifice of feeling'. Exclusion from participation —and this relates him to other Jamesian characters, such as Strether—is 'the price of the secret success, the lonely liberty and the intellectual joy'. It is what his 'priceless pearl of an inquiry' costs—to save it he is willing to 'harden my heart'. Pearl and crystal in preference to—a live woman? We are at least allowed the hint and should take away with us some sense of the price the narrator talks about. But if his willingness to pay the price is not simply obsessional, then his sense of necessary exclusion must be due to an awareness of some higher allegiance, some more exacting responsibility. His 'providential supervision' of the social world—even if it only goes on in his head—does have a value and is a real responsibility. For in some way he is the one who strives to see among the blind, the upholder of consciousness among the unconscious.

Excluded from the frame of society, he is its artist: denied its physical embraces, he is its conscience. He is what Conrad said James himself was: 'the preserver, the keeper, the expounder of human experience.'[2] That is why his 'curiosity matters'. Not only because it is the only way he can appease his inner drives—'the satisfaction of my curiosity is the pacification of my mind'—but also because even among the wreck of his theory he can salvage his 'understanding'. And this is an important passage. 'I couldn't save Mrs. Server, and I couldn't save poor Briss; I *could*, however, guard, to the last grain of gold, my precious sense of their loss, their disintegration and their doom.' Curiosity leads to under- standing—and only understanding can develop a sense of values. The narrator is not, after all, a nosey-parker—rather he is the person whose heightened awareness and delicate sensibility in- troduce into the callous indifference of unconscious life a sense of good things spoiled and cruelties perpetrated, of fine things de- stroyed and horrors achieved. He is accused in the book of not only seeing 'horrors' but of liking them, and it is possible to see some of his curiosity as illicit, almost prurient: but his own answer is that before condemning them he likes to 'look them first well in the face'. But if 'knowing', whether through inference or in imagination, is his vocation, then a proper distribution of pity is closely involved with it. The speculation might not be for the sake of sympathy, but there is sympathy in the speculator and in the very manner of the speculation. And this idea that there might be different ways of looking at the world, different kinds of curiosity, different modes of speculation, even different kinds of knowledge, brings us to what I think is one of the most important tenets in James's work.

There is a moment early in the book when the narrator per- suades Mrs. Brissenden to share his theory about the hidden source of Long's improvement. But as he listens to *her* speculating he suddenly has a sense of the cruelty in her being so 'keen' to indict Mrs. Server. Perhaps in this he is only seeing his own fault writ large, perhaps he is emotionally involved with Mrs. Server, or perhaps he is realizing that there are at least two different kinds of 'attention' that one can pay the world. He defends observation, speculation, reflection—but he is shocked at the gleam of cruelty in Mrs. Brissenden's manner of mentally pouncing on victims and

[2] *Notes on Life and Letters* (London, 1949), p. 17.

fools. She lacks the artistic, the sympathetic motive.

To emphasize these two different ways of looking at the world, I would refer back to the relatively simple story *The Patagonia*. There is also a narrator to that story, and he tells of an ocean crossing made in the company of Mrs. Nettlepoint, her son Jasper, and a rather lonely girl called Grace Mavis who is crossing with them in order to marry her fiancé in France. The narrator is also an observer, and there is something in his character that 'makes me, in any situation, just inordinately and submissively *see* things'. In the curious atmosphere of the boat—detached from land entanglements as Newmarch is detached from the material limitations and impositions of day-to-day city existence—his speculations take on an almost creative resonance. The ship becomes a stage:

> The clean boards of the deck turn to the stage of a play that amuses, the personal drama of the voyage, the movement and interaction, in the strong sea-light, of figures that end by representing something— something moreover of which the interest is never, even in its keenness, too great to suffer you to slumber. I at any rate dozed to excess, stretched on my rug with a French novel, and when I opened my eyes I generally saw Jasper Nettlepoint pass with the young woman confided to his mother's care on his arm. Somehow at these moments, between sleeping and waking, I consequently felt that my French novel had set them in motion.

Yet in this dreamy proto-fictional world on which the narrator finds it so interesting to 'exercise' his mind, a real event of palpable physical tragedy is germinating. For Grace Mavis is obviously falling in love with Jasper—a selfish young man who is sporting with her to pass the time—and as obviously dreads her impending marriage. The narrator, sympathetic through his very speculations about her state of mind, takes it upon himself to issue some advice and admonishment to Jasper, who is offended but then leaves the girl alone. Very alone. 'There was an odd pang in seeing her move about alone; I felt somehow responsible for it and asked myself why I couldn't have kept my hands off.' Is he an interfering busybody, or does he act from insight, pity and imagination? I think we are made to feel more of the latter. Certainly when the dream is over reality intrudes in the ugliest way. The narrator says to Grace shortly before the ship docks: 'The first sight of land, at sea, changes everything . . . It always affects me as waking up from a dream. It's a return to reality.' The dream-like French romance gives way to a tragic suicide—for Grace Mavis jumps from the ship at night.

It is such events, such unpleasant cruel twists to existence that James alluded to in his famous phrase—'the Medusa face of life'. These are things which art is helpless to prevent and unable fully to explain: it can only console by recording the loss and lamenting the waste. That is the narrator's function. His type of observation and curiosity in one sense do a great service to life: they provide that sort of sympathetic generosity of appreciation and the 'dignity of judgement' without which life remains an unreclaimed and unrecorded mess. But there is another kind of observation at work on the boat. The loathsome Mrs. Peck who is the busy-body supreme, hungry for derogatory tit-bits, quick to spread damning rumours, always keen to spot out something to castigate in public with malicious glee: she also pays attention, is an observer, and perhaps a 'creator' of sorts since her vicious gossip may have driven the lonely Grace Mavis to suicide. The narrator's benevolent meditative speculation bestows a benediction on life—he endows it with significance and invests it with an inner emotional logic where the surface shows only a squandering chaos. He may perhaps be mocked a little because he is 'so full of signification' but at least, as he himself protests, 'I had taken no such ferocious . . . note as Mrs. Peck.' In contrast to his artistic speculations there is a ferocity of attention which mars what it touches, which destroys what it regards. This sort of attention has a withering effect —it takes life away.

In summing up the virtues which these narrators—and the artist in general—represented for James, I would pick on Natalia Haldin's compliment to the old western language teacher in *Under Western Eyes:* 'There is a way of looking on which is valuable.' And if Conrad seems too different a writer to compare with James, I would point to some of Conrad's statements which seem to corroborate the Jamesian idea of the artist. Thus in *A Personal Record* where he defends himself against the charge of 'resignation': 'But resignation is not indifference . . . I would fain claim for myself the faculty of so much insight as can be expressed in a voice of sympathy and compassion.' He returns to the point. 'Resignation, not mystic, not detached, but resignation open-eyed, conscious, and informed by love, is the only one of our feelings for which it is impossible to become a sham.' The Jamesian narrator could not remain detached to the point of indifference, and it is certainly intimated that love and pity were the cause of this inability. More, he too insists on looking at horrors 'open-eyed' and he too upholds the claims of consciousness. The narrator, or perhaps we should now simply say James himself, could claim, as Conrad does, that his art has its origins in 'a sentiment akin to piety'. For James, like Conrad, was one of those few men who, to use Conrad's fine phrase, 'know how to look at their kind'.

Obviously some basic aesthetic problems have been raised here: what is the way the artist looks at the world, does it differ from other modes of visual appropriation of the phenomenological universe, what is the relation between the artist's vision of form and the form-evading empirical data which endlessly claim his attention? I suggest that we see James's parable of the artist against the larger philosophical background. We could begin by considering Shaftesbury's opposition to empiricism.[3] Against the Baconian ideal of *scientia propter potentiam*—knowledge for the sake of power—he set up an ideal of *amor non mercenarius*—non-mercenary love. The beauty of an object is only really felt, Shaftesbury maintained, when all thoughts of possessing, enjoying, or controlling it are absent. Devotion not dominion, meditation not mastery, contemplation not conquest—these are his preferred attitudes. Thus he maintains that 'The Bridegroom-Doge' 'who in his stately *Bucentaur* floats on the Bosom of his THETIS, has less *possession* than the poor *Shepherd*, who from a hanging Rock, or Point of some high Promontory, stretch'd at his ease, forgets his feeding Flocks, while he admires *her Beauty*'.

Admiration not appetite is the true manner of 'possessing' the beauty of the world: this is almost exactly James's own position. It is at least partially for this reason that Strether refuses participation in the European arena of the senses—he prefers to wonder at it in his own non-interfering manner. Appreciation as opposed to appropriation. For the neo-platonists—such as Shaftesbury was and James might have been—it was the part of animals to act according to the 'provoked senses', it was the high vocation of man to transcend his appetites and relish the formal principles at work

[3] The following passages from Shaftesbury (*Characteristics of Men and Manners*, 1711, incorporating *The Moralist*, 1709, and *Soliloquy*, 1710) are quoted in Ernest Cassirer's *The Platonic Renaissance in England*.

in the universe. *'The Beautiful, the Fair, the Comely,* were never in the *Matter* but in the *Art* and *Design,* never in the *Body,* itself, but in the *Form* or *Forming Power.'*

Shaftesbury's concept of 'disinterested pleasure' has a profound influence on all the later German aestheticians and thus back to Coleridge, Emerson and New England culture in general. But here I would point out that the Shaftesburian artist does not interfere with the seen world, nor does he merely celebrate the surfaces of material things. By appreciating the hidden forming powers at work in the universe he is able to perceive and produce forms where the ordinary man might see only random matter open to legislation and exploitation. Because of his superior insight the artist is not bound by the gratuitous configurations of the empirical world. But to get at the difference between the matter of the world and the matter of art I would turn briefly to a modern aesthetician —Henri Focillon: and during the following quotations[4] I suggest that the narrator of *The Sacred Fount* be kept in mind.

> There is consequently between the matters or substances of art and the substances of nature a divorce, even when they are bound together by the strictest formal propriety. A new order is established, within which there are two distinct realms. . . . The wood of the statue is no longer the wood of the tree; sculptured marble is no longer the marble of the quarry; melted and hammered gold becomes an altogether new and different metal; bricks that have been baked and then built into a wall bear no relation to the clay of the clay-pit. The colour, the integument, all the values that affect the sight have changed. Things without a surface, whether once hidden in the bark, buried in the mountain, imprisoned in the nugget, or swallowed in the mud, have become wholly separated from chaos. They have acquired an integument; they adhere to space; they welcome a daylight that works freely upon them.

It is perhaps the aim of all artists to 'separate things from chaos' and we could say that the intention of the narrator of *The Sacred Fount* is to take his raw material from the social world and reform it into a more orderly dispensation. Focillon further maintains that 'the life of forms is never at a loss to create any matter, any substance whatsoever of which it stands in need'. He insists that it is the normal ambition of man's mind to give form to what it sees and he then defines the artist's difference from ordinary man: 'the artist develops, under our eyes, the very technique of the mind; he

[4]From *La vie des formes en art.*

gives us a kind of mould or cast which we can both see and touch. But this high privilege is not merely that of being an accurate and skilful moulder of casts. He is not manufacturing a collection of solids for some psychological laboratory; he is creating a world— a world that is complex, coherent, and concrete.' The artist is not restricted to observed phenomena: he can create what the exigencies of his formal ideas demand. Shaftesbury also insisted that artistic genius does not imitate created nature: it imitates the creative genius of the universe itself. This is Shaftesbury's definition of the artist: 'Like that Sovereign Artist or universal Plastick Nature, he forms *a Whole*, coherent and proportion'd in itself, with due Subjection and Subordinacy of constituent Parts. He notes the Boundarys of the Passions, and knows their exact *Tones* and *Measures;* by which he justly represents them, marks *the Sublime* of Sentiments and Action, and distinguishes *the Beautiful* from *the Deform'd, the Amiable* from *the Odious.'*

This is not an attempt to force James into some invented tradition: rather I wish to suggest that in *The Sacred Fount*—and elsewhere—he was probing and exploring a profound aesthetic issue and that his notion of non-participatory speculation is related to the ancient and persistent idea of the artist as a man who creates forms which might be truer than the truth—the truth, that is, as apprehended by those immersed in the 'destructive element' seeking only to satisfy their 'provoked senses'. If his creations are lies, then they are lies not like truth, but better than the truth. The narrator of *The Sacred Fount* is at least eligible for Shaftesbury's definition of the artist as 'a second maker; a just Prometheus under Jove.' It is James's peculiarly modern insight—think of Mann's *Doctor Faustus*—to allow the suggestion that the activities of the artist might be allied to insanity. But then, who should have the last word on health in a disease-damaged world? Perhaps here we should recall the moving dying words of the artist Dencombe in *The Middle Years:* there can be little doubt that he speaks for James. 'We work in the dark—we do what we can—we give what we have. Our doubt is our passion and our passion is our task. The rest is the madness of art.'

THE WINGS
OF THE DOVE

1902

"The Wings of the Dove"

DOROTHEA KROOK*

My heart is sore pained within me: and the terrors of death are fallen upon me. Fearfulness and trembling are come upon me, and horror hath over-whelmed me. And I said, Oh that I had wings like a dove! then would I fly away, and be at rest.

Psalm 55

The dove descending breaks the air
With flame of incandescent terror
Of which the tongues declare
The one discharge from sin and error.
T. S. Eliot, Little Gidding

In an essay entitled *Henry James, Melodramatist* Mr Jacques Barzun drew attention to an important element of James's art which, he claimed, is as prominent in the works of the late period as in those of the early and midldle periods.[1] Mr Barzun calls it "melodramatic," a term exactly applicable to the early and middle works—*The American*, for instance, the *dénouement* of *The Bostonians, The Princess Casamassima*—but only (I believe) with certain reservations to the late. In the latter, this element is per-haps more properly described as "legendary" or even "heroic": the simplifications of the melodramatic mode, which by their na-ture exclude complexity, here give way to the simplicities of the heroic, which incorporate all complexity; and this development is

*From THE ORDEAL OF CONSCIOUSNESS IN HENRY JAMES by Dorothea Krook. Copyright 1962, by the Cambridge University Press. Reprinted by permission of the author and the publisher.

significantly linked with other aspects of James's art in the late works. Nevertheless, Mr Barzun's term applies admirably to the bare plot of *The Wings of the Dove*, and it is worth exposing to view the remarkably simple melodramatic framework of this most heroic of James's late works.

There are four principal *dramatis personae:* the English lovers, Kate Croy and Merton Densher; Mrs Lowder (Aunt Maud), Kate's wealthy aunt and patroness; and Milly Theale, the Dove, an American millionairess. The principal minor characters are Lionel Croy, Kate's father, an elegant wastrel, who appears only in the first scene of the novel, but whose absent presence hangs over large stretches of the action; Kate's sister Marian, widow of the Rev. Mr Condrip, who lives with her four young children in a mean little house in Chelsea; Lord Mark, an English nobleman of high rank; and Mrs Susan Stringham, formerly a Boston journalist, who is Milly's friend and confidante.

Aunt Maud, who is as magnificently vulgar, witty and heartless as she is magnificently rich, offers to adopt her beautiful and brilliant niece Kate Croy and give her all the riches of the world—a charming set of rooms in her big house at Lancaster Gate, the finest robes and jewels, the most splendid society and the most distinguished husband (Lord Mark)—on condition that she severs all connexion with her odious father and sister, and gives up her lover Merton Densher, a clever but poor journalist, who (Aunt Maud knows) will never do anything remarkable in the world. The first condition is explicit and unqualified; the second, though equally binding, is tacit: Aunt Maud believes she can safely leave its fulfilment to Kate's honour and good sense. Kate submits to the first condition, under the merciless pressure of the father and sister themselves, who hope to gain everything from her connexion with Aunt Maud; she goes to live at Lancaster Gate; and soon finds that the great world is exceedingly delightful. But she does not give up Merton Densher; and from this crucial decision springs the main action of the story. The great game now begins—the game, as they call it, of "squaring" Aunt Maud, that is, of somehow rendering Merton Densher acceptable to her so that they may have each other and Aunt Maud's money too. This proves to be no easy task; and a stalemate appears to have been reached when the fourth principal, Milly Theale, enters the story.

Milly Theale, American millionairess, the Heir of all the Ages, the Fairy Princess, the Poor Little Rich Girl, and ultimately also the Dove, appears at Lancaster Gate accompanied by her hand-maiden, Mrs Susan Stringham. She becomes Kate Croy's dearest friend, Aunt Maud's moneyed darling, Lord Mark's adorable Bronzino, and the toast of the London *beau monde*. But she is stricken with a mortal disease, knows that she must die young, and communicates this information to Kate Croy. By doing this, she provides the missing piece for the success of Kate's great design to have her cake and eat it. Since Milly very much "likes" Densher (which in the Jamesian idiom means she is fifty fathoms deep in love with him), and since she knows nothing (and need know nothing) about his being secretly engaged to Kate, Densher is to make love to Milly, who will respond with the desperate passion of the sick girl "conscious of a great capacity for life, but . . . condemned to die under short respite, while enamoured of the world." They will marry; Milly will die; Densher will inherit her money and marry Kate; and in this way Aunt Maud will be at once "squared" and "dished." This is Kate's remarkable plan. It is car-ried forward to its penultimate stage, but is at the last moment frustrated by Lord Mark, who gives the game away to Milly. Milly, in her hired palace in Venice, turns her face to the wall and dies. But before dying, she calls Densher to a last interview, at which something extraordinary happens which Densher after-wards finds it very difficult to describe; and she leaves him a great deal of money. But the interview with Milly has made it impossible for Densher to take the money; and when he goes back to Kate, it is to offer himself without the money, or the money without himself. Kate, it seems, in the end chooses the second alternative; but the suspense is maintained to the very last line of the book:

> He only said: "I'll marry you, mind you, in an hour."
> "As we were?"
> "As we were."
> But she turned to the door, and her headshake was now the end. "We shall never be again as we were!"

This is the skeleton, melodramatic indeed, that lies beneath the skin of the work that many will account James's masterpiece. The ultimate grounds of its greatness are to be discussed in their place; what more immediately claims our attention is that aspect of its greatness which turns upon the curious generality (or "abstractness," as it is more commonly called) of its total effect. This appears to be the result chiefly of what may be described as a fusion, at maximum pressure, of all the principal Jamesian themes that had previously been treated separately and at a lower intensity. Of these, the international theme (incorporating among its component parts the American national character, the English national character and London society) is the most conspicuous. We have already learnt that this is one of James's principal "objective correlatives" for his experience of the condition of modern man; and in *The Wings of the Dove* it is treated on a scale surpassing every previous attempt in magnitude and grandeur. All the familiar elements, we find, are there; but they are so magnified, heightened and intensified—so intensely "idealised"—that they assume virtually heroic proportions. Everything is larger than life, and in that sense of heroic stature; and everything has about it that air of the legendary which is inseparable from the heroic.

This is true, to begin with, of the famous Jamesian "types" that here as elsewhere sustain the international theme. They all stand to James's earlier renderings of the same types as the ideal to the actual. Milly Theale, the American Girl in Europe; Kate Croy, the English Girl of the pure Gainsborough breed; Merton Densher, the Young Man of developed sensibility and reflective mind who "consecrates by his appreciation"; Mrs Lowder, the *grande dame* who (like Mrs Newsome in *The Ambassadors*) makes her impact by her lack of imagination; Lord Mark, the barely articulate English nobleman, who seems merely stupid but is in fact sinister; Susan Stringham, the lady journalist from Boston: it is impossible not to see them palimpsestically, written over their predecessors, and irresistibly fascinating beyond their intrinsic interest for their "hereditary" characteristics.

The development of the new out of the old is, however, characteristically Jamesian in being not the addition of new elements to the old but, rather, a feat of generalisation. The old elements are all there by implication, "assumed as known"; what is new is the scale and scope of their ordering—the comprehensiveness of the framework in which they are contained, the breadth and height, the sheer "elevation," of the standpoint from which they are viewed. Nor does the quasi-logical character of the achievement injure in the minutest degree its life as a novel. The implied elements are all there, poetically realised, concretely "pictured"; for the act of generalisation here is not the logician's kind (which ought properly to be called "abstraction"), but the artist's which involves no loss of concreteness. It remains vivid, because it does not empty the final vision of the particular perceptions from which it draws its life but contains them in their full primitive intensity.

There is no certainty, of course, that James himself saw his later novels in this light—as generalisations, in the sense indicated, of the principal themes and characters of his earlier works; though it is conceivable (in view of his own sensitiveness to logical relations expressed in the recurrent logical or quasi-logical terms, expressions and images in his later works) that he would at least not have been surprised to find them viewed in this way. But whether James was or was not conscious of it, and, if conscious, to what degree, this quasi-logical view does suggest an explanation of what would otherwise remain a baffling peculiarity of *The Wings of the Dove* along with the other late novels—the intense generality of the picture (misdescribed as "abstract") with the intense concreteness; and it does in any case help us to a better understanding of some of its more remarkable achievements.

Among the chief of them is the portrayal of Milly Theale. Milly is at once the most heroic, most legendary, element in this heroic and legendary tale and also the most real and exemplary for exhibiting one of the deepest aspects of James's mature vision of the human condition. We have already encountered this aspect in *The Awkward Age.* The principal tragic theme of *The Wings of the Dove,* like that of *The Awkward Age,* is the impact of the worldly world upon the unworldly—its power to undermine, reduce, and (in this instance) finally to destroy those who cannot accommodate themselves to its values. The chief weapon that the world here, as in *The Awkward Age,* employs for this work of destruction is the characteristic virtues of the victims themselves—their innocence, ignorance and good faith, their generosity and tenderness; and, again as in *The Awkward Age,* what is chiefly held up for exposure is the worldly world's rapacity and ruthlessness springing from its terrible single-mindedness in the pursuit of pleasure or power or both. These are the defining features of the world represented by the Lancaster Gate circle in *The Wings of the Dove* just as they were of Mrs Brookenham's circle in *The Awkward Age;* and, as in that supremely civilised society so in this, the rapacity and the ruthlessness are not something distinct from the charm, intelligence and civility in which Lancaster Gate, like Buckingham Crescent, abounds. On the contrary, they are so inseparably bound up with each other that it is difficult, indeed impossible, for the victims to recognise the rapacity and ruthlessness in the charm, the intelligence and the brilliance; and being unable so much as to recognise them, they are of course left helpless against their destructive power.

This was the case of Nanda Brookenham in *The Awkward Age*, and it is again the case of Milly Theale, the principal vessel of consciousness in *The Wings of the Dove*. Milly Theale, we soon discover, incorporates all the long line of Jamesian American Girls from Daisy Miller and Bessie Alden in *An International Episode* to Isabel Archer in *The Portrait of a Lady*. She is as lovely as the lovely lady in the Bronzino portrait that she is taken to see by her friend Lord Mark. She is tender, generous, gay, and full of the zest for "life"—for knowledge, that is, and friendship and love, which she passionately desires to have in abundance and in the greatest possible intensity. She is solitary, having lost in rapid succession her parents and all other near relations; she is stricken (we have already learnt) by a mysterious but mortal disease, which must cause her to die young; and above everything, she is rich—colossally, unbelievably rich.

There are two short passages that admirably evoke this high-legendary quality of Milly Theale against the background of her personal history. The first is Susan Stringham's recollected first impression of Milly:[2]

> Mrs Stringham was never to forget—for the moment had not faded, nor the infinitely fine vibration it set up in any degree ceased—her own first sight of the striking apparition, then unheralded and unexplained: the slim, constantly pale, delicately haggard, anomalously, agreeably angular young person, of not more than two-and-twenty summers in spite of her marks, whose hair was somehow exceptionally red even for the real thing, which it innocently confessed to being, and whose clothes were remarkably black even for robes of mourning, which was the meaning they expressed. It was New York mourning, it was New York hair, it was a New York history, confused as yet, but multitudinous, of the loss of parents, brothers, sisters, almost every human appendage, all on a scale and with a sweep that had required the greater stage; it was a New York legend of affecting, of romantic

isolation, and, beyond everything, it was by most accounts, in respect to the mass of money so piled on the girl's back, a set of New York possibilities.[3]

A similar impression of Milly and her wildly romantic personal background is received by Kate Croy, her English friend, who is to play such a devastating part in Milly's life:

> They had talked, in long drives, and quantities of history had not been wanting—in the light of which Mrs Lowder's niece might superficially seem to have had the best of the argument. Her visitor's American references, with their bewildering immensities, their confounding moneyed New York, their excitements of high pressure, their opportunities of wild freedom, their record of used-up relatives, parents, clever eager fair slim brothers—these the most loved—all engaged, as well as successive superseded guardians, in a high extravagance of speculation and dissipation that had left this exquisite being her black dress, her white face and her vivid hair as the mere last broken link: such a picture quite threw into the shade the brief biography, however sketchily amplified, of a mere middle-class nobody in Bayswater[4]

The story of Milly Theale, we have already learnt, properly begins when, accompanied by Mrs Stringham, she descends upon London in the manner common, it seems, to rich young Americans in James's day, and is there instantly drawn into the heart of "the world," represented by the big house in Lancaster Gate. The presiding daemon, the supreme symbol of its worldliness, is the terrible Mrs Lowder, Kate Croy's Aunt Maud, who is Mrs Touchett in *The Portrait of a Lady*, Mrs Brookenham (and the Duchess) in *The Awkward Age*, Mrs Newsome in *The Ambassadors* and a host of other earlier Jamesian *grandes dames* rolled into one; and being the quintessential *grande dame*, she is of course incomparably more deadly and dangerous than any of her predecessors. Mrs Lowder is ably supported in her role of presiding daemon by a large anonymous cast of minor daemons, who circle in and out of the big house at Lancaster Gate as friends, relations or guests at the innumerable luncheon-parties and dinner-parties that form the background to the intense personal drama in which the main actors are Milly Theale, Kate Croy and Merton Densher.

What this central drama is we already know, at least in bare outline, and further discussion of the dénouement—Densher's last interview with Milly Theale before she turns her face to the wall,

and its remarkable consequences for the world of Lancaster Gate
—must for the present be reserved. The more immediate critical
task in respect to James's rendering of Milly Theale is to determine what exactly it is that exposes her to the destructive power
of Lancaster Gate even to the point of death; and this brings us
directly back to the international theme, the encompassing framework of the central tragic experience of *The Wings of the
Dove.*

What we perceive at once and with the least difficulty is that it
is her American "innocence" which in the first place lays Milly
open to the rapacity and ruthlessness of her English friends. As in
her predecessors among James's American Girls, this innocence
in her springs from a fatal ignorance of the complex pressures
operative in the complex world of Lancaster Gate—an ignorance
due in the first instance, of course, to her American background.
James speaks here of "the immense profusion, but the few varieties
and thin development" of the America of Milly Theale's day, and
does not fail to draw again the familiar moral of the international
theme, namely, the disabling effects upon the American mind of
the simplicities and freedoms of American life, and their effect in
particular of placing Americans at a severe disadvantage in their
intercourse with the English and the Europeans.

This precisely is what happens to Milly Theale when she is
thrown among the English. Her disability is plainly that she has
no experience of the pressures, in particular the economic, to
which the individual in such a society is perpetually exposed. As
in *The Awkward Age,* these economic pressures never show on the
surface of the gracious living in the big house at Lancaster Gate;
but they are the most powerful subterranean force in the life of a
society struggling to maintain a traditionally high standard of life
on perpetually dwindling resources. The uneasy relation between
an America growing steadily richer and a Britain growing steadily
poorer which has become one of the commonplaces of Anglo-
American relations since James's day was, it seems, already sufficiently apparent then, at any rate to his discerning eye; and it is
this economic fact (with all its moral implications) that lies behind
the long sigh of ecstasy and envy that is to be heard in Lancaster
Gate every time Milly Theale's English friends touch upon the
subject of what they call her good luck. Her "good luck" is, simply,
her money: which they desire, of course, not for its own vulgar

sake but for its precious power to secure the freedom they long for —the freedom to enjoy without impediment all that Lancaster Gate would so much like to enjoy, and would know so well how to enjoy.

But Milly knows nothing of these material pressures that lie beneath the gracious surface, and therefore knows nothing of their demoralising effects upon the human spirit, even the most intelligent, most cultivated, most imaginative of human spirits. Indeed particularly (this is James's grand point) upon the intelligent and imaginative—like Milly's dear friend Kate Croy, whose range of enjoyments so greatly exceeds that of the less intelligent and less imaginative, and whose appetite therefore for the power to procure these enjoyments exceeds correspondingly. Lacking such knowledge, Milly Theale is accordingly very slow to see herself, the fabulously rich American, as a proper object of exploitation.

Besides this, however, what makes it so difficult for her to see herself as Lancaster Gate sees her is that the exploitation is not in the least vulgar; nor is it purely mercenary. What is so difficult and puzzling (and profoundly deceptive) is that the exploitation is perfectly compatible, it seems, with the most genuine devotion to Milly herself. Aunt Maud worships the very air she breathes, and is genuinely stricken when she hears of the death of the poor "moneyed darling." Kate Croy is genuinely enchanted with Milly: when she says that Milly is as charming as she is queer and as queer as she is charming,[5] she speaks with complete sincerity; and she enjoys their friendship with the most genuine ardour. And Merton Densher, whom Milly so much "likes," treats her with the most tender deference; and Lord Mark, who makes a point of showing her the Bronzino that everyone says she resembles, intimates in his inexpressive English way that she really ought to "let a fellow who isn't a fool take care of [her] a little";[6] and all the anonymous guests at the luncheon-parties and dinner-parties can't make enough fuss of her. Everybody in Lancaster Gate, in short, is as charming as possible to her; and here (James wishes us to understand) is another of the characteristic features of the English of that class, another aspect of "the fathomless depths of English equivocation": that they can feel the most genuine, most sincere, most whole-hearted devotion for those who can serve their interests, and can as genuinely, as sincerely and whole-heartedly cast them off the moment they have ceased to serve their interests—

or, alternatively, have begun to make demands that are inconvenient or irksome or just boring.

Of all this Milly Theale has no inkling when she first arrives at Lancaster Gate. She learns most of it, very painfully and slowly, as the story advances, and the most devastating thing of all only at the point of death. She acquires her knowledge in the most incidental, or seemingly incidental, flashes; James's dramatic genius ensures that they shall appear as incidental as in life itself. One of the early flashes occurs when she is talking to Lord Mark at her first dinner-party at Lancaster Gate, and presently discerns that, in spite of his deference and his seeming interest in her, he finds her only diverting, only "funny"—"a mere little American, a cheap exotic, imported almost wholesale," who has no power to challenge his real interest, and certainly none to engage his stronger feelings.[7] Another, very important, flash occurs when she discovers that Kate Croy cannot endure her friend Susan Stringham. The reason (she discovers on analysis) is, astonishingly, that Kate has in her a streak of brutality—the kind of brutality which enables her to dismiss another human being with the easiest contempt when that human being happens merely to violate her standard of good breeding. Yet this brutality (Milly also discovers) is characteristically English, in that it has nothing to do with primitive cruelty and everything to do with what in the modern jargon is called a "defence-mechanism." It is an instrument of self-preservation, Milly discerns; and pursues her analysis in a passage that is as good an instance as any of the sheer quantity of analytical insight, perfectly dramatised, that can be packed into a few characteristic sentences of James's late style:

> Mrs Lowder didn't feel it, and Kate Croy felt it with ease; yet in the end . . . she grasped the reason, and the reason enriched her mind. Wasn't it sufficiently the reason that the handsome girl was, with twenty other splendid qualities, the least bit brutal too, and didn't she suggest, as no one yet had ever done to her new friend, that there might be a wild beauty in that, and even a strange grace? Kate wasn't brutally brutal—which Milly had hitherto benightedly supposed the only way; she wasn't even aggressively so, but rather indifferently, defensively and, as might be said, by the habit of anticipation. She simplified in advance, was beforehand with her doubts, and knew with singular quickness what she wasn't, as they said in New York, going to like. In that way at least people were clearly quicker in England

than at home; and Milly could quite see, after a little, how such instincts might become usual in a world in which dangers abounded. There were clearly more dangers round about Lancaster Gate than one suspected in New York or could dream of in Boston. At all events, with more sense of them, there were more precautions, and it was a remarkable world altogether in which there could be precautions, on whatever ground, against Susie.[8]

This is the kind of insight into the complex world of Lancaster Gate that Milly is liable to receive from her most casual encounters with her English friends. Her mind, however, is to be still further enriched by her intimacy with Kate Croy. In a great scene at a critical point in the story, Kate "lets herself go" (as Milly puts it to herself) "in irony, in confidence, in extravagance" on those qualities of the American Mind, as represented in her friend Milly Theale, that she has come to find peculiarly exasperating—chiefly, its crude naive empiricism, its seemingly inexhaustible capacity for "exaggerated ecstasy" and "disproportionate shock," and its consequent propensity to produce upon more developed minds the effects of boredom and irritation. It is an exposure as brilliant as it is bold; and Milly "follows" it, participates in it, with an intelligence, an appreciation of all Kate's finest shades of veracity, and an irony to match Kate's own, which sets her apart from all her predecessors in the line of James's American Girls and gives her a unique place in the ranks of the late-Jamesian vessels of consciousness:

The beauty and the marvel of it was that she [Kate] had never been so frank: being a person of such a calibre, as Milly would have said, that, even while "dealing" with you and thereby, as it were, picking her steps, she could let herself go, could, in irony, in confidence, in extravagance, tell you things she had never told before. That was the impression—that she was telling things, and quite conceivably for her own relief as well; almost as if the errors of vision, the mistakes of proportion, the residuary innocence of spirit still to be remedied on the part of her auditor had their moments of proving too much for her nerves. She went at them just now, these sources of irritation, with an amused energy that it would have been open to Milly to regard as cynical and that was nevertheless called for—as to this the other was distinct—by the way that in certain connexions the American mind broke down. It seemed at least—the American mind as sitting there thrilled and dazzled in Milly—not to understand English society without a separate confrontation with *all* the cases. It couldn't proceed by

—there was some technical term she lacked until Milly suggested both analogy and induction, and then, differently, instinct, none of which were right: it had to be led up to and introduced to each aspect of the monster, enabled to walk all round it, whether for the consequent exaggerated ecstasy or for the still more (as appeared to this critic) disproportionate shock. It might, the monster, Kate conceded, loom large for those born amid forms less developed and therefore no doubt less amusing; it might on some sides be a strange and dreadful monster, calculated to devour the unwary, to abase the proud, to scandalise the good; but if one had to live with it one must, not to be for ever sitting up, learn how: which was virtually in short to-night what the handsome girl showed herself as teaching.[9]

This is Kate Croy's anatomy of the famous American innocence and ignorance; and as such it is uniquely instructive to Milly. But it is intended also to illuminate the complexities of Kate's own nature, in particular her boldness, her audacity, her strange, "perverse" courage. For Kate by this time is already in the process of conceiving her diabolical design against Milly, and the rest of her "speech," from the most interesting mixture of motives, is intended also as a warning to Milly—to get out of Lancaster Gate before she is destroyed.[10] Milly, of course, misses the warning, and is consequently doomed; and this submerged tragic irony does much to intensify the powerful dramatic impact of the whole scene.

So Kate Croy, at any rate, is in no doubt that it is Milly Theale's American ignorance and innocence that in the first instance expose her to the destructive power of Lancaster Gate. There are, however, other more subtle reasons that contribute to this condition of exposure. The ignorance and innocence indeed might by themselves have proved a kind of protection, at any rate against the *conscious* knowledge of her final deception and betrayal. But their potential power to protect is perpetually cancelled out by her very powers of appreciation: by her intelligence, her sensibility, her imagination; and above everything by her passion for "knowledge"—her fatal curiosity. These together make Lancaster Gate irresistibly fascinating and delightful to her; and by the same token weaken her resistance to its destructive power.

What chiefly weakens her resistance in fact is her supreme Jamesian quality, her self-consciousness. For Milly Theale's passion for knowledge is principally a passion for self-knowledge; and it is for this, more than anything, that she is prepared to suffer pain, confusion and humiliation, and finally total deprivation and loss. That is why (for instance) she participates, in the way we saw, in Kate's analysis of the American mind, entering into Kate's view of herself with an avidity of interest that would be almost masochistic if it were not what it in fact is—the disinterested passion for self-knowledge, characteristic of all the great Jamesian heroes and heroines. The same is true also of her deeply intelligent understanding of the English point of view in other connexions: of the reasons for Kate Croy's streak of brutality; and for Lord Mark's indifference to her; and, most painfully (before she is made to believe he is in love with her), for Merton Densher's indifference. Having received from Kate Croy an unforgettable light on her disabilities as an American Girl, and presently also on her still graver disability, that of being a Dove (*"That* was what was the matter with her. She was a dove"), she has already by the time Densher returns from America begun to see herself through the eyes of Lancaster Gate; and in the quarter of an hour's talk she has with him alone after their first meeting in the National Gallery, she recognises simultaneously both how much she "likes" him and how much therefore she regrets that he should share "the view" of her:

> She could have dreamed of his not having *the view,* of his having something or other, if need be quite viewless, of his own. The defect of it [the "view"] in general—if she might so ungraciously criticise— was that, by its sweet universality, it made relations rather prosaically a matter of course. It anticipated and superseded the—likewise sweet —operation of real affinities. It was this that was doubtless marked in her power to keep him now—this and her glassy lustre of attention to his pleasantness about the scenery in the Rockies.[11]

Again and again in *The Wings of the Dove* we receive such testimonies to the range and depth of Milly Theale's self-knowledge.[12] Its tragic implications, however, are not fully disclosed until she has learnt from the great doctor that she is very sick and, on seeking to communicate her secret to Kate Croy, meets with a rebuff that is the more desolating for being so bright and brisk.[13] Then Milly also becomes fully conscious of her own ultimate solitude amidst the buzz of admiration and adulation of the Lancaster Gate circle; and it is this knowledge that adds the last intolerable weight to the burden of her self-consciousness. Her self-consciousness is her glory (James wishes us to understand): Milly is not merely the American Girl "acting out" her nature unconsciously, like Daisy Miller and the other American girls in James's earlier stories. She is the American Girl grown conscious of herself as acting out the character of the American Girl; and it is this capacity at once for "being" and "seeing," for at once suffering intensely and being intensely conscious of the suffering, that defines the kind and quality of her tragedy.

Milly's desperate isolation is created in the first instance, of course, by the combination of her "good luck," as the English call it, with her "queerness"—that she should be so rich and yet such a saint, a dove, an exquisite thing. More plainly, what Lancaster Gate finds astonishing beyond comprehension is that Milly Theale should be so little the "great personage" she ought by virtue of her fabulous good luck to be: that she should, besides being munificently generous, be so mild, so humble, so eager, so "funny"—in fact, so *good*—when she could so easily afford not to be. They cannot stop marvelling at this; and they do in fact treat her as a great personage, thus consigning her to the lonely eminence symbolised in an early scene in the Swiss Alps.[14] To this even her dear devoted Susan Stringham contributes:

> The girl was conscious of how she [Susan] dropped at times into inscrutable impenetrable deferences—attitudes that, though without at all intending it, made a difference for familiarity, for the ease of intimacy. It was as if she recalled herself to manners, to the law of court-etiquette.[15]

In this aspect, Milly's story may be seen as James's rehandling of another grand melodramatic theme, that of the Poor Little Rich girl.[16] She is "rich" in virtue of her money, her exalted position, and the expectations of bliss that these spread all around her. She is poor and deprived because through this thick cloud of expectations, this mass of blinding preconceptions about her "happiness," no human love can penetrate.

What, however, intensifies her solitude to the tragic pitch is her mysterious mortal disease. It is this that finally isolates her from the world she so passionately desires to know and to enjoy. When Lord Mark takes her up to the Bronzino she is supposed to resemble she looks at it with tears in her eyes ("the lady in question

. . . was a very great personage—only unaccompanied by a joy. And she was dead, dead, dead"); and Lord Mark, "though he didn't understand her was as nice as if he had." [17] Presently in the same scene Kate comes up, and Milly asks her to accompany her on her first visit to Sir Luke Strett, the doctor:

> Kate fixed her with deep eyes. "What in the world is the matter with you?" It had inevitably a sound of impatience, as if it had been a challenge really to produce something; so that Milly felt her for the moment only as a much older person, standing above her a little, doubting the imagined ailments, suspecting the easy complains, of ignorant youth. It somewhat checked her.[18]

She is to receive a further and final check after her second visit to the doctor, this time alone. She has spent an afternoon of anguish in Regent's Park pondering with "her little lonely acuteness" the great man's advice, trying to make out how sick she really is, and deciding that she must, in view of all he had said, be very sick indeed. Back at her hotel Milly awaits Kate's visit. Kate arrives; and her first words of enquiry are, "Well, what?"

> The inquiry bore of course . . . on the issue of the morning's scene, the great man's latest wisdom, and it doubtless affected Milly a little as the cheerful demand for news is apt to affect troubled spirits when news is not, in one of the neater forms, prepared for delivery. She couldn't have said what it was exactly that, on the instant, determined her; the nearest description of it would perhaps have been as the more vivid impression of all her friend took for granted. The contrast between this free quantity and the maze of possibilities through which, for hours, she had been picking her way, put on, in short, for the moment, a grossness that even friendly forms scarce lightened: it helped forward in fact the revelation to herself that she absolutely had nothing to tell. . . . Almost before she knew it she was answering, and answering beautifully, with no consciousness of fraud, only as with a sudden flare of the famous "will-power" she had heard about, read about, and which was what her medical adviser had mainly thrown her back on. "Oh it's all right. He's lovely." [19]

After this, there are no further direct references to Milly's sickness; but there is one final comment upon the inaccessibility to death of the living. "I'm a brute about illness. I hate it," says Kate Croy to Densher, telling him about Milly's case; and adds, "It's well for you, my dear, that you're as sound as a bell."

"Thank you!" Densher laughed. "It's rather good then for yourself too that you're as strong as the sea."

She looked at him now a moment as for the selfish gladness of their young immunities. It was all they had together, but they had it at least without a flaw—each had the beauty, the physical felicity, the personal virtue, love and desire of the other. Yet it was as if this very consciousness threw them back the next moment into pity for the poor girl who had everything else in the world, the great genial good they, alas, didn't have, but failed on the other hand of this. "How we're talking about her!" Kate compunctiously sighed. But there were the facts. "From illness I keep away." [20]

This inaccessibility of the living to the experience of death and dying is the immediate cause of Milly's tragic deprivation.[21] The living of Lancaster Gate admire and adore Milly Theale; but they all withhold from her the one thing that would relieve the terrors of her state—their participation, at once intelligent and generous, in "the ordeal of consciousness" from hour to hour of a young creature with a great capacity for life condemned to die while hating and fearing death. From this terror of Milly Theale's condition they all, like Kate Croy, withdraw. They are all prodigiously intelligent, but not intelligent enough to know what such a condition means; and they are all brave, but not so brave as to risk participation in the twilight life of a soul awaiting death. This, we are meant to see, is the last dreadful infirmity of the brave and beautiful souls that inhabit Lancaster Gate. A final incapacity for love is intimately linked with a final incapacity to confront the fact of death; and, conversely, the incapacity to confront death is the final measure of the coldness, ruthlessness and egotism of the worldly world figured here.

Milly Theale on her side responds to the indifference with her own last infirmity, which is the sin of pride. She refuses to speak of her illness; she is determined to die (as Kate puts it) "without smelling of drugs or tasting of medicines." It is of course a sublime virtue, this perfect exercise of fortitude in the face of death: but it is also the last temptation of the devil. For it isolates her more completely than ever from her fellow creatures, cutting her off from her last chance to draw some remnant of loving-kindness out of the cold heart of the world. If Milly Theale (like Maggie Verver in *The Golden Bowl*) had been humble enough, or fearless enough, to renounce her pride, a saving connexion might have been established between herself and the enemy—enough at any rate to render impossible the diabolical design that finally kills her. But she does not renounce it, and thus deprives herself of the last possibility of being saved.

These accordingly are the qualities that together incapacitate Milly Theale against the powers of Lancaster Gate—her American innocence and ignorance, her appreciation, her consciousness, her solitude, her pride. And her mysterious disease is perhaps best seen as at once "real" and "symbolic," physical and spiritual. On the one hand, it is a real sickness of the body, which saps her physical resistance; on the other, it is a sickness of the spirit, induced in the first instance by her early intimations, vividly communicated to us by the scene in the Swiss Alps,[22] of the lonely, loveless condition to which she is condemned in spite of (or because of) her fabulous "luck." Her spiritual sickness is presently intensified by her experience of the world, and finally confirmed by the ultimate betrayal which causes her to turn her face to the wall and die. She would live if she could be happy, Sir Luke Strett had said;[23] but Milly Theale is so constituted that she cannot wrest happiness out of a world by its nature implacably hostile to her very being. Though she longs to the very last moment to be happy and to live, no mutual accommodation is possible between her and the world she inhabits; and with no physical, "animal" strength to fall back upon when, for the last time, she struggles to live after the knowledge of her betrayal by her dearest friends Kate Croy and Merton Densher, there is no escape for her from death.

The question that has still to be answered is why the story is called *The Wings of the Dove.* This turns our attention more directly to the world of Lancaster Gate and, in particular, to Kate Croy and her diabolical design. That the design shall finally be judged to be diabolical James sufficiently (but not more than sufficiently) ensures by his use of one of the time-honoured devices of the tragic dramatist—he shows us the slaughter of the innocent by the wicked followed by the just punishment of the wicked in the last scene of the drama. It does not help Densher that he should have been moved to repentance and expiation by his victim's forgiveness; he still has to lose the prize for which the sin was committed. Nor does it help Kate that her design should have been a miracle of intelligence, courage, good sense, good will—everything in fact that the world ever asks of any worldly design, provided that it succeeds; she still has to lose Densher, for whose sake the courage, lucidity and self-command were so superbly exercised. In the Preface to *The Portrait of a Lady* James tells us that he deliberately forswore the use of those aids to "interest" of which the older dramatists have always availed themselves—the "comic relief and underplots," the "murders and battles and the great mutations of the world." There is no lack of great mutations in James's dramas, but they are solely those of the moral world; and the murders and battles all take place upon the ground of the moral consciousness of his protagonists. The defeat of Kate's design is the Actium of these most magnificent of James's lovers, and their parting in the last scene a re-enactment of the parting in the Monument.

Kate's design is central to James's fable, for by means of it he accomplishes one of his principal purposes: to exhibit the worldly world in the perfection of its horror and its glory, and thus as a world prepared for the descent of the Dove. The horror is in the fact that a design so dreadful should find such a natural place in this world—that the beautiful, gracious circle of Lancaster Gate should find it so damnably, so infernally, easy to accommodate this piece of evil; the glory is in the treasures of intelligence, courage, good will and good humour with which it renders its homage to the devil. If on the one side any part of the bright beauty of Kate Croy and Merton Densher is missed or minimised, or on the other any shade of the horror in the diabolism of Kate Croy's design, so much in either case is lost of James's achievement. Here supremely James has made the "difficulty" as great as possible for himself; for the design is at once as monstrous as any that passion conjoined with the love of pleasure and power could devise, and is presented with a surface as brilliant and a style as great, and protected by justifications as deep and sound and satisfying, as only a great novelist could imagine and execute.

The justifications (or "motivation") in this part of the story testify again to James's profound sense of the conditional character of our knowledge of the world and the life of man. The wonderful early scenes of the novel unforgettably fix in our minds the outrage that Kate's domestic pieties—her "narrow little family feeling," as she calls them—received from a cold mercenary father and a selfish mean-spirited sister; and are afterwards meant to remind us constantly that it was their combined pressure that in the first place precipitated her into Aunt Maud's world. We are also expected never to forget that the whole design began as a fine, "amusing" game, that of "squaring" Aunt Maud, and by nothing more reprehensible than the exercise of natural wit and the neatest, cleverest diplomacy. Who being Kate Croy, who "always gave Densher finer things than anyone to think about and banished the talk of other women . . . to the dull desert of the conventional," would *not* be tempted to outwit Aunt Maud in this way? Who would not agree that Aunt Maud thoroughly deserved to be so outwitted—for a dozen reasons, but chiefly for the prodigious cynicism with which she can admit to liking Densher, oh liking him immensely, only for herself, not Kate? [24] And who being Densher would not respond to the daring and the fun of the thing —Densher with his developed aesthetic sense, to whom "it had really, her sketch of the affair, a high colour and a great style, at all of which he gazed . . . as at a picture by a master." [25] The challenge to two such people as Kate Croy and Densher really is irresistible, and to fail to take it up would be—well, rather stupid, rather spiritless; showing a narrow, unimaginative kind of rectitude, a mean sort of pusillanimity. James, in short, by the high colour and great style of his opening sketch of the lovers wins us over entirely to their side.

But Aunt Maud resists squaring; Milly Theale with her money and her mortal disease appears on the scene; and what began as a daring piece of fun is slowly transformed into the diabolical design. And here, where the going becomes more and more difficult, the justifications press most irresistibly. Is not Milly passionately, desperately, in love with Densher? Is she not to die very soon? Would not the illusion of Densher's love do as much for her last happiness as the reality? Would it not therefore be an act of loving-kindness to "give" her Densher for that time, in order that she might die in the blissful belief of having "lived"? Where is the harm? asks Kate Croy, with all the sincerity and good faith with which the worldly always ask the question whenever there are, or seem to be, vast splendours of power and pleasure to be gained by means only minutely tainted. All one needs is singleness of purpose, a cool head, strong nerves, and (where possible) a decent sincere regret that there should be even so minute a taint as there is in the whole magnificent business. "I don't like it," says Kate

Croy to Densher on the night of Milly's great reception in the Palazzo Leporelli, while their hostess stands on the other side of the *sala* smiling towards them: "I don't like it, but I'm a person, thank goodness, who can do what I don't like." [26]

When we reach this point in the story, we may well feel that here is the extreme verge of the world. It is "extreme" in a quasi-logical sense: for here the logical implications of the values of the world are drawn out, ineluctably, to their last particle of meaning. It is "extreme" poetically: for here is the world of appearances presented with colours so intense, lines so sharp, qualities, tones and cadences so finely discriminated and rendered with such a felicity as to give an intelligible meaning to the notion of an absolute in poetic achievement. And it is also "extreme" in the deepest moral sense—a world *in extremis* from its own perfection of beauty and freedom. It has reached its *non ultra*, with no taint of the decay that we are soon to meet in *The Golden Bowl;* and beyond lies that of which neither Kate Croy nor Merton Densher nor Aunt Maud have any knowledge or imagination. Into this world, stretched to its limit and taut for the impact, the Dove descends. The meaning, indeed, is obscure:

> He saw a young man far off and in a relation inconceivable, saw him hushed, passive, staying his breath, but half understanding, yet dimly conscious of something immense and holding himself painfully together not to lose it ... The essence was that something had happened to him too beautiful and too sacred to describe. He had been, to his recovered sense, forgiven, dedicated, blessed; but this he couldn't coherently express.[27]

That is all we are told—that Densher, in his last interview with Milly Theale, when she knew that he and Kate had hideously deceived and betrayed her, had been "forgiven, dedicated, blessed." It becomes plain, however, from the subsequent course of the fable, that this interview marks the descent of the Dove into the world of Lancaster Gate. Not indeed with flame of incandescent terror; but quietly and unobtrusively the Dove descends, covering them all (as Kate herself puts it) with its wings.

After that, it seems, Lancaster Gate is no longer the same. Nothing spectacular happens, of course: there are no confessions, no conversions, no breast-beatings, no guilt or shame: Lancaster Gate continues to behave as beautifully as ever, with perfect lucidity and composure; and Densher still wants more than ever to marry Kate Croy, and Kate still wants to marry Densher. But the action of the Dove is known by its effects; and the ending of James's fable leaves us in no doubt that these have been shattering. Kate Croy and Merton Densher find in the end that they cannot after all marry. Densher still desires it to the last moment; but Kate, superior to the last in her clear-headedness, knows that it is no longer possible. The last dialogue between them, with which the book ends, makes it plain that Kate at least has discerned the full effect of the Dove's descent—though, characteristically, she cannot assign the proper cause to the effect. Densher is still begging her to marry him, and Kate is apparently still wavering:

> "Your word of honour (she says to Densher) that you're not in love with her memory?"
>
> "Oh—her memory!"
>
> "Ah"—she made a high gesture—"don't speak of it as if you couldn't be. *I* could, in your place; and you're one for whom it will do. Her memory's your love. You *want* no other."
>
> He heard her out in stillness, watching her face, but not moving. Then he only said: "I'll marry you, mind you, in an hour."
>
> "As we were?"
>
> "As we were."
>
> But she turned to the door, and her headshake was now the end. "We shall never be again as we were!" [28]

In that last sentence Kate Croy, speaking for Lancaster Gate and so for all the unredeemed world, proclaims that the Dove has triumphed. It has triumphed, not indeed by redeeming the world —for James's fable of redemption we have to wait until *The Golden Bowl;* but by injecting into it its first knowledge of an order of goodness and power greater than any this world by itself can show.[29] As the religious might put it: by the holy life and holy death of one Milly Theale, God has too evidently made foolish the wisdom of the world; and Lancaster Gate, being as intelligent as it is, does not fail to grasp the point.

This is the deepest theme of *The Wings of the Dove;* and if (as I suggest elsewhere) the story of Milly Theale is intended not only as a final commemoration of the beloved cousin Minny Temple but also as an expiation of the young Henry James's refusal to "reconcile her to a world to which she was essentially hostile," it has to be allowed that the expiation is handsome indeed. The

Jamesian moral passion seems here to reach a pitch, the Jamesian vision of human possibility to acquire a depth and a breadth, which brings it to the edge of the religious. If in the end it remains on this side of the dividing line, the parallels with the religious are nevertheless striking: in the use, to begin with, of the Dove as a central image; but even more in the conception of the tragic conflict as a clash between the powers of light and darkness—between the power of the world, figured in Lancaster Gate, to undermine and destroy the noble and the good, and the power of the good, figured in the person of Milly Theale, to abase the proud by answering it with forgiveness, loving-kindness and sacrificial death.

What is perhaps more masterly than anything else in this master-novel is James's handling of the whole difficult *dénouement* in the last book, which begins with Densher's return to London after the momentous events in Venice and ends with his final parting from Kate Croy. Here Densher is the central figure: it is as if James, having cast him for the part of the male lead to the second leading lady of the drama and kept him strictly subordinate to her up to this point, at last gives him the centre of the stage; and it is wonderful to see how he is "brought out" in the process—how all that before was implicit or only intimated is now made fully explicit, and how this justifies the special kind and quality of interest that Merton Densher had invited from the start.

Viewed palimpsestically,[30] Densher shows most clearly the lineaments of that long and distinguished line of Jamesian heroes "who consecrate by their appreciation," which starts with Roland Mallett in *Roderick Hudson*, includes Ralph Touchett, "little" Hyacinth Robinson (and in some aspects also Nick Dormer), and reaches its apotheosis in Gray Fielder in *The Ivory Tower* and Lambert Strether in *The Ambassadors*. This is James's opening sketch of Densher:

> He was a longish, leanish, fairish young Englishman, not unamenable, on certain sides, to classification—as for instance by being a gentleman, by being rather specifically one of the educated, one of the generally sound and generally civil; yet, though to that degree neither extraordinary nor abnormal, he would have failed to play straight into an observer's hands. He was young for the House of Commons, he was loose for the Army. He was refined, as might have been said, for the

City, and, quite apart from the cut of his cloth, he was skeptical, it might have been felt, for the Church. On the other hand he was credulous for diplomacy, or perhaps even for science, while he was perhaps at the same too much in his mere senses for poetry and yet too little in them for art. You would have got fairly near him by making out in his eyes the potential recognition of ideas . . . [31]

What establishes Densher's place in the brotherhood, we soon learn, is "his weakness for life, his strength merely for thought." Thus, in respect to Kate Croy,

> Merton Densher had repeatedly said to himself—and from far back —that he should be a fool not to marry a woman whose value would be in her differences. . . . Having so often concluded on the fact of his weakness, as he called it, for life—his strength merely for thought— life, he logically opined, was what he must somehow arrange to annex and possess. This was so much a necessity that thought by itself only went on in the void; it was from the immediate air of life that it must draw its breath. So the young man, ingenious but large, critical but ardent too, made out both his case and Kate Croy's.[32]

But what links him with Lambert Strether in particular is the quality of "intellect," as distinct from mere intelligence. Like Strether he is a "writer," a journalist of the superior breed not uncommon, it seems, in James's day; the difference is that in Densher this quality is more integral to the man and more actively important than it ever really is in Strether. It enters intimately, for instance, into his relationship with Kate; she too, on her side, we learn, "had quickly recognised in the young man a precious unlikeness":

> He represented what her life had never given her and certainly, without some such aid as his, never would give her; all the high dim things she lumped together as of the mind. It was on the side of the mind that Densher was rich for her and mysterious and strong; and he had rendered her in especial the sovereign service of making that element real. She had had all her days to take it terribly on trust, no creature she had ever encountered having been able in any degree to testify for it directly. Vague rumours of its existence had made their precarious way to her; but nothing had, on the whole, struck her as more likely than that she should live and die without the chance to verify them. The chance had come—it was an extraordinary one—on the day she first met Densher; and it was to the girl's lasting honour that she knew on the spot what she was in the presence of.[33]

Densher, however, is also over-written with another "line" of Jamesian heroes, which includes some members of the previous line but is distinct from it. This, in the works already discussed, is represented principally by Vanderbank in *The Awkward Age;* and it is to culminate in the Prince in *The Golden Bowl.* As we have already learnt from the case of Van, the common characteristic of this fraternity is its combination of the most engaging personal charm and the most sincere goodwill and good faith with a constitutional dispositon to evade moral issues—or, rather, moral decisions. The weakness is an inseparable part of the charm, goodwill and good faith; and being for this reason so difficult to isolate as a weakness, it is exceedingly dangerous to its victims. In *The Wings of the Dove* Densher has this sacred terror chiefly, of course, for Milly; for Kate it is reinforced by the "intellect" (which is absent in Van) and even more by the passion, the distinctively male quality which is absent in all the Jamesian heroes of this line before Densher.[34]

In any case, it is this moral personality of Merton Densher in which intellect, sensibility and passion co-exist with a fatal moral indecisiveness that is chiefly brought out in Book X. We have, of course, seen it repeatedly before this. We remember Densher at his most Van-like when, at a crucial point in his relationship with Milly when he knows that to call on her alone would commit him irrevocably to Kate's plan, he contrives nevertheless to talk himself into the necessity, the desirability, the simple decency of doing so:

> It wasn't so much that he failed of being the kind of man who "chucked," for he knew himself as the kind of man wise enough to mark the case in which chucking might be the minor evil and the least cruelty. It was that he liked too much everyone concerned willingly to show himself merely impracticable. He liked Kate, goodness knew, and he also clearly enough liked Mrs Lowder. He liked in particular Milly herself; and hadn't it come up for him the evening before that he quite liked even Susan Shepherd? He had never known himself so generally merciful. It was a footing, at all events, whatever accounted for it, on which he would surely be rather a muff not to manage by one turn or another to escape disobliging.[35]

The moral indecisiveness appears conspicuously at another crucial point in the story when, reflecting on the fearful implications of Kate's design in one of his interior monologues, Densher explicitly recognises that so far as he was concerned, "Kate's design was something so extraordinarily special to Kate that he felt himself shrink from the complications involved in judging it." [36] In Book X, however, these characteristics expose themselves most fully because tested in the most challenging situation of Densher's life. There accordingly we have Vanderbank writ large; there James "goes behind" his hero as he did not in *The Awkward Age,* and as a consequence brings to light new facets of the type, of its graces and virtues equally with its weaknesses, which in the end make Densher one of the principal triumphs of the book. The chief of the new facets disclosed is, we shall see, the sustained self-deception that a man like Densher is capable of when life thrusts upon him an experience that demands a total reorientation of his previous attitudes and beliefs; and this extraordinary power of self-deception, though a function of the moral weakness, is shown to be at the same time a function of his developed moral sensibility (his "conscience"), his intelligence, his charm and his passion.

The anatomy of Merton Densher actually begins before the opening of Book X when he is left alone in Venice to bring Kate's scheme to its consummation and finds himself, suddenly, portentously, and at first unaccountably, denied access to Milly. As he wanders about in the cold lashing rain, he sees Lord Mark sitting in Florian's, guesses what has happened, and is at first stricken. But presently:

> His business, he had settled . . . was to keep thoroughly still; and he asked himself why it should prevent this that he could feel, in connexion with the crisis, so remarkably blameless. He gave the appearances before him all the benefit of being critical, so that if blame were to accrue he shouldn't feel he had dodged it. But it wasn't a bit he who, that day, had touched her [Milly], and if she was upset it wasn't a bit his act. The ability so to think about it amounted for Densher during several hours to a kind of exhilaration. The exhilaration was heightened fairly, besides, by the visible conditions—sharp, striking, ugly to him—of Lord Mark's return. . . . He didn't need, for seeing it as evil, seeing it as, to a certainty, in a high degree "nasty," to know more about it than he had so easily and so wonderfully picked up. You couldn't drop on the poor girl that way without, by the fact, being brutal. Such a visit was a descent, an invasion, an aggression, constituting precisely one or other of the stupid shocks that he himself had so decently sought to spare her. Densher had indeed drifted by the next morning to the reflection . . . that the only delicate and honourable way

of treating a person in such a state was to treat her as *he*, Merton Densher, did. With time, actually—for the impression but deepened —this sense of the contrast, to the advantage of Merton Densher, became a sense of relief, and that in turn a sense of escape.[37]

He cannot, of course, sustain this mood of "exhilaration," and accordingly, a few chapters on, when he meets Sir Luke Strett who has just come away from Milly, finds the sweetest consolation in Sir Luke's complete and (as Densher interprets it) gentlemanly abstention from any reference to Milly or Milly's condition or Densher's relation to her:

> He had hoped for it, had sat in his room there waiting for it, because he had thus divined in it, should it come, some power to let him off. He was *being* let off; dealt with in the only way that didn't aggravate his responsibility. The beauty was also that this wasn't on system or any basis of intimate knowledge; it was just by being a man of the world and by knowing life, by feeling the real, that Sir Luke did him good. There had been in all the case too many women. A man's sense of it, another man's, changed the air; and he wondered what man, had he chosen, would have been more to his purpose than this one. He was large and easy—that was the benediction; he knew what mattered and what didn't; he distinguished between the essence and the shell, the just grounds and the unjust for fussing.[38]

Sir Luke, however, just before he boards his train, tells him that Milly has asked to see him, and Book IX ends with Densher arriving at the palace for the last fateful interview.

The first line of Book X inform us that Densher has been back in London for a fortnight and has only just called to see Kate at Lancaster Gate. The colloquy that follows confirms this first hint of the abyss that has opened between Kate and Densher as a result of his last interview with Milly. Yet throughout the scene (we are told) Kate's beauty, high sobriety and exquisite self-command have lost none of their power for him; on the contrary, with the memory of the consummation of their passion in Venice still un-forgettably present to his mind, they inspire in him a joy, pride, tenderness and gratitude greater than ever before; and it is this, we soon perceive, as in all the succeeding scenes between them, that pulls against his growing knowledge of the change in their relation-ship, perpetually threatening it with extinction.

But the knowledge does come, against all resistance. In the course of their first meeting, Densher tells Kate that it was Lord

Mark's visit that had made Milly turn her face to the wall. Kate instantly asks him why he did not deny what Lord Mark had told Milly:

> "To tell her he lied?" [asks Densher].
> "To tell her he's mistaken" [answers Kate].
> Densher stared—he was stupefied: the "possible" thus glanced at by Kate being exactly the alternative he had had to face in Venice and to put utterly away from him. Nothing was stranger than such a difference in their view of it. . . . Of course, it was to be remembered, she had always simplified, and it brought back his sense of the degree in which, to her energy as compared with his own, many things were easy; the very sense that so often before had moved him to admiration. "Well, if you must know—and I want you to be clear about it—I didn't even seriously think of a denial to her face. The question of it—*as* possibly saving her—was put to me definitely enough; but to turn it over was only to dismiss it. Besides," he added, "it wouldn't have done any good." [39]

What this discloses, among other things, is Densher's special kind of "stupidity"—the intellectual counterpart, so to speak, of his moral weakness of which we are to have repeated evidence in Book X. Why, if he knows Kate (as by this time he has every reason to know her), should he "stare" and be "stupefied" by her suggesting something that is perfectly consistent with the grand scheme in which, up to that point, he had actively participated, and is also, granted the validity of the scheme (which he *had* implicitly granted), perfectly reasonable and "moral"—at any rate as reasonable and moral as any of the other consequences of Kate's scheme that he had previously assented to? The answer, or one part of it, is that his mind, here as elsewhere, is as confused and self-contradictory as Kate's is clear and rigorously self-consistent; that his right hand appears not to know what his left is doing; and that he is as "stupid" in this as Kate is in her tendency to "simplify."

But what we are also expected to see is that this stupidity, though present in Densher from the beginning, is now, since the shattering experience of his last meeting with Milly, acutely intensified by the bitter remorse, grief and horror with which the experience has impressed him. He is here so confused and contradictory because, still wanting Kate and still needing therefore to persuade himself that he remains loyal to her and her design, he will not recognise that he has, since he was "forgiven, dedicated, blessed" by Milly Theale, totally repudiated the dreadful design and with it Kate herself. And that is why in this scene he "stares" and is "stupefied" at Kate's suggestion. It is his way of trying, characteristically, to have his cake and eat it: at once to remain loyal to Kate and to repudiate her design—an endeavour in which he is defeated, as we learn in the last line of the book, by Kate's implacable clear-headedness and consistency. This in fact is the *leitmotif* of the whole of Book X: to show Densher, on his side, as incorrigibly confused and inconsistent, and persistently—literally to the last line of the book—refusing to acknowledge with his mind what he has recognised with his moral sensibility, that his last meeting with Milly has made a radical alteration in his relationship with Kate; while Kate, on her side, is shown to be totally deficient in moral sensibility in having to the end no knowledge of what Densher's transforming experience might have been (and probably no great curiosity to know), yet being perfectly clear and self-consistent throughout, and capable both of inferring accurately from the minimal signs she receives what the experience has done to him and of drawing the inescapable conclusions—in particular the most inescapable, that "we shall never be again as we were."

If the principal interest of Book X is this gradual, painful disclosure of the differences between Kate Croy and Merton Densher who had seemed such a mutual pair, what makes it especially instructive and poignant is the further disclosure that the differences had been there from the beginning, had previously been obscured by their common participation in the life of the world, but had now been brought to light by the spiritual crisis created for Densher by Milly Theale's extraordinary act of loving kindness. And this (the religious would say) is the characteristic effect of the irruption of the divine order into the natural. It pierces through the appearances, exposing to view the reality that lies beneath—the real identities and differences constituting the natural order; and by the sheer truth of its revelation in the end commands the obedience of those who have received it.

On the view of *The Wings of the Dove* proposed in this chapter, this, or something like it, would seem to be the ultimate meaning of the theme of Book X. If this is the meaning, the power and authority with which it is enunciated is due entirely to James's art —which here, as elsewhere, succeeds in projecting the theme as fully articulated drama. As in *The Awkward Age* and all the works of the late period, the style re-creates or re-enacts the succession of minute steps, each by itself barely cognisable, by which the momentous alteration is effected: Densher's flashes of recognition alternating with his withdrawals and evasions;[40] the stresses and tensions that hover all the time below the surface of their mutual consideration, admiration, enjoyment; and towards the end, when their suppressed knowledge can barely any longer be held down, the delicate, desperate subterfuges to which they resort in the effort to hide from themselves what is happening. And, with all this and in spite of it, we also have conveyed to us a powerful sense of the bond of passion that still holds them together right to the end. It is expressed in their essential candour with each other through all the subterfuges and evasions, in their loyalty to each other, and in a kind of toughness or resiliency, which is the ulti-mate expression of their marvellous vitality, and succeeds—as in *Antony and Cleopatra*—in turning, or almost turning, their final defeat into a triumph. The effect, if one follows the process closely enough, is as overwhelming as it is in *Antony and Cleopatra*, and leaves one with the same sense of an affirmation of life so powerful as to transcend the proper limits of tragedy.

But the tragic is there, whether or not *The Wings of the Dove* as a whole is to be accounted a tragedy. It makes its unmistakable impact in those moments when the suppressed disharmonies, misunderstandings, hostilities gathering between them momen-tarily break the surface: when at their first meeting, for instance, Densher tells Kate that he could not have denied to Milly what Lord Mark had told her "only to take it back afterwards," and Kate, "her colour flaming" as she grasps his meaning, replies "You would have broken with me to make your denial a truth? You would have 'chucked' me to save your conscience?" [41] Or when, in a later scene, having listened to Kate's explanation of Lord Mark's presence in London, Densher remarks "You see in everything, and you always did, something that, while I'm with you at least, I always take from you as the truth itself," and Kate, "consciously and even carefully extracting the sting of his reserva-tion," presently answers ("with a quiet gravity") "Thank you." [42] Again the sense of a marriage of true minds irreparably shattered is never stronger than in the passage in which we learn of Den-sher's secret, silent grieving over the unread letter that Milly wrote him before she died;[43] and it is perhaps most poignant in the moment in which Densher perceives how "damned civil" he and Kate are being to each other, and how their passion is now a way not of showing but of concealing their knowledge of each other, expressing "the need to bury in the dark blindness of each other's arms the knowledge of each other that they couldn't undo." [44] When one remembers the beauty and the freshness of that early scene in Kensington Gardens when Kate pledged him every spark of her faith, every drop of her life, and he responded with breathed words and murmured sounds and lighted eyes,[45] it is hardly possible to question the tragic intention of the denouement; it remains only to admire again the way in which James succeeds in suggesting a redemption of the suffering and loss by the saving power of a human passion reinforced by courage, dignity, intelligence, and good faith.

NOTES

1 Jacques Barzun, "Henry James, Melodramatist," in *The Question of Henry James*, ed. F. W. Dupee, 1947.

2 Mrs. Stringham, the former Boston journalist who is now Milly's confidante and handmaiden, may be seen, partly at least, as a fresh and more complex version of Henrietta Stackpole in *The Portrait of a Lady*.

3 *The Wings of the Dove*, I, iii, 1, p. 95.

4 *Ibid.*, I, iv, 2, p. 154.

5 *Ibid.*, I, iv, 2, p. 156.

6 *Ibid.*, I, v, 2, p. 194.

7 *Ibid.*, I, iv, 1, p. 147.

8 *Ibid.*, I, iv, 2, pp. 160-61.

9 *Ibid.*, I, v, 6, pp. 243-44.

10 *Ibid.*, I, v, 6, pp. 244-45, 247-48.

11 *Ibid.*, I, v, 7, p. 265.

12 In view of the displayed intelligence of Milly Theale, it is astonishing indeed to learn that such a critic as Marius Bewley finds her "stupid," and another, F. R. Leavis, both stupid and "embarrassingly sentimental." One can only guess at the kind of reading of *The Wings of the Dove* that could issue in such judgements; but surely it must have been literal-minded to a degree no serious reading of the later James can afford to be.

13 See below, p. 256.

14 *The Wings of the Dove*, I, iii, 1.

15 *Ibid.*, I, v, 4, p. 225.

16 The phrase is virtually used at one point in Milly's meditation in Regent's Park after her second visit to the doctor (*The Wings of the Dove*, I, v, 4, pp. 227-28).

17 *Ibid.*, I, v, 2, pp. 195-96.

18 *Ibid.*, I, v, 2, pp. 200-01.

19 *Ibid.*, I, v, 4, pp. 227-28.

20 *Ibid.*, II, vi, 4, pp. 48-49.

21 Readers of Mr Lionel Trilling's novel *The Middle of the Journey* will remember that the immunity of the strong and healthy to the experience of death and dying is one of its principal themes, and is handled by Mr Trilling with a penetration and a delicacy that one likes to think James would have admired.

22 *The Wings of the Dove*, I, iii, 1, pp. 110-13.

23 *Ibid.*, II, vii, 1, p. 99.

24 *The Wings of the Dove*, II, vii, 1, pp. 107-08. One of the richest, subtlest strokes of the Jamesian irony occurs in the scene between Mrs Lowder and Mrs Stringham in which the two ladies settle the futures of their respective "girls." Having exhibited to Mrs Stringham (and to us) the breathtaking scope of her machiavellian diplomacy, and having concluded her "beautiful" pact with Mrs Stringham—that she, Mrs Lowder, will help her, Mrs Stringham's, girl Milly to get what she wants, *viz.* Densher, if she, Mrs Stringham, in turn will help her, Mrs Lowder's, girl Kate *not* to get what she wants, *viz.* again Densher—Mrs Lowder pronounces their pawn Densher to be "charming" nevertheless; and then, reflectively, and with perfect seriousness and sincerity, throws out the aside which explains the pious principle on which she has acted and the renunciations she has made for its sake. "One lives for others," she says to Mrs Stringham. "*You* do that. If I were living for myself I shouldn't at all mind him. . . . Of course he's all right in himself." (*Ibid.*, II, vii, 1, p. 107).

25 *Ibid.*, I, ii, 1, p. 66.

26 *Ibid.*, II, viii, 3, p. 203.

27 *Ibid.*, II, x, 2, pp. 304-05.

28 *Ibid.*, II, x, 6, pp. 358-59.

29 This is the phrase used by James to describe the religious spirit of his father, the elder Henry James (*Notes of a Son and Brother*, ch. 6, p. 335).

30 Cp. p. 246 above.

31 *The Wings of the Dove*, I, ii, 1, p. 44.

32 *Ibid.*, I, ii, 1, pp. 46-47.

33 *Ibid.*, I, ii, 1, p. 46.

34 It is present only in the rough-diamond heroes, like Basil Ransom in *The Bostonians* and Caspar Goodwood in *The Portrait of a Lady*. That Densher has the "sacred terror" for Milly is clearly intimated in the scene of the luncheon party at Milly's hotel after her meeting with Densher and Kate in

the National Gallery when she grieves secretly over his, too, having "the view" of her (see p. 255 above), and recognises that "whatever he did or he didn't, [she] knew she should still like him—there was no alternative to that." (I, v, 7, pp. 264-65). It is powerfully confirmed by Kate at the end when she says to Densher, "She never wanted the truth. She wanted *you*. She would have taken from you what you could give her, and been glad of it, even if she had known it false. You might have lied to her from pity, and she have seen you and felt you lie, and yet—since it was all for tenderness—she would have thanked you and blessed you and clung to you but the more. For that was your strength . . . —that she loves you with passion." (II, x, 1, p. 291).

35 *The Wings of the Dove*, II, vi, 5, p. 63.

36 *Ibid.*, II, vi, 5, p. 68.

37 *Ibid.*, II, ix, 2, pp. 236-37.

38 *Ibid.*, II, ix, 4, p. 271.

39 *Ibid.*, II, x, 1, pp. 287-88.

40 For instance, when Densher feels at one point "a horror, almost of her [Kate's] lucidity," but by the end of the scene finds that she still "prevented irresistibly . . . the waste of his passion" (II, x, 1, p. 311); or when he finds himself tacitly acquiescing in Mrs Lowder's view of him as "the stricken suitor of another person," and spending more and more time with her because she does not know the truth and less and less with Kate because she does know it (II, x, 2, pp. 298 ff.).

41 *The Wings of the Dove*, II, x, 1, p. 290.

42 *Ibid.*, II, x, 5, p. 336.

43 *Ibid.*, II, x, 6, pp. 350-51.

44 *Ibid.*, II, x, 6, p. 347.

45 *Ibid.*, I, ii, 2, pp. 85-86.

"The Wings of the Dove"

LAURENCE B. HOLLAND*

I

It was not till afterwards that, going back to it, I was to read into
[Kate's] speech a kind of heroic ring, a note of a character that
belittled [Densher's] own incapacity for action. Yet he saw indeed
even at the time the greatness of knowing so well what one
wanted." The quoted sentences, drawing attention to the heroism
of one character (Kate Croy) and comparing it to the passivity of
the novel's hero (Kate's fiancé, Merton Densher), occur at the
height of the scene which constitutes the drama of *The Wings of
the Dove* by bringing the novel's crisis to its culmination and at the
same time providing the basis for its resolution. At so crucial a
point, James speaks, in the first American edition, for the only
time when his voice emerges in the first person to help bring an
important matter, Kate's heroism, into definite focus; Densher's
ready admiration for her at the time enforces a tribute felt later but
openly by James. In the first English edition as in the subsequent
New York collection, the "I" is replaced by "he," whether because
James detected a typographer's error, corrected his own mistake,
or decided on second thought to substitute one form of expression
for another.[1] In any case, the "muffled majesty of authorship" and
the entire insight into Kate's heroism are delegated in the revisions

*From THE EXPENSE OF VISION by Laurence B. Holland. Copyright 1964 by Prince-
ton University Press. Reprinted by permission of the author and the publisher.

to Densher—his "bland Hermes," as James was to call him in the preface, the god of theft and commerce who gave Apollo his lyre.[2] In all versions the tribute to Kate helps to define the novel's form by straining it, in an effort to encompass both a prospective and a retrospective view, so as to define an act of confession of which the quoted sentences are part. (II, 226).

The act of looking ahead or anticipating the completion of the action and the act of reconsidering it in memory, whether performed ostensibly by James or ostensibly by Densher, are joined in a tribute to Kate's heroism at the moment when she has expressed a willingness to " 'do what I don't like' " in encouraging her own fiancé to marry a dying and wealthy American girl, Milly Theale. James's intervention at this point to pay tribute to Kate, in the unrevised version, would implicate him explicitly in the plot, thus associating him intimately with Kate's and Densher's deed. But the tribute assigned wholly to Densher in the revision is a degree of consciousness and conscience *imputed* to him by James, and it is likewise an effort to confess James's responsibility for the action and to confess as well his form's involvement in the action and his intimate involvement with his medium.

The narrative convention of *The Wings of the Dove* is founded on neither the author's voice alone nor on the center of consciousness alone but on the intimate connection between them, on the shared burden and responsibility which the narrative's gestures confess; it is articulated consistently and frequently, in all versions, when the narrative momentarily reveals James's presence in such carefully unobtrusive phrases as "I say" or "our analysis," "our young lady" and "our subject." Being the very image of the vicarious imagination, the narrative exercises authority by delegating authority and confessing responsibility for it, and the scene which includes the tribute to Kate's heroism twice reveals explicitly, then again veils, James's presence in the phrase "we know."[3] (I, 275, 141, 157; II, 204, 222.)

James's emergence intermittently in the first person is paradoxically both a lapse or flaw in the "guarded objectivity" of his drama and the fulfillment of its logic as a novel which builds, as the preface was to point out, on its own failure. His acknowledgment of the role of narrator, the pretentious "majesty of authorship," is the flaw in his form and a questionable commitment, matching that of Kate and Densher, which must be answered and redeemed. Yet it articulates also James's confession of his commitment. But James's confessed presence is revealed more profoundly, in all versions, in the projected *action* of the scene, for what Kate and Densher do on that occasion—what they do for James—is to "suit the action to the word, the word to the action" of James's novel by agreeing to enact its plot, with Kate forcing Densher to put her plan into words and then joining him in the phrasing of it. Moreover James's complicity and the involvement of his form are revealed implicitly also in the rendering of other characters who are James's instruments and who contribute along with Kate and Densher to the plot. Indeed, the very behavior of language itself as an instrument is revealed to be one of the sources of the novel's tragic vision.

If it inheres in the very nature of a language, as Santayana has written, that it gives "perspective" to experience but in that act also "vitiates the experience it expresses," the "kindly infidelities" of language, as Santayana called them, define the verbal action which mediates the tragic vision of *The Wings of the Dove:*[4] the behavior of a medium which at once expresses and betrays its subject or vision and accordingly is inseparable, in *The Wings of the Dove*, from the tragic action it renders. The novel's language is shaped by three principal vocabularies—one commercial, one religious, and one aesthetic—which are defined by characteristic metaphors or phrases: for instance, the phrase "a capital case" which a doctor uses to describe the dying and wealthy heroine; or the description of doves who are "picking up the crumbs of perpetual feasts" in the square before a Christian church in Venice; or the description of the heroine as "embodied poetry." Each of the phrases, and each of the larger vocabularies of which it is part, helps define the novel's relevance to the actual world beyond it— to the institutions, attitudes, formulations of value, and forms that comprise the culture of capitalism, or the Judaeo-Christian tradition, or the fine arts. But the field of relevance they define is a field of behavior in which they act, not a safely remote and independent realm of actualities to which they refer, and the language functions so as to draw the practices and values it suggests *into* the "crucible" of the imagination and into the fictive action, to include them in the world it creates, and, conversely, to bring the "penetrating imagination" into an intimate encounter with its materials, the actualities in the world of which it is part.

The consequence is that the language, as an instrument, is subject not only to all the pressures which have already endowed it with the conventional implications that it brings into the novel but to the pressures it undergoes as the mediating instrument of James's imagination. Its behavior is far from the "merely referential" function which James was to disparage in the preface to *The Ambassadors*, in being at once more anxious or apprehensive and more powerful. It is closer rather to the exploratative maneuvers he attributed to himself, as a "wary adventurer," in the preface to *The Wings of the Dove*, "standing off" from the "situation" of the wealthy dying girl, but then "coming back to it," walking "round and round" the "case" that "invited and mystified" his fascination.[5] The language does not so much stipulate its meanings or describe its action as *suspend* them in a mode which is epitomized by the novel's opening sentences, where Kate Croy's hesitation between departing or remaining, between going away or staying to see and help her father, presents the first version of the novel's central action and its basic rhythm. The paleness, the waiting, and the decision to stay, here touched on for the first time, are crucial motives in the novel, and the opening sentences virtually postpone Kate's decision to remain, suspending it in tension with the temptation to go away so as to evade a confrontation with her father, while literally pausing and lingering over her name, the detail of the mirror above the mantel, and her momentarily pale face: "She waited, Kate Croy, for her father to come in, but he kept her unconscionably, and there were moments when she showed herself, in the glass over the mantel, a face positively pale with the irritation that had brought her to the point of going away without sight of him. It was at this point, however, that she remained. . . ." (I, 3.)

While the language, in this dramatic suspension, both expresses and betrays its subject, rendering it by approaching it but holding off from it, the prose serves the several functions that are paramount for James's art and govern his characters as well as his language. The prose can be as intimate and compressed in its irony for James as it is for Kate, with her desire when talking of her family's predicament "to work off, for her own relief, her constant perception of the incongruity of things," and to devise, for intimate conversation with her fiancé, a shorthand of "fantastic" phrases and "the happy language of exaggeration," exaggerations which constitute their intimacy and manage to be more true than the less intimate make-believe which they indulge in public. In its analytic probing the prose risks the cruelty of exposure which Kate fears when she learns that she might be written up in a book: " 'Chop me up fine or serve me whole'—it was a way of being got at that Kate professed she dreaded." Yet if it is intimate in its devious exaggerations and painfully close in its exposure of the characters it depicts, the language is, nevertheless, conspicuously restrained even when subservient to James's analytic strategy, as when sheer observation of the ailing heroine becomes a risky adventure for her hired traveling companion, Mrs. Susan Stringham, whose watchful care is dangerous and is inseparable from the reader's and James's own. She knows that she would not (or at least "shouldn't") *lunge* at the girl in her efforts to keep track of her and watch for symptoms of her illness, but she has "almost the sense of tracking her young friend as if at a given moment to pounce" and fears that her aid is "secretive" that her "observation" is "scientific." She fears that she is "hovering like a spy, applying tests, laying traps, concealing signs," and while she continues to do this nevertheless, satisfied because "to watch" is "a way of clinging to the girl" and gives access to her "beauty," she does so with the tact of reticence and with restraint. The same probing analysis which risks exposing or chopping up Kate, and spying on or trapping Milly, is, in its restraint, a measure of solicitude and care. (I, 65-66; II, 46; I, 117.)

So infused is the language itself with the creative aim it serves and the drama it projects that it becomes at once a rich resource and a virtual fate, endangering and enclosing its subject in the very act of focusing loving attention on it, intimating what lies beyond its vocabularies but failing to free itself from them. The novel distinguishes the heroine's doctor's services from exclusively commercial ones, for instance, but does so in terms which remain distinctly pecuniary: "Sir Luke had appeared indeed to speak of purchase and payment, but in reference to a different sort of cash. Those were amounts not to be named or reckoned, and such moreover as [Milly] wasn't sure of having at her command." Whether because it clings perversely to the terminology of cash when it might try to abandon it, or because it dramatizes by that means art's inescapable dependence on its medium and the "kindly infidelities" which are unavoidable necessities inhering in the nature of language, the prose creates the very possibility of the impending tragedy, prepares the very "fallibility" James was to speak of in the preface as the foundation of artistic mastery, the failure of beguiling intentions which is made part of the very creative process and helps stage the destruction and transformation through wastage—in sum, the tragedy—of Milly Theale. (II, 142.)

The "amounts" not "named" or "reckoned" and the failure to name and reckon them are so central to the tragedy that the "kindly infidelities" of words, the verbal drama suspended in the movement of the prose, virtually defines the plot of the novel, when Densher tries to define in his own case the relations among words and action and inaction, telling a lie and "acting it out," telling the truth and keeping it secret. He decides that truth and candor inhere only in naming the names and declaring the reckoning, in openly "speaking the particular word," and that measured by this standard, any behavior short of it—silences, verbal evasions, and inaction as well as overt action—is "acting" in the sense of histrionic illusion or affectation, and that such "acting" in his case makes him responsible for acting out a lie. Accordingly, the very sentences which suspend, postpone, and prolong their import and action, the "kindly infidelities" of the prose which hovers "round and round" its subject in a verbal drama and holds off from naming and reckoning, are, in their style, part of the very drama they help enact. Indeed, the "particular word" that Densher speaks of is a secret that is crucial for the novel's plot—the fact that Kate still is in love with Densher—and Densher goes on to pledge himself to continued silence out of loyalty to Kate and a consequent loyalty to her "design," a design which at that point in the novel has not been fully divulged to Densher, has not been made explicit to the reader, and *may* not even be fully formulated yet by Kate. But that emerging "design" is crucial in James's novel, for it is his own plot which, along with the prose, helps to project the tragic action. It helps to create the design and the movement which James was to call, in the preface to *The Ambassadors*, the full "process of vision," the firm "march" of his novel's "action."[6] (II, 76-77.)

II

The plot has one origin in the fact that Kate and Densher, the English writer she loves, have not enough money to marry. Nor can they get help from Kate's wealthy Aunt Maud, a philistine social climber who will share her money only if Kate marries the impecunious aristocrat Lord Mark. For obvious reasons, Kate's widowed sister and ruined father want her to please her rich aunt, and Densher's meager salary provides no satisfactory alternative. Accordingly, Kate, whose family "piety" is genuine and whose assessment of her predicament is astute, resorts with Densher to a familiar strategy of deception, a secret engagement. Kate will pretend to oblige Maud, to favor Mark, and to remain indifferent to Densher while she and her fiancé wait out their secret engagement in hope of winning all of Maud's consent and at least some of her cash. (I, 71.)

Much later Kate stumbles on an unexpected opportunity in the novel's heroine Milly Theale, a young American orphan who is fabulously rich and who seems, and later proves, to be dying. Kate alters her scheme so as to do justice not only to the need for deceiving Maud and acquiring money but to the genuine pity and affection she feels for her friend. She will induce Densher to be friendly with Milly, helping with his attentions to give Milly the strength to live. Milly will be encouraged, through Maud and Susan, to think that Kate is not interested in Densher. Then Kate will induce Densher to pay court to her and marry the dying girl. Though there is a risk that Densher might genuinely fall in love with Milly and that Milly might live, Kate makes the gamble: Milly will die; Densher will inherit her cash; he and Kate can marry.

As enterprising schemes have a way of doing, this one works, even though it is threatened twice by contingencies Kate had not anticipated or had hoped to avoid. One is Densher's demand, to which she consents, that she pay for his cooperation by sleeping with him. The second is Mark's shrewd guess that Kate and Densher are engaged, a fact he reveals to Milly in hope of gaining her hand and her purse for himself: in his unthinking crudeness he precipitates her death. But Milly has come to love Densher, she agrees to see him before going away, she forgives him in a letter and bequeathes him a fortune when she dies. In the last chapters,

Kate and Densher confront the fortune which has become for them, as it became for Milly, a tragic destiny.

That portentous destiny is established as an immanent possibility in the earliest elaborations of the plot, the early configurations which ominously, however tentatively, sound the note of bargaining, bankruptcy, and sacrifice. All but vulgar and forceful Aunt Maud (she is "Britannia of the market-place," secure as a "lioness" in the "cage" that is her "counting-house") are shown to be rootless and insecure in the social environment James labels "middle-class." Kate's widowed sister, pinching pennies with her four "greasy children" in grubby quarters, has shown that marriage for love can be like being squeezed through a funnel. Though Kate's penniless and shifty father seems "the fortunate settled normal person," he deals out lies like cards from a "greasy old pack"; Kate can virtually taste the sordidness, the " 'something wicked' " which his late wife made a successful secret of, his "failure of fortune and of honor." (I, 30, 174, 65, 7-8, 67, 4.)

His faked pretense of willingness to sacrifice himself for his daughter's advancement introduces one of the novel's earliest motifs of sacrifice, as does indeed his name Croy, which Kate feels to be a "bleeding wound." In the first chapter Kate is genuinely willing to sacrifice herself to help her father, and even when he spurns the offered gift the prospect of sacrifice still threatens. Haunted and menaced by her relatives, in their eyes a commodity or "tangible value" that is "chalk-marked for the auction," Kate likens herself "to a trembling kid" being saved to feed her aunt, and she reflects "that the more you gave yourself the less of you was left. There were always people to snatch at you, and it would never occur to *them* that they were eating you up. They did that without tasting." In one argumentative conversation about whom she should marry, Kate can be reduced to denying "everything and every one," even, as a conversational gambit, to "paying with the sacrifice of Mr. Densher." (I, 6, 32, 9, 6, 30, 33, 44.)

If the language of feasting and auctions suggests the possibilities that threaten in Kate's world, so does the vocabulary of the arts. Maud's furnishings are vulgar "signs and symbols" which "syllabled [Densher's] hostess' story." Lionel Croy's letter to Kate announcing that he is too sick to leave his room and asking help is called "the sketch of a design" lacking even "the moderate finish required for deception." Densher's journalistic mission to America (when he first meets Milly Theale) is called "parenthesis" in an otherwise ordinary "sentence" on "a great grey page of print." Indeed, Kate lives not only in Chelsea and Kensington but in the space defined by a virtually Faulknerian sentence which is nevertheless the medium of James's own syntax: Kate's family "history . . . had the effect of some fine florid voluminous phrase, say even a musical, that dropped first into words and notes without sense and then, hanging unfinished, into no words nor any notes at all." With her admirable determination, she plans to survive even the test of Jamesian prose: "She hadn't given up yet, and the broken sentence, if she was the last word, *would* end with a sort of meaning." (I, 76, 6; II, 11; I, 4, 6.)

Kate will have the novel's last word, but she can scarcely anticipate that with certainty on page six. The tempest that rumbles in Aunt Maud's world threatens also within the contrivances of a magician-artist. No wonder that Kate hopes, by her strategy of deception, to avoid for herself, her family, and Densher the sacrifice that threatens: " 'I shall sacrifice nobody and nothing, and that's just my situation, that I want and that I shall try for everything.' " No wonder that the rootless engaged couple, each raised as a child on the Continent by transient impecunious families, should have acquired what Kate recognizes as most highly developed in Densher: the "religion of foreign things." One wonders only at the "process of vision," the "march of the action," when the foreigner from America with her ample checkbook, her hunger for cultivation and affection, and her strange beauty descends into the broken sentences of James's novel and onto Aunt Maud's London; there, in search of a doctor, she takes her place in Kate's design. (I, 73, 92.)

It is at this point that the novel extends the range and renders more precise the evocations of its medium, speaking more frequently now of imagined realms, of "imagination" and "fancy" and "legend" associated with Milly. It begins to focus on the realm in which her "New York history" and her "New York legend" coalesce, namely her manner. It is the medium of forms which both reveals and shapes her character, because the manner is created in response to inner pressures of will, moral intent, and aspiration and outer pressures of decorum, social accommodation, and moral strictures. There are four components in Milly's manner, merely acquired at first but then possessed more consciously and used articulately in the course of the novel's development. (I, 104-106.)

One of these (and one of civilization's most problematic creations) is her money, a symbol always of the economic power it represents, in this case power which Milly simply inherited as the " 'survivor of a general wreck,' " pecuniary power which is the speaking record of its sources, "the record" namely "of used-up relatives, parents, clever eager fair slim brothers . . . all engaged . . . in a high extravagance of speculation and dissipation that had left this exquisite being her black dress, her white face and her vivid hair as the mere last broken link. . . ." As all can see who notice her clothes and other visible signs of her affluence, Milly is an " 'angel with a thumping bank-account,' " and as her companion Susan knows, "the girl couldn't get away from her wealth," she "couldn't have lost it if she had tried." On one occasion the costly pearls she could afford to purchase are acknowledged to lend something to her "style." (I, 241, 174; II, 51; I, 121; II, 217.)

To be so clearly the " 'capital case' " is, as her doctor recognizes, to be the American, and Milly is imaged as an explorer and adventurer, at once naïve and empirical. Wanting in culture, odd looking and new, she is the "potential heiress of all the ages" that it took Europe centuries to produce—the American, that is, of history and legend whom Densher calls simply "the American girl" and whom the novel renders in terms of "spontaneity" and simplicity, with her way of doing always "the natural thing." (I, 242, 109; II, 215; I, 295-296.)

Yet this simplicity of temperament and manner is a formed one and comes to be the cultivated and artful one of a civilized showpiece. When on display at Lord Mark's party or in the National Gallery, she displays the "bland stare" of conventional society that she has learned to adopt, and a "glassy lustre of attention" as a social conversationalist. As she looks over the ornamental objects in her doctor's office while waiting for him, she wonders what gift she will give him in gratitude, and imagines that she should be "one of the circle of eminent contemporaries, photographed, engraved, signatured, and in particular framed and glazed, who made up the rest of the decoration." The girl who may one day hang in this office behind glass is later referred to as "embodied poetry." She is imaged as a cloistered princess of Byzantium, an image as stylized, as rigidly two-dimensional as the courtly figures against a gilt background in the Ravenna mosaics that the novel mentions. (I, 219, 301, 237; II, 217; I, 256.)

To have one's place like the Empress Theodora in the Ravenna mosaics, however, is to have a place in a church, and Milly's manner is that of a cloistered princess and an object of worship in a world of ceremonious decorum, in a novel where offices and houses are called temples and Kate's hoped-for marriage with Densher is called "a temple" without a street running up to it. Milly at one time is imaged as a communicant, at another as "a priestess." When she is first introduced, sitting on a ledge overlooking a valley in the Alps, her calm self-possession is likened to Christ's in the face of Satan's demand that he prove his divinity by leaping from the steeple or Satan's tempting offer of the kingdoms of the earth; her companion, Susan, is relieved to find that Milly was not driven by some "horrible hidden obsession" to commit "suicide" in a "flying leap" and that if she was overlooking the "kingdoms of the earth" it was because she felt no intention of "renouncing them" but, already in a state of "unlimited possession," was prepared to accept the "human predicament" and take "full in the face the whole assault of life." Kate declares very early that " 'we all adore you' " and recognizes Milly as a dove, calling her a dove "not with familiarity or as a liberty taken, but almost ceremonially as in the manner of an *accolade.*" (I, 241; II, 146; I, 59; II, 135; I, 123-125, 228, 283.)

While these are the patterns of Milly's manner, bestowed by her past and by Kate's naming of them, Milly's way of acting with them is equally part of the manner. The phrase for this is given in connection with the empirical procedure and comforting bedside manner of her doctor, Sir Luke. Milly notices that he gives her no facts about her illness, and that he is perpetrating a "beautiful beneficent dishonesty" in pretending to be her friend; but she senses also that, when he assures her she will not suffer " 'a bit,' " he is probably trying to "let the patient down easily" in his mission to the doomed, that he is " 'acting,' as they said at home, as if she did matter" medically, acting as if she were seriously ill. (I, 252, 240, 246, 253.)

And *acting as if,* or playing a role, characterizes precisely Milly's conduct. With the motifs of wealth so clearly, if tastefully, a part of her, she begins to act the part. She had to begin with "no manner at all" about her money; unlike Maud who sits "in the midst of her money" and had a clever "high manner about it," Milly sits on the frontier of her fortune and one can "get at her nature" without having to cross "any piece of her property." But the anticipation that Milly might eventually acquire a "motive" in using her money and that "then she might very well have, like Aunt Maud, a manner" is fulfilled when Milly begins to think consciously of her money, begins to measure its impact on others, and plans finally to use it to buy her rented palace in Venice as a last "counter-move to fate." Also, she begins to look and act the part of the spontaneous American, sounding at will "her own native woodnote" in making conversation with Densher: "She still had reserves of spontaneity . . . so that all this cash in hand could now find employment. She became as spontaneous as possible and as American as it might conveniently appeal to Mr. Densher . . . to find her." When she sees the conventional "bland" stare of polite society, she adopts it. (I, 196-197; II, 142; I, 295-296.)

When, finally, Kate calls her a dove, Milly adopts it as "the revealed truth. . . . *That* was the matter with her. She was a dove. Oh, *wasn't* she? " And she "studied . . . the dovelike," beginning to act out the role named for her by Kate. She'll be kind, she'll protect her friends' interests and feelings, even by telling lies. Chiefly she does this by the lie that her health is better than she feels it is, though she creates this illusion "with no consciousness of fraud, only as with a sudden flare of the famous 'will-power' . . . which was what her medical adviser had mainly thrown her back on." If she will lie to help others, she will also muster courage and tact so as to help her doctor treat her: "him too she would help to help her, if that could possibly be," virtually becoming a "physician" to help him as "patient." Moreover she will accept the attentions and deferences with which they honor her. If her doctor and companion offer her "devotion" on a platter, she will "consume it as the dressed and served dish. . . ." For "devotion" her "appetite would be of the best. Gross, greedy, ravenous—these were no doubt the proper names for her." (I, 283-284, 258; II, 124-125; I, 261.)

The adoption and gradual perfection of a manner by Milly accompanies her initiation into the complexities of the society she confronts and her growing understanding of it. Indeed, the development of her manner is shown to be inseparable from her initiation, her deepening understanding, and her consequent gain in self-possession. Not only does Milly learn from her immersion in Maud's world: she illuminates and begins to mold *it*, revealing a process of ferment which is altering a stratified society, a process which her presence and manner quicken and eventually govern. It is profoundly significant that in presenting Milly's confrontation of unfamiliar social realities James reveals a British society in which some of the marked contours seem arbitrary and are subject to challenge and alteration while being nonetheless oppressively real. The society, moreover, is one in which the "manner" devised merely to *adjust* to *given* social differences displays the latent capacity for a more creative social function, that of salvaging or reconstituting the very basis of a community which is threatened by intermissions and cleavages within it.

Unfamiliar in America with the differences in social "position" which prevail in England and the "awfully good manner" which functions to "bridge" the distance between them, Milly arrives in Europe stripped by death even of her immediate family and, with an isolation enforced by her huge fortune, she is " 'independent,' " as Kate declares enviously, of the " 'tiers and tiers' " of groups in an "hierarchical, an aristocratic order." One thing her native society lacks is the vast "interval" between classes, which is associated metaphorically by James with blocks of "skipped" pages in a book or "social atlas." Another thing it lacks is a "manner" —accompanied by a "sinking" or repressing of the "consciousness" (but not the ignoring) of social intervals by both the privileged and unprivileged classes but particularly by the privileged— a manner which bridges the intervals, acknowledging the intervals by the fact of bridging them but repressing the awareness of the differences so as to be able to bridge the intervals at all. In the world of Matcham and Lancaster Gate, social distinctions are still to *some* extent founded on settled arrangements but are also founded on the manipulations, powerful and enterprising of middle-class Aunt Maud. Not only is she devoting her money, talents, and practiced manner to gaining higher status in the traditional "order" for Kate, and an attractive well-financed wife for the aristocratic Lord Mark; she has brought about by willed effort, virtually created, an otherwise nonexistent social distinction between Kate and her widowed sister Marian—a distinction which to Milly seems forced. (I, 191-192, 281.)

Though the position of the Croys was once "settled" in the

successful middle class, static *status* is no longer the apt term for Lionel Croy's precarious and shifting position as he moves downward through bankruptcy toward oblivion, and though Marian Croy may have married beneath her station while Kate is being groomed for higher things, James's treatment of the "social atlas" suggests that the "order" is no longer fixed under the impact of Maud's counting-house, that Kate and her sister have not simply fallen or been sorted into different fixed social positions but that a position for Marian has been "established" by Maud's maneuvering, exaggerating whatever interval might otherwise extend between the two sisters, a feat which will be completed if Kate marries the impecunious Lord Mark. The "vast interval" which places Marian on virtually a different "map," in "quite another geography," is defined by skipping, willfully and habitually, "page after page" of the actual social fabric; to locate and acknowledge Marian in the book at all (with a benevolent " 'Here!' " to mark the discovery) is virtually to salvage a community of pages from which she was otherwise willfully excluded. Status and class divisions seem falsely sharp, yet appear more malleable than fixed, in Maud's England as the governing fact of her money produces ferment and the prospect of change. Milly confronts not the old "hierarchical . . . order" of settled divisions but its remnants, in a middle class world which subjects everything to change in its struggle for power and secure position, and where everyone talks (as Milly notices) of money and threatens to put people and opportunities (as Kate warns Milly)to "use." (I, 191, 281.)

James's rendering of Milly's explorative reaction to the world of the Croys and Aunt Maud reveals a characteristic American view in speaking of social divisions as gaps or voids rather than as tangible barriers, as spaces that can be spanned by a manner which responds to the need for it instead of as walled enclosures. The suggestion is not that the intervals are unreal or inconsequential but that they are not impassable. Furthermore, to bridge them (rather than either to obliterate or fortify them) is to define a community which will encompass several geographies without relegating one to another atlas and which will compensate for the "skipped leaves" or pages in the total community—the network of social distinctions and the continuities between them—which the larger contours of class division and Maud's forced exaggerations obscure.

The metaphor of a book—conceived both as an integral whole and as a series of discrete pages—governs James's analysis of Milly's initiation into English society and enables him to define the complex and unresolved relation between that social world and both his heroine's action and his novel's action in it. The glaring, cruel, operative distinctions are there for Milly to discover and confront, the manner which bridges gaps by suppressing consciousness of them is there to emulate. The full sequence of the "atlas" from page to page is there to suggest the density of the existing community behind its more obvious cleavages, but to suggest also the long chain of intervals between pages which must be bridged by a "manner" if the society or book (with its broken sentences and parentheses) is to hold together at elemental levels and attain beyond that the full coherence it seeks. Milly's American manner, like James's, is adopted in the process of coming to understand society and its sharp divisions and, while moderating her consciousness of them, to bridge the intervals which separate her from it or from the groups and individuals in it whom she encounters. In the process, her manner has the effect of enabling Milly to play a role in her world and to share in altering and shaping it. Vulnerable in her illness but powerful with her money, she begins with her manner to take precedence over Aunt Maud and to become the governing center for the schemes and aspirations of the world which begins to form around her under the impact of her power and presence.

Both her impact on that world and her gain in understanding and self-possession are vivid in the scene when Lord Mark unexpectedly proposes marriage to her and Milly discerns an "ugly motive" dimly and briefly showing in his request. But she suppresses the recognition that the combination of her money and "the ravage of her disease" together make her attractive to him, decides that his "motive shouldn't matter" because he was "kindly, . . . humanly, concerned for her" anyway, and with perfect ease and candor tells him openly that she is " 'very badly ill,' " doing so out of kindness to soften the blow of her refusal. Her dove-like concern for his feelings is combined not only with a repressed understanding of his motives but with firm self-possession and with an exercise of her influence; she now can bring herself to talk openly of her illness and impending death and can *use* her influence, enforcing Aunt Maud's desire by suggesting that

Mark seeks to marry Kate. (II, 149-150, 155, 165.)

Eventually Milly's self-possession, power, and manner survive an even firmer test at a time when Milly so dominates the lives of the others that Densher feels it is Milly who accomplishes everything, governing, even purging, his and Kate's relation to her (if indeed "practically purged it was"): it was Milly herself, "Milly's hospitality, and Milly's manner"—it was "Milly's character, and perhaps still more than anything else, Milly's imagination" that worked in his and Kate's interest; and "not to profit by it, so far as profit could be reckoned, would have been to go directly against" it and against the "spirit of generosity" which Milly instills in him. In his last conversation with Milly before the exposure of his engagement, Densher faces Milly's second request that she visit his rooms for tea, planning to refuse a second time because he thinks of his rooms as sacred to Kate alone. His own manner falters in awkwardness as he inadvertently alludes to Milly's illness; Milly, by contrast, registers first "for twenty seconds an exquisite pale glare" and then declares that she is " 'splendid' " and " 'capable of life,' " declaring that she " *'can'* " and " 'will' " live in a tone that converts the solemn "weight" of her determination into "mere light and sound." Moments later, when Milly asks again to visit Densher's rooms for tea, the "sense of her own reality" which overwhelms Densher as he consents is not adequately revealed in "his face or his manner," and Milly takes his reaction for bored politeness instead and withdraws her request, speaking not with the "hand-to-mouth" improvisations which characterize Densher's attempt to help *her* but "gently" and with the smile that characterizes the kindness, ease, and assurance of her American and dove-like manner. As Milly questions him finally about his motives for staying on in Italy, his "anxiety" and "vagueness" are countered by her determination to help and by the grace with which she draws back from further questions out of kindness, and phrases an answer for him: " 'You stay because you've got to.' " In her mercy she lets him depart with the simple and genial but forceful declaration that will later become a formidable burden and tax his conscience: she says lightly that he "must judge" whether, as he has suggested, it is " 'enough, whatever may be one's other complications, to stay after all' " for her. (II, 239, 245-250.)

In Milly's *acting as if* and in the patterns of her action are the manner which yields the appearance, at least, if not the very image of Milly herself. Yet it is the very fact of having a manner and using it, however, that the novel develops into ambivalent and disconcerting expectations for the reader. They and the actions which occasion them establish the main rhythm of the novel, one movement of which is revealed fully when Milly, at a party in her honor, confronts a portrait by the Mannerist painter Bronzino which everyone says looks just like her.[7] Moved in her excitement to tears, Milly senses, in a feeling which the novel suggests has nothing to do with the portrait's subject, that the woman is "dead, dead, dead," and says " 'I shall never be better than this.' " She is reminded, of course, of her own death that she fears is imminent, but the reader is also reminded of a sense in which any work of art, no matter how brilliant, is dead, all art being lifeless in a way which the gestures, postures, and high finish of Mannerist painting display in a particular and extreme version: no blood flows through a painting or novel and no breath breathes there; one can smear greasy oil upon a yielding canvas, but no womb will conceive new life. The association of the realm of art with death is reinforced instantly, for it is immediately afterward that Milly, her illness upon her, sinks fainting into a chair. In this incident, however, Milly willingly takes passive refuge in her sickness—"in a manner plunge[s] into it"—overcome by envious resentment toward Kate who seems so familiarly the friend of Densher. (I, 221, 225.)

This action gives one of the novel's main movements: the anguished withdrawal from life into death, a movement that is confirmed and deepened by one of the evocations of the novel's title, Psalm 55. There, in fear and trembling at "the oppression of the wicked," a voice cries out: "O that I had wings like a dove! / Then would I fly away and be at rest. / Lo, then would I wander far off, / I would lodge in the wilderness. / I would haste me to a shelter / From the stormy wind and tempest." The voice then asks the psalmist's God to "Destroy, O Lord, and divide their tongue . . . For it was not an enemy that reproached me— / Then I could have borne it— / Neither was it he that hated me that did magnify himself against me—/ Then I would have hid myself from him— / But it was thou, a man mine equal, / My companion, and my familiar friend. / We took sweet counsel together, / We walked in the house of God with the throng. / Let death come suddenly upon them, let them go down alive into the pit: / For wickedness is in their dwelling, in the midst of them."

Counter to this movement is the other: not to withdraw but to stay, to live on "for a long time" as she declares "with her eyes again on her painted sister's" in Bronzino's portrait, to live by an act of will and, as the doctor urges, to " 'accept any form in which happiness may come,' " to turn her "anxiety" and utter uncertainty into a "great adventure, a big dim experiment" and with whatever resources she can muster to act out her role as "the American girl." This is the dove hailed in Psalm 68 as Jehovah leads his favored nation into the promised land: " 'Kings of armies flee, they flee, / And she that tarrieth at home divideth the spoil' — / 'Will ye lie among the sheepfolds?'— / 'The wings of a dove covered with silver and her pinions with yellow gold'—." (I, 227-228, 242, 250, 248.)

To the extent that a resolution of this tension is prefigured in the first half of the novel, it is in the gesture Milly makes to Kate after feeling so resentful of her. Recognizing that Kate has a right to friends, Milly makes up for her silent injustice by a gesture of devotion to the friend whom, in her momentary withdrawal, she had left behind; in a gesture of devotion, she asks Kate to accompany her to her London doctor's office, pledging her to join in the " 'wicked and false' " deed of keeping the visit secret, and adopting her clearly as a companion and friend. (I, 226.)

It is not in London, however, where the novel approaches its final crisis, but in Venice, the declining city of luxury and intrigue which James had called (in 1882 in an early piece on Venice) a "great bazaar," a "curiosity shop" itself like the many "halls of humbug" which it harbored. In 1907 in *The American Scene*, Venice was to remind James of New York City and Venice's annual ceremony of marriage to the sea was to seem the analogue of New York City's welcome to the immigrants who sought a new life there. It is in Venice that James's New York heroine confronts the ultimate crisis of her adventure and presents to the friends who follow her there the ultimate challenge of their lives. The drama hinges finally on three crucial scenes. Of these, the third is never described, that in which Kate spends the night with Densher in his rented rooms. The first, however, is one of the most brilliantly rendered in the novel; it is the occasion when Densher, frustrated and impatient, makes his request of Kate. He had broached the subject before in London—protesting against the need to improvise furtive meetings with Kate and to see her always in public places or at Aunt Maud's Lancaster Gate or Milly's apartments, and proposing to Kate that instead she " 'come to *me.* ' "Then, out of pity he drew back from his request. Now he makes it a demand as part of a desperate bargain.[8] (II, 5, 29.)

Milly is too sick to go on an outing, but Maud and Susan, Kate and Densher, make a trip to the great St. Mark's Square. Gradually the architecture of the scene comes into view. Three sides of the Square are surrounded by shops, and it is shopping that Susan and Maud plan to accomplish and spend the chapter doing. The fourth side is dominated by the huge cathedral, the "biggest booth" in the "bazaar" of Venice (James had written in 1882), filled with Renaissance paintings and Byzantine mosaics and with the bread and wine sacred to the claims of Christian communions. Densher and Kate do not plan to shop; they plan to have a "look-in," as Densher says, at the cathedral. Early in the chapter they do, though the novel scarcely mentions it. Then they come out and walk about the Square, which, since the Venetians are having breakfast is deserted except for the "pigeons picking up the crumbs of perpetual feasts." As Kate and Densher talk, Densher insists on his impatience and threatens to leave Venice. At the chapter's end, with Kate turned so that she twirls her parasol in the direction of the cathedral, Densher makes his proposition. She dodges his question, turns toward the shops, and is rescued when Maud and Susan, their commercial errand over, emerge from the stores and interrupt the private conversation. Though he has not yet received an answer, Densher takes satisfaction in the masculine ascendancy he has now asserted and feels certain that Kate will oblige him.[9] (II, 190.)

In the next chapter comes the dramatic scene for which the entire novel has been preparing. Possibilities which have been latent in the action since the beginning now materialize and are revealed in their full depth and power, their furthest implications embodied in the very simples of a party scene which present by intimating the sacrificial drama which the novel's action has become.

Densher drops around at Milly's palace as usual and is asked to stay to dinner and then for a party afterward in honor of Sir Luke who has just arrived in Venice. Milly is too sick to come down for dinner, but she does come down for the party. There are musicians hired for the occasion, and Milly gives them instructions and spends the rest of the time mingling with her guests. Densher and Kate both serve as delegated centers of consciousness, joined for the occasion to make a "represented community of vision," as James called it in the preface, in a chapter which bears the "double pressure" of "picture" and dramatic "scene." During most of the scene, Densher and Kate stand in the foreground watching Milly and talking to each other.[10]

The foreground in which they stand is one of immense scope as is suggested by remarks Susan makes when asking Densher to stay for the party—remarks about one of James's favorite painters, Paolo Cagliari, the expatriate who was known in the Venice where he flourished by the state where he was born, Veronese. To John Addington Symonds, Veronese was "precisely the painter suited to a nation of merchants," who depicted religious martyrs as "composed, serious, courtly, well-fed personages who like people of the world accidently overtaken by some tragic misfortune, do not stoop to distortion or express more than a grave surprise, a decorous sense of pain." For Berenson, writing in the fourth quarter of the last century, Veronese displayed a "happy combination of ceremony and splendour with almost childlike naturalness of feeling," a "frank and joyous worldliness, the qualities . . . we find in his huge pictures of feasts. . . ." Two of Veronese's huge feasts became for James, in one of the boldest appropriations of his expressionism, the instrumental forms for the making of his own composition.[11]

The two are introduced by Susan's reply to Densher's remark about the festive decorations of Milly's palace. She says: " 'bringing out all the glory of the place—makes [Milly] really happy. It's a Veronese picture, as near as can be, with me as the inevitable dwarf, the small blackamoor, put into a corner of the foreground for effect.' " She should have a " 'hawk or hound' " or borrow a " 'big red cockatoo' " to " 'perch on [her] thumb for the evening.' " Though Densher feels out of place in so grand a "composition," Susan insists: " 'Besides you're in the picture. . . . You'll be the grand young man who surpasses the others and holds up his head and the winecup.' " (II, 206-207.)

One of the paintings is evoked by Susan's echo of Veronese's defense when summoned before the Inquisition (Ruskin had printed a transcript of the proceedings in his guide to the Academy at Venice); it was and is known as *The Supper in the House of Levi*.

As recounted in the Bible (Luke v, 27-35), Christ was entertained on that occasion by his wealthy tax-collecting disciple Matthew, along with a company of publicans and sinners. When asked why he associated with such persons, Jesus replied: "They that are whole need not a physician; but they that are sick"; Jesus declared that he came "not to call the righteous, but sinners to repentance," and warned against the day "when the bridegroom shall be taken away."

In Veronese's treatment of the tale, a dwarf stands in the left foreground. (The dwarf aroused the Inquisition's suspicion, but it was placed there, Veronese informed the Inquisitors, "For ornament, as is usually done.") A blackamoor reaches for the bird perched on the dwarf's wrist. Above them on the landing of a staircase in a Venetian palace, in a strikingly mannered pose, stands a figure in green who seems about to descend the stairs and depart; he affords an analogy to Densher. At dinner, far in the background but centered, is the doomed and sacred figure of Christ; he, and his wealthy host, afford analogies to Milly.[12]

The second painting is *The Marriage Feast at Cana*. On that occasion, singled out as Christ's first miracle by the Gospel of John (II, 1-11) and regarded as one of the precedents for the Christian sacrament, Jesus and his mother attended a wedding banquet where the host ran out of wine. Asked to help, Christ first refused, then instructed servants privately to fill the jugs with water and serve that; it proved to be a very fine wine indeed. After tasting it, the banquet's steward made a speech, explaining that most hosts serve their best wine first, then offer cheaper kinds when guests can less easily taste the difference; this host, by contrast, had saved the best wine till the last.

In Veronese's picture (the Louvre version which James knew), a dark-skinned dwarf, with his bird, stands inconspicuously in the left foreground of a sumptuous banquet scene. On the right, holding up a wine cup, stands the steward; he is the figure Susan associates with Densher. Dominating the composition in the center foreground is a small group of musicians, including a portrait of Titian and a self-portrait of Veronese. They draw the eye in the direction of the figures directly behind, but, in their business as performing artists, they distract attention from the others; behind them at dinner, analogous in their position to Milly, are Mary and Christ.

These are the instrumental forms introduced early in the chapter by Susan's remarks. Later Densher speaks of "the Veronese painting . . . as not quite constituted," but by the end of the chapter the import of Veronese's subjects and the compositional patterns of his canvases have been constituted as part of James's medium, and they inform the composition of James's own canvas and the drama they reveal. (II, 213.)

The chapter's central action is enclosed in a frame outside itself (by the proposition which precedes and the assignation which follows) and by one within it. It opens with Susan's urgent request that Densher stay for the party and stay in Venice; it ends with Densher and Kate making urgent requests to each other and consenting. Kate urges Densher to remain in Venice, to pay court to Milly and marry her. Densher agrees to stay. But in return, Densher presses his demand that Kate sleep with him in his rooms, and Kate, reluctantly but without flinching, agrees to do it.

But within this frame of requests and answers, demands and commitments, a proposition and an assignation, lies a vision of Milly which it is the burden of the chapter, and indeed of the entire novel, to make vividly present, a vision which she makes real by enacting it and which sinks so deeply into Densher's consciousness that he can never get away from it, even though at the time he does not fully appreciate it.

It is rendered entirely through Kate's and Densher's perceptions, and while they spend much of the time watching Milly, talking and thinking about her, Milly herself is scarcely even seen. She is far off in the background most of the time, almost obscured in any literal sense by Kate and Densher, the writer, in the foreground. Only once does Milly pass close to the pair and then only to say three words which are not given: it is a "single bright look and the three gay words (all ostensibly of the last lightness) with which her confessed consciousness brushed by him." Densher admires in her the infectious geniality of a civilized hostess and, feeling that she has never before been so much "the American girl," he sees her "as diffusing, in wide warm waves, the spell of a general, a kind of beatific mildness." In the deep waters of that spell, he feels that all of them are swimming around "like fishes in a crystal pool." She is like a " 'new book,' an uncut volume of the highest, the rarest quality," and Densher feels "again and again" the "thrill of turning the page." Later in the chapter, Milly communicates again specifically with Kate and Densher; from across the room she sends a silent message, "all the candour of her smile, the lustre of her pearls, the value of her life, the essence of her wealth." (II, 214, 215, 213, 222, 229.)

The closest view of Milly herself, actually, is a look at her costly pearls. Kate points them out to Densher and they both stare at them; the "long, priceless chain, wound twice around the neck, hung, heavy and pure, down the front of the wearer's breast." Looking at these pearls of great price, Kate remarks: " 'She's a dove . . . and one somehow doesn't think of doves as bejewelled. Yet they suit her to the ground.' " Densher agrees, and, as the novel says, a dove "was the figure for her, though it most applied to her spirit." (II, 217-218.)

What lies revealed in the impress of Kate and Densher's experience is that Milly, though sick, has put on the superlative performance of her career so far, as the sumptuous hostess, the spontaneous American, the dove. It is revealed, too, that she has become one with the role she began earlier to play, for the illusion is so amply complete, so intensely and tangibly real, that one of Densher's phrases for her is perfectly apt: he thinks of her as "embodied poetry." And in becoming one with what she seems, she wears a dress whose color Densher notices, for the first time appearing, like Christ at the moment of his transfiguration, in white. The embodied poem, the wealthy dying dove, has become the perfect host. She has spent more lavishly of her money for the party—Densher noticed more candles burning when he entered her " 'temple to taste' "—and she has been spending more lavishly of her energy, her life. Milly has had to miss dinner to save strength for the party, and Densher could even *taste* the question of her health when he entered the palace; toward the end of the chapter, Kate insists that Milly's health is worse. The entire chapter, in its form or composition, focuses attention on Milly while not showing her directly to reveal and shield the torment of her triumph as host, the agony within a radiantly glad and splendid surface. Milly has been inspired by the occasion (chiefly, Densher notices, when Sir Luke arrives), and it is under the nourishing stimulus of this ceremonious affair that she diffuses her "beatific mildness." And while she is finding sustenance in the occasion, Kate and Densher feast their eyes on her. Although Densher at best only half grasps, and Kate now scarcely appreciates at all, what is before their eyes, Milly has become the sacrament, the sacred thing, prefigured in the temples, histories, and legends which the novel evokes but embodied now in its stricken heroine, the treasure, dove, and muse of James's imagination. (II, 217, 146, 203.)

Milly's sheer presence in this chapter has two important effects on Kate and Densher, even though she speaks to them only once and looks at them only twice. First, her sheer presence makes Densher aware of Kate's limitations; judgment is passed against Kate through Densher's consciousness. By comparison with Milly's strange beauty, he reflects, Kate would be more appropriately dressed in black. Then he feels that Kate, when looking at Milly's pearls, is thinking not of their purity and genuineness and what they reflect in Milly, but of the cash value which they also represent while lending something to Milly's "style." And to this measurable extent, Kate and Densher are momentarily separated and their "community of vision" is threatened. Judgment is passed against Kate without Milly's saying a word or even knowing that it happens. She does not condemn Kate or try to separate the two, but her sheer presence brings it about. Momentarily the close intimacy of Kate and Densher is destroyed, and divided is their tongue.

The other effect of Milly's sheer presence proves to be disastrous for Milly. Part of her triumph has been to bring people together, to make them, as Densher says, "more finely genial." The effect of this is to bring Kate and Densher closer together too. When Milly sends across the room "all the candour of her smile, the lustre of her pearls, the value of her life, the essence of her wealth," the tragic consequence is that it brings Kate and Densher more intimately together than they have ever been before. They have begun to talk over whether Densher should stay in Venice, and it has dawned on Densher what Kate has been scheming for so long. At Kate's insistence, he invests with words, as he does in deeds, the design that unwittingly he has been enabling Kate to realize. And Kate, as listener and participant, knowing that Densher is now "in possession," finds courage to "pronounce the words she hadn't pronounced"; she breaks "the grace of silence" to join him with the echoing responses which seal their union. " 'Since she's to die I'm to marry her?' " Densher asks; Kate replies " 'To marry her.' " " 'So that when her death has taken place I shall in the natural course have money?' " " 'You'll in the natural course have money. We shall in the natural course be free.' " (II, 213, 225.)

It is at the precise moment when Densher is struggling with Kate's proposal that Milly happens, by chance accident and James's careful management, to smile at them: her smile "brought them together again with faces made fairly grave by the reality she brought into their plan." Within a matter of minutes, under the protective "cover" of the music of Milly's orchestra, Densher has agreed to stay, to pay court to Milly under false pretenses, and to propose marriage to her if she lives long enough and seems to give him the opportunity. With her smile as well as with her cash, with the "essence of her wealth" and her benign manner as well as with her money, Milly has tempted her two friends and helped to bring them together in Kate's design. Moreover, by sustaining and making vivid the beauty of her role, she not only tempts Densher but makes it easier, virtually helping him, to betray her. Milly will not cough blood, seize her heart, or show herself to be wracked with pain. For her friends who are feasting on her she will not (as Kate has known she would not) " 'smell . . . of drugs' " or " 'taste . . . of medicine.' " Kate reminds Densher that " 'She isn't for you as if she's dying.' " It is in the full face of the vision Milly now embodies that the reader is forced to witness this betrayal by her own equals, her companions, her familiar friends. (II, 53, 229.)

But if together they so betray Milly in accordance with Kate's evil plan, Densher compounds the outrage by adding another: his betrayal of Kate. For the first time he applies successfully a strong pressure to Kate, asserts his dominance, and forces her consent to surrender her body to him. Impatient and frustrated, he has begun to fear that Kate, succumbing to Aunt Maud's arguments, may abandon him for Mark, and he feels that if he is to bargain his integrity for Milly's money, he prefers a partner to share the responsibilities and risks: Kate too should spend and pay. The assignation is the payment he demands. And this demand is not only an assault on the sexual scruples which the two so far have respected, it is a challenge to Kate's sincerity in their engagement and to the ardor of her love for him. While she is not shocked in the conventional sense, she seizes on pretexts, trying to evade the question at the end of the scene. But Densher, pleased with his new-found mastery and admiring Kate's ability to rise to the occasion, persuades her. He will stay in attendance at Milly's rented palace if Kate will accede, just once, to his demand. " 'You'll come?' " he asks. And the chapter closes with Kate's answer: " 'I'll come.' " (II, 231.)

This double betrayal is the very action that promises at the same time to be a triple guarantee. For by promising to insure the success of Kate and Densher's terrible deception, it promises to gain them the money and entrance into the "temple" of marriage, and it promises also to sustain the beautiful illusion of loving adoration for Milly which they have helped to create and to which they have already given more substance than they know, the illusion founded to begin with, as Milly knew, on sheer pity, but now become the vision of the life to which Milly clings so desperately. In persuading Densher to stay in Venice, Kate insists, with genuinely affectionate concern for Milly and even more point, that to break up their act now would be a heartless cruelty: it would kill Milly. Susan, too, wants Densher to stay for Milly's sake. When Densher agrees to stay in Venice, he agrees to perpetrate the fraud which is Milly's betrayal, fixing himself squarely in the picture at *The Supper in the House of Levi*, there to hear the call to repentance. Yet the same action, staying in the picture at Venice, fixes him squarely as the admiring young man with the wine cup, still sampling the sacred wine in *The Marriage Feast at Cana*.

III

It is the echo of that call and the aftertaste of that wine which dominate the last two books of the novel. In being the mere echo and aftertaste, however, they call into question the novel's very form. Why does it not give directly the scene which precipitates the final crisis, the scene where Lord Mark (whose thoughtless brutality is the very cruelty which Kate and Densher strove to avoid) tells Milly of the secret engagement? Why does it not show Milly's final visit with Densher, or the agony of her last days alive? Why does it give, instead, the stricken conscience and tortured feelings of Densher, and why is it through these only, in fragments based on hearsay, memory, and imaginings, that it renders the final crisis of Milly's tragedy? The novel takes this form for the reason that its governing perspective is what the Narrator in *The Sacred Fount* called " 'the torch' " of " 'analogy.' " Instead of the central passion it gives the analogies or embodied likenesses in which the mysterious passion itself is refracted.

To do so becomes the burden of a passage near the novel's end, where, even when it is wrenched from context, one can imagine an unspoken statement of Milly to Densher, as she leaves him to face alone her doom:

> "She had throughout never a word for what went on at home. She came out of that and she returned to it, but her nearest reference was the look with which, each time, she bade him good-bye. . . . 'It's what I *have* to see and to know—so don't touch it. That but wakes up the old evil, which I keep still, in my way, by sitting by it. I go now—leave me alone!—to sit by it again. The way to pity me—if that's what you want—is to believe in me. If we could really *do* anything it would be another matter.' "

There is the form of Milly's passion, rendered by a passage which describes not Milly, but Kate, the look Kate gives Densher to say that she must leave him to sit alone by her penniless, sick and ruined father. And her suffering, so similar to Milly's yet so different, is so precisely analogous to Milly's that the same passage can give the form for both. Yet that form is resilient enough to sustain the immense difference between the two friends, for Kate's suffering is imaged not as the dove's but as the "bleeding wound" she carries in her name, and Croy, in a dialect of the penny-pinching Scots, means the legal penalty paid, whether in goods or cash, for murder. (II, 394-395.)

The refractions of analogy, in phrase after phrase, play about the textures of the prose, which serves to distend, in the taut lucidity of its simplifications and abstractions, the paradoxes which yield its tragic vision. When, for instance, Milly sits in the park in meditation after seeing her doctor, she is surrounded by impoverished people in whom she recognizes the likeness of her own predicament; *she* is "a poor girl—with her rent to pay" and shares with them "their great common anxiety," and the phrase on which the poor have been taught to base their desperate hopes—"they could live if they would"—echoes in diction and syntax the phrase which sounds the imminence of a common doom: "they would live if they could." Terror and compassion become inseparable when the phrase which renders Milly's substance and integrity, her generosity and aspirations—*"That* was the matter with her—she was a dove. Oh, *wasn't* she? "—renders also the other things which matter for the reader as they do for Maud and Kate and Densher, for anxious Susan and Sir Luke: "the matter with Milly" is her money or her mortal illness, the prospect of her dying. (I, 250, 253-254, 117, 209, 253.)

The same task of refracting Milly's passion through analogous enactments becomes the burden of the novel's action. Milly's sacrifice and Kate's sexual surrender to Densher in his rooms are shown, without being identified, to be each the likeness of the other. A garbled sentence in James's preface testifies to the power of the analogy which joins Kate's sacrifice to Milly's and suggests the importance of the analogy to the novel's structure: "heaven forbid we should 'know' anything more of our ravaged sister [Milly] than what Densher darkly pieces together, or than what Kate Croy pays, heroically, it must be owned, at the hour of her visit alone to Densher's lodging. . . ."[13] A profound analogy links Milly's "mercy"—which by the end of the novel has shamed Kate and Densher and split them asunder—to Mark's cruel bluntness when he discloses the fact (which he has guessed) of Kate's and Densher's secret engagement, exposing Milly's naïveté to shame yet *saving* her from being duped and used unwittingly by the other two. These actions are prefigured earlier in Sir Luke's "merciful" concern for Milly which, during her meditation in the park, she finds nonetheless "chilling," his "compassion" which is "divesting, denuding, exposing." And these actions are echoed in the analogous incidents which occur in the closing chapters, when Densher's effort to repay Kate for her act of devotion in Venice and to salvage their love is combined with a cruel test of her affection and moral fiber—which pains her as if she were a sick patient being examined by an "exploring medical hand" probing to locate an illness or injury. Then indeed Kate and Densher's attempt to redeem their efforts echoes at every turn the analogous attempt by Milly. (II, 242; I, 252-253; II, 398.)

One of the formal triumphs of the novel is that, despite the disproportion between the two halves for which James apologized in the preface,[14] the early action in its main dimensions prefigures the later action by establishing the basis for exploratory analogous forms which join the two parts and reveal the actions of Lionel Croy, Kate and Densher, and Maud to be part of the very matrix of Milly's effort to redeem the world in which they live. Lionel

Croy, surviving his secret "failure of fortune and of honor" with his pretense of self-sacrifice, his lies, his letter to Kate containing the "sketch of a design," finds not only his moral opposite but his tragic and transforming likeness in the American girl who survives for a while *her* "general wreck," tells lies while studying "the dove-like" to help her friends, and, while she " 'can't make a bargain,' " finally writes a letter and uses her wealth in a last "countermove to fate." Kate—with her secret engagement, her immense vitality, her brutality which is nonetheless a "strange grace," and with the "bleeding wound" in her name—and Milly —with her mysterious illness and her dove-like radiance—are not so much opposed or divorced from each other as joined, in different measure, in a tragic action; and Kate's efforts to please and beguile Maud early in the novel are the same efforts which later please and beguile Milly and help create the crisis which Milly undertakes to redeem. (II, 161; I, 182.)

Even Aunt Maud, though she lacks Susan's depth of tenderness and Sir Luke's professional insight, is joined in a community of interest with Milly finally, despite the opposition between her effort to separate Kate and Densher and Milly's attempt to protect them. Though Maud is a " 'vulture' " rather than a dove, she is also an " 'eagle—with a gilded beak . . . and with wings for great flights' " who can eventually share sympathetically in the tragedy of the gilded dove. With Milly's money "fairly giving poetry to the life Milly clung to," and with Milly's vision of the " 'might have been,' " the "possibilities" which life might have afforded, so "at one" with Maud's own view, Maud is moved to tears at the time of Milly's dying and recognizes in the "cruelty of the event" a "cruelty, of a sort, to herself." It is with Maud that Densher can bring himself to speak of Milly's farewell to him and of her "unapproachable terror" as she "held with passion to her dream of a future" and then was torn from it "as one might imagine some noble young victim of the scaffold, in the French Revolution, separated at the prison-door from some object clutched for resistance." These conversations with Maud he keeps secret from Kate, as later he keeps secret his exchange of letters (his "transatlantic commerce") with Susan, finding in that duplicity the only rock to cling to in a vast "waste of waters," the "grey expanse" of stark, drab candor. (I, 73; II, 341-432, 391.)

All these dimensions of the action and all the probing analogies are most revealing and moving when the reader tries to make out what Milly saw in the dark shadows of her last days alive, and to imagine what she made out of the life that consumed her.

She made two things simultaneously which were joined in the process of her making: the final passionate surrender of devotion, and the image of it, as she acted out, with genuine passion, the complex role she had been playing and now filled completely. It is this double action which the novel can not allow the reader to see and will not allow him to glimpse (shielding the privacy of Milly's shame and the mystery of her agony), but which, with all the power at its command, it urges him to imagine. First, Milly put into words which the novel does not give the lie Densher has been acting out: she told Mark the lie that Densher's motives were genuine, and Mark returned to London duped by this delusion which he passed on to Maud, for he had paid Milly the tribute of believing her. Then Milly " 'turned her face to the wall' "—her pride injured her folly denuded and exposed—excluding Densher and shaming him. Since her money and her life proved to be both a blessing and a curse, she told Susan and her Italian doctor to leave her alone and to " 'talk of the price of provisions.' " (II, 270, 276.)

That anguished statement is, in this profoundly economic novel, the turning point in the novel's drama, for while marking the catastrophe, it reveals Milly's recognition of the meaning of her "dim experiment." Knowing finally the "price of provisions," she began in her dying days to pay it and to act it out. She agreed to see Densher again and mercifully "let him off" (to use one of the novel's recurring terms for kindness and mercy) by not asking him to state openly his motives, her mercy enabling him to evade the choice between herself and Kate; in her mercy she held back from creating the occasion when Densher would be forced actually to make that choice—in which case, as he remembered it later and declared to Kate, he would have lied to Milly in affirming his love for her, would have " 'denied' " Kate, and then redeemed his lies, made them true, by sticking to them. In her mercy Milly has saved him from the cruelty of that choice but ironically has created for him the cruelty of a later choice which he faces in the closing pages of the novel. She did the kind and cruel thing, the civilized, dove-like, and naïve thing in mercifully forgiving him. Then, like a civilized person and like the adored princess who feeds on the devotion of others, she acknowledged the devotion in a letter to Densher, sending him a message and arranging that it arrive on Christmas Eve from across the interval of silence which now separates them. (II, 301, 325.)

Finally she did the dove-like thing which is the civilized and naïve and American thing: she spent her money, spent it lavishly, in the act of giving it away to Densher. She took possession of herself and of her money, in her act of spending them to give away, bequeathing to Densher an image of her love for him. She joined in her friends' commerce, completed their transaction, redeemed their enterprise by transforming it into a gift, making her loving surrender to her tragic fortune and joining to "the imagination of expenditure," which Kate had early attributed to her, the "imagination of terror, of thrift, the imagination . . . of a conscious dependence on others," which for Milly is of more recent acquisition. (I, 175.)

In this action Milly gave final form to what had been the rhythm of her life, suspended as she was between moments in which she encountered, recognized, and accepted her impending doom and moments when, mustering the "famous 'will power' . . . which was what her medical adviser had mainly thrown her back on," she struggled to live. While she had succumbed willingly to her illness at Matcham before the Bronzino portrait, she had on other occasions as a "counter-move to fate" turned away from death and had clung to her appointed role as "the American girl"; the end of the first volume had left her feigning an interest in the American West because Densher wanted to talk about the States, prolonging the conversation and clinging to "the Rockies" so as to avoid facing her doom. At her death she clung again to her role as the American girl and dove, clinging as a "counter-move to fate" to the illusion she was making real. When she died, only the three images which embodied the illusion were left: her letter, her money, and the memory of her. But she now made at the same time an anguished withdrawal *into* her doom, her death, accompanying it by a tribute of devotion to the life which brought on her death and which she left behind. It was a tribute to Densher, whom she then knew fully and nonetheless loved. And it was a tribute also to the illusion of love which he, more intimately than anyone else, had helped to sustain. (I, 301-302.)

To speak of this rhythm, however, is to speak of the novel's form, though to speak thus is to "act as if" the form and the substance of the novel were completely separate, which is the lie we tell, the murderous violence we must risk, in any act of historical and critical analysis. In the rhythm of *The Wings of the Dove* the form is made to be analogous to the action which the novel is about. Instead of merely describing its subject, the form acts it out. The form enacts the passion which lies at the novel's center and is revealed, chiefly through Milly's sacrifice, in the action which she, helped by the others, brings to pass. The novel tacitly acknowledges that it cannot completely or directly embrace the ultimate reality—neither the ultimate horror nor the ultimate beauty, neither the pulsing actuality of life beyond art, nor the completely imagined vision which was the novel's origin or muse before, in the dance of James's imagination, it was wooed, seduced, and made into the rhythm of his words. But the novel is not content to acknowledge this by saying it. Instead it acts as if its vision lay within the presence but beyond the reach of language: as if its horrors were unspeakable horrors and its beauties too beautiful for words, the novel intimately acknowledges the fact in the contortions of expressive movement, the rhythm of approach and withdrawal as a tribute of devotion to what it leaves behind. As a gesture of love, this rhythmical form falls short of the full communion it manages nonetheless to intimate and celebrate; as an act of devotion it reveals by betraying the life and sacred presence it adores.

Early and again late, it presses close to Lionel Croy, then draws back from the terrible—and pitiful—truth about him. Twice it moves toward temples—St. Mark's and later the Oratory in London—and sends Kate and Densher, then Densher alone, into them, but itself withdraws without entering them. It presses toward Kate's assignation, but draws back without entering that scene. It draws close to Milly's illness but leaves it unnamed, just as it presses closer and closer to her suffering but even at her party scarcely shows it at all. And the novel makes an anguished withdrawal from the crisis occasioned by Mark's visit in Venice, and from both the utter horror and the utter beauty of Milly's final agony—and in this very withdrawal it pays tribute to what it leaves behind: to what Milly actually suffered, to the validity of the role she enacted, and to the created vision which she finally made, in dying, out of the life that consumed her.

But in approaching Milly only to draw back from her, even while paying tribute to her, it becomes what Densher calls the action they all have been engaged in: just before exclaiming " 'the mere aesthetic instinct of mankind!' " he calls their action "a conspiracy of silence" which has suppressed "the great smudge of mortality across the picture," and has surrounded "the truth . . . about Milly" in an "expensive vagueness," and "impenetrable ring fence" made up, with Milly's help, of "smiles and silences and beautiful fictions." The novel enacts the other dimension of its passion: in failing to do justice to Milly, it betrays her. It draws back into a world which has only fragments and images of Milly, and set against her actual suffering and the envisioned glory she embodied, the novel confesses in guilty terror the necessity it accentuates and gives assent to. Like the rich color and gilt background of a Byzantine painting, like the hard stony glasses of a mosaic, like the mannered art of the Bronzino painting, it is in the candor of its own confession "dead, dead, dead." As in the case of the pictures in Sir Luke's office, which were "in particular framed and glazed," so Milly is *framed* as well as glazed by the novel which takes her to use as the subject of its chilled embrace, and arranges, in the eighth book, that "her death" shall have "taken place." She is betrayed by the very fiction that enshrines her. (II, 298-299.)

This is the form—the design and the movement—that gives shape to what otherwise would be a miscellany of irrelevant notations: The fact that Milly is placed in canvases of Veronese whose compositional modes are like James's own. The fact that in the circle of her friends Milly numbers two professional writers, Densher and Susan. The fact that, in the rite which constitutes her worship, she acknowledges two friends who carry the names of devoted writers: Mark, the patron saint of Venice and author of the Second Gospel; and Luke, the physician-evangelist, the patron saint of painters, and author of the Third Gospel. The fact, finally, that a remark of Densher's early in the novel reveals in Kate's scheme or plot, the plot, the design in deed, of art. He had been admiring Kate's plan to deceive Maud, the plan that was broadened to embrace Milly: "It had, [Kate's] sketch of the affair, a high colour and a great style; at all of which he gazed a minute as at a picture by a master." (I, 74.)

For the novel, like all its characters, is caught in the tragic passion it celebrates. In varying degrees they all, even Mark, pay Milly the tribute of devotion which she exacts, but together and at the same time they all, even Susan and Luke, "frame" her and betray her. For novel and characters alike are consumed in the tragic passion which the novel reveals life to be: this world which mercifully gives life, hope, love, and even money to Milly, enabling her to envision the complete life, only to make these things cruelly impossible of full attainment and to waste them. By the end of the novel, life—with the help of Milly's "disconcerting poetry," her "inscrutable" mercy, and what Maud calls " 'the mere *money* of her' "—has done that to Kate and Densher too. It is a world which is enlightened and ennobled by its suffering but which is also ruined and consumed by it. And it is this consuming passion, the tribute of devotion joined with the betrayal, that the novel's form enacts. The consuming passions of life and art were joined in Milly and they are joined by *The Wings of the Dove* in the "sacrament" which "marries" form and content, for the passion is enacted by the form, which is the telling likeness of it. (II, 184, 242, 341.)

It is with the novel's form in view that one is moved by its withdrawal into the agony of Densher, which transpires on the stage of Densher's memory as he recalls his last sight of Milly, seated talking to him in a room that was "all gaiety and gilt," instilling in him the sense that he has been "forgiven, dedicated, blessed" in a "scene" which he relives in memory as if reading it "from the page of a book." Then on the stage of memory he imagines the torment of Milly's death and tries to redeem at once his love for Kate and his devotion to Milly. His effort, along with the reactions of Kate and Maud, the novel can pretend to give with comparative directness. Moreover, it is chiefly through the sensitive medium of Densher's conscience and imagination that the novel can undertake its most difficult task: to make a likeness of the passion it cannot embrace directly, revealing it in the likeness of analogy. Like Milly, Densher feels intense shame. Like Milly, he feels that "while the days melted, something rare went with them." Like Milly he must face as closely as he is allowed, and as a living person can, the horror of her death, "the price of provisions." Like Milly, at the end, he creates a moral crisis for the living person he loves by trying to give Milly's letter and then the money to Kate, trying to surrender them in honor of the memory he adores. It is because Densher's suffering, and to some extent

Kate's and Maud's, is so like Milly's that Milly's tragic presence hovers over the closing chapters even though she is never otherwise seen. (II, 342-343, 395.)

And it is because Densher's and Kate's predicament and suffering are so like the central predicament and passion of the novel that the last two chapters not only complete the novel, as they must, but do what words and novels can do only when they achieve in narrative prose the movement and power of the drama: they not only complete the novel but virtually reenact the entire work.

Life before had surrounded Milly and the others with actual opportunities for life and love along with visions of even more glorious possibilities. Now Kate and Densher confront the actual opportunity they have longed for, the opportunity for their marriage. And they try, despite the widening gap between them—the momentary scorn, the disgust, the recriminations, and the "dim terror" of their final confrontation—to prevent the waste of their passion. But they confront also the images of more glorious possibilities which constitute Milly's last "counter-move to fate." They confront her letter, and then they confront her cash. That money is, as Shaw wrote in his preface to *Major Barbara*, "the most important thing in the world"; it affords the enabling condition which will permit them to have the civilized life and married love they want. The money is, at the same time, a sacred symbol, important (again as Shaw knew) for the very reason that it is a symbol of economic power and that, in modern commercial society, it is made a symbol of the "health, strength, honor, generosity and beauty" which it "represents." In a world which needs and worships the almighty dollar, a world where Milly's compassionate devotion and last "counter-move to fate" find in a gift of cash the necessary form that reveals and makes them possible, that money is made a sacrament, a sacred symbol "set apart and sanctified," as Melville wrote of the doubloon, "to one awe-striking end." It is a symbol, sanctioned now by James's art, of the finest possibilities, revealed in Milly, that they want to pay tribute to. And it is intimately bound to the memory of Milly (with "the mass of money so piled on the girl's back" she "couldn't have lost it if she had tried"), bound to the image of her which is embodied in the memories of Kate and Densher and the others. Milly had had to decide what to do about her memories and had paid them the tribute of devotion; now Kate and Densher must decide what to do about theirs.[15] (II, 401; I, 106, 121.)

Even in situation and setting, the last two chapters are a reenactment of the whole. Maud is still around, touched to the heart, still confident, and still, thanks now to Milly, deceived. Mark is still available, though Kate has turned him down once; he is simply a bit poorer and closer at hand. Lionel Croy is back, a more ominous and pathetic presence than before. And the setting returns in one chapter to the environment where it began—to the dingy quarters of Kate's family. There Kate and Densher confront Milly's letter of forgiveness on Christmas Day.

With the knowledge of himself that he cannot bury, and with his devotion to Milly, Densher feels he would desecrate the letter by opening it, and he refuses to read it: in a tribute of devotion to Milly, he draws back from the "undisclosed work of her hand," just as Milly, in her tribute of devotion to life and to Densher, drew away and bequeathed him an image of something so glorious and shaming that it insures his refusal of it. (II, 388.)

Then Densher makes a gift to Kate of Milly's letter, making it a " 'tribute' " and " 'sacrifice' " and " 'symbol' " of his gratitude for Kate's " 'sacrifice,' " the " 'act of splendid generosity' " she performed when surrendering her body to him in Venice. And Kate proceeds to reenact the crime which she and the world have been committing for some time in an incident which has the terrifying power of the scene in Ibsen's *Hedda Gabler* when Hedda ruthlessly destroys the manuscript which had been inspired by Thea's love for Lövborg, whispering "Now I am burning your child, Thea! . . . Your child and Eilert Lövborg's . . . I am burning your child." Kate, accepting what the letter surely promises, "with a quick gesture . . . jerked the thing into the flame," the "thing" being the "sacred script," the still "undisclosed work of [Milly's] hand." In that action Kate betrays life and betrays herself, for at the novel's end she has, finally, paid with "the sacrifice of Mr. Densher." And Densher suffers the letter's loss, keeping the "pang" of memory wrapped in a "sacred corner" of his room and undoing the wrappings, "handling" the memory "as a father, baffled and tender, might handle a maimed child." His imagination "filled out" the distinctive tone and manner of Milly's letter, and the loss of the "revelation" he imagined is like "the sight of a precious pearl cast before his eyes—his pledge given not to save it. . . ." It was "like the sacrifice of something sentient and throbbing" which "might have been audible as a faint far wail." He clings to the memory so that it might "prevail" as long as it can before the "inevitable sounds of life . . . comparatively coarse and harsh," would "smother and deaden it" and "officiously heal the ache in his soul that was somehow one with it."[16] (II, 385-387, 395-396.)

Then a few months later, as the seasons move (without ever getting there) toward the full bloom of spring, the money comes and Kate and Densher confront that, the novel recalling insistently that they are, once again, alone in Densher's rooms. And Kate, who if no one else in the novel can see, sees now the glory of Milly's love and asserts her claim to having helped prepare for it: " 'she died for you then that you might understand her. From that hour you *did.* . . . And I do now. She did it *for* us. . . . That's what I give to you. . . . That's what I've done for you.' " The only proper tribute to Milly's generosity is to take the money; to "refuse to profit by it" would be to deny Milly and the life she clung to so passionately; it would be to spurn the offered gift, as Lionel Croy had done when Kate offered her help to him. Milly gave Densher the condition of life that he might have it: To take the money. But Densher who if no one else in the novel now can feel, feels that to take the money would be to complete his betrayal of what the money symbolizes. To take the dim reflection and soil it with his lips would betray the impassioned love it represents: Not to take the money. Then, to prevent the waste of his and Kate's passion, Densher like Milly tries to give away the money to the living person he loves, adding out of his devotion to Milly the stipulation that Kate in turn renounce the cash. (II, 403-404.)

This action, in which Kate agrees to join, is at once a tribute to their own love and to Milly's memory, but at the same time it is a refusal of the cash which would enable them to marry and a refusal of Milly's generosity: it is a tribute of devotion, but it is also an assignation. Accordingly, as Densher awaits Kate's decision, the novel evokes as a memory the earlier assignation, never described, in Densher's rooms: "Strange it was for him then that she stood in his own rooms doing it, while, with an intensity now beyond any that had ever made his breath come slow, he waited for her act." As before, Kate consents, determined if she can to prevent the waste of their passion, but consenting only on one condition: " 'Your word of honor that you're not in love with her memory.' " She demands that he deny the dead image of a girl now dead, but an image of a passion beyond any he could otherwise imagine. Densher squirms in making an exclamation which tries to hide, without openly denying, the memory that now possesses him: " 'Oh—her memory!' " But within that exclamation Kate sees instantly the truth that separates them: " 'Her memory's your love. You *want* no other.' " When Densher offers again to marry her, and stands, without moving, awaiting her answer, Kate "turned toward the door, and her headshake was now the end." She has withdrawn from a passion which, she knows, is spent. They have made an anguished withdrawal into the sterile isolation of their lives apart while paying a desperate tribute to the passion —their own and Milly's—which they leave behind. (II, 404-405.)

Densher is left with the memory of what the novel, with Densher, calls in genuine seriousness the " 'act of splendid generosity' " performed by Kate in his rooms in Venice. Both have the memory of the marriage they had hoped for, that institution a temple still and still without a street running up to it. And each has the memory of the money which sits on the table at the novel's end, the check not acknowledged or endorsed, the gift still not possessed, the grace of forgiveness and love still operative but balked of fulfillment: it is "untouchable and immaculate," like Melville's doubloon, and wasted. And each has the memory of the American girl who made on the occasion of her party a "brief sacrifice to society" in a world where "ripeness is all," a world which cannot make the most out of its money.[17] (II, 295.)

Every attempt Kate and Densher have made at the end to salvage their love and pay tribute to Milly's has involved them in the throes of transformation, in the process which Milly's suffering brought to light and which her redemptive imagination created in partial fulfillments for herself and for her friends. But these efforts, finally failing, have inescapably divided and destroyed them at the same time, revealing the possible *might-be* in the form of the *might-have-been* and its betrayal, rendering the world not redeemed but redeemable in the process of its tragic wastage. The double burden of this double recognition is carried by Kate's closing cry, the novel's last sentence before, "hanging unfinished," it drops "into no words nor any notes at all." Kate says simply: " 'We shall never be again as we were!' " The novel's vision yields itself, as the form reveals itself, in its spendthrift waste of passion—their own and Milly's—the tragic waste which is the appalling cost of Milly's tragic triumph. The novel's action spends itself, as the form completes itself, in the consuming passion with all its waste which James found life and art to be.

NOTES

1. *The Wings of the Dove*, 2 vol. (New York, 1902), II, 241; *ibid.*, 2 vol. in one (Westminster, 1902), II, 434. Subsequent references to James's fiction, enclosed in parentheses in the text, are, unless otherwise identified, to the New York Edition, *The Wings of the Dove* being volumes XIX and XX of that collection.
2. *The Art of the Novel*, p. 298.
3. Cf. the American version, I, 300, 157, 175; II, 223, 243.
4. George Santayana, *Reason in Art* (New York, 1905), p. 82.
5. *The Art of the Novel*, p. 288.
6. *Ibid.*, p. 308.
7. Miriam Allott identified the portrait as that of Lucrezia Panciatichi in "The Bronzino Portrait in *The Wings of the Dove*," *Modern Language Notes*, LXVIII (January, 1953), 23-25.
8. *Portraits of Places* (Boston, 1884), p. 9; *The American Scene*, pp. 184, 206.
9. *Portraits of Places*, p. 9.
10. *The Art of the Novel*, p. 300.
11. Symonds, *The Renaissance in Italy: the Fine Arts* (American Edition, New York, 1888), p. 373; Bernard Berenson, *Venetian Painters of the Renaissance* (New York, 1895), p. 64.
12. John Ruskin, *Guide to the Principal Pictures in the Academy at Venice* (rev. ed., London, 1891), p. 55.
13. *The Art of the Novel*, p. 301.
14. *Ibid.*, p. 302.
15. George Bernard Shaw, *John Bull's Other Island and Major Barbara* (New York, 1907), p. 271. Herman Melville, *Moby-Dick*, eds. Luther P. Mansfield and Howard P. Vincent (New York, 1952), p. 427.
16. *Eleven Plays of Henrik Ibsen* (New York: Modern Library, n.d.), p. 287.
17. Melville, *Moby-Dick*, p. 427.

THE AMBASSADORS

1903

"The Ambassadors"

FREDERICK C. CREWS*

I.

It is a fact perhaps too well known that James's later novels are not easy to read. If we approach them with anything less than the closest and most patient attention, or with an expectation of being entertained as Fielding and Dickens and Thackeray can entertain us, we shall neither understand nor enjoy them. There is little that is "lifelike" about them in the ordinary use of that term. The strategy of James's later style was not to represent but to disguise the "lifelike touches" which abound in his own early works. Critics who have disliked the ambiguities, hesitations, and lengthy periods of the later style have been inclined to set these things down to inadvertence, to a loss of the power to be concrete. However, James himself regarded them as deliberate and necessary elements in the total effect of his novels. Obscurity was not something to be avoided but rather to be cultivated, in order to secure the highest intensity of interest on the reader's part. The luxury of art is greatest, he wrote in his preface to *The Wings of the Dove*, "when we feel the surface, like the thick ice of the skater's pond, bear without cracking the strongest pressure we throw on it."[1] This is an ideal not of noncommunication, but rather of inviting as much communication as possible.

The depth of the later novels is achieved in part by a restriction

*From THE TRAGEDY OF MANNERS by Frederick C. Crews. Copyright 1957 by Yale University Press. Reprinted by permission of the publisher.

of their width. They record no historical crises, show us a mini-
mum of background scenery, and contain no philosophical reflections irrelevant to the scenes at hand. Instead, they begin with a
basic practical situation and then explore every influence that the
situation can have upon the few characters who are involved in it.
The means to complexity lies in the characters themselves. They
are enormously sensitive to moral and intellectual shades of meaning that would remain unperceived by ordinary people. In effect
they are superhuman, larger than life, but they perceive nothing
that is not latent in the situation before them. Given their exceptional capacity for reflection and analysis, we cannot say that they
misrepresent the truth of their experience, for that experience is
conditioned by their very receptivity.[2] Although they concentrate
only on their relations with each other, they bring such extraordinary sensitiveness to bear on those relations that the simplest facts
become charged with significance.

James's technical ideal in these books was to eliminate every
extraneous factor from the situation at hand. Hazard, whim, coincidence—these were tricks of plotting to which the novelist should
not resort. As he wrote in "The Art of Fiction," "What is character
but the determination of incident? What is incident but the illus-
tration of character?"[3] It is possible to see most of the differences
between the earlier and later novels as deriving from the serious
application of this concept in the later works. With a very few
exceptions there are no unexpected, externally caused events to
complicate or change the characters' attitudes.[4] Rather, each
event results from an improvement in comprehension of events
that have gone before. The question is not, as in most novels,
"What is going to happen next?" but rather "What is the meaning
of that which has already happened?" At any given point James
professes to know only as much as his characters do. The reader
and the characters together are coaxed into ever larger realizations, yet always with the sense of their perceptual limits before
them. We are forever on the verge of solving a crucial mystery, or
rather by solving it we enable ourselves to see further mysteries
behind it. Like Proust and Kafka, James thus presents us with a
world in which reality is kept just around the corner. His characters, by being remarkably perceptive and yet finding themselves
still ignorant of the most important facts, illustrate his belief that
no single awareness of life is adequate in itself. The elaborate,

groping, often ambiguous sentences in which these novels are written serve this feeling directly. Completely aside from action, method alone becomes an instrument of meaning.

James's concern for strength of surface is shared by his characters, who insist on preserving their good manners at all times. Each of the major figures feels obliged to be polite to the others, even when it means suppressing the most urgent feelings. In effect this is a method of complicating and intensifying the drama, for it makes it difficult for each character (and for the reader) to tell what the others are thinking. It is common practice for resolute enemies to take considerable pains for each other's comfort and to express the tenderest mutual sentiments. Only in the slightest gestures, the barest inconsistencies of politeness is the real emotional drama beneath the surface perceived. The language of good manners thus provides a kind of circumlocution for the action it hides, and when simple facts do finally emerge, they seem all the more stark by contrast with the pervading atmosphere of courtesy. But since James does not contradict his characters when they use their good manners hypocritically, it is hard to decide who is sincere and who isn't. However, it is significant that the basic moral contrasts of the early novels are repeated in the later ones; if we are sufficiently familiar with the moral issue we can follow the logic of the action.

What is it that James's true heroes have in common? We saw at the end of *The Princess Casamassima* that Hyacinth Robinson had achieved a moral superiority to every influence in his past life. He became a moral hero not by rejecting his previous imperfect ideals but by acknowledging their destructive grasp on him. He ended in a selfless passion for knowledge, an awareness of life-as-a-whole (designated below as "Life") rather than an endorsement of one way of living against another. We shall see this pattern repeated in the later novels. The true hero has an aesthetic sense of Life's vastness and diversity, and he prizes this vision above every other goal. He will do anything to preserve it. In practice this means that he will look for a measure of validity in every attitude that he meets, including those of his worldly enemies. His point of view, which I shall call "inclusiveness," thus seems near to a Christian one, for it counsels a tolerance that borders on Christian love. However, the hero does not love his neighbor for Jesus' sake but for the sake of filling his own consciousness with truth. Yet a kind of Christian humility is the end result of his attitude. Believing as he does that other people have an acquaintance with Life that is as valid as his own, and recognizing his relative unimportance in the great panorama that he sees, he is characterized above all by magnanimity. He believes in everything as a part of Life but in nothing as a final version of it.

In contrast, the Jamesian villain—I use the word only for want of a more accurate one—is "practical." Gilbert Osmond may be taken as a model of the type. He looks on society as a field of battle, and instead of seeking the truth he is concerned only to use his social weapons to best advantage. He may or may not have the intellectual and moral capacity for inclusiveness, but he finds it imprudent to train his sights beyond any immediate goal. His ends supposedly justify his means. On the level of the action his sin is an exploitation of the hero's inexperience and good faith. Metaphysically he is sinning against truth itself, for in effect he is attempting to deny the value of a disinterested zeal for knowledge. Inclusiveness and practicality are the opposite poles in a moral world whose supreme virtue is an open mind.

The Americans who appear in James's "international" novels have a more or less fixed set of possible roles in this contrast of values. The American is a visitor from a world of relative ingenuousness. His civilization is so young that it hasn't had time to develop social gestures that will represent its characteristic perceptions about reality. He is often inarticulate; he feels the tension created by his insufficient ability to express himself in terms that the European can understand. Christopher Newman in *The American* is the example most often cited, but any number of others could be mentioned. In Jamesian language they are "empty" of social refinements, while the European is full to overflowing with them. But human nature abhors a vacuum: the American often compensates for his spiritual loneliness with a "sacred rage," a reliance on moral righteousness instead of worldliness. This righteousness can run in the broadest or narrowest channels. Christopher Newman is able to achieve a kind of magnanimity by virtue of his belief in his moral superiority to France, but Sarah Pocock in *The Ambassadors* uses the same conviction as a basis for the meanest sort of prejudice. In other characters—Madame de Mauves, for example—the American righteousness is treated with a deliberate moral ambivalence. Although we admire Madame de

Mauves's firm integrity, we are left wondering at the end whether this very integrity may not be to blame for the unnecessary death of her husband. At any rate, there is an important similarity in the case of every American who has not renounced his nationality: he is incapable of living in an amoral, "realistic" manner. As Philip Rahv says, in a slightly different connection, "The principle of realism presupposes a thoroughly secularized relationship between the ego and experience."[5] Most Americans, even as ruthless businessmen, cannot be secular in this sense. They are always making moral estimates of their actions, always justifying or condemning themselves according to some unseen standard. At his best the American lives on principles; at his worst, on moralistic half-truths. He cannot cultivate emotions as a pastime, or relax in a bath of history and tradition. He is by definition intense.

In Europe the American is particularly reminded of his social homelessness. As a remedy he is inclined either to adopt a foreign pattern of social observances, as Gilbert Osmond does, or to intensify his moral strictness, as Waymarsh does in *The Ambassadors,* or to attempt a comprehensive grasp of everything he touches, by a special effort of his intellect or heart. In this third group are the truly inclusive heroes. If Europe offers the American a chance to renounce his country, it may also challenge him to fall back on the best qualities of his "empty" and hence uncorrupted American soul. It is revealing that while the morally purest characters in our three late novels are all Americans, in two cases the most unsavory characters are American as well. This whole situation will be seen to tie in with the philosophical problem raised by Madame Merle. The International Theme—naïve America versus sophisticated Europe—remains the context of James's drama, but the moral question becomes more complex as naïveté comes less and less to be regarded as a virtue in itself. Is purity of imagination compatible with the highest inclusive heroism? James raises this question with increasing stress in *The Ambassadors, The Wings of the Dove,* and *The Golden Bowl,* and I feel that in each successive novel he moved closer to a full statement of his attitude.

II.

The plot of *The Ambassadors* centers about Chad Newsome, the rebellious heir to an unspecified industry in Woollett, Massachusetts, who has spurned his family and fortune and secluded himself in Paris, presumably in the clutches of an "evil woman." His widowed mother sends Lambert Strether, to whom she is informally engaged, to persuade Chad to accept his obligations. Instead of being reformed by Strether, an unexpectedly civilized Chad converts Strether to his own point of view. Strether himself falls in love, intellectually, with Chad's Madame de Vionnet, and for her sake actually prevents Chad from returning to Woollett with Mrs. Newsome's second platoon of ambassadors, the Pococks. Alienated from Mrs. Newsome and presented with the opportunity of marrying Maria Gostrey, an attractive woman who loves him, Strether nevertheless decides to return to America.

Lambert Strether is the hero of the book, and all the action is seen through his eyes. He is a widower of fifty-five who thinks that life has passed him by, as indeed it has, and when he gets to Europe he begins to understand what the trouble has been. Mrs. Newsome, the Woollett dowager who is paying for his trip, has very subtly dominated his mind with her own narrow outlook on life. Superficially she is all beneficence. By allowing him to edit a small review whose debts she pays, she provides him not only with a means of living but with a moderate portion of "fame" and "culture" as well. Furthermore, she intends to take the hero out of his financial misery for good, by marrying him. But once Strether has put some geographical and moral distance between himself and Mrs. Newsome he is able to see that her apparent generosity has had a restricting effect on his consciousness, and indeed that the whole society represented by Woollett, Massachusetts, has restricted him. In Paris he is confronted with the image of a world which now seems at least as real as Woollett and a good deal more interesting; yet he has never had a chance to take it into account, for Woollett has had nothing to do with it. Strether, like Hyacinth, wants to know rather than to enjoy this new life—or more precisely, he wants to enjoy it only in order to know it. Paris becomes a symbol of everything he has felt lacking in himself, and he pursues the ideal of self-cultivation with religious fervor. It is too late to make his life over, but it is not too late to dedicate himself to an openness of spirit that he might have developed long ago, had he only suspected how large and various the world beyond Woollett actually was. James in his preface states the issue as it appears to Strether:

Would there yet perhaps be time for reparation?—reparation, that is, for the injury done his character; for the affront, he is quite ready to say, so stupidly put upon it and in which he has even himself had so clumsy a hand? The answer to which is that he now at all events *sees;* so that the business of my tale and the march of my action, not to say the precious moral of everything, is just my demonstration of this process of vision.[6]

The result of the process of vision is inclusiveness.

Strether's career is morally parallel to Hyacinth's, and some idea of the degree of understatement in James's later method can be gained from the reflection that whereas Hyacinth pays for his vision with his life, Strether achieves exactly the same goal by merely deciding quietly not to accept the offer of a comfortable way of living. Although this is in some sense a neutralization of dramatic possibilities, it does bring the question of values into sharper focus than before. Strether's advanced age and his recurring awareness of it prevent us from confusing his moral growth with mere factionalism; he has nothing ultimately at stake but the expansion of his awareness of Life. In what James called the central passage in the book, as well as the inspiration for the whole, Strether makes a little speech about freedom which negates any hope of his own for a new start: "One's consciousness is poured —so that one 'takes' the form . . . and is more or less compactly held by it: one lives, in fine, as one can." (p. 150) Immediately afterward he exhorts the young American painter Bilham to cultivate the illusion of freedom, and later in the novel he thinks of Chad as free, but he can never forget for long that he himself is running out of time. In effect he defies his own deterministic philosophy by breaking out of his Woollett "mould," but his success is entirely on an intellectual, philosophical level.

Strether meets the inevitable Jamesian confidante, Maria Gostrey, at the very outset upon his arrival in England, and the implicit contrast between Maria and Strether's companion from America, Waymarsh, immediately dramatizes the two extremes between which he will find himself for the rest of the novel. Waymarsh is a satiric figure throughout the book, but there are undertones of genuine respect in James's attitude toward him. He is a personification of New World austerity, simplicity, and discomfort. What Strether says of Woollett is also true of Waymarsh: he isn't sure he *ought* to enjoy things. In the eyes of Milrose, Connecticut, he leads a "full life," which is to say that he has narrowly escaped a nervous breakdown from overwork. His friends in Europe refer to him affectionately as "Sitting Bull," and his, specifically, is the sacred rage against the nice European distinctions which strike the democratic soul as invidious. All things foreign seem to him to be interconnected in a conspiracy against good will, as this reflection bears out: "The Catholic church, for Waymarsh—that was to say the enemy, the monster of bulging eyes and far-reaching, quivering, groping tentacles—was exactly society, exactly the multiplication of shibboleths, exactly the discrimination of types and tones, exactly the wicked old Rows of Chester, rank with feudalism; exactly, in short, Europe." (p. 29) He is as helpless and uneasy in Europe as a revival preacher in an art gallery. Everything should be either black or white; why all these intermediate shades?

Maria Gostrey represents an opposite attitude. She is an American who appears at first to have overcome every trait in the national character, through constant exposure to Europe. Yet her type is as genuine as Waymarsh's. James mentions in his notebook that "She is inordinately modern, the fruit of actual, international conditions, of the growing polyglot Babel."[7] She seems to be the perfectly adjusted expatriate, living for the cultivation of her tastes and the exercise of her sympathies. Her actual loneliness emerges only gradually, as we come to realize how dependent she is upon her role as Strether's guide. Strether recognizes at once the usefulness of her companionship, not merely as an aid in "seeing the sights," but in accustoming him to a European manner of thinking. In her presence he becomes more conscious than before of Waymarsh's shortcomings, and together they are amused—but also impressed—by his sacred rage. It would be stretching the point to say for Strether, as we could say for the influences in Hyacinth's life, that he is composed of "Waymarsh-forces" and "Maria-forces." His two companions suggest, rather, his past and his future. Waymarsh's bluntness reminds him of the New England he is leaving behind, a New England he is increasingly tempted to regard in caricature. Maria's superior perceptiveness shows him the subtlety of the world he is about to enter. He is not really torn between Waymarsh and Maria; he gravitates instinctively to Maria.

This is an initial victory not directly for Europe but for the cause of self-cultivation. Strether has not yet realized that a commitment to the latter implies an acceptance of the former. His mental conflict at this early point is between Maria's worldliness and his sense of obligation to Mrs. Newsome. He too isn't sure he ought to enjoy things, and the fact that he is capable of being seduced by the Old World only sharpens his painful sense of duty. When he gets to Paris and begins to appreciate the attractiveness of the place, he alters his religious interpretation of this mission: "Was it at all possible, for instance, to like Paris enough without liking it too much? He luckily, however, hadn't promised Mrs. Newsome not to like it at all. He was ready to recognize at this stage that such an engagement *would* have tied his hands. . . . The only engagement he had taken, when he looked the thing in the face, was to do what he reasonably could." (p. 62) Shortly afterward he has gone much further: "He wasn't there to dip, to consume—he was there to reconstruct. He wasn't there for his own profit—not, that is, the direct; he was there on some chance of feeling the brush of the wing of the stray spirit of youth." (p. 65) This process of compromise and revision is going on, largely between the lines, from the first day of Strether's acquaintance with Maria. He finds himself ashamed to tell her that he is from no more outstanding a home than Woollett, Massachusetts. (p. 11) When she asks if Mrs. Newsome is in Europe, he expresses relief that she is safely isolated at home. And when he dines with Maria he is given over to "uncontrolled perceptions" (p. 36), which add up to the conclusion that Maria's company is strikingly different from, and more exciting than, that of Mrs. Newsome. From the point of view of sensuous appeal, Maria and Europe seem to be winning the battle hands down.

But Strether is not so easily wooed. Before he has met Chad he remains convinced that however provincial Mrs. Newsome may appear, her moral ideas and purpose are completely sound. To think that Strether's eye immediately dictates to his heart is to forget the basic Puritan distrust of the flesh; for Strether is, in spite of himself, a descendant of the Puritans. This is brought out only in suggestion, but the suggestions are deliberate and important. Strether's sense of sin is out of all proportion to his sins. Like Mrs. Newsome ("to lie was beyond her art"; p. 66) he looks upon his vows as sacred obligations. Witness, for example, his need to rationalize his enjoyment of Europe, even on the most innocent

level. He has, as he later accuses himself, an "odious ascetic suspicion of any form of beauty." (p. 133) Even his vocabulary shows
traces of Calvinism. For example, Chad appeals to him as a "pagan," though a pagan whom Woollett would do well to tolerate.
Waymarsh, the personified survival of New England's fiercest asceticism, is called a "Hebrew prophet" (p. 79) by his English
benefactress, Miss Barrace. Strether's apparent shift of allegiance
can be viewed in part as a movement from a Calvinistic to a more
secular view of human pleasures.

Strether's perceptions are no less restricted by his background
than Hyacinth's were. At first, to Maria Gostrey's considerable
amusement, all things European strike him as elegant and grand.
And he begins with none of Maria's talent for the crucial business
of guessing what the other characters are thinking. But with Maria's help he gradually learns to make the proper distinctions, and
by the middle of the book his judgment has been so improved that
he can find his way through the maze of true and false hints with
no aid at all. However, it is significant that his moral background,
in fixing his interpretation of the word "virtue," prevents him from
grasping the most important—and to Maria's mind the most obvious—fact about Madame de Vionnet's attachment to Chad.
Strether is constantly forced to temper the extremity of his values,
for Paris is a place where "what seemed all surface one moment
seemed all depth the next." (p. 62) It defies the compartmentaliz-
ing mind. Before the city is through with Strether he will have
admitted by implication that all his previous beliefs were mere
prejudices, and the fact that he does so with an acquiescence
approaching zeal proves not only that he is covetous of the truth,
but also that as an American he is thoroughly aware of his emptiness. Once he has been emancipated from a few superstitions there
is nothing left to sustain him in the comfortable belief that his ideas
at any given point correspond to realities. The very earnestness
with which he denounces Woollett can be traced to an insufficiency that Woollett instilled in him. His inadequacies spur him
on to deeper penetrations, just as, in a lesser sense, Waymarsh's
inadequacies lead to grander gestures of defiance. There is something distinctly noble in such reactions. It is what Maria means
when she says, "We're abysmal—but may we never fill up!" (p.
295)

The pervasive *motif* of youth versus age, of hovering opportunity and lost opportunity, crystallizes in Strether's acquaintance with "Little Bilham," Chad's companion. While Chad is conveniently absent from Paris, Maria's task of "softening up" the ambassador is transferred to Bilham. James suggests this schematic arrangement in the last paragraph of Part II, before Strether has so much as spoken to Bilham. Maria is still in England, so that ". . . Waymarsh . . . struck him as the present alternative to the young man [Bilham] in the balcony. When he did move it was fairly to escape that alternative. Taking his way over the streets at last and passing through the *porte-cochère* of the house was like consciously leaving Waymarsh out." (p. 68) In other words, Strether symbolically rejects Waymarsh's manner of life in preference to an ideal first embodied in Maria and now to be represented by Bilham.

His attitude toward Bilham is friendly but equivocal. Bilham reminds him of his own youth, and Bilham's case history contains an interesting parallel to his own. They are both artists in temperament, but both have despaired of producing works of art. Strether has always lamented his failure, but Bilham is distinctly different. He is both "intense" and "serene" in Strether's eyes.

> It was by little Bilham's amazing serenity that he had been at first affected, but he had inevitably, in his circumspection, felt it as the trail of the serpent, the corruption, as he might conveniently have said, of Europe; whereas the promptness with which it came up for Miss Gostrey as but a special little form of the oldest thing they knew justified it, to his own vision as well, on the spot. He wanted to be able to like his specimen with a clear good conscience, and this fully permitted it. What had muddled him was precisely the small artist-man's way—it was so complete—of being more American than anybody. [pp. 86f.]

If Bilham is an "abysmal" American, he no longer shows it. His is an unusual case, and one whose characteristically American quality James does not bother to explain. He is serene, paradoxically, by virtue of his emptiness. "The amiable youth, then, looked out, as it had first struck Strether, at a world in respect to which he hadn't a prejudice. The one our friend most instantly missed was the usual one in favor of an occupation accepted. Little Bilham had an occupation, but it was only an occupation declined; and it was by his general exemption from alarm, anxiety, or remorse on this score that the impression of his serenity was made." (p. 87)

Bilham had come to Paris in the first place to learn how to paint, but like many another prospective artist he found that his high standards of taste prevented him from taking his own work seriously: "his productive power faltered in proportion as his knowledge grew." (p. 87) Thus his unwillingness to paint suggests something more than a personal inadequacy; it is a form of tribute to the Old Masters. Although "he had not saved from his shipwreck a scrap of anything but his beautiful intelligence and his confirmed habit of Paris" (p. 87), these things suffice. He is content to exchange most of the ordinary comforts of life for the privilege of collecting knowledge passively, of seeing Life as a disinterested spectator. His implicit philosophy is that to *live* one's vision of Life, in the strictest sense and concerning the broadest vision, involves abstaining from *doing* things at all.

This thrusts us into an area where James is not generally considered to be on firm ground. Few critics are willing to see any sort of idleness as a virtue. Bilham's case is only one of three in *The Ambassadors,* the other "idlers" being Chad and eventually Strether himself. We cannot attempt to justify or condemn James's position—if indeed it is his position—until all the evidence has been taken into account. But it should be apparent already that James is not dealing with industry versus laziness, but with ways of seeing. Bilham, like Hyacinth, is mentally active by virtue of being uncommitted to a narrowing form of life. His "activity" is the exercise of his expansive imagination, which he refuses to compromise. The intensity which I have called a necessary term in the definition of an American operates here in a new way: it reinforces an essentially European manner of living.

However, there is nothing truly European about Bilham. By virtue of his intensity he is "one of us," as Maria announces. This is why Strether is interested in seeing him make the most of his life. Strether understands the national want of fulfillment, and he knows from his own example that the way to profit from Life is not to watch it drifting away from you. He passionately exhorts Bilham not to "miss things," and later on he urges him to get married, first to Jeanne de Vionnet and then, when that appears unlikely, to Mamie Pocock. He wants Bilham to participate in, not merely observe, the great panorama, for participation is the richest means of seeing. The heart as well as the mind must be involved. No one is able to capture Life in its totality, in Strether's view, but everyone is entitled to try, and the only way to succeed moderately is to make a full-scale effort. The central passage of the book, already quoted in part, makes Strether's position clear:

> "The affair—I mean the affair of life—couldn't . . . have been different for me; for it's, at the best, a tin mould, either fluted and embossed, with ornamental excrescences, or else smooth and dreadfully plain, into which, a helpless jelly, one's consciousness is poured—so that one 'takes' the form . . . and is more or less compactly held by it . . . Still, one has the illusion of freedom; therefore don't be, like me, without the memory of that illusion. I was either, at the right time, too stupid or too intelligent to have it; I don't quite know which." [p. 150]

Although at any given point one is no better than his past circumstances have made him, he nevertheless has had a measure of influence over those circumstances. If one admits at the start that he has no hope of escaping the bounds of his education, he will be likely to despair of making that education as complete as it might be. "The illusion of freedom" can carry one along to something very close to actual freedom—an exposure to circumstances so various that any single mould will no longer determine one's sense of truth. The "fluted and embossed" mould can be construed as the refined, Parisian way of life, and the "smooth and dreadfully plain" one as Woollett's. Neither is substantially larger than the other. Paris, indeed, provides an incentive for making fine distinctions, but it also provides a kind of ready-made smugness, an attitude of moral neutrality speciously derived from "experience." The beauty of the American's life in Europe is that he can, if he so chooses, gather knowledge of a more complicated world than his own without abandoning his basic sense of values. Unlike the American in America he is encouraged to exercise his taste, and unlike the native European he can be directed in his self-cultivation by a clear awareness of his needs. But as Strether insists, he must aspire not merely to understand but to become a part of the Life he sees.

Although Bilham is perceptibly influenced by Strether and is anxious to take his advice, it is the younger man who seems to do most of the influencing. This relationship is curious. The fact that Bilham reminds Strether of his own younger days not only provokes Strether to forewarn him, it turns Strether himself toward Bilham's present way of thinking. He has found his "chance of

feeling the brush, of the wing of the stray spirit of youth." By the
moment of Chad's appearance on the scene Strether has realized
that his association with Maria, with Europe, with Bilham, and
even, by contrast, with Waymarsh, has left him "quite, already, in
Chad's hands." (p. 92) Bilham's presence has been the decisive
influence, and Strether's knowledge that this was premeditated by
Chad only makes Chad himself seem all the more remarkable.
Bilham has graciously introduced Strether to Chad's unexpectedly
well-mannered and agreeable form of life, and by means of his
extreme tact he has discouraged all embarrassing questions about
Chad's private affairs. As Strether tries to explain to Waymarsh—
and this is evidence of Europe's superiority in conversational battle—"You can't make out over here what people do know." (p. 75)
This inspires a classic outburst of Waymarsh's, ending in the pre-
cept, "People don't take a fine-tooth comb to groom a horse." (p.
75) Waymarsh sees a simple case of adultery as the essence of the
matter, and doesn't consider it worth the soiling of honest hands
to intervene. But Strether's thinking has been diverted from such
lines. When Chad arrives, sophisticated and genial, the ambassador is already somewhat ashamed of his mission.

Chad's character is left ambiguous until the story is almost over.
What we see is his high European polish, his ability to control any
situation with good-natured delicacy. He was, we are told, a
"brute," a "monster" of willfulness before he went abroad. The
unspoken question in Strether's mind, when he sees him so altered
in manner, is whether he has really changed inwardly. By degrees
Chad convinces him that he has. This is easy for Chad in the same
way that it was easy for Osmond to impress Isabel and for the
Princess to impress Hyacinth: being unfamiliar with Chad's conti-
nental manners, Strether has no way of telling true nobility from
false. He has been prepared to argue with Chad on frank American
terms, but he finds to his dismay that Chad has adopted a different
set of rules—rules of good manners which Strether can only admire and fall victim to. "You could deal with a man as himself—
you couldn't deal with him as somebody else." (p. 94)

Favorably inclined as he has now become to a world where
surfaces and depths seem interchangeable, Strether is greatly impressed by Chad's social developments. Even on the level of simple physical appearance the changes seem uniformly to be for the
better:

Chad was brown and thick and strong, and, of old, Chad had been rough. Was all the difference therefore that he was actually smooth? Possibly; for that he *was* smooth was as marked as in the taste of a sauce or in the rub of a hand. The effect of it was general—it had retouched his features, drawn them with a cleaner line. It had cleared his eyes and settled his color and polished his fine square teeth—the main ornament of his face; and at the same time that it had given him a form and a surface, almost a design, it had toned his voice, established his accent, encouraged his smile to more play and his other motions to less. He had formerly, with a great deal of action, expressed very little; and he now expressed whatever was necessary with almost none at all. It was as if, in short, he had really, copious perhaps, but shapeless, been put into a firm mould and turned successfully out. [p. 104]

This last sentence should come to the reader's mind when he meets Strether's slightly later sermon on moulds, fluted and plain. The implicit question is this: does Strether's identical image for describing Chad and describing the limitations of human consciousness mean that he is aware of the restrictions of Chad's new "form"? The answer is perhaps both yes and no. In his clearest moments Strether knows that Chad is no freer in the strictly metaphysical sense of the word. His new manner is the stamp of a mould like any other. Still, Strether has been carefully brought around to a feeling that Chad's new form is far supeior to his old one—or rather, to his previous lack of one. Chad is perfectly adapted to his environment, and the environment in question appears to Strether, at his present stage of awareness, as a whole universe of wonders. He believes in Chad's metamorphosis so thoroughly that at times he thinks of him specifically as "free": "His changed state, his lovely home, his beautiful things, his easy talk . . . what were such marked matters all but the notes of his freedom?" (p. 114) It would be unfair to say that Strether means exactly "free will" here. Compared to his old self Chad *is* free— he is free *from* his old self—and it is this comparison that seems uppermost in Strether's mind.

From this point onward the novel becomes an elaborate guessing game, a detective story whose mysteries are expressed in, and approached by means of, the slightest outward hints. Strether perceives that Chad is "a man marked out by women," and the chief mystery thus becomes "what woman or women?" The field is soon narrowed to two, Madame de Vionnet and her daughter Jeanne. Strether first suspects Jeanne of being Chad's beloved, but this error, fostered by Chad and Madame de Vionnet, is quickly rejected. It is Madame de Vionnet herself, a middle-aged woman with no immediate air of distinction, who has "formed" Chad. She appears to be genuinely in love with him, and the reader assumes that her affection is returned. When this much has been established in Strether's mind, Chad has only to convince him of Madame de Vionnet's worthiness in order to convert him utterly to his own point of view.

This is accomplished by Madame de Vionnet herself, and with the greatest of ease. Strether's gradual progression from a Puritan to an Epicurean frame of mind has weakened him for the final assault. Madame de Vionnet, as he discovers when his first impression of her has faded, is the epitome of civilized Gallic taste. Her taste is so sure that she rarely feels obliged to display it in public. As James remarks in his prospectus for the novel, the cleverest thing about her is that she does not seem "dazzlingly clever."[8] Her art lies in masking things so casually, with such an appearance of consistent frankness, that few or no traces of the hidden facts can be found; or, when forced into a corner, she can admit the bald and unpleasant truth with such delicacy that her inquisitor can be charmed out of his anger. "As she presented things the ugliness —goodness knew why—went out of them; none the less too that she could present them, with an art of her own, by not so much as touching them." (p. 398) She is a master at conversational politics, not merely in her easy duplicity but also in her manner of gently forcing people to pledge their allegiance to her. Strether in particular finds himself unable to resist her pleas for help. Such promises cost Madame de Vionnet a secret or two, but nothing that would seriously compromise her. She so impresses Strether with the difficulty of her own plight—caught as she is between Mrs. Newsome's pressure on Chad and, as we come to suspect, Chad's own business ambitions—that Strether ignores his own equally urgent predicament. He too is trapped; his indebtedness to Mrs. Newsome cannot be reconciled with his growing sympathy with the Frenchwoman. Strether, who has learned some duplicity himself, originally has no intention of keeping his promise to "save" Madame de Vionnet, as close attention to the motivation of his vow will bear out: "So it was that the way to meet her—and the way, as well, in a manner, to get off—came over him. He heard himself use the exorbitant word, the very sound of which helped to determine his flight. 'I'll save you if I can.' " (p. 177) He is convinced at this point that he *cannot* save her. But Madame de Vionnet, in James's image, drives the golden nail in a little farther at each opportunity, until Strether finds himself securely fastened and no longer minding it.

The thing especially to note in their relationship is that Strether is fully conscious of being "used" by his adversary. It is just her masterful way of ensnaring him that he admires. His reaction to her is aesthetic rather than moral, but his new dedication to "taste" is applied with a kind of moral earnestness. He fills up his social vacuum by placing good manners above everything else, including his self-interest—something that few Europeans, however cultured, would think of doing. Strether knows well enough that manners can be used for selfish ends. He simply doesn't care, as Waymarsh does, to conclude that all manners are base or noble according only to the ends in mind. The end in this case, the continuation of a love affair of dubious propriety, interests Strether far less than the tactics that Chad and Madame de Vionnet are employing with him. But if one decided that means justify ends for Strether, he would be thinking more schematically than Strether himself does. At this stage he is not entirely aware of the moral issue: he lets his "taste" blind him to it. This is a fault, no doubt, but it is not the same as saying that he is frankly condoning adultery.

It is tempting to regard this phase of Strether's development, in which he has become even more Gallic than Chad in moral outlook, as an ethical nadir. Certainly he has suffered from having abandoned one moral system without fully understanding its substitute. But some critics have gone further and said that this mistake is a sign of insufficiency in *The Ambassadors* as a whole. Yvor Winters, for example, inveighs against James for bothering with the idle, worthless existence of Chad in Paris, and is especially disappointed with Strether for being so impressed by him. Chad, Winters says, is not worth "the expenditure of quite so much moral heroism as Strether expends upon him." "The central issue," he concludes, "does not quite support the dramatics."[9] This statement is based on the mistaken assumption that nothing more is at stake than the future career of Chad Newsome. The issue is ethical, and of the highest order: it is the relationship of principle to taste. Winters would probably say, with Waymarsh, that principle transcends taste, and that it is immoral to think otherwise. Madame de Vionnet might be said to exemplify the possibility that taste may replace principle. But where does Strether stand? This, I submit, is the most difficult and crucial problem in the book. Although Strether's values at this point are still imperfectly formed, we can get some idea of his position by reviewing his opinion of the three characters who are contending for his approval.

Very little can be said in behalf of Mrs. Newsome. The fact that she never appears in person and yet is ever present in the minds of the New England characters makes us feel her almost as an abstract force, a principle of repression. Her correspondence with Strether, which seems so friendly and patient at first, begins to take on sinister overtones when we realize that he is being subtly compelled to justify all of his actions, and indeed his thoughts, according to her particular standards. She is the mythical figure we have come to recognize as "Mom"—"a *moral* swell" (p. 47), as Maria calls her. She "doesn't admit surprises." (p. 358) In contrast to her intensely abysmal countrymen she is "filled as full, packed as tight, as she'll hold." (p. 358) Strether eventually decides that there is but one way to deal successfully with her: "You've got morally and intellectually to get rid of her." (p. 358) And with her goes Woollett, Massachusetts, and its habit of narrow moralizing.

Chad and Madame de Vionnet are not so easily judged. One thing is certain: Chad has derived great benefit from her love. Although Yvor Winters suggests that she has corrupted Chad's values,[10] quite the opposite is true, as everyone in the novel except Sarah Pocock is perfectly able to recognize. Chad has been transformed from a nasty young adventurer into a gentleman. Whatever sense of obligation he has acquired, whatever tact and decency and tolerance are due to Madame de Vionnet's deliberate influence. Furthermore, these developments are not accompanied by any of the overtones James is so adept at suggesting in a relationship where one party is guilty of tyrannizing another's mind. Madame de Vionnet has "freed" Chad and even though she wants his presence desperately, she will give him up rather than use his real indebtedness to her as a means of keeping him. When Strether learns that Chad is ready to desert her and return to

Woollett, the case for America's symbolic value looks extremely poor. As Elizabeth Stevenson puts it—although perhaps too neatly —"In this novel the young American is the cruel exploiter, and the older, experienced European woman is the gentle victim."[11]

By the time the Pococks, Mrs. Newsome's second-string ambassadors, have descended upon Paris, Strether has his conclusions about the above relationships well in mind. He feels that Chad owes everything to Madame de Vionnet, and that neither he nor Chad owes anything to Mrs. Newsome. He expects that the arrival of Sarah and Jim Pocock, Chad's sister and brother-in-law, and Mamie Pocock, Jim's sister and Chad's prospective wife, will bring only confusion and ill feeling. America's symbolic fortunes may be said to take an upward turn when Strether meets the Pococks and finds them not so fierce after all. Furthermore, he is immediately reminded of Mrs. Newsome's special forgotten charm, which these envoys seem somehow able to project:

> The woman at home, the woman to whom he was attached, was before him just long enough to give him again the measure of the wretchedness, in fact really of the shame, of their having to recognize the formation, between them, of a "split." He had taken this measure in solitude and meditation; but the catastrophe, as Sarah steamed up, looked, for its few seconds, unprecedentedly dreadful—or proved, more exactly, absolutely unthinkable; so that his finding something free and familiar to respond to brought with it an instant renewal of his loyalty. He had suddenly sounded the whole depth, had gasped at what he might have lost. [pp. 252f.]

This reversal is only temporary, however. Its real function is to remind Strether and ourselves of how much is at stake in his decision to defend Madame de Vionnet. Sarah Pocock, who is less sophisticated than her mother but is essentially a faithful embodiment of her mother's attitudes, quickly loses Strether's sympathy by refusing to see that Chad's new virtues are due to Madame de Vionnet's care. She looks upon that lady as a kind of sorceress, and upon Strether as a bewitched apprentice. When Sarah blithely insists that she "knows" Paris, as if the city were only an assortment of tourist attractions, Strether's revulsion becomes complete. America as represented by Sarah soon falls back into disrepute.

Mamie's effect is more impressive. She too evokes old and pleasant sentiments. "There were positively five minutes in which the last word seemed of necessity to abide with a Woollett represented

by a Mamie." (p. 253) But Mamie, unlike Sarah, stands for something to which Strether is permanently rather than occasionally
dedicated. This is our friend, the abysmal American soul: "he felt
satisfied that her consciousness was, after all, empty for its size,
rather too simple than too mixed, and that the kind way with her
would be not to take many things out of it, but to put as many as
possible in." (p. 254) Strether finds Mamie quite able to stand a
comparison with her French contemporary, Jeanne de Vionnet.
Jeanne is perfectly bred and charmingly innocent, in the sincerely
lifeless way that only convent-educated girls can be innocent.
Mamie's innocence is of a richer and fuller sort. She faces every
situation honestly and realistically, regardless of its hazards.
Jeanne, by contrast, is all fragility and discretion. The difference
is something like that between a sunflower and a lily; if not the
lovelier of the two, Mamie is unquestionably the taller and stur-
dier. But she finds herself rendered no less helpless by Chad's new
manners than Strether was. She is able to perceive at a glance that
Chad has altered for the better, and she lets the implications of this
fact influence her so deeply that she relinquishes her claim to him.
She sees that Madame de Vionnet has already accomplished her
project of "reforming" Chad, and that he is no longer in need of
her maternal patience. Mamie's saving grace, in Strether's eyes, is
that her sense of justice is stronger than her Woollett prudishness.
Evil or not, Madame de Vionnet has done wonders for Chad, and
once Mamie has seen him she never for a moment entertains the
evangelical notion of converting him back to "Americanism."

This is a blow to Strether, who has never before realized the
degree of incompatibility between Chad's world and Mamie's.
Believing as he still does in the "virtuous attachment," he has
hoped that a match between Chad and Mamie would reconcile the
opposing parties. Indeed, he sees it as his own last opportunity for
a reconciliation. But there is no more chance of converting Mamie
to Chad's ways than there appears to be of converting Chad back
to Mamie's. The ocean flows between them. Admiring Mamie in
spite of his general sympathy with the French attitude, Strether
hesitates at moments between the two. His association with Jim
Pocock at this point reinforces his attachment to Woollett in a
unique way. Jim, to be sure, is easygoing and empty headed, and
his immediate approval of Chad's cause provides little more than

comic relief. He has no influence with his moralistic wife, and no conception of the values at stake. But he sees the affair on a marvelously simple level that Strether concedes to be at least partly justified by the facts. As Strether explains, "He understands . . . that Chad and I have above all wanted to have a good time, and his view is simple and sharp. Nothing will persuade him—in the light, that is, of my behavior—that I really didn't, quite as much as Chad, come over to have one before it was too late. He wouldn't have expected it of me; but men of my age, at Woollett —and especially the least likely ones—have been noted as liable to strange outbreaks, belated, uncanny clutches at the unusual, the ideal." (p. 284) Jim is himself a caricatured example of the type, and insofar as Strether is forced to agree that Jim's escape is similar to his own, he must disbelieve in the absolute, almost occult significance of Paris. When he begins to think of his whole adventure as an outlet for grievances, a binge, the desire is reborn in him to get back to simple American realities. His hope of matching Bilham and Mamie is offered as a kind of expiation, a reaffirming of Woollett's moral power: "I've been sacrificing so to strange gods that I feel I want to put on record, somehow, my fidelity—fundamentally unchanged, after all—to our own." (p. 319)

This "return to religion" is also inspired in part by his disgust at the news of Jeanne de Vionnet's impending marriage to a French nobleman whom he has never met, and whom Jeanne knows scarcely better. He learns that Chad has been instrumental in arranging the match, a marriage of pure convenience on Madame de Vionnet's side in more respects than one. Strether's reaction is twofold. In the first place, the impersonal handling of the affair gives him an immediate sense of the potential cruelty of custom. The question of whether Jeanne loves her fiancé is, de- spite Madame de Vionnet's assurances, left open, and we never know for certain that she hasn't loved Chad all along. Strether is burdened with the sense that this fine, delicate creature is being sold for the sake of a title. Nothing could be more appalling to the romantic American soul. Strether feels for the first time that he has probed through the veil of manners and reached their ugly signifi- cance: "He had allowed for depths, but these were greater: and it was as if, oppressively—indeed absurdly—he was responsible for what they had now thrown up to the surface. It was—through something ancient and cold in it—what he would have called the real thing." (p. 291) Strether is now jolted from his faith in the interchangeability of surfaces and depths. He has finally allowed his idea of evil to settle upon the French as well as the American way of doing things.

The other result of the news is similar. Strether is suddenly aware that Chad and Madame de Vionnet are unscrupulous in the exercise of their social powers. It is convenient for them to have Jeanne safely married, especially if, as is quite possible, she really is in love with Chad.[12] Looking backward, we can see that they have "used" her all along, first as a decoy to confuse Strether, and then as an example of French purity to impress (unsuccessfully) Sarah Pocock. This is all fair and normal in Madame de Vionnet's moral world, as Strether reluctantly observes. But he has not expected to find that Chad, the American, is not only an accomplice to the cynical marriage but actually its most diligent promoter. At this point Chad begins to take on some of the sinister hues of Gilbert Osmond.

Madame de Vionnet attempts to justify the matter to Strether by hinting that Jeanne is, after all, better off reasonably married than she would have been as a spinster pining away for Chad. Strether himself should supposedly approve of the match, for it ought to allay his fears that Jeanne is being undeservedly left out of things. But this line of heartless rationalization does not produce the desired effect. When Madame de Vionnet intimates that the marriage was arranged partly in order to please Strether himself, he is more enlightened and disturbed than ever. "Thus she could talk to him of what, of her innermost life—for that was what it came to—he must 'accept'; thus she could extraordinarily speak as if, in such an affair, his being satisfied had an importance. It was all a wonder, and it made the whole case larger." (p. 292) At the end of this conversation Strether is at least persuaded that everyone's convenience has been considered; but until this time he hadn't suspected that everyone's convenience *should* be considered in the marriage of one's daughter. The scene ends on a note of high tension. Madame de Vionnet has realized that Strether has been temporarily, perhaps permanently disillusioned with her methods, and Strether in his turn is on the brink of condoning or condemning Chad.

With one major exception, the stage has now been set for the climactic scene. The exception is Sarah Pocock's blunt ultimatum to Strether. With what would appear to be subtle wisdom Chad has placed the question of his staying or leaving entirely in Strether's hands. James suggests in his prospectus that this is simply the result of having worked Strether over to Chad's side, but in the novel itself a quite different motive is ascribed. Chad is weary of carrying the burden of choice. He has already made up his mind that he wants to return to Woollett and go into business; ironically enough, it has been his contact with Strether that has turned his thoughts homeward, but Strether's admiration for Madame de Vionnet that has kept him in France. Morally Chad is obligated both to Madame de Vionnet and to his mother, but much more strongly and immediately to the former. Strether can not only save him from returning if he wants to stay, he can "force" him to return, thus saving him the embarrassment of breaking openly with Madame de Vionnet on his own initiative. Chad is really hoping that Strether will decree his return. He puts his fate in Strether's hands not simply because he wants to leave—for he must surely be aware that Strether wants him to stay—but because his own hands are tied. Strether is his only hope of success. When Strether is, as a consequence, faced with a direct assault from Sarah, her outburst against his hesitation imprints on his mind an indelible image of the crudity of spirit that she and Mrs. Newsome represent. In short, he has been disillusioned with Woollett once and for all.

The discovery that Chad really wants to go home is another important step in Strether's disappointment with him, and yet it helps Strether to judge him realistically. In his opinion anyone who cannot see the full importance of Madame de Vionnet's gift is sadly deficient in imagination. He has placed Mrs. Newsome and Sarah on this list, and now he finds that he must include Chad himself. But this does serve to clear Chad of the suspicion of evil intentions. He is devoid of a moral imagination of either good or evil. Chad has a natural assertiveness and charm which, tempered by his new command of manners, serve his interests as it were automatically, without his ever deliberately planning to hurt others. He more or less inadvertently inspires good faith. Maria sums it up: "There's nothing so magnificent—for making others feel you —as to have no imagination." (p. 359) In the symbolic battle between Paris and Woollett this is a further gain for Paris, for Strether now feels that no one is doing justice to Madame de Vionnet, including Chad. Then again, he is reminded by Chad's blindness that Madame de Vionnet's achievement has not been so complete as he once thought. The issue has reached a stalemate and Strether, exhausted with fixing his ideals first on one party and then another, takes a train into the country for a day's rest.

Here, in one of James's truly great scenes, Strether finds Chad and Madame de Vionnet together under circumstances which imply their physical intimacy discreetly but irrefutably. Strether has been made increasingly aware of the true state of affairs, but this comes as a tremendous shock. "He recognized at last that he had really been trying, all along, to suppose nothing. Verily, verily, his labor had been lost. He found himself supposing everything." (p. 389) What this self-deception had signified was an effort to reconcile Woollett and Paris by means of the "virtuous attachment" theory; if Madame de Vionnet were truly disinterested, she could deserve the approval of Strether's chaste New England moral sense. Madame de Vionnet is not at all disinterested, and Strether realizes with a jolt that the fact of adultery has in itself no moral connotations for her. France must be deemed amoral even in the most liberal American perspective. The question hence becomes: is Strether going to condone Madame de Vionnet's amorality because she is French, and in deference to her civilizing influence, or is he going to condemn her flatly as a sinner?

While Strether is still in a condition of spiritual numbness from his discovery, he finds himself an actor in a delicate social comedy, the author and heroine of which is Madame de Vionnet. Instead of recognizing the obvious fact that she and Chad have been "found out," she plays her part to the hilt, pretending that she and her "good friend" have merely been passing a harmless afternoon in the country, not a whole weekend. Unfortunately, some of the essential props are absent, and all three actors are aware that the presentation is unconvincing. Still, by maintaining her pretense Madame de Vionnet gains a kind of triumph over the laws of evidence and logic. Looking back on it, Strether sees that her performance has been heroic rather than cowardly, and in a sense, in spite of everything, disinterested. She has preserved the decorum of the situation out of an innate respect for decorum itself: "He perceived soon enough at least that, however reasonable she might be, she was not vulgarly confused, and it herewith pressed upon him that their eminent 'lie,' Chad's and hers, was simply . . . such an inevitable tribute to good taste as he couldn't have wished them not to render. . . . once more and yet once more, he could trust her. That is he could trust her to make deception right." (p. 398)

This is Madame de Vionnet's saving grace, and it is not so immoral as it may sound. Strether now has it clearly in mind that the essential human relationships are not much different in Paris than in Woollett. The real difference is that whereas Woollett has refused to admit their existence, Paris has learned how to clothe them acceptably and live with them. Strether's sympathy leans toward Madame de Vionnet in spite of all he has learned. This sympathy is firmly and finally sanctioned when Madame de Vionnet confesses to him, in her wonderfully circumspect way, how thoroughly she loves Chad, and reluctantly begs him not to take Chad away. She realizes that such a decision will alienate Strether from his old world, and she shows a genuine sense of guilt at her persistence: "What I hate is myself—when I think that one has to take so much, to be happy, out of the lives of others, and that one isn't happy even then. . . . The wretched self is always there, always making one somehow a fresh anxiety. What it comes to is that it's not, that it's never, a happiness, any happiness at all, to *take*. The only safe thing is to give." (pp. 401f.) This defines the real poignancy of her situation. She is and has always been sensitive to her impositions on Strether and to the fact that she has been keeping Chad in Paris against his will. In fact, she seems to grasp these things more surely than the benefits which atone for them. Her dilemma is that she can see the unreasonableness of her demands and yet simultaneously feel driven by her love for Chad to persist in them. She has watched her sense of ethics fall victim to her passion, and she suffers for it. When Strether shows his awareness that her equilibrium hangs by the slender thread of Chad's not deserting her, she breaks into tears, "giving up all attempt at a manner." (p. 403) This is the final proof of her humanity. Her love, "mature, abysmal,[13] pitiful" (p. 404), when considered with the hopelessness of her future and her consciousness of having enlightened Strether too much for his own good, transforms her into a pathetic figure: "he could see her there as vulgarly troubled ... as a maidservant crying for her young man. The only thing was that she judged herself as the maidservant wouldn't; the weakness of which wisdom too, the dishonor of which judgment, seemed but to sink her lower." (p. 404) Her tears not only betray her despair, they remove Strether's last trace of belief that surfaces and depths can really be interchanged. Paris, the town of surfaces only, is now as far from being an image of reality as Woollett is. Strether has been left high and dry, a man without a home.

This is not to say that he rates Paris and Woollett equally as places in which to live. Paris in this respect is still a fairyland, and Woollett more than ever a penal colony. Furthermore, it is fair to say that the French heroine has attracted more of his admiration —his love, in fact—than any American character has. This is not the point at all. What really matters is that Strether, like Hyacinth, has found that neither of his potential homes is large enough to accommodate his sense of reality. That sense has been nursed by Paris and stunted by Woollett, and in this respect the book is "anti-American." Also, his previous belief that the "real" people, in contrast to merely "well-mannered" people, are all Americans has crumbled in his discovery of Madame de Vionnet's sensitive conscience and Chad's lack of it. But the central judgment of the novel is that both systems are inadequate. Neither Woollett's abstemious Puritanism nor Paris' amoral secularism can account for the sense of Life that Strether has achieved through the expansion of his social and moral awareness.

Strether ends his adventure in controversial fashion. Maria Gostrey has hinted that she would accept a proposal of marriage from him. Nothing seems to stand in the way of Strether's proposing, least of all his natural inclination, yet he announces instead that he will return to America, for the peculiar reason that he feels he shouldn't "get anything" out of his embassy. Some critics look upon this as simple ingratitude. Winters, whose desire to expose the guilty obliges him to read James on the lowest level, calls Strether's return a "sacrifice of morality to appearances," "so that he may not seem in Woollett to have got anything for himself from a situation in which he will seem to his friends in Woollett to have betrayed his trust."[14] Calmer observers (F. O. Matthiessen, for example) suspect that Strether here betrays an instinctive resurgence of Puritan sentiment in reaction to Europe's corruption. But the most reliable authority on the subject, to my mind, is James himself in his prospectus:

> He *can't* accept or assent. He won't. He doesn't. It's too late. It mightn't have been, sooner—but it is, yes, distinctly, now. He has come so far through his total little experience that he has come out on the other side—on the other side, even, of a union with Miss Gostrey. He must go back as he came—or rather, really, so quite other that, in comparison, marrying Miss Gostrey would be almost of the old order.[15]

This passage may superficially admit of the interpretation that it is Strether's American asceticism that stands in his way. However, this does not take his "total little experience" into account. What really obstructs him—and wouldn't have done so earlier, as James notes—is his final awareness that either way of life is insufficient tribute to Life. To marry Miss Gostrey would not in itself destroy his independence, but it would be a symbolic avowal that her world, the European one, corresponds to what he wants.[16] Europe comes closer than America, perhaps, but both fall so far short of the ideal that Strether prefers to forego them both. Like Hyacinth's suicide, this is a gesture of affirmation at the same time that it is the only choice he can make, considering the strength and nature of his vision. Strether is more heroic than Hyacinth, because his sacrifice is not demanded by a physical threat. His return to a life that can hold few pleasures, no comfortable illusions, no righteous prejudices, little in short except a continuous stream of insult to his widened consciousness, is his supreme tribute to Life as a whole. Marrying Miss Gostrey would have committed him to a manner of living which, a few weeks before, he felt perfectly prepared to enjoy, and to which he could still easily habituate himself. But this would be false to his vision. Strether has indeed emerged, as James says, "on the other side" of his social adventure. His final renunciation, so subtly couched in a refusal to hide from Woollett, is the perfect, necessary conclusion to the gradual extension of his awareness. Again we arrive at the supreme Jamesian irony, that a full appreciation of Life is incompatible with the everyday business of living. Strether, like Hyacinth, refuses to save himself from the war of his two societies. His vision is worth its price.

NOTES

1. *The Art of the Novel*, pp. 304f.
2. James's idea of the subjective nature of truth in human perception may be suggested by this passage from "The Art of Fiction": "Experience is never limited, and it is never complete; it is an immense sensibility, a kind of huge spider-web of the finest silken threads suspended in the chamber of consciousness, and catching every air-borne particle in its tissue. It is the very atmosphere of the mind; and when the mind is imaginative . . . it [the mind] takes to itself the faintest hints of life, it converts the very pulses of the air into revelations." (Reprinted in *Criticism: the Foundations of Modern Literary Judgment*, eds. Mark Schorer et al. New York, Harcourt, Brace, 1948, p. 48). Experience is not an external chain of events but "an immense sensibility"; it is inseparable from the texture of one's mind. If the mind is extremely receptive, it will find truth in impressions that other minds do not receive at all. Thus for James there is no such thing as a restricted body of experiences that are "true to life."
3. "The Art of Fiction," p. 50.
4. When coincidences do occur, they have been elaborately prepared for on a symbolic level, so that they appear to be determined by the natural development of the situation. For example, Maggie Verver's finding of the same cracked golden bowl that was almost given her as a wedding present by her adulterous husband and his mistress signifies her final awareness of the adultery. In *The Ambassadors*, Strether's unexpected meeting of Chad and Madame de Vionnet in the country has the same force. "What he saw was exactly the right thing . . . It was suddenly as if these figures, or something like them, had been wanted in the picture, had been wanted, more or less, all day, and had now drifted into sight, with the slow current, on purpose to fill up the measure." *The Ambassadors* (New York, Harper, 1948), p. 382.
5. Philip Rahv, *Image and Idea* (Norfolk, Conn., New Directions, 1949), p. 13.
6. *The Art of the Novel*, p. 308. In his prospectus of 1900 for *The Ambassadors*, James emphasized a more specific reason for Strether's seriousness. Many years previous to his "embassy" Strether had buried an adolescent son whom he had greatly misunderstood through an unwillingness to make allowances for the boy's "strangeness." When the boy died Strether blamed his own narrow-mindedness for his son's unhappy life, and as a result he developed a compulsive desire to remind himself of his failure. "Deep and silent penance has he privately performed ever since." *(Notebooks*, p. 382) However, James does not stress this circumstance in the novel itself.
7. *Notebooks*, p. 378.
8. *Notebooks*, p. 392.

9. Yvor Winters, *Maule's Curse* (Norfolk, Conn., New Directions, 1938), p. 206.

10. *Ibid.*, p. 184.

11. Elizabeth Stevenson, *The Crooked Corridor* (New York, Macmillan, 1949), p. 60.

12. It is conceivable that Jeanne, loving Chad but taking in the extremity of her mother's predicament, willingly sacrifices herself by professing enthusiasm for her marriage to another man. But James never suggests it, and I am not sure that Jeanne possesses such strength of will. In any case her unblinking obedience to *maman* produces the desired results.

13. The key word "abysmal" here suggests to me that Madame de Vionnet is in some sense "American" in spirit. Her strong love for Chad provides her with an intensity which, while it can hardly be classified as a sacred rage, nevertheless deprives her of the common European confusion of manners and morals. She, no less than Waymarsh and much more than Strether, is able to recognize that means do not really justify ends. The fact that her means are graceful does not convince her that they atone in any way for her less praiseworthy ends. Of all the characters in the book she is the most dispassionately severe in judging herself.

14. *Maule's Curse*, p. 207.

15. *Notebooks*, p. 415.

16. James confessed to Grace Norton: "One's attitude toward marriage is . . . the most characteristic part doubtless of one's general attitude toward life . . . If I were to marry I should be guilty in my own eyes of inconsistency—I should pretend to think quite a little better of life than I really do." Quoted by F. O. Matthiessen, *Henry James: the Major Phase* (New York, Oxford University Press, 1944), p. 50.

"The New England Conscience, Henry James, and Ambassador Strether"

AUSTIN WARREN*

The 'New England conscience' I cannot find used by any writer before Henry James used it in his *Notebooks*—an 1895 entry; yet, as James five years later used the phrase in single quotes, it was presumably an already current phrase. But it does not appear in Hawthorne or in Mrs. Stowe's New England novels: they describe the phenomenon but never name it. It seems probable that, like 'Puritan', it was first devised by an outside observer or critic,—and that it may have first been used pejoratively,—by those who did not regard the private conscience (if I may be tautological) as both infallible and inexorable. Whether or no this conjecture be accurate, by the end of the nineteenth century New Englanders came to pride themselves on the possession of this high and morbid ethicality.

Such stringency of conscience is, of course, not limited to New Englanders. Matthew Arnold has wise things to say about it in his *Culture and Anarchy* (1869) when he speaks of a "strict conscience" as the pride of English Puritanism,—a term which he chronologically extends to include the Nonconformists of his own time. Recommending that the Hebraic conscience be supple-

*From *The Minnesota Review*, II, Winter, 1962. Copyright 1961, *The Minnesota Review*. Reprinted by permission of the author and *The Minnesota Review*.

mented by the Hellenic consciousness, he appositely quotes the eighteenth century Anglican Bishop Wilson's maxim, "Never go against the best light you have, [but] take care that your light be not darkness." I understand this maxim to mean—as I think Arnold took it to mean—that conscience is a man's ethical light and moral imperative, and must be followed, but that a second and equal—or better say, almost equal—duty is to regard the conscience as educable.

It would be a mistake also to suppose that over-conscientiousness to be purely a Protestant phenomenon. The Catholic Church knows it and calls it 'scrupulosity'—a perpetual self-scrutiny, such a concern about details of conduct and purity of intention as leaves the penitent always uncertain whether he has confessed all his sins and whether his absolution is valid since he is not sure whether he has been truly or adequately enough penitent.

None the less, the fussy and overexacting conscience is, in my judgment, commoner among Protestants than among Catholics, and commonest among those who are 'ethnically' rather than theologically Protestant. The seventeenth century Puritan, like the Orthodox Jew, had an intricate and manifold series of duties prescribed by the infallible Bible and the almost infallible clergy; but the latter-day Protestant has no Church to prescribe his major duties and no confessional save his own journals. He is still under the Law, or rather the Laws, and cannot apprehend that Love is the fulfilling of the Law.

Now comes an important distinction. Suffering for conscience's sake is not to be confounded with suffering from conscience. The former,—the lot sometimes unchosen and sometimes rather perversely chosen—by Christians among pagans, by Catholics among Protestants, by Puritans among Anglicans, by Quakers and Seekers among Puritans—consists in being beaten, imprisoned, sent into exile, or put to death, and has its own reward in the martyr's crown. Such persons are what we now call 'conscientious objectors.' They are not tormented by their own consciences but by rival theologies and rival ecclesiasticisms.

The second group are those who suffer interiorly. They are tormented by doubts and scruples, feel the mixed—and, hence, impure—motives which prompt them to perform what, externally considered, are 'good works', never feel worthy enough to 'join the church', never, however many duties they may have performed, feel that they have adequately done their Duty, never feel their contrition adequate to the assurance of Divine pardon.

The immigrant Fathers of New England appear to have been untroubled by conscience in this second sense. Converted either from religious indifference or from the 'imperfectly reformed' Church of England, they felt no serious doubt of their being, in the language of St. Paul's Epistle to the Romans, 'saints' and the 'elect'. They had suffered imprisonment or, at any event, silencing at the mandates of Archbishop Laud, suffered again the journey, which they forever compared to the Israelites' journey through the wilderness to Canaan, which brought them to a place where they could found a truly theocratic state; and at last they were, as they delighted to repeat, a "city set upon a hill," an exemplar to the rest of the world.

The Journals of Michael Wigglesworth, an early Harvard graduate, and of Cotton Mather, grandson of immigrant clergy, show much self-chastisement—and, in the case of Mather—many instances of 'special providences'—self-glorifications viewed as signs of angelic, if not Divine, visitations; but in both cases,—and especially Mather's—it is difficult to distinguish between rhetoric and the desire to edify posterity on the one hand and, on the other, sincere pangs of conscience.

Jonathan Edwards is the beginning of a new theological and ethical era. No one can read his Resolutions and his Diary without feeling that they are straightforward wrestlings of the soul; and I cannot doubt that he was a saint in that more special and Catholic sense unintended by the Pauline and Puritan use of 'saints' as meaning all members of the visible churches of Christ. With Edwards and his *Treatise on the Religious Affections*, and with his disciples, Hopkins, Bellamy and Emmons, the New England conscience as directed against oneself instead of against others begins to take shape. It is manifest in Mrs. Marvyn, a chief figure in Mrs. Stowe's *The Minister's Wooing*—Mrs. Marvyn, who sits weekly under the once famous Dr. Hopkins' Edwardsean sermons, is scrupulous in the performance of every duty, yet can never feel that God has elected her to salvation. It is manifest in Dr. Hopkins' own celebrated test of sanctity: that one should be willing to be damned for the glory of God. That was a test which certainly never occurred to seventeenth century Puritans. Indeed, in the whole period of Edwardsean theology, so distinct from the earlier so-called Calvinism of the immigrant Fathers, one sees conscience turning from the testimony that one is elect to the doubt whether one is not only damned but worthy of damnation.

Unitarianism, of the benign Boston variety, might be expected to mitigate the New England conscience. But here comes another turn of the screw. Legalism and theological system give their own security. To dissolve and discharge them leaves men free to worldliness or to antinomianism or to moralism, but also to self-doubt and self-scrutiny and self-laceration.

Emerson was an innocent antinomian. Says the father of the Jameses, Emerson "never felt a movement of the life of conscience from the day of his birth till that of his death." And James adds, "if we are still to go on cherishing any such luxury as a private conscience toward God, I greatly prefer for my own part that it should be an evil conscience. Conscience was always intended as a rebuke and never as an exhilaration to the private citizen." Emerson knew youthful depression and sense of inferiority, but he never knew either of the two religious realizations of man,—the sense of sin of the Western Church or the sense of finiteness of the Eastern Church. He was, as William James said in *The Varieties*, once-born.

Yet Emerson is not a representative of the New England conscience. Eventually, the New England conscience is left faced, not with serene and blithe innocence but with the impersonal concept of Duty,—not with some naturalistic or humanistic version of Grace but with the Moral Law, a concept and a tyrant more rigid and all-searching, of a rectitude to which one can never attain because it is a perfection both of taste, manners, conduct, and motives. And, as with the ancient Jews, Law does not separate itself from Laws. There are so many high principles to be followed that the high principles themselves conflict, and every case becomes a 'case of conscience'—that is, an attempt to discover which high principle must take precedence over what other high principle. The hedonist may be happy; the saint may say with St. Augustine, "Love and do what you will"; but either the lower or the higher spontaneity is ruled out by the supremacy of Duty.

Howells' novel of 1891 is called *An Imperative Duty;* but to the mind of one like his character, Mrs. Meredith, whom he first met in company of "a serious young clergyman, sojourning in Florence after a journey to the Holy Land," every duty is in turn an imperative, for she has "a conscience of prodigious magnifying force, cultivated to the last degree by constant training upon the ethical problems of fiction" such as George Eliot's.

Henry James, who was not a New Englander by birth but who was a curious and attentive observer and analyst of its conscience, even before, in 1866, he met Howells, also not of New England origins but a convert to Boston and its conscience, notably employed himself in the definition of something at once alien and repellent but also, with whatever civilized improvements, an ineradicable part of himself.

In that little masterpiece, *The Europeans: A Sketch* (1878), he dealt with the Unitarian New England "upwards of thirty years since"—that is, the 1840's, the age of Channing Unitarianism as well as of Transcendentalism. The 'Europeans' are expatriate Americans whose uncle is the New England gentleman, Mr. Wentworth; and James sees the Wentworths through the expatriates' eyes and the expatriates through the Wentworths' and those of their Unitarian pastor, Mr. Brand. James already anticipates Mr. Wentworth's judgment when he describes expatriate Felix as having a face "at once benevolent and picturesque" but "not at all serious."

Gertrude Wentworth is a rebellious New England girl who is introduced in conjunction with her serious sister and her serious young pastor. It is Sunday morning, and she is not going to church. Her sister is, and when Gertrude criticizes her sister's hairdo, her sister replies, "I don't think one should ever try to look pretty." The clergyman thinks she is staying at home because she is depressed. Gertrude replies, "Depressed. I am never depressed." "Oh, surely, sometimes," he replies, as if he thought this a regrettable account of oneself. "I am never depressed," Gertrude repeated. "But I am sometimes wicked. When I am wicked I am in high spirits."

Reporting his introductory visit to his sister, Felix, the 'European', meets her comment: "They must be Puritans to their fingertips; anything but gay." "No, they are not gay," he admits. "They are sober; they are even severe. They are of a pensive cast; they take things hard . . . they have some melancholy memory or some *depressing expectation*. It's not the epicurean temperament. My uncle, Mr. Wentworth, is a tremendously high-toned old fellow; he looks as if he were undergoing martyrdom, not by fire."

When the sister, morganatic wife of a German Prince, comes to call with her brother, Mr. Wentworth looks "very rigid and grave" and "almost cadaverous"; but Felix's "light imagination had gained a glimpse of Mr. Wentworth's spiritual mechanism, and taught him that the old man being *infinitely conscientious*, the special operating conscience within him announced itself by several of the indications of physical faintness." This is naturally a grave occasion for a man infinitely conscientious: how to treat a lady so aristocratic, so unhappy and also, presumably, as a Catholic and European, so refinedly corrupt.

So much for the Wentworths of the 1840's.

In 1895, a young friend's mention of Howells in Paris' where he "had scarcely been . . . even in former days" and of Howells' sadly serious injunction to the young friend, "Live all you can: it's a mistake not to . . . I haven't done so—and now I'm old. It's too late," starts in James' mind the theme of *The Ambassadors*. His long *Notebook* entry of 1895 and his 20,000 word Prospectus for the novel, sent about 1900 to Harpers and published in the *Notebooks*, make clear the extent to which this novel was James' most serious as well as final dealing with the New England conscience.

The *Notebook* entries are conceptual and explicit in a way James as an artist would never be—and is not—in his novel. His hero, suggested by Howells, the convert to Boston, is a man "who hasn't 'lived', hasn't at all in the sense of sensations, passions, impulses, pleasures. . . . He has never really enjoyed—he has lived only for Duty [capitalized] and *conscience—his conception of them; . . .* lived for effort, for surrender, abstention, sacrifice." "He has married very young, and austerely. Happily enough, but charmlessly and oh, so conscientiously: a wife replete with the New England conscience." Now long a widower, he has been taken under the financial and moral protection of a New England and wealthy widow, an imposing figure in her city,—some place like Providence, Worcester, or Hartford. She is, says James, a reflection of Strether's pre-European initiation; and, as befits the American world, the woman is "of the strenuous pattern,"—Strether of the passive. She is will without imagination—unlike "poor Strether," who, despite his conscientiousness, has "imagination," that is, can conceive of other ways of being right than in his own suffering way.

Both Mrs. Newsome and Strether have New England consciences; but their consciences are of different species. Strether is said, in *The Ambassadors*, to arrive in Paris weary, perhaps on the verge of breakdown; but the representation scarcely bears out the assertion: he is, rather, frustrate at the ineffectuality of his life's efforts and mildly puzzled that being good has not made him happy.

Mrs. Newsome has no qualms on that score. She knows that we were not put here on earth to be happy; and her worries are not puzzles about herself. She must expiate, by her philanthropy, the unscrupulous ways by which her late husband left her wealthy; she must save her son, who has been for a few years in Paris, studying art and love, and who is presumably detained from returning to the unscrupulous promotion of her late husband's business by a sordid sexual attachment; she also is a woman of what used to be called 'culture and refinement', and hence unavoidably distressed by, as well as with familial piety attached to, her daughter, not so cultured and refined, and her daughter's husband, who is even less so.

As a woman of force, Mrs. Newsome is a kind of New England counterpart of Aunt Maud Lowder in *The Wings of the Dove;* but the difference between two types of Anglo-Saxons is rendered perfectly and—not at all strangely—in accord with Hawthorne's impressions of the two in *Our Old Home.* Mrs. Lowder is untroubled by conscience or nerves: she is Britannia seated on her money-bags and ruling the waves while Mrs. Newsome is a beautiful specimen of one kind of late nineteenth century American woman: when James says, in his characteristic way, that she is "a really remarkable woman" he does not mean to praise her but to delight in her being so remarkably pure a specimen of a type. She is "high, strenuous, nervous, 'intense' (oh, a type)—*full of ideals and activities*"—a delicious phrase. "She is many other things besides; invalidic, exalted, depressed, at once shrill and muffled, at once abounding and extremely narrow . . . she is a particularly intense and energetic invalid," ever active, by virtue of her "restless conscience"—one, of course, directed towards others—in charities, reforms, and good works.

Mrs. Newsome loves Strether, "poor fine melancholy, missing, striving, Strether": all of James' later sensitively passive men are Strethers; but he is not reported in the *Notebooks* as doing more than admiring and esteeming her. Indeed—though James can never bring either himself or Strether to say so, they both almost certainly fear and somewhat dislike her, though James has the advantage over Strether of seeing her as comic as well as—what Strether comes to see her as—narrow and unimaginatively righteous. Talking of her to Maria Gostrey, "his eyes might have been fixing some particularly large iceberg in a cool blue northern sea." Maria rejoins, "There's nothing so magnificent—for making others feel you—as to have no imagination." With full confidence in truth, undeniable in the sense intended, James successfully makes Mrs. Newsome, the unimaginative, present in the novel only through the force she exerts on the imaginative.

At the instigation of Mrs. Newsome, Strether sets out for Paris to rescue Chad from his un-New England ways. The manifest irony is that, finding Chad vastly—and, for the reader, somewhat incredibly—improved over his earlier self,—now indeed, at least temporarily, and in Strether's eyes—Strether is forced to a conception of salvation opposite to that with which he came. To save Chad is not to take him back to Worcester, Mass., but to keep him from returning. In this he finally fails. Chad's somewhat incredible elegance is attributable to the influence upon him of a Catholic noblewoman who, by her code, cannot marry him. As the *Notebooks* make more explicit than the novel, there is much of the unscrupulous late Mr. Newsome in Chad; and at the end of the novel he is fascinatedly studying that peculiarly unsavory American art, the art of advertising, and about to become a successful business man at Worcester.

But Chad's failure to be—only to seem—a man of imagination; the passive, borrowed, and temporary quality of his civilizing—is only incidental to James' book. Its real subject, as well as its point of view, is Strether. Its real theme is the inadequacy of the famous New England conscience. Strether—and apparently Mrs. Newsome—are not even Unitarians; but, as for conscience, each has been accustomed to accuse the other of being "morbid"—that is, over-beset by the sense of guilt and the sense of duty; and they both hold inflexibly to the conception that all adultery is a sin and that happiness is dangerous—if not indeed evil.

What occurs to Strether in his three or four months in Europe can be called either the development of conscience into consciousness,—or the change from the view of conscience as identical with its early presuppositions and mandates to the view that conscience is educable.

James calls his novel *The Ambassadors*, for the sake of the comic and the ironic; but it might, more seriously, have been called *The Instructors* or—had not he earlier used that title with delicate irony for a delicate and masterful *nouvelle*, "The Pupil." The novel is a novel of initiation, a *Bildungsroman*. Strether's instructors are Miss Gostrey, Chad, little Bilham, Mme. de Vionnet.

The first-named is the most explicit and pedagogic. She takes her disciple in hand from his arrival at Liverpool and relinquishes her commentaries only when she feels sure that he can "toddle alone"; and she establishes immediately an intellectual intimacy which makes him feel disloyal to the betrothed Mrs. Newsome.

Miss Gostrey directly sets to work on Strether. Strolling with her through Chester, Strether feels delight in the picturesque, dim memories of his former visit at twenty-five, but also conscience. "It was with Waymarsh he should have shared" this experience; and he was now, then, taking from Waymarsh "something that was his due." His observant mentor quickly comments, "You're doing something that you think not right." The dialogue on the sin of even pleasure goes on, with Strether's question, "Am I enjoying it as much as that?" and Maria's replying, adapting herself to a New Englander by reminding him that pleasure may be a duty, "You're not enjoying it, I think, so much as you ought," and Strether's presently saying, "Woollett [the name finally adopted for Worcester] isn't sure it ought to enjoy." His guide responds, "I wish you would let me show you how" to enjoy.

But, thus committing himself, he confesses to fearing; and he further expands the plight of the man beset by duties: "I'm always considering something else, something else, I mean, than the thing of the moment." Rebuked, he says, he knows he shouldn't. "If only I could! But that's the deuce of it—that I never can."

Paris abounds in surprises for Strether. He attempts to do his manifest duty. He indites long letters to Mrs. Newsome, long ambassadorial reports on things seen and heard; and as regularly for a time receives long replies from Woollett. But the time comes when Woollett letters cease, and a cable demands the ambassador's immediate return. He defies it, only to learn that his post is to be occupied by newly appointed and more sturdy legates. They come; before they depart, Mrs. Newsome's daughter Sarah summons Strether that he may make his submission. As Mrs. Newsome is "essentially all moral pressure," so, through Sarah, she "reaches him by the lengthened arm of the spirit." Still he resists; and Sarah has to remonstrate against his attitude toward the relation between Chad and Mme. de Vionnet—his acting as though there could be a doubt—as between Chad's loyalties—of Chad's duty. Strether has to ponder not only the question but "the sore abysses it revealed" before he can bravely answer, "Of course they're totally different sorts of duty"—an abstract reply which might be intelligible to the New England mind were it not followed by an affronting explication to the effect that Strether's state of mind, and—by polite, if not ironic, inclusion, pre-European—Sarah's proceeded from "our queer New England ignorance, our queer misconceptions and confusions—from which, since then, an inexorable tide of light seems to have floated us into our perhaps still queerer knowledge."

Sarah and party leave indignantly and virtuously for the Alps: and now Strether faces, in Book XI, a new trial of conscience and consciousness. He has had earlier adjustments to make—for eminent example that it is a married mother and not her daughter with whom Chad is in love. Yet he has been sustained by a formula which he has been careful not to test too rigorously—little Bilham's formula that what was under scrutiny was "an innocent attachment." Now he is called upon to witness not indeed the act of adultery but a situation which can scarcely be interpreted by easy inference as other; and his consciousness is forced to admit both that the relationship between Chad and Mme. de Vionnet has never been purely 'spiritual' and yet that little Bilham's delicate ambiguity of an "innocent attachment" was, in a sense which he can no longer deny, true. If there can be a conflict between duties, so there can be a distinction between sexual relations,—a point made, to Anglo-Saxon distress, by Swedenborg in his book, *Conjugial Love.*

Mme. de Vionnet does her subtle best at face-saving, not for her sake or Chad's but for Strether's; yet he is left with three pains, —the "quantity of make-believe involved, and so vividly exemplified, that most disagreed with his spiritual stomach," and, in one of those "vain vigils," those sleepless nights, so often attributed to 'poor Strether', with the pity that the make-belief should be "so much like lying," and, lastly, with the contrast the intimacy of others thus revealed and his own cold loneliness.

Now Strether's conscience has been educated, stretched, as far as it can go. He has learned to distinguish, in the case of others, tints and shades between white and black. And to this new-found ability to distinguish—or to admit to his consciousness that he can distinguish—he has sacrificed his chance of returning to Woollett, his marriage to Mrs. Newsome, his thus acquired economic security, although perhaps the first two were not severe losses but partly releases. Miss Gostrey must test out whether his knowledge of the "virtuous attachment" 's real nature, a knowledge she had all along possessed but felt he was conceivably not ready to take, has made "an arrest of his independence . . . , a revulsion in favor of the principles of Woollett"; she discovers it has not. He has arrived at one of the latest refinements of the New England conscience: that one can charitably allow others to do what one wouldn't do oneself, or, to put it another way, that one's public conscience is emancipated beyond one's private.

There are no very credible reasons why Strether must return to New England. Mme. de Vionnet, represented as to him the most attractive of women, would accept him as her lover; Chad would support him; Maria Gostrey wants to marry him, and in her he would have a sympathetic and intelligent companion. This rejection of Miss Gostrey is not eased for the reader by James' calling her the novel's *ficelle;* and Strether's rejection of her proposal— Strether must always be proposed to—certainly appears—if one wants to phrase it so—as failure to do a duty. But still Strether must return. The only reason he can give Maria is that he must go "to be right" and that "to be right" is, "out of the whole affair, not to have got anything for myself."

The last scenes with both Mme. de Vionnet and Miss Gostrey are masterly in the women's shrewd appraisals of Strether. According to the former, to feel himself victimized is evidently the way he must live. The latter reminds him that he has got something for himself—his "wonderful impressions" but, when reminded that he has not got, because not asked for, her, charmingly asks, "But why should you be so dreadfully right?"

James manages to shift the emphasis in the final lines of dialogue by having Miss Gostrey pun on the word *right.* In her question, *right* meant *good;* and *good* means *self-sacrificing;* in her final and, as James calls it, her "defeated protest," the word shifts its meaning to 'true to type'. "It isn't so much you're being 'right'—it's your horrible sharp eye for what makes you so."

Yet Miss Gostrey's question remains,—Why does Strether have to be so "dreadfully right?" And perhaps not less her comment. Strether's emancipated conscience in judging others,—an emancipation painful to him in the process and hardly joyful in the end —has still left him pride—his pride in the supererogatory rigors of his own, his New England, conscience.

THE GOLDEN BOWL

1904

"The Function of Slang in the Dramatic Poetry of the 'Golden Bowl'"

H. K. GIRLING*

In *The Golden Bowl*, Henry James demonstrates the mastery of his technique by presenting a polished solution of a problem which vexes every serious novelist: how to construct a narrative which will not display the marks of craftsman's tools. The usual affectation of omniscience has sometimes seemed to a novelist like a hood, assumed for the sake of anonymity, which has the effect of obscuring the vision; so he abandons his story to a single observer in an autobiographical novel, or interpolates a narrator as his agent. After disengaging himself from the scene with greater and greater success in earlier novels, James, in *The Golden Bowl*, entrusts the entire exhibition of his own "manifold delicate things, the shy and illusive, the inscrutable, the indefinable . . ."[1] to his characters. The "effect of representation, [his] irrepressible ideal," is to reach the reader through "a consciousness highly susceptible of registration," rather than through the "mere muffled majesty of irresponsible 'authorship.' "[2] The author leaves the stage, and the novel is in the hands of his actors, from whom directly come those perceptions and judgments which are to be as much part of the fiction as the events. The novelist allows himself only a playwright's interest in the irreducible residue of the text: the fable, the development of the action and the dramatic language.

The fable James worked out in some detail twelve years before he published the novel. His notebooks in the entry for November 28, 1892, give a full outline of the plot; while on February 19, 1895, referring to the plot again, he revels in "the divine principle of the

*Copyright c 1956, by The Regents of the University of California. Reprinted from NINETEENTH-CENTURY FICTION, XI, 130-147 by permission of The Regents.
[1] *The Golden Bowl* (Pocket ed.), 2 vols. (London: Macmillan, 1923), I, xxiv.
[2] I, vi.

Scenario." Another entry, on December 21, 1895, gives the synopsis of the plot in one sentence: *"The Marriages* (what a pity I've used that name!): the Father and Daughter, with the husband of the one and the wife of the other entangled in a mutual passion, an intrigue."[3]

The fable, then, no doubt in the form of a scenario, was completely worked out before James wrote the novel, where it lies embedded as the story. Dramatically, the divisions in *The Golden Bowl* are not so clearly marked as the scenes in *The Ambassadors* or *The Awkward Age.* But the novel proceeds in a series of confrontations, where the clash of motives in action is presented in forms which the author has purposely made external—in conversation, and in the analysis of appearances as they enter the consciousness of a single character. This is an enlargement of dramatic representation, in that both the spoken words and the silent movements of thought are in the script. The four main characters are all of princely stature, one by virtue of his ancient aristocratic lineage, two by virtue of their plutocratic wealth, the other by her beauty and aristocratic *savoir-faire;* and their conflicts are as intense as the desperate encounters in Renaissance tragedy. There remains to add the poetry.

The style of James's late novels is peculiarly his own. It is a vehicle of intense and subtle imaginings, hairbreadth analysis, and fine moral discriminations. Just as Shakespeare's blank verse was the medium which encompassed the whole of experience, from the trivial to the tragic, so James's prose immerses motive and action and significance in a medium of translucent consistency through which they are interpreted. The medium affords the possibility of wide dramatic differentiation, it enables each character to be intensely himself, but speech and thought and action are all viewed from an infinite distance by the universalizing eye of their creator. The record remains continuous, because vivid moments of actuality and protracted speculations are all measured in discrete fractions of time by the progress of events. The novels flow with the inevitability of dramatic colloquy. Not even an unuttered thought goes without its riposte or qualification in the active consciousness of his "registering" characters. The debate is swift, in conversation or in speculation. Each word is meant to be sounded; the prose has

[3] *The Notebooks of Henry James,* ed. F. O. Matthiessen and Kenneth B. Murdock (New York, 1947), p. 233.

the cadence of a speaking voice, echoing the distant accents of the author.

In Shakespeare's dramatic poetry, many of the profoundest insights and most piercing moments are recorded in the simplest and most familiar words: "Put out the light"; "Yet here's a spot"; "Pray, do not mock me." All these words belong to a very elementary vocabulary, but when they come together in a particular dramatic situation, they shine with the searing light of a revelation. James's vocabulary is not lacking in polysyllabic words, but frequently, at critical moments in his novels, he feels the need for a simplicity comparable to Shakespeare's, and rummaging through the battered words of daily speech, he emerges with treasures of slang.

To demonstrate the part played by slang in *The Golden Bowl*, it will be necessary to consider some of the general problems of the novel. Slang, with its aura of the esoteric, is an important element in the presentation of these problems, which are all connected with comprehension. Within the novel, in the relations between the characters, and outside the novel, in the perceptions of the reader, the quest is for a perfect understanding: of the events of the story and its resolution, of the motives which direct the plot, and most significantly, of those traces which inner conflicts imprint upon outer appearances. These traces are observed primarily in conversation, where a shared understanding is everything, secondly through the interpretation of facial expression and of gestures, and thirdly in the movements of the shadows which apprehensions and expectations cast upon graceful social occasions moment by moment. The outermost manifestation, the spoken word, gives a preliminary clue to the other modes of comprehension.

Vernacular differences offer possibilities of eccentricity in conversational idiom. There are several variations from a standard language, which is the polite idiom of upper-class England. Maggie Verver, who becomes the Princess, and Mrs. Assingham, both American born, are the only conversationalists who remain within the conventional bounds of "standard" English. Colonel Assingham, the only Englishman in the main group, serves chiefly as a stage confidant in prompting Mrs. Assingham's commentaries on the others, though in addition, his laconic questions and comments frequently point the issues at stake, and help the groping reader to follow the stages of Mrs. Assingham's swiftly moving analyses and speculations. Adam Verver, the millionaire connoisseur, is accredited only with a command of pure "American." Many of his expressions are clipped and oblique, and give an air of the legendary magnate, a Carnegie or a Rockefeller, full of latent inflexibility and power, though they do not mask his essential simplicity of appearance and manner, and his primal innocence of intention. Amerigo, the Italian prince who marries Maggie, and Charlotte, her penniless friend who becomes her father's wife, are, on the other hand, polyglots. They could display their accomplishments in French or Italian as well as English, although only odd phrases in their conversation exhibit this talent.

The variations in idiom, now facilitating communication, now obstructing it, are essential devices in the author's manipulation of situation, and hence they are of importance in the shaping of the plot, of which the design is largely an antithetical comparison between the rewards of the high understanding of Maggie and her father, and the punishments of the low conspiracy of the Prince and Charlotte. But even among these highly articulate creatures, James, according to his habit, allows many communications to be delivered in silence. No doubt he chooses to leave his revelations to be inferred, rather than to put himself under the obligation of stating them; but apart from this, the central situation in *The Golden Bowl* is controlled by Maggie's silence. In silence she observes, she suffers, she reconciles, and she triumphs. The final settlement could not have come about if she had given the smallest audible expression to her hopes and fears. She and her father, and her husband and her father's wife have in the end swerved from the brink of tragedy by remaining silent: ". . . the note was struck indeed; the note of that strange accepted finality of relation, as from couple to couple, which almost escaped an awkwardness only by not attempting a gloss."[4] Each has not dared to make an explicit confession of understanding the motives of any other person. Even to the end, the reader is not sure whether Adam Verver's complicity in the obscuring silence is due to his innocent ignorance or to his suppressed knowledge. Maggie's whole task is to prevent her father from giving expression to his speculations. She has succeeded by a hair's breadth. Contemplating the tranquillity of the last meeting of the two couples, she concludes: ". . . how

[4] II, 318.

impossible such a passage would have been to them, how it would have torn them to pieces, if they had so much as suffered its suppressed relations to peep out of their eyes."[5]

On two occasions the depths are stirred up by speech. Once, Maggie, driven to desperation in her anguish and fear, asks Mrs. Assingham in brutal words: " 'What awfulness, in heaven's name, is there between them [Amerigo and Charlotte]? What do you believe, what do you *know.?* ' " [6] Mrs. Assingham, at the sword's point, lies as heroically as Little Bilham lied to Strether in *The Ambassadors*. Maggie, however, is not deceived; she soon accepts the falsehood in the spirit in which it was intended, not to blind her suspicions, but to sustain her in the pretense that she has none. Mrs. Assingham's lie gives Maggie her positive answer; it also confirms and strengthens her determination to play out her role in silence.

On the other occasion, at Fawns, after Maggie has been face to face with the bitterest agony, Charlotte breaks the silence. Maggie has had a sudden vision of "the horror of finding evil seated all at its ease where she had only dreamed of good; the horror of the thing hideously *behind*, behind so much trusted, so much pretended, nobleness, cleverness, tenderness."[7] Then, on the terrace, Charlotte, desperate to discover how much Maggie knows about her association with Amerigo, asks if she and Maggie have become estranged. Maggie, in full retreat from explanation, and only too glad to give a false denial to the imputation, knows by Charlotte's question that she has been right to keep silence. Charlotte's motives are by now stripped bare, and all initiative has passed from her hands. The outcome of the situation depends upon Maggie's determination, beneath her quiet vigilance, to win back the Prince. Charlotte's outburst has betrayed her helplessness, and opened the way to Maggie's reconciling settlement, but Maggie has still kept the extent of her knowledge secret.

Silence can speak louder than words, and the words, as they issue from the mouths of the characters, often lift no more than a corner of the veil which hides their thoughts. James is prepared to reveal their inner contemplations at length, but each utterance, though it but graze with a fingernail the contextual situation,

[5]II, 319.
[6]II, 95.
[7]II, 209.

affects in some degree the extremely delicate balance of interrelations. Each word is an act playing its part as ponderably as a dagger thrust. Yet clearly, many of the words as they are spoken in conversation, seem merely polite or conventionally affable. To show the meaningfulness of them all, the speeches must be arranged in a pattern dominated by those phrases in which motives intersect or collide. Then the courteous exchanges assume the shape of the situation into which comprehension or the lack of it significantly intervenes.

Many important acts of understanding dispense with explicit statement. Maggie takes her cue from her husband about the way to deal with Charlotte, without words uttered; and the communication between Maggie and her father which results in the Ververs' decision to go to America, is framed in words designed as much to conceal their anxieties as to reveal their hopes. Difficulties of comprehension extend to idioms of thought as well as idioms of speech. The Prince, feeling excluded from the mutual understanding of Maggie and her father, thinks in the following terms:

> Those people—and his free synthesis lumped together capitalists and bankers, retired men of business, illustrious collectors, American fathers-in-law, American fathers, little American daughters, little American wives—those people were of the same large lucky group, as one might say; they were all at least of the same general species and had the same general instincts; they hung together, they passed each other the word, they spoke each other's language, they did each other "turns."[8]

Whatever idiom the Ververs employ, the Prince feels a stranger, faced with barriers of usage which no linguistic accomplishments can cross. He admits to Charlotte: " 'The difficulty is, and will always be, that I don't understand them. I didn't at first, but I thought I should learn to.' " Through the miraculous powers of Maggie's goodness, the Prince is redeemed and at last is able to understand his wife.

Is there a comparable outcome for Charlotte after *her* failure of comprehension? The novel ends with the Ververs' departure for American City, where Charlotte will heroically undertake the missionary work of the connoisseur's wife. Her heroism must be led up to, for throughout the novel it is painfully clear that for a

[8] I, 261-262.

creature like Charlotte, America is the darkness of limbo. When Adam Verver first intimates to Maggie his idea of returning there with Charlotte, Maggie is dazzled: "It was a blur of light in the midst of which she saw Charlotte like some object marked by contrast in blackness, saw her waver in the field of vision, saw her removed, transported, doomed."[9] Charlotte herself, in looking forward to what Maggie imagines as "her doom, the awful place over there—awful for *her,*"is driven to despair. She escapes one afternoon "to let her horror of what was before her play up without witnesses."[10] When Maggie follows her, their encounter in the garden teaches Maggie how to connive in the saving tact of Charlotte's plan to pretend that Maggie has come between her and her husband, whom she now claims for herself. This resolution, elaborated with courage and pride, places Charlotte in an attitude of heroic abnegation which Maggie and Adam, in the last scene, can call "great."

But "greatness" and redemption are not the same; and Adam Verver has not offered Charlotte what Maggie offered the Prince —redemption on the London scene. The only explanation can be that Charlotte never attained to the Prince's knowledge. He, with a *galantuomo's* mobility of affectionate attention, was not so entirely wrapped up in his love affair that he could not respond to Maggie's sudden access of fascination, which came through her developing knowledge of the situation. Charlotte, on the other hand, remained totally centered and dependent upon the Prince. Benighted and groping as he was, her only means of understanding Maggie—and through her, Adam—was through his perceptions; and in the critical testing time, he was holding back from her his discovery of Maggie's knowledge. In effect Maggie and the Prince were playing on her incomprehension; and the "invisible silken cord" which held her to Adam was woven as much from her ignorance as from Adam's unspoken and undefined knowledge. On the eve of her dispatch to American City, the Prince ungallantly betrays her to Maggie: " 'She ought to have *known* you. That's what's present to me. She ought to have understood you better. . . . She not only doesn't understand you more than I, she understands you ever so much less.' "[11] Then, to supply poor

[9]II, 239.
[10]II, 275.
[11]II, 306.

Charlotte's epitaph, " 'She's stupid,' he abruptly opined."

This is also a moral condemnation. A final promise of Charlotte's purification is offered by the combined influences of Adam Verver, American City, and the garnered *objets d'art;* but morally and intellectually she has been found wanting, and one default includes the other, as Mrs. Assingham announced, early in the novel: " '. . . stupidity pushed to a certain point *is*, you know, immorality. Just so what is morality but high intelligence?' "[12]

With morality, intelligence, and comprehension so interdependent how did James set about finding the words which would preserve the balance of situation, expose the wrong, defend the right, and display alternatively perspicuity or obtuseness on the part of extremely sophisticated utterers? The subtleties of James's conception could not have been realized if the resources of his prose had not responded to the demands which usually only dramatic poetry can fulfill. He deploys all the craft of his ambiguity and symbolism, and extracts the maximum support from action and situation. Beyond this, his slang phrases—though often they are faded ones—provide specimens of his dramatic and poetic language. These phrases often crystallize in a few words the complexities of the contextual situation.

James approaches a slang expression in one of two ways. He pretends that its metaphor is so rich that he can play it as a theme with variations; or he treats it as if its meaning were so comprehensive that it can contain in a single phrase all his accumulated implications. In the first manner, when Verver proposes to Charlotte, the image of burning boats is a constant background to his hesitations. In a similar way, the Prince extends the phrase "in the same boat" until all its possibilities are exhausted. At the great ball where Amerigo and Charlotte make their first appearance without their respective spouses, Mrs. Assingham has the experience of hearing first Charlotte, and then the Prince, explain how they intend to behave in the strange position in which they find themselves. Charlotte tells her that " 'Maggie thinks more on the whole of fathers than of husbands.' " The Prince, a few minutes later, concludes his remarks by saying, about Adam Verver: " 'What I really don't see is why, from his own point of view—given, that is, his conditions, so fortunate as they stood—he should have

[12]I, 79.

wished to marry at all.' ''[13] Both are announcing to Mrs. Assingham that their situation gives them a free hand. She, feeling so responsible for their marriages, is horror-stricken by the possibilities they seem to be suggesting to her. With his air of friendly confidence, the Prince hints to Mrs. Assingham that his cynicism is as boundless as his charm, and Mrs. Assingham can only gasp in distress at the future events he seems to be announcing so clearly.

He connects himself with Charlotte first through Adam Verver: '' '. . . besides, there *is* always the fact that we're of the same connexion, of—what is your word?—the same "concern." We're certainly not, with the relation of our respective *sposi*, simply formal acquaintances. We're in the same boat. . . .' ''[14] The "boat," he hastens to add, is "Mr. Verver's boat," and after James has extended some of Mrs. Assingham's speculations about flotation, the Prince elaborates:

> "The 'boat,' you see"—the Prince explained it no less considerately and lucidly—"is a good deal tied up at the dock, or anchored, if you like, out in the stream. I have to jump out from time to time to stretch my legs, and you'll probably perceive, if you give it your attention, that Charlotte really can't help occasionally doing the same. It isn't even a question, sometimes, of one's getting to the dock—one has to take a header and splash about in the water."[15]

These variations on the theme of "boat" take the phrase further and further from its slang origin. The "boat" is first something in which the four central characters in the story are so brought together that they must sink or float as one. Then it is a vessel of possibilities going to waste because of the timorousness or caution of those who tie it to the safety of the dock, or only allow it to pull against the anchor in the channel. Also it is a symbol of adventure on the open sea, which calls so clearly to frustrated dockbound mariners that they have to leap over the side to find a freedom for their limbs. Since the community of interest among the four, in guilt and innocence, in agony and in joy, which is broken only at the end of the novel, is the essential reference of the phrase, "in the same boat," it would seem that this primary meaning is soon passed over. But the variations from the main theme are them-

[13] I, 243.
[14] I, 238.
[15] I, 241.

selves symbolic of the whole novel. The Prince and Charlotte chafe at the reluctance of Maggie and her father to make use of the high facilities offered by their position and by Adam Verver's wealth. The accumulation of rare treasures is for them too lifeless an expression of power and position. And their guilty association is made possible by their duty of representing the joint families at Matcham and elsewhere, when they are tempted to head for adventure, in order to escape from the cramping goodness of Maggie and Adam. In his conversation with Mrs. Assingham, the Prince concludes his variations on the theme: " 'We shan't drown, we shan't sink—at least I can answer for myself. Mrs. Verver too moreover—to do her justice—visibly knows how to swim.' "[16] Here speaks the *galantuomo* in the flower of his confidence. He has yet to learn what pain his self-confessed deficiency—that of a moral sense—will inflict on all of them. And in view of later developments in his affair with Charlotte, his conclusion is bitterly ironic. He and Charlotte both swim, and swim for their lives, when they are swept into the wide ocean of uncertainty, until from Maggie's rescuing vessel there is thrown to them the rope of understanding.[17]

On one occasion James uses two slang phrases in his second, comprehensive manner, and introduces them with a comment on the Prince's power of using slang. Maggie, her suspicions about the Prince and Charlotte aroused, has noticed that she is being immersed in a bath of considerateness. Against her will, or at least without her acquiescence, she is being treated to the tortures of their pitying kindness and her suffering is aggravated by their assumption that she is not clever enough to realize why they are doing it. In genuine and high-minded commiseration with Maggie's plight, Amerigo and Charlotte are going to all lengths to avoid wounding or alarming her or her father. Their belief that she can be soothed in this way is the refinement of their cruelty. There is a sudden change in the social habits of the quartet. Charlotte pays much more attention to her than before, while the Prince is assiduous in his attendance on her father; and Maggie realizes that the two have, without consultation, arrived at a common plan of action:

[16]I, 241.

[17]In a happier sense, Maggie and her father also get "together into some boat" when they wish to escape from their worries and "only *know* each other henceforth in the unmarried relation" (II, 225).

Charlotte's alacrity in meeting her had in one sense operated slightly overmuch as an intervention: it had begun to reabsorb her at the very hour of her husband's showing her that to be all there, as the phrase was, he likewise only required—as one of the other phrases was too —the straight tip. She had heard him talk about the straight tip in his moods of amusement at English slang, in his remarkable displays of assimilative power, power worthy of better causes and higher inspirations; and he had taken it from her at need in a way that, certainly in the first glow of relief, had made her brief interval seem large.[18]

The slang phrase "to be all there" may be interpreted as "to be fully and actively understanding." At this juncture, however, in spite of his agility in spinning to the breeze of Maggie's moods, the Prince is not understanding Maggie at all. All that is "there" is his physical presence, engaged in diverting Adam Verver or in answering with a silent caress the questions of Maggie for which he is unable to find replies. A "straight tip" is a revelation accepted as authentic information. But, as anybody who has ever received one knows, it only too often sends one to the wrong horse. Maggie's unaccustomed action in returning home to wait her "brief interval" for her husband's return from the Matcham house party, was understood by Amerigo as a "straight tip" that she required more attention. Accordingly she received it in full measure, both from Charlotte and Amerigo. But the very unanimity of their concerted effort to entertain her and to defer to her, gave rise to suspicions of their complicity. The course of action prompted by the "straight tip" stirred up the reactions it should have allayed. Maggie's original action was certainly a "tip," and the explanation her husband seized on was as plausible as a tipster could make it. But as an attempt to divert Maggie's suspicions, the endeavors of Amerigo and Charlotte were lamentably misguided. Their kindness exacerbated her misery, and intensified her anguished realization that only a profound change in Amerigo, his acceptance of moral responsibility, would bring her any relief.[19]

Toward the end of the novel, there is a moment when Charlotte's suffering strikes Maggie and her father simultaneously. Unable to penetrate Maggie's silence, baffled by Amerigo, she falls back on her primary security and devotes her time to her husband's

[18] II, 34.

[19] Not long before, Colonel Assingham had "got the tip [from his wife] and the tip was all he wanted." On this occasion, the tip was indeed "straight," though it lacked the adjective: ". . . that Charlotte and the Prince must be saved . . ." (I, 339).

interests. She has common ground with Adam in their cultivated tastes: "Maggie had in due course seen her begin to 'work' this fortunately natural source of sympathy for all it was worth."[20] So she begins to follow Adam round his collection, attached to him by the "silken halter" of subjection and misery. Then, deserted by the Prince, who can stand the sight of her suffering no longer, she busies herself showing visitors round the collection of Verver treasures. While she is doing so, Maggie suddenly feels that a quaver in Charlotte's voice sounds "like the shriek of a soul in pain."[21] Maggie turns to her father with a start. His glance seems to show that he shares her emotion, so that she senses in his expression a comment on Charlotte's shame:

> "Poor thing, poor thing"—it reached straight—"*isn't* she, for one's credit, on the swagger?" After which, as held thus together they had still another strained minute, the shame, the pity, the bitter knowledge, the smothered protest, the divined anguish even, so overcame him that, blushing to the eyes, he turned short away."[22]

The words are not spoken, but they are as clearly present as if they had found utterance. "On the swagger" represents the deprecatory shrug of the collector who does not need to have his "credit" or reputation increased by such petty means, to whom the act of showing gaping neighbors round the gallery is an act of unnecessary ostentation. The phrase also conveys an impression of the crushing burden Charlotte is suffering. She is having more difficulty than any of the others in keeping a brave face amidst their anxieties. Her guilt was no greater than Amerigo's, but whereas he can escape to London, and in any case has the comfort of Maggie's unspoken agreement in keeping Maggie's knowledge from Charlotte, Charlotte stands alone, with her doom opening before her. Her gallant and pathetic determination to pretend that she is not on the rack requires the outer courage of bravado. "Swagger" it must be, since her bravery cannot express itself in natural forms; the grotesqueness of her endeavor is matched by the vulgarity of the slang phrase. However unliteral the "swagger," this description of Charlotte is debasing. And at the same time it stands here for the greatest compassion of which James is capable. Kate Croy and Mme. de Vionnet also hold their heads high in the hour of

[20]II, 252.
[21]II, 257.
[22]II, 257.

retribution. The creatures who have taken the wrong course must meet their deserts, but when such high souls meet disaster with courage and resolution the sight of the expiation required from them cannot but inspire admiration and pity.

The moral imbroglio of Amerigo and Charlotte is most of the fable, and their decisions activate the plot. The conflicts of Maggie and Adam, however, are not represented in the detail of action, but in large oppositions for which the setting is the whole novel. Unlike the others, who have to learn "goodness," they have the peculiarly American variety of moral probity which so often appears in James, and they need to learn the deficiencies of their perceptual apparatus. They can teach the content of moral judgments, but they have also to recognize the aesthetic shape of the moral order. Their views are originally stuffy and provincial. Maggie's aesthetic "reflected her small still passion for order and symmetry, for objects with their backs to the walls, and spoke even of some probable reference in her American blood to dusting and polishing New England grandmothers."[23] Adam Verver also, however celebrated for his immaculate collector's taste, was concerned rather with the bric-a-brac of art than its inner spirit.

> It was all at bottom in him, the esthetic principle, planted where it could burn with a cold still flame; where it fed almost wholly on the material directly involved, on the idea (followed by appropriation) of plastic beauty, of the thing visibly perfect in its kind . . .[24]

Maggie and her father are locked together in complacent happiness by natural affection, by wealth, position, and good taste; but their satisfactions seem to lack palpable form. The occasions of deepest communion between them are rendered in phrases so inexplicit and so general that they seem almost empty. It was clearly James's design that this "vacancy" should be a sign of a richness of meaning which could be supplied only by the whole work, and which might be diminished by any attempt to capture it in a few words. The method, however, has its possible drawbacks, in the strain it imposes on the reader's imagination, and even perhaps in the reader's sense, on one or two occasions, of an excitement finely worked up, only to be let down by the absence of a clinching and illuminating expression of the moment of climax.

[23]II, 134.
[24]I, 175.

In the scene in which Maggie and Verver resolve that the solution of all their problems is to ship Charlotte with Verver off to America, they discuss their marriages and their aspirations more thoroughly than at any other time. The hint of impending separation makes each clutch at the qualities of the other more overtly than at any other juncture in the novel. When Maggie tells her father of her love for the Prince, he feels that he can share in her passion:

> The beauty of her condition was keeping him at any rate, as he might feel, in sight of the sea, where, though his personal dips were over, the whole thing could shine at him and the air and the plash and the play become for him too a sensation. That couldn't be fixed upon him as missing; since if it wasn't personally floating, if it wasn't even sitting in the sand, it could yet pass very well for breathing the bliss, in a communicated irresistible way—for tasting the balm. It could pass further for knowing—for knowing that without him nothing might have been: which would have been missing least of all.[25]

The limit of Maggie's articulate expression is reached by her tribute to him " 'Oh it's you, father, who are what I call beyond everything. Nothing can pull *you* down.' " His reply is first a silence. "He might have been seeing things to say and others, whether of a type presumptuous or not, doubtless better kept back. So he settled on the merely obvious. 'Well then we make a pair. We're all right.' "[26]

In view of the immediate context of this phrase, and of the importance of the agreement, the words "We're all right" are monumentally inadequate. Insofar as the "rightness" of Maggie and Adam has been demonstrated by the whole novel, the phrase has meaning. Otherwise it indicates a completeness of communication between two people, and presumes an intensity of mutual comprehension. It may indeed represent that place where communication is so complete that it passes beyond words or gestures. The affectionate understanding of Maggie and her father has been frequently represented in long colloquies, and the phrase is offered as a symbol of a communion already exhibited. But the intensity of this blinding moment calls for a sudden incision of poetic insight. The phrase, poetic in force and intention, bearing the most severe stress which James has imposed on any words, yet does not

[25] II, 232.
[26] II, 232-233.

function as poetry. Words in poetry cannot receive so much more from their context than they supply to it. "All right" seems to depend so entirely on the context that a good deal of the necessary poetic penetration is lacking.

The final agreement between Maggie and her father is couched in the same words. Adam is speaking of a Florentine picture he gave to Maggie at the time of her marriage, and which he admires greatly.

> "It's all right, eh?"
> "Oh my dear—rather!"
> He had applied the question to the great fact of the picture, as she had spoken for the picture in reply, but it was as if their words for an instant afterwards symbolised another truth, so that they looked about at everything else to give them this extension.[27]

The "truth" is immediately discovered in "the triumph of selection"—in a view that ranges from the furniture and the cabinets to the art treasures, and settles upon Amerigo and Charlotte seated upon a sofa.

> . . . Mrs Verver and the Prince fairly "placed" themselves, however unwittingly, as high expressions of the kind of human furniture required esthetically by such a scene. The fusion of their presence with the decorative elements, their contribution to the triumph of selection, was complete and admirable; though to a lingering view, a view more penetrating than the occasion really demanded, they also might have figured as concrete attestations of a rare power of purchase.[28]

The shade of irony which might adhere to the phrase "power of purchase" is not felt in the context. "Power" refers rather to the discrimination of the purchaser than to his capacity for acquisition as reflected by his bank balance. The "rightness," however, now refers to the perfection of their arrangements, just as the previous "rightness" had applied to the perfection of their attitudes. As a final judgment, "all right" is still inadequate; as before, James has placed the phrase with every care, but it seems not quite to have carried out the task he entrusted to it.

The use of slang amounts to quite a small part of James's techniques of dramatic representation. Because, however, of the conflict in the slang phrases between their originally wide and

[27] II, 317.
[28] II, 317.

imprecise meanings, and the accuracy which James expects from them, they can be regarded as nodal points in his task of exhibiting through words his profound and delicate analysis. Like a poet, he attempted to find the exact joint of denotation and connotation, and balanced the counterclaims of clear definition and wide association. Few poets, even dramatic poets, have cared to observe the phenomenon of human speech as devotedly as they have perceived the wonders of the natural world. Speech is apprehended by one of the bluntest of the five senses, and a vigorous receptivity on the part of the hearer is required if it is to be related to moral and aesthetic discriminations. James's ear, moreover, was not tuned to oratory, or even to the accents of passion, but to the coloquial conversation of a very fluent society.

He detected in its elements of ambiguity, allusiveness, and symbolism the possibilities of a poetic language suitable for his drama of human passions and moral values. In *The Golden Bowl*, the passions and the judgments are not separated. They are exhibited, to the life, in a form which allows the author to stand aside, as in drama, but still to remain present in every word uttered, as in poetry. Not reproducing the colloquial, but refashioning it for his own high purposes, James, through a vision comparable with the poet's apprehension of common objects, transmuted the commonest parts of speech into aesthetic order.

"The Golden Bowl"

DOROTHEA KROOK*

Or ever the silver cord be loosed, or the golden bowl be broken, or the pitcher be broken at the fountain, or the wheel be broken at the cistern: then shall the dust return to the earth as it was: and the spirit shall return to God who gave it.

Ecclesiastes, xii, 6-7

I

The story of *The Golden Bowl* is even more simple, bare and melodramatic than that of *The Wings of the Dove*. There are again just four principal personages: Adam Verver, American millionaire and art-collector; his daughter Maggie; Prince Amerigo, scion of an ancient Roman house, who marries Maggie Verver at the opening of the story; and Charlotte Stant, American *cosmopolite*, former mistress of the Prince and Maggie's dearest friend, who is presently to marry Adam Verver and become Maggie's stepmother. Of the two subsidiary characters only one is fully articulate. Colonel Assingham is an Englishman, his wife Fanny an expatriate New Yorker who is a devoted friend to all the principals and passionately concerned in their affairs; he is as unimpressionable and seemingly unresponsive as his wife is vivacious and expressive; and between them they perform admirably the function of a sustained choric commentary on the main action.

This rigid economy in the matter of *dramatis personae* is one

*From THE ORDEAL OF CONSCIOUSNESS IN HENRY JAMES by Dorothea Krook. Copyright 1962, by the Cambridge University Press. Reprinted by permission of the author and the publisher.

aspect in which *The Golden Bowl* resembles the classical Greek drama. Another is the intense singleness and simplicity ("unity") of the action, in Aristotle's sense of the word; and in both aspects its quasi-classical character is reinforced by an almost text-book observance—for a modern novelist, at any rate—of the unity of place: the scene of the action moves strictly between Fawns, the Ververs' country-house, and their town-houses in Eaton Square and Portland Place, the only exceptions being an excursion to Brighton (where Mr Verver makes his proposal of marriage to Charlotte) and a memorable week-end party at a country-house called Matcham. These, however, are only the external or technical signs of the grand classic style and scope of *The Golden Bowl.* The more significant, and distnctively Jamesian, signs are to be referred to that generality and comprehensiveness of the creative impulse and passion which James speaks of in a passage in the Preface;[1] and if the degree of achieved generality and comprehensiveness is indeed the measure of poetic excellence, *The Golden Bowl* may stand as James's most ambitiously conceived and most brilliantly executed long poem.

The terms "general" and "comprehensive" are to be interpreted in a quasi-logical sense not commonly intended when they are used by literary critics. There is a sense in which the experience of *The Golden Bowl*, like that of *The Wings of the Dove*, presupposes all that has gone before in James's poetic experience, and all that went before implies what is unfolded here. This aspect is conveniently illustrated by a short passage in the First Book in which the Prince, standing on the terrace at Matcham, reflects upon the English national character. Like other Jamesian foreigners before him, he is especially struck, it seems, by "the fathomless depths of English equivocation":

> He knew them all, as was said, "well"; he had lived with them, stayed with them, dined, hunted, shot and done various other things with them; but the number of questions about them he couldn't have answered had much rather grown than shrunken, so that experience struck him for the most part as having left in him but one residual impression. They didn't like *les situations nettes*—that was all he was sure of. They wouldn't have them at any price; it had been their national genius and their national success to avoid them at every point. They called it themselves, with complacency, their wonderful spirit of compromise—the very influence of which actually so hung

about him here from moment to moment that the earth and the air, the light and the colour, the fields and the hills and the sky, the blue-green counties and the cold cathedrals, owed to it every accent of their tone. Verily, as one had to feel in presence of such a picture, it had succeeded; it had made, up to now, for that seated solidity, in the rich sea-mist on which the garish, the supposedly envious, peoples have ever cooled their eyes. But it was at the same time precisely why even much initiation left one at given moments so puzzled as to the elements of staleness in all the freshness and of freshness in all the staleness, of innocence in the guilt and of guilt in the innocence. There were other marble terraces, sweeping more purple prospects, on which he would have known what to think, and would have enjoyed thereby at least the small intellectual fillip of a discerned relation between a given appearance and a taken meaning. The inquiring mind, in these present conditions, might it was true, be more sharply challenged; but the result of its attention and its ingenuity, it had unluckily learned to know, was too often to be confronted with a mere dead wall, a lapse of logic, a confirmed bewilderment.[2]

The passage may be seen as a recapitulation or synopsis, at a pitch of generality not previously attempted, of all that has been exhibited *in extenso* of the English national character in such earlier stories as *The Tragic Muse, The Awkward Age, What Maisie Knew, The Spoils of Poynton*, and the Lancaster Gate portions of *The Wings of the Dove*. What is remarkable about it is that it really does seem to recover the multiplicity of particular perceptions, judgments and generalisations contained in those earlier works in their full vivid particularity. "They didn't like *les situations nettes;* they wouldn't have them at any price": that, one feels, explains as comprehensively as may be desired the British hatred of art that was exposed in *The Tragic Muse,* where Nick Dormer (we remember) incurred ridicule and hostility precisely because he would insist on pursuing his portrait-painting as *une situation nette;* and it explains also, with the same satisfying completeness, a good many other British antipathies. The puzzle about "the elements of staleness in all the freshness and of freshness in all the staleness, of innocence in the guilt and of guilt in the innocence," is the very puzzle that is so intensively explored and so instructively exhibited in *The Awkward Age* and *The Wings of the Dove.* What is it, after all, but the freshness in her staleness that makes the terrible Mrs Lowder so irresistible; and before Mrs Lowder, Mrs Brookenham in *The Awkward Age,* Mrs Gereth in *The Spoils of Poynton,*

Sir Claude in *What Maisie Knew* and even Ida Beale and Mrs. Beale? Then—catching one's breath a little at the sheer quantity of illumination contained in the simple phrases—one recognises how often indeed in English society the enquiring mind is confronted in the end "with a mere dead wall, a lapse of logic, a confirmed bewilderment"; and one recalls a dozen other delightful instances in James's works of this bewilderment of the British mind in the presence of "ideas"—Lord Lambeth's in *An International Episode*, Mrs Ambient's in *The Author of Beltraffio*, Lady Agnes's and Julia Dallow's in *The Tragic Muse*, Lord Mark's in *The Wings of the Dove*. Finally, one understands also why the enquiring mind of a clever foreigner like the Prince should crave in that intellectual desert for even so humble a pleasure as "the small intellectual fillip of a discerned relation between a given appearance and a taken meaning." He wouldn't mind not understanding the English (as he did understand his Europeans), he wouldn't care that in this instance his "taken meaning" should be a total misreading of the "given appearance," so long as the gap itself might be admitted as matter for enquiry, the "relation" between the given situation and his own misreading of it open to the free play of mind. For then it would be at least a relation "discerned," and as such something to sustain a mind to which criticism and analysis came as naturally as leaves on a tree.

The high generality or "universality" of *The Golden Bowl* is also intimately connected with the principles and method of James's later works, which are here supremely exemplified. The principle of internal relations, for instance, is observed with an ideal completeness unparalleled in any previous work of James's maturity. Everything in the world of this novel is involved in everything else, everything is modified by everything else, and this "rich interpenetration" defines its very essence. Similarly, the principle which James called his "law of successive aspects" is here observed with a rigour of economy not previously attempted. There are but two centres of consciousness, the Prince in the First Book, Maggie Verver in the Second, and they are used strictly in succession, without recourse to the relief of alternation. The other two principals, Charlotte Stant and Adam Verver, are never at any crucial point in the story directly exhibited—or (as James prefers to put it) are never exposed to "that officious explanation which we know as 'going behind' ";[3] and the Assinghams are there merely to assist in "going behind" the Prince and Maggie Verver. Finally, the indirect method of presentation predominates here to the almost complete exclusion of direct statement; and as one grunts and sweats one's way through this most late of Jamesian works, perpetually losing one's way amidst the qualifications and parentheses, struggling to keep a hold on the proliferating subleties of analysis, the relentlessly sustained metaphors, the tormenting crypto-statements of the elliptical, allusive, digressive dialogues, one has reason to believe that James meant what he said when, in a letter to Hugh Walpole at about this time in reply to some unforgivable question Walpole had asked about *The Ambassadors,* he commented, "How can you say I do anything so foul and abject as to 'state'?"[4]

The generality of vision projected by these means does indeed produce an air as rarefied as any we have yet been asked to breathe in James's works. To adopt his own metaphor about *The Awkward Age,*[5] his "process" here, as there, has been "to pump the case gaspingly dry, dry not only of superfluous moisture, but absolutely . . . of breathable air"; and the "exemplary closeness," the compression "ferocious, really quite heroic" which James proudly remarks in *The Awkward Age,* are many times more exemplary, ferocious and heroic in *The Golden Bowl.* Indeed it is for the later masterpiece rather than the earlier that one would wish to reserve the superlative praise that James bestows upon *The Awkward Age,* that it is "triumphantly scientific."[6]

In what sense *The Golden Bowl* is supremely "scientific," in what sense it exemplifies and vindicates James's conception of the logic of the perfect novel, is best shown by tracing in outline the development of the central story.

Charlotte Stant, brilliant, accomplished, and beautiful in the Florentine style of "the great time," and Prince Amerigo, Roman *galantuomo,* with a taste particularly inclined to the art of the great time, have been before the opening of the story passionately and splendidly in love with each other. But because (like Kate Croy and Merton Densher) they are both poor and both too "great" to live without money, they do not marry; and it is evident to all, but especially to their intimate friend Mrs Assingham, that each must make a suitably splendid marriage. This is the first premise or *donnée* of the story. The first necessary consequence is that the Prince marries Maggie Verver, who is the daughter of Adam Verver, American millionaire and famous collector, whose collection of European art-treasures is finally to be taken back to American City, there to be enshrined in the greatest art-museum the continent has yet seen. Maggie adores her husband, and is blissfully happy. But she also adores her father, with whom since her mother's death she has enjoyed a tender and deeply harmonious intimacy of companionship; and she is now full of anxious fear that her marriage will leave her father solitary and sad. Goaded by this anxiety—"her stupid little idol," as she is afterwards to call it—she urges her father to marry her dear friend Charlotte. This marriage, which is the second necessary consequence of the first premise, also in due course takes place; and it is now generally felt that the best possible solution has been reached to the problems of everyone concerned. Charlotte Stant has made her splendid marriage; Adam Verver has been supplied with the best of companions to compensate him for the loss of Maggie; Maggie's own stupid little anxiety has been relieved; and the Prince is in the agreeable position of having the best of wives, the best of fathers-in-law, and now also the best of former mistresses more or less on the premises. Maggie and her father know nothing, of course, of the Prince's former relations with Charlotte.

These consequences, however, themselves produce a set of fresh relations, from which the rest of the "argument" follows by a necessity equally ineluctable. The admirable situation created by the two marriages begins gradually to alter its character; and the alteration is all in the direction of an ironical reversal of everyone's expectations. Maggie and her father, so far from being separated by their respective marriages, are drawn together more closely than before, in particular after the birth of Maggie's son, who sets the bloom of perfection, so to speak, on their domestic happiness; and as a consequence of this increased intimacy between the father and daughter, the former lovers, the Prince and Charlotte, are in their turn thrown more and more together. The grand irony of the situation is that it is all a perfectly open secret. It had been one of Maggie's main arguments at the time she was urging her father to marry Charlotte that Charlotte would supply them with what she called "greatness"—meaning by this a certain high distinction, in the sphere of social relations in particular, that Charlotte possessed in a pre-eminent degree and the Ververs not at all. She and her father accordingly now take the comfortable, cosy view of themselves as the dear old stay-at-homes whose special office it is to form the domestic background to the brilliant public appearances of the Prince and Charlotte; and they in turn, with the comfortable complacent approval of the Ververs, take every opportunity to exercise their developed social gifts in the interests of the two families. They appear at all the season's most important receptions, banquets and balls, while Maggie and her father remain at home, sitting together by the cradle of the Principino, rejoicing in the child, each other, their absent *sposi*, and the whole happy arrangement. Maggie and her father on their side honestly believe that the arrangement can continue indefinitely; and the Prince and Charlotte on theirs honestly desire that it may so continue.

But, of course, it can't, and doesn't. The Prince and Charlotte cannot indefinitely continue to "go about" (as the Prince puts it to himself in a crucial interior monologue) in "the state of our primitive parents before the Fall." It becomes too absurd in the end that such a mutual pair as they more and more find themselves to be should continue to go about in this way. And so, partly because the situation itself is so absurd, partly because they are still bound by their old passion, and in spite of their resolution to be sane and sensible and to remember the advantages they both enjoy from not being married to each other, Charlotte and the Prince become lovers again; and this in the story of *The Golden Bowl* constitutes the act of betrayal which is presently to precipitate the suffering of Maggie Verver, the principal vessel of the central tragic experience. The fact is disclosed to us at a grand reception, at which the Prince and Charlotte encounter the Assinghams and the Prince gives Mrs. Assingham "a quintessential wink," which makes it plain to that well-intentioned lady what has happened and sends her back in terror to her husband to communicate it all to him in a monlogue longer and more intensely analytical than any she has yet embarked upon. Presently, when the Prince and Charlotte, having gone to a grand house-party at a grand country-house, stay away longer than is natural or proper, Maggie's own eyes are at last opened to the true state of affairs; and this discovery ends the first part of the story, entitled *The Prince*. The second part, entitled *The Princess*, is concerned to show, through Maggie's consciousness alone, how what has been lost is restored: how the Prince is restored to Maggie, Charlotte to Adam Verver; and how this is accomplished entirely, or almost entirely, by Maggie's solitary effort.

This, in bare outline, is the story of *The Golden Bowl,* the telling of which occupies more than eight hundred pages of the closest late-Jamesian writing. What emerges from it is a great fable—one of the greatest in modern European literature—of the redemption of man by the transforming power of human love. The instrument of the redemptive act is Maggie Verver; its ultimate source, her father; the principal recipient of the grace, her husband the Prince. But the fourth principal, Charlotte Stant, also enjoys its beneficent influence in ways accommodated to her needs and capacities; and the way in which this is accomplished by Maggie Verver, drawing her power from her father, is the heart of James's tale.

In the story the redemptive theme is contracted into a simple act of *restoration:* Maggie Verver has to restore what has been lost, or fatally impaired, by the adultery of her husband the Prince with her friend Charlotte Stant. In the concrete human situation, this means that she must draw her husband back to herself, separate him from Charlotte, and restore Charlotte to her father; and on this plane Maggie's act of restoration is characteristically simple, personal and domestic. It consistently maintains this character, with never the breath of a suggestion, never an intrusive hint, that it is anything but what it appears to be. Yet it is more; and *The Golden Bowl* is a triumph of the poet's art because it succeeds in projecting the universal in and through the intensely concrete and particular. By the profundity and intensity of his insight into the private domestic suffering of Maggie Verver, and by his power to render the felt quality of that suffering with a poet's fullness, minuteness and exactness, James exhibits to us the representative or "exemplary" nature of that suffering; and since to be representative or exemplary in this sense is to be universal, Maggie Verver's act of restoration becomes a "figure" (as the older critics would have called it) of a larger act—a restoration of the universal moral order which has been disordered by the immorality of an ugly betrayal.

On this view, what has disordered the moral universe in *The Golden Bowl* is the destructive passion of lust figured in the adultery of the Prince and Charlotte. The nature of this "lust," however, is not simple but exceedingly complex, and the act of betrayal that springs from it is correspondingly complicated. Its several immediate causes are to be traced back to a single source —the fundamental clash between the moral code of the Ververs and that of the Prince and Charlotte. This indeed is the mainspring of the whole drama, and accordingly requires to be closely examined.

Prince Amerigo, we soon discern, is James's quintessential Aesthetic Man. Compared with the Prince's aestheticism, that (for instance) of Gilbert Osmond, which had seemed to go so far in sophistication and so deep in its power to dominate his life, appears crude and superficial; and also artificial, "acquired," in a way in which the Prince's, the product of centuries of breeding, is not. The Prince's aestheticism also has nothing to do with "fine things" as such; nor is it tainted, as it was in Osmond, by a mean, shabby conventionality, a concern about mere social appearances. The Prince's aestheticism is pre-eminently a view of life, dangerously complete and coherent, whose basic, unexamined assumption is that the aesthetic criterion, "the touchstone of taste" (as the Prince himself is to call it at a crucial point in the story), is the ultimate criterion in the conduct of life. The aesthetic, on this view, is the measure of the good; the good is a function of the beautiful; and the beautiful, in this context, means something uncommonly large and comprehensive. It is the product of intelligence, sensibility and imagination, all developed to the highest degree; and in personal relationships it expresses itself in the pursuit not merely of the graceful and charming but also, and indeed chiefly, of the bold, the imaginative, the brilliant. That is how people are measured by the touchstone of taste—by their free play of mind, by their sense of the irony of things, by the high style in which they conduct their lives.

We receive the full flavour of this style at Matcham, the stately home from which the Prince and Charlotte make their fateful expedition to Gloucester:

> Every voice in the great bright house was a call to the ingenuities and impunities of pleasure; every echo was a defiance of difficulty, doubt

or danger; every aspect of the picture, a glowing plea for the immediate. . . . For a world so constituted was governed by a spell, that of the smile of the gods and the favour of the powers; the only handsome, the only gallant, in fact the only intelligent acceptance of which was a faith in its guarantees and a high spirit for its chances.[7]

The Prince, we learn, possesses in full measure this faith in its guarantees and high spirit for its chances. As he stands on the terrace waiting for Charlotte to come down, he defines to himself the nature of his extraordinary good luck:

The upshot of everything for him, alike of the less and of the more, was that the exquisite day bloomed there like a large fragrant flower that he had only to gather. . . . He knew [now] why he had tried from the first of his marriage with such patience for such conformity; he knew why he had given up so much and bored himself so much. . . . It had been just in order that his—well, what on earth should he call it but his freedom?—should at present be as perfect and rounded and lustrous as some huge precious pearl. He hadn't struggled nor snatched; he was taking but what had been given him; the pearl dropped itself, with its exquisite quality and rarity, straight into his hand.[8]

When the sense of the beautiful goes as far and as deep as this, one might suppose it really was enough for all the ends of life, even the most exalted. One might suppose that the perfection of taste, when it comprehended so much, was indeed co-extensive with all human virtue and *a fortiori* with moral virtue. Yet (we learn as the story advances) it is not: these two, the aesthetic and the moral, though intimately bound up with each other, are yet not the same; indeed they can even, in certain circumstances, be mutually exclusive. We receive our first hint of this at the very beginning of the story, in a significant exchange between the Prince and Mrs Assingham in which the Prince in his charming, easy way confesses that he believes himself to be lacking in a moral sense:

"I should be interested," she presently remarked, "to see some sense *you* don't possess."

Well, he produced one on the spot. "The moral, dear Mrs Assingham. I mean always as you others consider it. I've of course something that in our poor dear backward old Rome sufficiently passes for it. But it's no more like yours than the tortuous stone staircase—half-ruined into the bargain!—in some castle of our *quattrocento* is like the 'lightning elevator' in one of Mr Verver's fifteen-storey buildings. Your moral sense works by steam—it sends you up like a rocket. Ours is slow and steep and unlighted, with so many of the steps missing that —well, that it's as short, in almost any case, to turn round and come down again."

"Trusting," Mrs Assingham smiled, "to get up some other way?"

"Yes—or not to have to get up at all. However," he added, "I told you that at the beginning."[9]

We receive a further and fuller hint of the possible incompatibility of the aesthetic and the moral in another early colloquy, that between the Prince and Charlotte on their memorable shopping expedition the day before the Prince's wedding. They are talking about Maggie and the wedding gift Charlotte wants to buy her. Charlotte says, "Anything, of course, dear as she is, *will* do for her. I mean if I were to give her a pin-cushion from the Baker Street Bazaar"; the Prince, laughing, agrees; and Charlotte goes on:

"But it isn't a reason. In that case one would never do anything for her. I mean," Charlotte explained, "if one took advantage of her character."

"Of her character?"

"We mustn't take advantage of her character," the girl, again unheeding, pursued. "One mustn't if not for *her*, at least for one's self. She saves one such trouble."

She had spoken thoughtfully, her eyes on her friend's; she might have been talking, preoccupied and practical, of some one with whom he was comparatively unconnected. "She certainly *gives* one no trouble," said the Prince. And then as if this were perhaps ambiguous or inadequate: "She's not selfish—God forgive her!—enough."

"That's what I mean," Charlotte instantly said, "She's not selfish enough. There's nothing, absolutely, that one *need* do for her. She's so modest," she developed—"she doesn't miss things. I mean if you love her—or, rather I should say, if she loves you. She lets it go."

The Prince frowned a little—as a tribute, after all, to seriousness. "She lets what—?"

"Anything—anything that you might do and that you don't. She lets everything go but her own disposition to be kind to you. It's of herself that she asks efforts—so far as she ever *has* to ask them. She hasn't much. She does everything herself. And that's terrible."

The Prince had listened; but, always with propriety, didn't commit himself. "Terrible?"

"Well, unless, one's almost as good as she. It makes too easy terms for one. It takes stuff within one so far as one's decency is concerned, to stand it. And nobody," Charlotte continued in the same manner, "is decent enough, good enough, to stand it—not without help from religion or something of that kind. Not without prayer and fasting— that is without taking great care. Certainly," she said, "such people as you and I are not."

The Prince, obligingly, thought an instant. "Not good enough to stand it?"

"Well, not good enough not rather to feel the strain. We happen each, I think, to be of the kind that are easily spoiled."

Her friend again, for propriety, followed the argument.

"Oh I don't know. May not one's affection for her do something more for one's decency, as you call it, than her own generosity—her own affection, *her* 'decency'—has the unfortunate virtue to undo?"

"Ah, of course it must be all in that."

But she had made her question, all the same, interesting to him. "What it comes to—one can see what you mean—is the way she believes in one. That is if she believes at all."

"Yes, that's what it comes to," said Charlotte Stant.

"And why," he asked, almost soothingly, "should it be terrible?" He couldn't at the worst, see that.

"Because it's always so—the idea of having to pity people."

"Not when there's also with it the idea of helping them."

"Yes, but if we can't help them?"

"We *can*—we always can. That is," he competently added, "if we care for them. And that's what we're talking about."

"Yes"—she on the whole assented. "It comes back then to our absolutely refusing to be spoiled."

"Certainly. But everything," the Prince laughed as they went on— "all your 'decency,' I mean—comes back to that."

She walked beside him a moment. "It's just what *I* meant," she then reasonably said.[10]

The passage discloses many significant things about Charlotte as well as the Prince; but we are concerned just now only with the Prince. What it shows is that he is a man of perfect breeding; that (like Vanderbank in *The Awkward Age)* he is thoroughly good-natured and charming; warmly affectionate; capable of the most sincere gratitude for all he has received, and is going to receive, from the Ververs; and, above everythng, full of humility, goodwill and good faith. He sincerely desires to do what is right, and genuinely believes himself capable of doing what is right without undue exertion on his part, or undue modification of his view of things.[11] Yet (as he himself has recognised) he has no moral sense. His persistent evasiveness in this scene, which is not the less ominous for being so charming, good-natured and good-humoured, is ample proof of this; and Charlotte further confirms it by her own doubts and misgivings. Charlotte, it is clear, does have an inkling of one of the important truths that the fable of *The Golden Bowl* is to disclose—that there is a difference between the moral and the aesthetic, and that by the aesthetic alone no man is saved. But though Charlotte dimly understands it while the Prince understands it not at all, Charlotte does not understand it enough to avert the catastrophe that is awaiting them; and this vital defect in the Prince and Charlotte is one efficient cause of the story of suffering, expiation and final redemption that follows.

What Charlotte Stant, however, principally has in common with Maggie's husband is that she, too, conducts her life in the light of the touchstone of taste. In her, it is true, the aestheticism is acquired rather than inherited; but it is so highly developed, and so intimate an expression of her personal genius, as to appear as natural as the Prince's. The presence of the aesthetic principle in Charlotte may be discerned, first, in the kind and quality of her beauty, to the interest of which the Prince handsomely testifies;[12] and, second, in the perfection of her social accomplishments. Her tact, her presence of mind, her "usefulness" in all social situations are never less than perfect; and her managerial capacities, though prodigious, never appear as managing but only as graceful. It may be discerned also in *minutiae* such as her dress, which is elegant in a way poor Maggie's never quite is. But, most of all, it is to be discerned in her taste for bold, free enjoyments of the kind in which, besides the boldness and freedom, the sensual element is also distinctly present; and it is this, more than anything perhaps, that defines the "greatness" repeatedly ascribed to her by the Ververs.

As the story develops and the Prince and Charlotte are thrown more and more together, it becomes evident that the principal (and most dangerous) bond between them is their free play of mind—their capacity to see the rich irony of things, and in particular the irony of their own situation *vis à vis* the Ververs. This situation, it has already been indicated, becomes to them in the end desperately exasperating; and though it is passion that in the first instance draws them together, it is sheer exasperation with the absurdity of their situation that, equally with the passion, finally leads them to become lovers again. Yet even as their exasperation grows, they still retain intact not only their composure and good humour but (remarkably) their good faith towards the Ververs; and it is precisely this razor's-edge balance—of their good nature, goodwill and genuine gratitude for benefits received with their supersophisticated sense of the irony of their situation—that they cannot in the end maintain. As the months pass the tension mounts and mounts, until the touchstone of taste finally triumphs and Charlotte and the Prince leap out of Mr Verver's boat and become lovers.

The interior monologue in which the Prince expresses, in the beautifully modulated accents of a *galantuomo*, his particular sense of outrage at the absurdity of his situation and the bottomless ignorance and innocence of the Ververs is among the really superb things in the book. At Matcham, where (we have already learnt) "every voice in the great bright house was a call to the ingenuities and impunities of pleasure; every echo was a defiance of difficulty, doubt or danger; every aspect of the picture, a glowing plea for the immediate,"

> There were only odd moments when the breath of the day, as it has been called, struck him so full in the face that he broke out with all the hilarity of "What indeed would *they* have made of it?" "They" were of course Maggie and her father, moping—so far as they ever consented to mope—in monotonous Eaton Square, but placid too in the belief that they knew beautifully what their expert companions were in for. They knew, it might have appeared in these lights, absolutely nothing on earth worth speaking of—whether beautifully or cynically; and they would perhaps sometimes be a little less trying if they would once for all peacefully admit that knowledge wasn't one of their needs and that they were in fact constitutionally inaccessible to it. . . . Deep at the heart of that resurgent unrest in our young man which we have had to content ourselves with calling his irritation—deep in the bosom of this falsity of position glowed the red spark of his inextinguishable sense of a higher and braver propriety. There were situations that were ridiculous, but that one couldn't yet help, as for instance when one's wife chose, in the most usual way, to make one so. Precisely here however was the difference; it had taken poor Maggie to invent a way so extremely unusual—yet to which none the less it would be too absurd that he should merely lend himself. Being thrust, systematically, with another woman, and a woman one happened, by the same token, exceedingly to like, and being so thrust that

the theory of it seemed to publish one as idiotic or incapable—this was a predicament of which the dignity depended all on one's own handling. What was supremely grotesque, in fact, was the essential opposition of theories—as if a galantuomo, as *he* at least constitutionally conceived galantuomini, could do anything *but* blush to "go about" at such a rate with such a person as Mrs Verver in a state of childlike innocence, the state of our primitive parents before the Fall. The grotesque theory, as he would have called it, was perhaps an odd one to resent with violence, and he did it—also as a man of the world—all merciful justice; but none the less assuredly there was but one way *really* to mark, and for his companion as much as for himself, the commiseration in which they held it.[13]

From this passage there emerges what must be one of the most curious—and most subtle and persuasive—justifications of adultery to be found anywhere in imaginative literature. It is precisely because the Prince is a *galantuomo*—a Gallant Man, a man of spirit, a man who guides his life by "the touchstone of taste," by the standard of "a higher and braver propriety" than any that the dear, innocent, ignorant, incorrigibly incorruptible and totally unimaginative Ververs could so much as dream of; and because, being such a man, he cannot bear the sheer ignominy of going about indefinitely "with such a person as Mrs Verver in a state of childlike innocence, the state of our primitive parents before the Fall," that he becomes Charlotte's lover. And this is how the touchstone of taste is seen not merely to sanction adultery but positively to insist on it—as the only intelligent, the only brave, the only decent thing to do in the circumstances.

In view of the *dénouement* of *The Golden Bowl* and the overriding importance of the redemptive theme, it is tempting to minimise the significance of the exposure of the Ververs contained in the Prince's *galantuomo* speech. The cruel light in which they stand exposed (it might be argued) is merely the specious light of Matcham; the price that allegedly has to be paid for their simplicity and goodness is entirely determined by the moral arithmetic of that world. The Ververs show up as badly as this only when (like the sycamore tree) they are observed by Charlotte and the Prince—when they are measured against *their* developed sensibilities governed by the touchstone of taste, their standard of a higher and braver propriety.

James, however, leaves us in no doubt that there really is a price to be paid, and that it is as heavy as it is genuine. The law of successive aspects may rule that no single aspect yields the whole truth. But it also rules that every aspect is an aspect of the truth; and what the Prince sees in the light of the touchstone of taste, though it is not the whole of what there is to see, is in fact there to be seen.

Adam Verver's unique Homeric quality, we already know, is his "simplicity." Though he is a multi-millionaire, and as such a Great Personage in the worldly world, he is shy, modest and simple— in particular simple; and one important aspect of his simplicity (we soon learn) is manifested in his attitude to the aesthetic, which is now theoretically the ruling passion of his life since he ceased money-making and became a collector. Adam Verver's passion for the beautiful, it transpires, is not a particularly exacting passion. It does not, it seems, involve any radical upheaval in his spiritual economy; on the contrary, it is all too easily accommodated to the habits and tastes formed in the first instance by the money-making activity:

> It was all at bottom in him, the esthetic principle, planted where it could burn with a still cold flame; where it fed almost wholly on the material directly involved, in the idea (followed by appropriation) of plastic beauty, of the thing visibly perfect in its kind; where, in short, in spite of the general tendency of the "devouring element" to spread, the rest of his spiritual furniture, modest, scattered and tended with unconscious care, escaped the consumption that in so many cases proceeds from the undue keeping-up of profane altar-fires. Adam Verver had, in other words, learnt the lesson of the senses, to the end of his own little book, without having for a day raised the smallest scandal in his economy at large; being in this particular not unlike those fortunate bachelors or other gentlemen of pleasure who so manage their entertainment of compromising company that even the austerest housekeeper, occupied and competent below stairs, never feels obliged to give warning.[14]

Or again, with the emphasis more explicitly on the acquisitive aspect of Adam Verver's love of the beautiful:

Nothing perhaps might affect us as queerer . . . than this application of the same measure of value to such different pieces of property as old Persian carpets, say, and new human acquisitions; all the more indeed that the amiable man was not without an inkling on his own side that he was, as a taster of life, economically constructed. He put into his one little glass everything he raised to his lips, and it was as if he had always carried in his pocket, like a tool of his trade, this receptacle, a little glass cut with a fineness of which the art had long since been lost. . . . As it had served him to satisfy himself, so to speak, both about Amerigo and about the Bernadino Luini he had happened to come to knowledge of at the time he was consenting to the announcement of his daughter's betrothal, so it served him at present [when he is about to propose to Charlotte] about Charlotte Stant and an extraordinary set of oriental tiles of which he had lately got wind."[15]

In respect to the Prince himself, what Mr Verver appears to find most irresistible is his exquisite breeding, which for him, the quintessential American collector, has all the beauty of its rarity value and all the rarity value of its perfect beauty. "You're round, my boy," he says to the Prince, "You're *all,* you're variously and inexhaustibly round, when you might, by all the chances, have been abominably square. . . . It's the sort of thing in you that one feels—or at least I do—with one's hand. . . . For living with, you're a pure and perfect crystal."[16] Yet the Prince's being like a pure and perfect crystal is for Adam Verver, it seems, perfectly compatible with his being also like a banker's draft. The Prince perceives this when at a dinner-party at the house in Eaton Square he catches his father-in-law's eye fixed upon him:

[Mr Verver's] directed regard rested at its ease, but it neither lingered nor penetrated, and was, to the Prince's fancy, much of the same order as any glance directed, for due attention, from the same quarter, to the figure of a cheque received in the course of business and about to be enclosed to a banker. It made sure of the amount—and just so, from time to time, the amount of the Prince was certified. He was being thus, in renewed instalments, perpetually paid in; he already reposed in the bank as a value, but subject, in this comfortable way, to infinite endorsement.[17]

The exposure of Adam Verver's curious philistinism is not the less deadly for being so amiable; and James is equally unsparing about the Ververs' provinciality, which (according to the Arnoldian doctrine) is inseparable from any philistinism however curious. This shows itself in their general attitude to the Prince:

> There were plenty of singular things they [Maggie and her father] were *not* enamoured of—flights of brilliancy, of audacity, of originality, that, speaking at least for the dear man and herself, were not at all in their line; but they liked to think they had given their life this unusual extension and this liberal form, which many families, many couples, and still more many pairs of couples, wouldn't have found workable.[18]

The edge of the criticism here is sharp indeed, especially when one takes in the note of self-congratulatory complacency along with the provinciality; and one can easily see how these features in particular of the good, kind Ververs might come to work on the Prince's patrician nerves.

Maggie herself, as we may expect, is treated more tenderly than her father in the matter of their common weaknesses. But—leaving aside for the moment the complex questions arising from certain Jamesian ambiguities in her attitude to the Prince and to Charlotte, which are to be taken up in a later section[19]—we are left in no doubt about the effect upon her husband and her friend of her American simplicities. She may be, like all James's American heroines, generous, tender and passionate; she may be lovely and thoroughly charming (the Prince compares her to "a little dancing-girl at rest, ever so light of movement but most often panting gently, even a shade compunctiously, on a bench"[20]). Yet, unavoidably, she is also "funny," in the special sense in which all James's American heroines are. In this comprehensive Jamesian sense, the word denotes an irreducible compound whose elements (we have seen) the sophisticated English and Europeans are particularly quick to discern, and always find fascinating and amusing when they do not find them excruciatingly boring. They are, first, the provinciality already noted; a moral rectitude remarkable—by metropolitan standards—for its simplicity, directness and candour; a passion for analysis and generalisation which is so "funny" because it is either terribly banal or surprisingly acute, and when acute nevertheless not in the least sophisticated; and a conspicuous absence of the higher social accomplishments. The last, though the least *sub specie aeternitatis,* is the most obtrusive in day-to-day intercourse. It shows itself in a certain absence of composure or "poise," both of the inward and the outward kind: in the light of the touchstone of taste, Maggie's numerous "little" anxieties—about her father's happiness, her husband's, her friend Charlotte's—would be a sign of the first kind, the inward lack of composure here being the product of an over-scrupulous conscience and an over-eager desire to do only what is right; while her anxiety about appearances—her dress, for instance (she is constantly tormented by the fear that her *toilet* on any given occasion will not measure up to Charlotte's exacting standards), is meant to show her lack of that outward poise which comes so naturally, it seems, to the Kate Croys and Charlotte Stants of her world. Mrs Assingham, immediately before the scene in which the golden bowl is broken, has occasion to note Maggie's "perfect little personal processes":

> Nothing more pathetic could be imagined than the refuge and disguise her [Maggie's] agitation had instinctively asked of the arts of dress, multiplied to extravagance, almost to incoherence. She had had visibly her idea—that of not betraying herself by inattentions into which she had never yet fallen, and she stood there circled about and furnished forth, as always, in a manner that testified to her perfect little personal processes. It had ever been her sign that she was for all occasions *found* ready, without loose ends or exposed accessories or unremoved superfluities; a suggestion of the swept and garnished, in her whole splendid yet thereby more or less encumbered and embroidered setting, that reflected her small still passion for order and symmetry, for objects with their backs to the walls, and spoke even of some probable reference in her American blood to dusting and polishing New England grandmothers.[21]

In the end, indeed, the "funniness" is seen to be merely another aspect of the familiar American innocence—the simple-heartedness which is so closely linked with the simple-mindedness as to be often (but not always) co-extensive with it. The story of *The Golden Bowl* is designed to show, among other things, how Maggie Verver starts by being as "funny" as may be desired—as simple-minded as she is simple-hearted; and ends still simple-hearted but no longer simple-minded.

The causes of the "act of shame" committed by the Prince and Charlotte are accordingly complex indeed. This complexity, of course, makes it very difficult to see their adultery as vicious at all, let alone as an act of shame. Yet the course of James's fable, and in particular the *dénouement,* can leave us in no doubt about the way in which we are meant to view it; and what the fable implicitly affirms is explicitly confirmed by a multitude of details designed to exhibit a fatal flaw in the relationship between the Prince and Charlotte which reduces it, in the final analysis, to a relationship of lust rather than love.[22] If this taint is in fact present, and if its proper name is lust, it is this that has violated the moral order in *The Golden Bowl;* and if lust is one of the deadliest of the deadly sins because it is so deceptively like the love that redeems while being in fact its diabolical counterpart, it is the lust figured in the adultery of the Prince and Charlotte that has to be exorcised in order that the moral order may be restored and reaffirmed.

This, taken at its highest pitch, is the ultimate scope of the fable. The restoration and reaffirmation of the moral order, we already know, is in fact accomplished. It is effected by Maggie Verver's love; and what we are shown in the second part of the story is the three-fold source of the redemptive power of her love. First, it is essentially selfless;[23] second, it is grounded in anguish and humiliation; third, it is informed by intelligence: it fights to win, and uses all the resources of the mind to accomplish its end.

Socrates' definition of love in the *Symposium* appears to be peculiarly applicable to the case of Maggie Verver. Diotima, says Socrates, had told him that love is the child of Penury and Resource. What she meant was that love is, in the first instance, "poor": poor in spirit, humble, submissive; even weak and wretched—prostrating itself before the beloved, "seeking that which it lacks," longing only to be filled by that which is the object of its desire. But love is also "resourceful": it knows what it wants; it seeks by all means to secure the object of its desire; and pursues its object with all the energy and purposefulness of a hunter in pursuit of his quarry. And this, which Diotima called Resource, is only another name for the intelligence by which love, the ragged pauper, is able to see its object steady and whole, and devise the means by which it may come into the blessed possession of the beloved.

Maggie Verver, when she embarks on her task of redemption and restoration, is likewise "poor." She is pitifully weak and wretched: pitifully diffident, of course, about her power to accomplish her task; and pitifully afraid of the three people—her husband, her father and her friend—she most cares for in the world. She is terrified, to begin with, of the Prince's "sovereign personal power," as she calls his sexual power. For the Prince (we have already discovered) is not only charming, good-natured and affectionate, gracefully compliant, and full of humility, gratitude and goodwill towards his benefactors. He is also, unexpectedly, powerful; and the source of his power is twofold. For his father-in-law Adam Verver, as we have seen, it is his breeding; for his wife Maggie it is his sexual virility. Though Prince Amerigo's breeding is so exquisite, he does not for that reason (like the men, for instance, in D. H. Lawrence's stories: Lou's husband in *St. Mawr*, or Clifford Chatterley and his circle in *Lady Chatterley's Lover)* suffer any loss or diminution of sexual energy; and though his sensuality is overlaid with his aestheticism, the aestheticism is plainly not debilitating. The passage in which Amerigo reflects on Charlotte's physical beauty at their first meeting in Mrs. Assingham's house is an early indication of the kind and quality of his sexuality:

> It was, strangely, as a cluster of possessions of his own that these things in Charlotte Stant now affected him; items in a full list, items recognised, each of them, as if, for the long interval, they had been "stored"—wrapped up, numbered, put away in a cabinet. . . . He saw again that her thick hair was, vulgarly speaking, brown, but that there was a shade of tawny autumn leaf in it for "appreciation"—a colour indescribable and of which he had known no other case, something that gave her at moments the sylvan head of a huntress. He saw the sleeves of her jacket drawn to her wrists, but he again made out the free arms within them to be of the completely rounded, the polished slimness that Florentine sculptors in the great age had loved and of which the apparent firmness is expressed in their old silver and old bronze. He knew her narrow hands, he knew her long fingers and the shape and colour of her finger-nails, he knew her special beauty of movement and line when she turned her back, and the perfect working of all her main attachments, that of some wonderful finished instrument, something intently made for exhibition, for a prize. He knew above all the extraordinary fineness of her flexible waist, the stem of an expanded flower, which gave her a likeness also to some long loose silk purse, well filled with gold pieces, but having been passed empty

through a finger-ring that held it together. It was as if, before she turned to him, he had weighed the whole thing in his open palm and even heard a little the chink of the metal.[24]

The aesthetic emphasis is of course unmistakable, and it blends smoothly, we observe, with the commercial and the erotic. It is a dangerous mixture; and in the Prince's attitude to Maggie this rare blend of sophisticated refinement with sexual power is made the more dangerous by the presence of a real tenderness, or at least affection, for her. These elements are beautifully distinguished in two important passages in the Second Book, in which the operation of the Prince's "sovereign personal power" is directly exhibited and its power to sap Maggie's resolution and strength for her redemptive task particularly emphasised. In their contexts the passages are as heart-rending for what they show of Maggie's heroic struggle against her own susceptibilities as they are terrifying for what they suggest of the power of the sexual element, in a man like Maggie's husband, to dominate and subdue:

> He had possession of her hands and was bending toward her, ever so kindly, as if to see, to understand more, or possibly give more—she didn't know which; and that had the effect of simply putting her, as she would have said, in his power. She gave up, let her idea go, let everything go; her one consciousness was that he was taking her again into his arms. It was not till afterwards that she discriminated as to this; felt how the act operated with him *instead* of the words he hadn't uttered—operated in his view as probably better than any words, as always better in fact at any time than anything. Her acceptance of it, her response to it, inevitable, foredoomed, came back to her, later on, as a virtual assent to the assumption he had thus made that there was really nothing such a demonstration didn't anticipate and didn't dispose of. . . . He had been right, overwhelmingly right, as to the felicity of his tenderness and the degree of her sensibility, but even while she felt these things sweep all others away she tasted of a sort of terror of the weakness they produced in her. It was still for her that she had positively something to do, and that she mustn't be weak for this, must much rather be strong.[25]

Presently again, in the carriage:

> What her husband's grasp really meant, as her very bones registered, was that she *should* give it up [her "idea"]: it was exactly for this that he had resorted to unfailing magic. He *knew how* to resort to it—he could be on occasion, as she had lately more than ever learned, so

munificent a lover: all of which was precisely a part of the character she had never ceased to regard in him as princely, a part of his large and beautiful ease, his genius for charm, for intercourse, for expression, for life. She should have but to lay her head back on his shoulder with a certain movement to make it definite for him that she didn't resist. To this as they went every throb of her consciousness prompted her—every throb, that is, but one, the throb of her deeper need to know where she "really" was. By the time she had uttered the rest of her idea therefore she was still keeping her head and intending to keep it; though she was also staring out of the carriage-window with eyes into which the tears of suffered pain had risen. . . . She was making an effort that horribly hurt her, and as she couldn't cry out her eyes swam in her silence.[26]

So Maggie is abjectly afraid of her husband's sexual power. But she is almost equally afraid of Charlotte's formidable managerial powers; and she lives in hourly terror, of course, of her father's coming to know what he must on no account know if they are not all to be ruined. Nor are her weakness and wretchedness diminished but rather increased by her passion. Her love of her father, always tender and passionate, is now reinforced by a fierce protectiveness of the "perfect little man" whose goodness, as she sees it, has been hideously betrayed by his wife and son-in-law. At the same time she adores the Prince her husband with an adoration that is incapacitating; she admires Charlotte's "greatness" with a generosity that her fear of Charlotte has no power to destroy; and while she is swamped and submerged in this way by her terror and her passion, she knows all the while that to the Prince and Charlotte she has no hope of appearing as anything but a fool— "saintly," of course, "rotten with goodness" (like Michy in *The Awkward Age),* but still a poor, simpleminded fool. This, it is indicated,[27] is what in fact happens after the Matcham episode: the Prince and Charlotte, now bound together by the most intimate of bonds, tacitly agree to treat Maggie with a compassionate consideration more cruel than contempt; and Maggie, being fully conscious of this, is spared none of its pain or humiliation.

All this, one might suppose, would already sufficiently disable Maggie Verver for the task of restoration she has assumed. But these disabilities are as nothing compared with her ultimate disability—the ultimate condition, supremely exacting and absolutely binding, under which she has to accomplish her task. She must effect it in such a way that the precious uniqueness of each of the three beloved persons concerned shall be unimpaired. The Prince must retain his adorable Roman "charm"; Charlotte must retain her "greatness"—her social gifts and high administrative abilities; and her father must retain his mysterious "simplicity," his beautiful "innocence": he must never know what has happened—never know the shameful act of betrayal that has been perpetrated under his eyes.

There can accordingly be no question of *exposing* the Prince and Charlotte. There is to be nothing so crude and mortal as an exposure; nor is there to be anything that would be tantamount to it. For to expose them (she comes to see in a crucial scene later in the story[28]) would be to reject them: to sever the connexion which (she discerns) is as precious to them as it is to her, and is the foundation of their common life together. To destroy this, the connexion and the common life, is what she cannot bring herself to do; and that is why the Prince and Charlotte are to be "spared," whatever the cost to herself.

The lengths to which Maggie is prepared to go to spare first her husband and presently also her friend are to be touched on in a later section.[29] In the meantime, the interest of this particular condition of Maggie's task is that it is the immediate (though not the only) cause of the extraordinary central situation that dominates the Second Book of *The Golden Bowl.* As this situation is James's main dramatic device for projecting simultaneously almost all the important aspects of his redemptive theme, it invites the closest attention.

Its simplicity is the first extraordinary thing about it. What "happens" is merely that Maggie, her father, the Prince and Charlotte maintain a total, unbroken silence about the drama in which they are all involved. After the Matcham episode, each "knows" that the other "knows"; or rather, each knows that the other knows something but none knows exactly what the other knows. Maggie herself does not know for certain until the incident with the golden bowl; up to then she is only in an anguish of doubt and uncertainty. Charlotte and the Prince do not know how much Maggie knows; and neither Charlotte nor the Prince even knows what the other knows of what Maggie knows, since (we are made to understand) they hold no private communication after their return from the Gloucester expedition. When the golden bowl is broken, the Prince in the subsequent scene[30] does indeed learn that his wife Maggie knows "everything." But immediately after that the silence is resumed; and in the critical period that follows at Fawns, Mr Verver's country-house, Maggie speaks never another word about it to the Prince, the Prince speaks never a word to Charlotte, Charlotte never a word either to the Prince or Maggie, and none of them, of course, utters a syllable to Adam Verver who knows (or appears to know) nothing whatever about the whole matter from the beginning to the end of the story.

So there they hang, the four of them, "in the upper air, united in the firmest abstention from pressure"—Maggie abstaining from pressure upon the Prince and Charlotte, they abstaining from pressure upon her and one another, and all of them abstaining from pressure upon Adam Verver; and it is in this condition of total silence about what concerns them all so intimately that Maggie accomplishes her task of restoration.

On the face of it, it is a situation so extraordinary as to seem almost grotesque. At first glance it looks like some huge super-subtle jest; and if this is what it is, the jest, being at the expense of a situation we are otherwise invited to treat with the utmost seriousness, would be in rather bad taste. Or (as some of James's more unsympathetic critics would urge), it might be merely another instance of that "hypertrophy of sensibility" which led James in his later works to lose all, or almost all, sense of reality and all sense of proportion in his treatment of human relationships, and to indulge his passion for elaboration and refinement as a mere exercise of technical virtuosity.

In fact, however, it is neither. As a dramatic device it is super-subtle indeed, but for reasons wholly creditable to James's genius; and it is of the first importance to understand the several complex ends it achieves in the total plan of *The Golden Bowl.*

The first of these is most conveniently approached by recalling one important theme in the account of *The Turn of the Screw* set out in an earlier chapter. The governess, it was suggested, failed in the end to accomplish her work of salvation because at a crucial point in the story she had insisted on extracting from little Miles a confession which in that situation it was sheer cruelty to insist upon. Goaded on (as she afterwards realised) by her mad "pride," her desire to bring her work to a decisive victory, she had pressed and harassed the child in her determination to "have all." She had been unable to let the knowledge of good and evil grow in him of itself, naturally and sweetly, until it should finally separate him from the powers of evil and restore him to the powers of good; and this in the governess was as much a failure of intelligence as of character. She did not in the first instance see that if love is to save it must be perfectly selfless; nor was she capable, it seems, of the effort of self-discipline that such love demands and (paradoxically) makes possible—in this instance, the power to abstain from pressure.

This is the failure which is gloriously redeemed by Maggie Verver in *The Golden Bowl*. Maggie's task, we gradually come to see, is accomplished precisely by not insisting: by not pressing or harassing her husband the Prince but, instead, simply letting him alone—to see for himself the shamefulness of his act of betrayal, to come by his own effort to the knowledge of good and evil, and so to supply himself in the end with that moral sense which (he had confessed to Mrs Assingham) he so lamentably lacked. By letting him alone,[31] moreover, the main condition of his transformation is also perfectly fulfilled—that it shall be accomplished without the smallest injury to his personal gifts and graces. His adorable Roman charm is to remain intact, the beautiful "pride of his manhood" (as Maggie later sees it) is to be left unimpaired. He must, in the common phrase, "remain himself" even while he is radically transformed by his new knowledge of good and evil; he must be humbled by the consciousness of his guilt but not diminished by it. The knowledge of good and evil must effect, in short, a transfiguration in a quasi-religious sense: the old elements are all to remain, but so glorified as to make a "new man" who, brought to birth in this way, will stand as a living testimony to the redeeming power of human love.

It is easy to see how the seemingly fantastic situation in the Second Part of *The Golden Bowl* perfectly dramatises this aspect of the theme. Maggie's total silence, her absolute abstention from pressure throughout the period in which the Prince is plunged in his dark night of the soul, is now seen to be the final measure of her love. It is because she loves him with a passion untainted by the spiritual greed of the governess in *The Turn of the Screw* that she can abstain from pressing him or harassing him or preaching to him; and it is by the strength of the same love that she can silently forgive him his trespass against her, silently suffer with him and watch over him in his anguish as he struggles to come to his knowledge of good and evil.

So this is the strength of Maggie Verver's love. Maggie herself, however, we already know, is a weak, timid, quavering girl. (Her voice always quavers in the most absurd way, especially when she is speaking to Charlotte.) In the pursuit of her redemptive task she accordingly passes through purgatorial fires of anguish, humiliation and terror, in a solitude more dark and dense even than any that Milly Theale had known; and the heroic effort it costs her to persist in her total abstention from pressure is repeatedly emphasised. As in the following passage, appropriately cast in a Waste Land image, in which the effort and the pain, the unnatural self-discipline, and the aching desire to relieve the solitude and re-establish the connexion she yearns for, are powerfully evoked:

> Maggie had become more conscious from week to week of his [the Prince's] ingenuities of intention to make up to her for their forfeiture, in so dire a degree, of any reality of frankness—a privation that had left on his lips perhaps a little of the same thirst with which she fairly felt her own distorted, the torment of the lost pilgrim who listens in the desert sands for the possible, the impossible splash of water. It was just this hampered state in him none the less that she kept before her when she wished most to find grounds of dignity for the hard little passion which nothing he had done could smother. There were hours enough, lonely hours, in which she let dignity go; then there were others when, clinging with her winged concentration to some deep cell of her heart, she stored away her hived tenderness as if she had gathered it all from flowers. He was walking ostensibly beside her, but in fact given over without a break to the grey medium in which he helplessly groped; a perception on her part which was a perpetual pang and might last what it would—for ever if need be—but which if relieved at all must be relieved by his act alone.[32]

This "perception," however, among others of the same order, follows as a consequence of the single, all-illuminating, perception that visits Maggie in an earlier scene. As in *The Portrait of a Lady* Isabel Archer's midnight vigil before the dying fire of her sitting-room marks the highest point of her growth in self-knowledge, so in *The Golden Bowl* Maggie Verver reaches her peak of self-knowledge as she walks on the terrace at Fawns passing and re-passing the smoking-room where her father, her stepmother and her husband sit playing their game of bridge.[33] Before coming out on to the terrace, as she sat on a sofa watching the players, she had been seized for a moment by a dreadful temptation to speak the word that would tear through the appearances they were all so wonderfully and prodigiously keeping up and expose once and for all the reality that lay behind:

> The amount of enjoyed or at least achieved security represented by so complete a conquest of appearances was what acted on her nerves precisely with a kind of provocative force. She found herself for five minutes thrilling to the idea of the prodigious effect that, just as she sat there near them, she had at her command; with the sense that if she were but different—oh, ever so different!—all this high decorum would hang by a hair. There reigned for her absolutely during these vertiginous moments that fascination of the monstrous, that temptation of the horribly possible, which we so often trace by its breaking out suddenly, lest it should go further, in unexplained retreats and reactions. . . . After it had been thus vividly before her for a little that, springing up under her wrong and making them all start, stare and turn pale, she might sound out their doom in a single sentence, a sentence easy to choose among several of the lurid—after she had faced that blinding light and felt it turn to blackness she rose from her place . . . and moved slowly round the room, passing the card-players and pausing an instant behind the chairs in turn.[34]

She meets the eyes of each of the four players (Mrs Assingham is the fourth) as she passes out of the room on to the terrace, conscious of "the secret behind every face," and receives her first intimation of her role as sufferer and redeemer. She reads in each pair of eyes

> an appeal, a positive confidence . . . that was deeper than any negation and that seemed to speak on the part of each of some relation to be contrived by her, a relation with herself, which would spare the individual the danger, the actual present strain, of the relation with the others. They thus tacitly put it upon her to be disposed of, the whole complexity of their peril, and she promptly saw why: because she was there, and there just *as* she was, to lift it off them and take it; to charge herself with it as the scapegoat of old, of whom she had once seen a terrible picture, had been charged with the sins of the people and had gone forth into the desert to sink under his burden and die.

They did not, however, want her to *die:*

That indeed wasn't *their* design and their interest, that she should sink under hers; it wouldn't be their feeling that she should do anything but live, live on somehow for their benefit, and even as much as possible in their company, to keep proving to them that they had truly escaped and that she was still there to simplify.[35]

Then, as she walks on the terrace, pondering the implications of this, she receives another great shock of recognition. She sees, at last, why she had all this time persisted in her chosen course, and what it was that had supported her through all the anguish, terror and humiliation. She sees why, from the beginning, there had been no question for her of succumbing to the more commonplace passions that her situation might, all too excusably, have provoked in another: why "she had been able to give herself from the first so little to the vulgar heat of her wrong"; why (though she had "yearned" for it) she had had to renounce "the straight vindictive view, the rights of resentment, the rages of jealousy, the protests of passion"; why, even, she had had to forgo the sense of horror itself—"the horror of finding evil seated all at its ease where she had only dreamed of good; the horror of the thing hideously *behind*, behind so much trusted, so much pretended, nobleness, cleverness, tenderness"; why, in short, she had been unable "to feel about them in any of the immediate, inevitable, assuaging ways, the ways usually open to innocence outraged and generosity betrayed." The reason, she discerns, was that to feel in any of these ways "would have been *to give them up*"—to reject them, to break the connexion; and this, "marvellously," never had been and was not now to be thought of. Her task all along, she now sees, had not been in the first instance to preserve her own dignity, her own self-respect, even her own integrity; nor had it been to preserve theirs. It had been, rather, to preserve the connexion itself, by guarding, jealously and tenderly, the very appearances she had a little while back wanted to tear apart—those "serenities, dignities and decencies" (as she now calls them) which were the common ground of their life together; and within this connexion and this common life to achieve a common salvation for them all.[36]

This, she now knows, is what had caused her on her sofa in the smoking-room to draw back "from that provocation of opportunity which had assaulted her . . . as a beast might have leaped at her throat";[37] and as she reaches this point in her meditation, she sees Charlotte standing in the empty drawing-room—"a splendid shining supple creature . . . out of the cage"—and knows that she is to be exposed in her role as scapegoat and redeemer to another terrifying, humiliating ordeal.

I return to the central situation in the Second Book of *The Golden Bowl* to suggest another aspect of its complex meaning. I mentioned in an earlier section that Henry James's particular contribution to the anatomy of love is the idea that love in the modern world must be informed by intelligence.[38] If the love of a Maggie Verver is to triumph in this world; if its redemptive work is to be accomplished, wholly and perfectly, within the human order and without reference to an order transcending the human; if, therefore, love is to triumph by the visible annihilation of death, and Maggie, the vessel of the redemptive love, is not (like the scapegoat of old) to die but to live, love must fight to win, and must win a visible victory. And to win such a victory requires not only humility and selflessness, and the power to forgive and to suffer— not only, that is, the saving virtues recommended by historic Christianity; it requires also a virtue not generally much emphasised in the Christian scheme and even held to be a little suspect.

The reason why Maggie Verver's love absolutely must be informed by intelligence is to be discovered by considering again the nature of the enemy she has to engage. Maggie is not, like Shakespeare's Desdemona or Cordelia, fighting the devil in the comparatively simple, tangible shape of an Iago or a Goneril and Regan. She is fighting him in a shape more subtle and insidious than any that even Shakespeare appears to have had any knowledge of—for the reason, perhaps, that it had not yet fully emerged in the consciousness of man at the time Shakespeare wrote. The destructive element that the Prince and Charlotte embody in the aesthetic principle, their "touchstone of taste," is a distinctly modern phenomenon, peculiar to the modern consciousness; and in the story of *The Golden Bowl*, its diabolical character is most fully exposed in that interior monologue of the Prince on the terrace at Matcham[39] in which the touchstone of taste says in effect "Evil be thou my good," and argues, with the utmost cogency and persuasiveness, that the Prince's adultery with Charlotte is not merely justified but is positively the only natural, the only decent, the only properly moral thing to do.

It is the touchstone of taste accordingly that Maggie must annihilate in order to accomplish her task. But since this is in its essence a function of the finest of human qualities—of sensibility and imagination, and of goodwill and good faith; since it looks so much like the work of God and not at all like the work of the devil, the difficulty of recognising it for what it is would seem almost beyond the power of human discernment. And perhaps it is beyond the power of human discernment, and perhaps (as the religious would say) Maggie Verver is acting by a power other than and greater than herself. But the fact is that she does discern, by whatever power, that the touchstone of taste must be annihilated.

Or rather, it must be transformed. The aesthetic must be superseded by the moral; yet the moral must, somehow, incorporate the aesthetic. For if the good is not also beautiful, and if it is not *seen* as beautiful, it will have no power to draw to itself those who are in the grip of the infernal principle. But the beautiful for the Prince and Charlotte, we already know, is inseparable from the intelligent (we remember the Prince on the terrace at Matcham reflecting bitterly on the dear good Ververs' constitutional inaccessibility to knowledge, and correspondingly rejoicing in Charlotte's free play of mind and rich sense of the irony of things); therefore the good must have the specific beauty of intelligence; and that is the first important reason why Maggie Verver's love has to be informed by this specific quality.

But, further (she also discerns), her intelligence must be the kind that the Prince will be able to recognise. It must be, in other words, the intelligence of "the world"—the Prince's world, the worldly world. Though directed to ends transcending in dignity and power anything that this world can conceive, it must yet be as acute, as shrewd, as calculating, as cool and self-possessed, and as perfectly disciplined as the intelligence that the world honours and understands; and since this, it seems, is the character that an intelligence animated by love has to assume in the modern world, it does in fact assume it when (like the divine love in the Pauline scheme) it is prepared to be all things to all men in order that it may by any means save some.

In the personal domestic story of Maggie Verver's struggle to regain the husband she lost, what this means is that Maggie has to prove to the Prince that she is not the charming simpleton he and Charlotte have taken her to be but a person (in the phraseology of the world) to be reckoned with. In this, we know, Maggie succeeds; she succeeds by the exercise precisely of the worldly qualities required; and in succeeding she satisfies the world's ultimate criterion of virtue. She achieves her triumph, however—and this is the point to be stressed—entirely within the framework of the strange situation she has created, by which she, her husband, her father and her friend are held together in the upper air, united by the firmest abstention from pressure; and to understand how she does it, and why, is to understand another aspect of the dramatic significance of this remarkable situation.

Having discovered that she has been betrayed by her husband and her friend, Maggie Verver abstains from pressure (we are now expected to see) because this is not only the most loving thing to do in the circumstances but also the most intelligent. To begin with, it is intelligent to exploit—yes, exploit—her husband's and her friend's terror of exposure. It is intelligent to exploit their compunction at what they have done. It is intelligent to hold them in an unbroken suspense, first, about how much Maggie knows and, presently, about what if anything she is going to do. It is supremely intelligent to keep them always in the wrong, herself always in the right—perpetually "one up" on them—by never breaking the silence she had resolved to maintain from the moment the golden bowl was broken and she said to the Prince "Find out the rest. Find out for yourself."[40] For by remaining absolutely and perfectly silent she can never provoke the kind of show-down in which they would certainly gain the mastery over her; she can never ask them for an explanation or excuse, and so never give them a chance to lie to her or snub her or in any other way put her in the wrong, themselves in the right. This, in the current phrase, is lifemanship; and this, it seems, is what a love informed by intelligence must know how to exercise in the modern world for the ends of salvation. In any case, it is by exercising her intelligence in this thoroughly worldly way that Maggie achieves her first decisive victory. She gains it by winning, in the phrase of the world, the Prince's "respect"—for her purposefulness, her shrewdness, her coolness, her self-possession; and in so doing, she completes the first necessary stage of her task of restoration and redemption.

There is, however, a further reason why Maggie's total silence, which is the pivot of the strange situation we are trying to understand, should gain for her the respect of her husband. For, simultaneously with its being an exercise of the worldly intelligence, it happens also to satisfy completely the touchstone of taste itself—that standard of a higher and braver propriety which, it appears, is so much too high and too brave for any simple-minded openness and candour. Is there not (one may imagine the Prince asking himself in the course of his silent brooding at Fawns) something extraordinarily delicate and charming about this silence of Maggie's—something so entirely expressive of the right sort of restraint, the right sort of forbearance, the right sort of abstention from every kind of tediousness? There had been no reproaches or recriminations (he would have noted to himself); no martyred airs, no moralising, no discussion or analysis even; nothing at all of what in the Prince's world variously adds up to being tedious. Apart from her matter-of-fact statement of what she "knew" when the golden bowl was broken, there had been only this perfect silence expressive of perfect civility, perfect composure, perfect good manners; and it is this that in the first instance must win the Prince's admiration and respect—that his wife should be capable of such scrupulously good manners in the face of (as he would put it) such a very trying situation. She is standing up to the touchstone of taste in a way completely unexpected, and to him thoroughly instructive.

Then, as his admiration and respect for her grow, he suddenly also finds her interesting, in the way Charlotte was interesting; and presently, indeed, more—positively more—interesting than Charlotte. For he begins to perceive, dimly and confusedly at first, but as the months pass more and more clearly, that her intelligence and her manners in this most trying of situations are not ends in themselves but are subordinated to another end. That end remains unnamed, and is perhaps unnameable; but though he never names it, he recognises it as something other than and superior to the touchstone of taste by which he has always conducted his life. The moment in which the Prince recognises this is climatic, and marks the resolution of one of James's principal themes in *The Golden Bowl*. Characteristically, it is given to us as casually and unemphatically as are all the great moments in James's greatest stories.[41] Maggie has announced to her husband that Mr Verver and Charlotte are coming to spend a last evening with them before they sail for America, and has suggested that he might like to

spend it alone with Charlotte. The Prince's first reaction is to let
Maggie see "that he took [this] for no cheap extravagance either
of irony or of oblivion."[42] Then, as he reflects intently on this offer
of "an opportunity to separate from Mrs Verver with the due
amount of form," he seeks grounds for condemning Maggie's
suggestion by an appeal to his touchstone of taste. But, for the first
time in his life, it fails him. He finds himself "in so pathetic a way,
unable to treat himself to a quarrel with it on the score of taste";
and the reason, we are explicitly told, is that:

> Taste in him as a touchstone was now all at sea; for who could say but
> that one of her [Maggie's] fifty ideas, or perhaps forty-nine of them,
> wouldn't be exactly that taste by itself, the taste he had always con-
> formed to, had no importance whatever?[43]

This is what the Prince has at last learnt, solely as a result of the
conduct of his wife. For her conduct, he now sees, has been motivated by love and by love alone; and by the side of such love, he
also sees, the touchstone of taste has indeed "no importance whatever."

There is soon after this, and following directly from it, another
climactic moment which is given to us even more economically.
The Prince, having seen what Maggie really is, is suddenly struck
with the fact that Charlotte does not see it. He registers this insight
to Maggie in a single simple sentence: "She's stupid," he says, in
a context that makes the pregnant reference of the statement plain
enough to Maggie.[44] Again it comes out as casually and unemphatically as any remark at the tea-table. But when one remembers
the weekend party at Matcham and the glory that had hung about
the Prince and Charlotte then; when one remembers in particular
their shared ironies at the expense of the poor simple-minded
Ververs, and their shared sense of that "higher and braver propriety" which had seemed to make their passion self-justifying,
this simple remark of the Prince has all the significance and force
of an illumination. As such, it marks his final repudiation of the
aesthetic standard and his final recognition of the moral—of the
surpassing dignity, power and beauty of the moral by which it
transcends the inferior dignity, power and beauty of the merely
aesthetic.

Maggie disputes her husband's judgment on Charlotte, and
presently succeeds in showing him that his rejection of Charlotte
is as unjust as it is unnecessary for the end of their common

salvation. This, however, is not the main point in the present context.[45] The point is that Maggie Verver has won back her husband and restored the right relations of their moral universe which had been disordered by his act of betrayal by bringing him to see the insufficiency of the touchstone of taste for the conduct of life—and thus effecting in him the final supersession of the aesthetic by the moral.

This process, however, it has already been indicated,[46] is in the nature of a transformation rather than an annihilation. In *The Golden Bowl* the aesthetic is indeed annihilated in the form in which it governs the life of the worldly world; but in the form in which the beautiful is always an intimate, inseparable part of the good, the touchstone of taste is not annihilated but incorporated into the greater and more glorious beauty of the good.

In an essay on Flaubert published in 1893, James speaks of the ultimate source of Flaubert's limitations as a lack of "faith in the power of the moral to offer a surface."[47] This memorable phrase exactly defines the faith he himself did possess—an absolute, inextinguishable faith in the supreme beauty of goodness, and in the consequent "power" of goodness to offer to the artist the richest opportunities for exhibiting this beauty; and in *The Golden Bowl* the power is conclusively shown and the faith triumphantly vindicated in the story of the moral transformation of the Prince by his wife's love.

That Maggie herself recognises the inseparable unity of the beautiful and the good is sufficiently proved by her passionate concern, already touched on,[48] to leave intact and inviolate her husband's princely "charm." He must acquire the moral sense he lacks, but he must not acquire it at the expense of his "personal serenity," his "incomparable superiority." She feels this very powerfully on the momentous occasion when the golden bowl is broken and the Prince's duplicity is about to be exposed. As she bends to gather up the pieces under his eyes, knowing that he now knows that she knows "everything,"

> There was even a minute . . . when her back was turned to him, during which she knew once more the strangeness of her desire to spare him, a strangeness that had already fifty times brushed her, in the depth of her trouble, as with the wild wing of some bird of the air who might blindly have swooped for an instant into the shaft of a well, darkening there by his momentary flutter the far-off round of sky.[49]

She accordingly finds herself silently entreating him to take all the *time* he needs to compose himself:

> "Take it, take it, take all you need of it; arrange yourself so as to suffer least, or to be at any rate least distorted and disfigured. Only *see*, see that *I* see, and make up your mind on this new basis at your conven- ience. . . . Above all don't show me, till you've got it well under, the dreadful blur, the ravage of suspense and embarrassment produced, and produced by my doing, in your personal serenity, your incompara- ble superiority."[50]

Presently, when the beginning of the end is in sight, we are given a vivid sense of the plenitude of peace, power and joy that flows for Maggie from her vision not, in the first instance, of the Prince's new moral goodness but of his moral *loveliness*—of "the beauty shining out of the humility, and the humility lurking in all the pride of his presence":

> It was as if she had passed in a time incredibly short from being nothing for him to being all; it was as if, rightly noted, every turn of his head, every tone of his voice, in these days, *might* mean that there was but one way in which a proud man reduced to abjection could hold himself. During those of Maggie's vigils in which that view loomed largest the image of her husband thus presented to her gave out a beauty for the revelation of which she struck herself as paying, if anything, too little. To make sure of it—to make sure of the beauty shining out of the humility and of the humility lurking in all the pride of his presence—she would have gone the length of paying more yet, of paying with difficulties and anxieties compared to which those actually before her might have been as superficial as headaches or rainy days.[51]

Finally, in the very last scene, when Adam Verver and Charlotte have gone and the love that has flowered between Maggie and her husband out of the depths and intensities of their new understand- ing of each other is about to be consummated in the body, she has a last spasm of anxiety for him. Amerigo enters the room, and

> His presence alone, as he paused to look at her, somehow made it [her reward] the highest, and even before he had spoken she had begun to be paid in full. With that consciousness in fact an extraordinary thing occurred; the assurance of her safety so making her terror drop that already within the minute it had been changed to concern for his own

anxiety, for everything that was deep in his being and everything that was fair in his face. . . . What instantly rose for her between the act and her acceptance was the sense that she must strike him as waiting for a confession. This, in turn, charged her with a new horror: if *that* was her proper payment she would go without money. . . . All she now knew accordingly was that she should be ashamed to listen to the uttered word; all, that is, but that she might dispose of it on the spot for ever.[52]

Here again, and for the last time, she cannot bear the thought of his being disfigured by anything so ugly as a "confession."

The Prince's recognition of the power of the moral to offer a surface is, of course, a vital part of his transformation. When he repudiates the touchstone of taste, he does so because he has perceived at last not only the goodness of Maggie's love but also the beauty of that goodness. This is what he means—or part of what he means—when he says of Charlotte "She's stupid" (not to see what Maggie is); and this is what is intimated again in his prolonged moment with Maggie in the scene just before the arrival of the Ververs on their last visit, when his passion almost overmasters his prudence about "waiting" until the Ververs have gone:

On him too however something had descended. . . . "Ah, but I shall see you—! No?" he said, coming nearer.

She had, with her hand still on the knob, her back against the door, so that her retreat under his approach must be less than a step, and yet she couldn't for her life with the other hand have pushed him away. He was so near now that she could touch him, taste him, smell him, kiss him, hold him; he almost pressed upon her, and the warmth of his face—frowning, smiling, she mightn't know which; only beautiful and strange—was bent upon her with the largeness with which objects loom in dreams. She closed her eyes to it, and so the next instant, against her purpose, she had put out her hand, which had met his own and which he held.[53]

So the touchstone of taste is finally transcended by incorporation into the moral, where beauty and goodness are, at last and indissolubly, one; and this is accomplished by Maggie Verver's love operating through her deeply intelligent scheme of maintaining a total unbroken silence about "everything." This, I believe, is the principal meaning of the situation in *The Golden Bowl* which had seemed at first sight so fantastic. There is, however, still another and final aspect to be discerned, which is in a sense comprehended by the other yet is also distinct from it.

One may call this the "social" aspect; and it is recognisably present already in the social themes of *The Awkward Age* and, further back, of *The Tragic Muse* and *The Portrait of a Lady.* This aspect is used by James to express a final criticism of modern society, meaning by "society" here as everywhere in James the ideally civilised, ideally sophisticated society of Buckingham Crescent, Lancaster Gate, and now also Matcham and Portland Place and Eaton Square.

In this aspect, the central situation in the Second Book of *The Golden Bowl* is, I believe, a colossal symbol, as audacious as it is brilliant, for expressing (in the Prince's phrase) the fathomless depths of equivocation that a sophisticated society is by its nature committed to. Reviewing the situation from such a point of view, what is the familiar picture that emerges? A calamitous thing, we know, has happened: Maggie Verver's adored husband has entered into an adulterous relationship with Maggie's beloved friend Charlotte Stant, who is also her father's wife. The calamity is, in the first instance, in the anguish of loss which Maggie herself suffers to satiety; but it is equally in the fact that the "serenities and dignities and decencies" of their common life appear, by the act of betrayal, to be shattered beyond repair. Yet everyone concerned remains, or appears to remain, perfectly unmoved. No one registers shock or horror, no one explains or apologises, no one so much as comments on what has happened or asks a single question about it. A perfect unbroken silence about it is maintained by everyone concerned. They remain perfectly easy and natural, perfectly civil to each other, chatting in the ordinary way, sharing their normal interest in each other and the world around them, carrying on the domestic and social round as if nothing whatever had happened.

Yet the calamity *has* occurred; and it is vitally necessary for the moral health and happiness of all concerned in it, and in order that the crooked may be made straight and the right relations of things restored, that it should be explicitly acknowledged and openly discussed. Nevertheless though there is nothing to prevent them from "speaking out"—telling what they know, asking what they want to know, challenging those who will neither tell nor ask—this is in fact the last thing any of them would dream of doing. In particular they would not dream of doing anything so simple, straightforward and candid as to ask. For though to ask and to receive an answer would instantly clear the air, yet it would also (we are made to understand) tear the little society to pieces by exposing it to itself in a way that would somehow bring it to ruin.[54] So the vital, saving question is never asked; there is never a showdown, never a face-to-face encounter; but everyone tries to read the answer in everyone else's eyes, to "find out" what he desperately wants and needs to know, while remaining totally silent.

We have already in James's later works met this particular object of his irony: most prominently in *The Awkward Age, The Sacred Fount* and *The Wings of the Dove;* but also in *The Turn of the Screw,* where the governess, we remember, cannot until the end bring herself to name Peter Quint and Miss Jessel to the children—cannot, that is, bring herself to challenge them directly about their relations with the dead servants. We have already, in other words, been invited to share the threefold aspect of James's vision of modern sophisticated societies: his profound sense of the prevailing absence of candour, the prevailing presence of obliqueness, evasiveness, "ambiguity"; his sense, equally profound, of its necessity—as, somehow, a means of corporate self-preservation; and his sense, finally, of its beauty. For there *is* a beauty (James here as elsewhere insists) in reticence, composure and civility inflexibly maintained, with every appearance of naturalness and ease, when the heart is being torn to pieces by anguish, terror and humiliation; and though the over-civilised—the Edwardian English, for instance—had perhaps too much of it, the under-civilised —James's simpler Americans—had too little; and James himself, we may suppose, would not have chosen to live among the more civilised rather than the less if he had not seen its beauty as well as its ugliness. Nothing in Henry James is ever made simpler than it is; but nowhere perhaps is his refusal to simplify and his fidelity to the experienced complexity of the actual more complete and more admirable than in his handlng of this theme in *The Golden Bowl.*

If, as James intimates, the necessity and the beauty, as well as the horror, of this prevailing lack of candour is to be observed at its richest and ripest in modern English society, it has to be added that it is more likely to be recognised by the perceptive foreigner than by the Englishmen concerned, whose degree of immersion in it (as James would have said) is generally as complete as it is unconscious. Nor, of course, will one ever see it in operation in real life as absolutely as in *The Golden Bowl*. But allowing for the difference between art and life, between the ideal perfection of the artistic situation and the imperfect approximations of life, the central situation in the Second Book may stand as James's most devastating comment on an aspect of civilised society that he had, from far back, found to be appalling, fascinating and illuminating all at once. As such, it is in one sense the super-subtle jest that some critics have taken it to be. But the jest in that case is a very serious one, and the irony (as in *The Awkward Age)* is predominantly tragic, not comic. For the main intention of the ironic exposure is to show the price in human suffering that may have to be paid for this lack of candour—which, we learn from the exemplary story of the four persons in *The Golden Bowl* who remained to the end united by the firmest abstention from pressure, can be colossal indeed.

II

In an illuminating chapter on *The Golden Bowl* in his little book on the later novels of Henry James,[55] Mr F. C. Crews remarks on the presence, in the later chapters in particular, of a "wealth of Christian overtones" which, he says, must be accounted for if we are to understand the "ultimate meaning" of the fable. The evidences he cites, though not exhaustive, are striking indeed. He notes that Maggie is "surrounded with images linking her to Christ," and that her function as "an agent of mercy" becomes increasingly prominent as the story draws to a close. He shows how Adam Verver's role as the God to Maggie's Christ, which has already been hinted at by the emphasis throughout the story on his power, and the "formlessness, colourness and inaccessibility" which are its essence, appears now to be reinforced by the suggestion that the power is unlimited; and he quotes passages in the later chapters that would seem to argue in James a deliberate intention to present Adam as a God figure whose relation to Maggie resembles in many important respects that of the Father to the Son in the Christian scheme.[56]

Mr Crews rightly declines to conclude from these admittedly challenging details that James is here writing as a Christian, or even in any strict sense projecting the Christian scheme of salvation; he contents himself with the observation that "by enlarging his characters through religious analogies he introduced the whole Christian system as an available means of moral judgment.[57] The sense in which Henry James might be regarded as a "religious humanist," and his later writings, in particular *The Golden Bowl*, as religious in that sense, is to be the subject of a separate enquiry.[58] In the meantime Mr Crews' formula, modest though it is, is of great value: first, in drawing attention to a dimension of meaning in *The Golden Bowl* that invites further examination; second, in suggesting the direction in which the answer to an important problem in the Second Book is to be sought. This turns upon the case of Charlotte Stant. Granted the interpretation of *The Golden Bowl* set out in the previous chapter, that it is predominantly a fable about the redemptive power of human love, the story of Charlotte in the Second Book clearly raises doubts and difficulties. What on this account are we to make of her fate? How in particular are we to explain what has been frequently noted as strange, unpleasant, and even repulsive in the last part of *The Golden Bowl*—the seeming injustice of Charlotte's "punishment," which is conspicuously more severe than that of her fellow-sinner the Prince, and so harsh as to seem cruel to the point of savagery?

The question of Charlotte's punishment, moreover, appears to be connected with other "unpleasant" elements in this part of the book. There are the numerous extended images of terror and shame surrounding not only Charlotte but Maggie as well.[59] There are the strange ambiguous conversations, between Maggie and Fanny Assingham and Maggie and Adam, in which Maggie's attitude to the "sinners," Charlotte and the Prince, seems often to carry a taint of self-righteousness, and her father's an even stronger taint of self-assertion, issuing in what appears to be a cruel, arbitrary exercise of power; and there are passages bearing specifically on Maggie's scheme for separating the Prince and Charlotte which suggest, or seem to suggest, a disturbing element of selfishness and possessiveness in her attitude of which neither she nor anyone else in the story appears to be conscious. The total impression left upon the reader is that in the later parts of *The Golden Bowl* there is a strain of grimness, pessimism, even bitterness in James's view of the human condition; and though this is hinted at by the title (and should therefore perhaps cause no surprise), it is at any rate not easy to reconcile with the positive redemptive theme of the story.

Before considering the scheme within which the seemingly contradictory aspects of *The Golden Bowl* might possibly be reconciled, I want to take up briefly the question of Maggie's "selfishness," in relation to the Prince in particular.

In an earlier section[60] I suggested that the most interesting thing about Maggie Verver's love was that it was at once completely selfless and thoroughly selfish, and that the sense in which it was selfish yet not therefore the less selfless needed to be understood if we were not to miss what was perhaps Henry James's most original contribution to the anatomy of love. The selfishness, in one word, is all in Maggie's wanting of her husband the Prince. She wants him passionately, possessively, jealously. Through all her anguished doubts and misgivings, it never for a moment occurs to her to concede Charlotte a prior or superior "right" to him. She too in fact, like Charlotte, regards her passion as self-justifying; she needs no further reason for wanting to get the Prince back from Charlotte than that she desperately, abjectly, abysmally wants him back. This is how she puts it to her father in the garden at Fawns:

> When you only love a little you're naturally not jealous—or are only jealous also a little, so that it doesn't matter. But when you love in a deeper and intenser way, then you're in the very same proportion jealous; your jealousy has intensity and, no doubt, ferocity. When however you love in the most abysmal and unutterable way of all— why then you're beyond everything, and nothing can pull you down.[61]

This is the selfishness of Maggie's love of the Prince; in this respect it is no different from Charlotte's; and the moral James perhaps means us to draw is that love by definition is grounded in and sustained by desire, and that, whatever else it may also have to be, it is not love at all if it does not spring from and is not perpetually nourished by want and wanting.

What then is the difference between Maggie's love and Charlotte's? Charlotte's is to be more fully discussed in a later section; for the present it is perhaps enough to say that her passion for the Prince (like his for her) is grounded in the aesthetic rather than the moral, that their marriage of true minds is sustained by their common allegiance to the touchstone of taste and the standard of a higher and braver propriety than (in their view) the merely moral can yield. In Maggie's love the aesthetic is, of course, not absent; on the contrary—as we saw in the scene in the carriage[62] where in the midst of her wretchedness she can still adore him for his "large and beautiful ease, his genius for charm, for intercourse, for expression, for life"—the aesthetic is an intimate part of it, and induces its own variety of passion. But it is not confined to the aesthetic. What she ultimately adores him for, what she finds peculiarly beautiful in him, is the moral loveliness she discerns in his charm, his tenderness, his good humour, good will, good faith —in everything that is most noble, most generous, most *good* in him. This, we will find, is what Charlotte happens to be most "stupid" about;[63] and it is also precisely what Maggie above everything wants to preserve (or restore) in the Prince. It is for this that she suffers terror, anguish and humiliation; renounces the pride of her knowledge, letting Charlotte think her a "fool" to the end; and is even ready, by one of the paradoxes of the true love, to lose the very object of her adoration rather than lose that which to her is most adorable in him: "He was walking ostensibly beside her, but in fact given over without a break to the grey medium in which he helplessly groped; a perception on her part which was a perpetual pang and which might last what it would—for ever if need be—but which if relieved at all must be relieved by his act alone."[64]

So Maggie's love is firmly grounded in the carnal, in want and wanting; yet it issues in something that transcends the carnal by incorporating it; and this is how the *eros* and the *agape* of the Christian account of love are reconciled in Henry James's account. But—and this is the last vital point—though (as we saw) Maggie's courage, intelligence and resolution have everything to do with the redemptive power of her love, it is her faith that ultimately guides and directs it. Maggie does not try to "teach" the Prince; she has no theories about making him better than he is; she is conscious of no desire to alter him. She clings to and acts by her faith alone —that is, by the simple belief that so long as she loves him for what is most beautiful and splendid in him, and so long as she wants him with passion, what she does will be, *must* be, right. Here again is the reconciliation of *eros* and *agape:* the wanting, "selfish" love— Socrates' ragged pauper in the *Symposium* pursuing the object of his desire and not resting until he possesses it; and the *agape,* the adoration of that which is most good and most beautiful in the beloved, issuing in a redemption of the beloved that is the more triumphantly found because it was never sought.

The grimmer, more pessimistic view of Maggie's "selfishness" is to be discussed in a later section.[65] In the meantime, I return to our main problem in the latter part of *The Golden Bowl*, that turning upon the fate of Charlotte Stant. To account for this, the framework of the redemptive theme set out in the previous chapter must, I believe, be enlarged to incorporate an aspect of the inherited Judaeo-Christian scheme of salvation (with all the necessary "humanist" modifications) which is perhaps more distinctively Judaeic than Christian and has a prominent place also in the view of the human condition of that other great source of spiritual wisdom in our civilisation, the Greek. The enlarged scheme turns upon the relation of love and justice, and the supremacy of justice in a world only imperfectly and incompletely redeemed by love. On this view, the defining task of justice is to ensure the right relations of things—their right relation to reality, whatever that reality may be; and in the moral sphere specifically, its task is to ensure the stability and perpetuity of the moral order, guarding it from violation or, when it has been violated, restoring it by the best means available to it in the circumstances. The defining task of love, on the other hand, is to alter reality—to transform it, transfigure it, perfect it; and because love possesses this power to alter or transform which justice does not possess, it is greater than justice, and the God of the Judaeo-Christian tradition is first and last a Loving God perpetually offering his prevenient grace to his creatures for their salvation by love.

But, though love by its nature has this power to transform and perfect reality and therefore the power to supersede justice by incorporating it into itself, and though in a world completely and perfectly redeemed by love justice would, finding its occupation gone, cease to exist as a separate and distinguishable entity, love never in fact, particularly when exercised by imperfect or limited human agents upon imperfect or sinful fellow humans, succeeds in accomplishing its redemptive task completely and perfectly. It never therefore succeeds in rendering justice supererogatory; and in a world incompletely and imperfectly redeemed by love—in the actual moral world, that is, as we know it—justice is for this reason supreme. For where love has failed, by reason of the imperfections of the agent or of the recipient or of both, there justice has to take over; and since in our world love never succeeds completely, justice always does have the last word, and is in that sense supreme. And that is why the God of Judaism and Christianity, besides being a God of Love, is also always a God of Justice who, knowing the disposition of his creatures perpetually to resist the grace of love, is perpetually compelled to exercise his power—the "wrath," the "judgement," of the Old Testament—as distinct from his love to restore and maintain the moral order against its perpetual violation by the creatures.

So although love has indeed the power to supersede and annihilate justice when it is exercised perfectly, where love fails, or is exercised only imperfectly, justice prevails; and a world, or that part of the world, in which justice prevails is likely to be sterner, harsher, grimmer than one which has been brought under the sweet dominion of love. As such, it may induce a profound "pessimism"; and we will presently examine more closely the evidences of this in *The Golden Bowl*. Meanwhile the general relevance of this view of the relation of love and justice to *The Golden Bowl* and the case of Charlotte Stant may be briefly indicated. What it suggests is that that part of the moral world in which Charlotte Stant is most prominent remains, for reasons to be examined, outside the dominion of love; that she accordingly comes under the dominion of justice; that Adam Verver is the executor of the justice, being, so to speak, a figure of the Just God of Judaism and Christianity as Maggie is a figure of the Loving God; and that Charlotte's fate at the end of the story, along with the other "unpleasant" elements we have noted, are to be explained as a function of the quasi-divine justice executed by Adam Verver by the exercise of his power.

An easy approach to the harsher, grimmer aspects of *The Golden Bowl* is to compare its prevailing moral atmosphere with that of *The Wings of the Dove*. Modern critics of Henry James— F. O. Matthiessen, for instance, and Quentin Anderson—have tended to treat the last three complete works as if they formed virtually a single unit; Mr Anderson indeed speaks of them as the parts of a "spiritual trilogy" each expressing a different aspect or phase of a single spiritual theme.[66] There is no doubt, of course, about the unifying preoccupations of these three works, nor about the peculiarities of the late style that they have in common. Yet the differences are as great, and as important, as the resemblances; and *The Golden Bowl* seems to me, in point of what I have called its moral atmosphere, to stand closer to *The Ivory Tower* and some of the very late stories—*The Bench of Desolation*, for instance— than to *The Wings of the Dove* and *The Ambassadors*.[67] At any rate, the peculiar moral atmosphere of *The Golden Bowl* may be discovered in a multitude of details which cumulatively give us the measure of its difference from *The Wings of the Dove*.

These, significantly, seem almost always to be connected with the Prince and Charlotte—with their own relationship or their relationship, singly or together, to the Ververs. What we sense very soon is that "the world" here—the worldly world—has passed beyond its climacteric. The odour of decay can already be scented; and though it does not yet hang as heavy as in *The Ivory Tower*, there is no mistaking the staleness here for the freshness of *The Wings of the Dove*. We notice before long, for instance, the absence of that primary passion which united Kate Croy and Densher in their infernal design; compared with them, Charlotte and the Prince, though they are of course "young" and though the talk at Matcham is all of "the bravery of youth and beauty," seem curiously middle-aged, somehow past their prime. Again, we notice the absence here of the prevailing note of discovery in *The Wings*—the perpetual freshness of surprise, wonder and excitement, shared in such abundance by Kate and Densher, by Kate and Milly, and even by Milly and Densher, which gives the relationships in that book the irrecoverable vibration of youth. Charlotte and the Prince give the impression of discovering only what they already knew from the beginning, and of being engaged for the most part in merely manipulating with superb competence their pre-existent knowledge. The Prince's reflections on the terrace at Matcham upon "the freshness in all the staleness and the staleness in all the freshness" have, we gradually come to see, an ironic double-reference: they refer in the first instance, of course, to the English *beau monde*, but implicitly also to his own relation with Charlotte as infected by the prevailing moral tone of that world.

There are more details of this sort to suggest the odour of decay in the moral atmosphere of *The Golden Bowl*. We receive early in the story a first hint of the Prince's "knowledge" of women: "He liked in these days to mark them off, the women to whom he hadn't made love: it represented . . . a different stage of existence from the time at which he liked to mark off the women to whom he had";[68] and we are jerked back to Merton Densher's lack of such knowledge, recalling how he had laughed with the excitement, intense though muted, of perpetually finding in Kate Croy's tone "something that banished the talk of other women, so far as he knew other women, to the dull desert of the conventional."[69] Again, when we hear Charlotte's banal, self-exhibitory chatter at tea with the Prince,[70] we discern at once that it is the "greatness" of the Princess Casamassima rather than that of Kate Croy that we are here invited to recognise. Or there is the shopping expedition of the two women, Maggie and Charlotte,[71] to yield some nice points of comparison with a similar expedition of the other two women, Milly Theale and Kate Croy.[72] Milly and Kate are so clearly *enjoying* themselves, even though on Kate's side the air of their friendship is already filled with the perturbations that are soon to grow into her infernal design. Their enjoyment nevertheless is real, and springs from the spontaneity of their liking for each other, the freshness of their mutual interest and curiosity—from the sheer contagion of friendship which the ardent young seem able to enjoy even in the felt presence of the destructive element. For Charlotte and Maggie there is no such saving exhilaration to come to the rescue. The Matcham episode has already taken place, and Charlotte, not knowing what Maggie "knows" or indeed whether she knows anything at all, seeks relief from the oppression of her anxiety and compunction by the warmest, sincerest civilities and affabilities to her victim. But nothing can turn appearance into reality. The air between them is rancid with Charlotte's guilt on the one side and Maggie's confusion and terror on the other; and all they can do is bravely to observe the forms of friendship, hoping and praying all the while that (as Maggie is to phrase it at the end[73]) reality may not break in to tear them both to pieces.

There are similar differences to be discerned between the passionate moments of Charlotte and the Prince and those of Kate Croy and Densher. The heavily patterned prose and the violence of the sexual imagery of the one stand in sufficient contrast with the directness and simplicity of the other to suggest the different qualities we are expected to take cognisance of:

They were silent at first, only facing and faced, only grasping and grasped, only meeting and met. "It's sacred," he said at last. "It's sacred," she breathed back to him. They vowed it, gave it out and took it in, drawn, by their intensity, more closely together. Then of a sudden, through this tightened circle, as at the issue of a narrow strait into the sea beyond, everything broke, broke down, gave way, melted and mingled. Their lips sought their lips, their pressure their response and their response their pressure; with a violence that had sighed itself the next moment to the longest and deepest of stillnesses they passionately sealed their pledge.[74]

He went on with that fantasy, but at this point Kate ceased to attend. He saw after a little that she had been following some thought of her own, and he had been feeling the growth of something determinant even through the extravagance of much of the pleasantry, the warm transparent irony, into which their livelier intimacy kept plunging like a confident swimmer. Suddenly she said to him with extraordinary beauty: "I engage myself to you for ever." The beauty was in everything, and he could have separated nothing—couldn't have thought of her face as distinct from the whole joy. Yet her face had a new light. "And I pledge you—I call God to witness!—every spark of my faith; I give you every drop of my life." That was all, for the moment, but it was enough, and it was almost as quiet as if it were nothing. They were in the open air, in an alley of the Gardens; the great space, which seemed to arch just then higher and spread wider for them, threw them back into deep concentration. They moved by a common instinct to a spot, within sight, that struck them as fairly sequestered, and there before their time together was spent, they had extorted from concentration every advance it could make them.[75]

Finally, Densher's encounter with Aunt Maud[76] may be compared with similar profit with the Prince's encounters with Mr Verver.[77] They both "like" their benefactors, they both find them tremendously "interesting"; and they both acquiesce, in ways we are invited to judge as equally culpable, in the conditions tacitly laid down for them. Yet the difference of man and man, the qualitative difference between the two complicities, is conveyed with the most convincing exactness. Everywhere we detect the staleness in the one, the freshness in the other, and in consequence the relative proportions of the guilt and the innocence in both.

With these preliminary suggestions about the moral atmosphere of *The Golden Bowl* present to our minds, we may look more closely at the Prince's relationship with Charlotte in an effort to determine in what sense, if any, the old-fashioned word "lust" may be applied to it.[78] The course of the fable, I have suggested, can leave us in no doubt about James's intention to present the relationship as, in some sense, evil. In spite of the powerful justification provided by the Ververs' culpable ignorance and innocence, it does remain, in some vital sense, an act of shame which has to be expiated by the suffering of the three persons most intimately concerned—first Maggie, then the Prince, finally Charlotte; and the problem is therefore to discover what, if anything, there is in the relationship itself—in the nature of the love or passion or whatever between the Prince and Charlotte—that renders it intrinsically self-destructive and therefore an act of betrayal *vis-à-vis* Maggie and Adam, an assault on the dignities, decencies and serenities of their common life, and ultimately also a violation of the universal moral order.

The answer, at this stage of our argument, is not difficult to find. To begin with, we have it on the authority of that invaluable choric commentator, Mrs Assingham, that the Prince does not really "care for" Charlotte. Her husband stares when she throws out this statement in the course of their long analytical session after the Matcham episode; so she explains: "Men don't when it has all been so easy. That's how, in nine cases out of ten, a woman *is* treated who has risked her life."[79] That Fanny Assingham is right about the Prince's never "really" having cared for Charlotte is most explicitly confirmed in the scene in which the golden bowl is broken and Maggie tells her husband what she "knows." As she reaches the point of explaining that she is now aware of the real reason for his shopping expedition with Charlotte the day before their wedding, Amerigo is listening intently. Maggie says: "The reason of that was that there had been so much between you before —before *I* came between you at all"; and Amerigo, who had been moving about the room, at this stands still "as to check any show of impatience," and answers: "You've never been more sacred to me than you were at that hour—unless perhaps you've become so at this one." From the "assurance of his speech" and the way in which he meets her eyes as he says it, and from the effect of the words upon Maggie ("it was as if something cold and momentarily unimaginable breathed upon her, from afar off, out of his strange consistency"), we are meant to infer that the declaration is as true as it is sincere.[80]

An apparently trivial episode earlier in the same scene further confirms the truth of Fanny Assingham's insight. Maggie is telling the Prince about the purchase of the bowl when, suddenly and seemingly irrelevantly, he asks her how much she paid for it. Maggie does not tell him because, she says, she is "rather ashamed to say"—it was so high; and does not, of course, attach any importance to the question except to find it "quaint."[81] But we are expected to know why Amerigo asks the question: we are expected to remember that on the day of the shopping expedition for the golden bowl, when Amerigo, on seeing the crack in the bowl, had stepped outside leaving Charlotte in the shop with the dealer, she had afterwards told him that the price of the bowl was remarkably low. "Five pounds," she had said, "Really so little"—though the man had in fact asked fifteen pounds and she had refused to take the bowl chiefly for this reason. "Five pounds?" Amerigo had asked. "Five pounds," Charlotte had firmly answered.[82] Amerigo, it seems, had suspected that she was lying, and had bethought himself at this moment with Maggie to confirm his suspicion; and though we may suppose that as a European he did not—or did not at the time—particularly mind the lie itself, we are surely meant to see a significance in the fact that it should have lingered still in his memory, and (more significantly) that it should have been recalled just at the moment when Maggie's own candour and directness were already making an impact on him very different from any that Charlotte had ever made.[83]

The most telling evidence of the Prince's not "really" having cared for Charlotte comes later: first, when after the episode of the broken bowl he deliberately withholds from Charlotte what Maggie now knows about their relationship, thus contributing more than anyone to her state of tormented fear and suspense; and finally, in the last scene but one, when he gives Maggie the brief assurance of his good faith from the beginning ("If ever a man, since the beginning of time, acted in good faith—!"). The first point is to be taken up again in another context; but it is already evident that there has been from the beginning some fatal flaw in the golden bowl of the Prince's and Charlotte's happiness, and that Fanny Assingham's diagnosis was cruelly accurate.

The reason Fanny had put forward was, however, equally accurate and even more cruel. "Men don't [care] when it has all been so easy," she had told her husband; and the truth of this too we are able to verify almost from the beginning of the story. Charlotte does indeed, all the time, make it too easy for the Prince—from the day of their shopping expedition for the golden bowl to the Matcham week-end which virtually ends their relationship. When on that shopping expedition they stop to rest in Hyde Park, and she openly declares her passion in a heart-searing speech in which she explicitly tells him that she doesn't ask anything of him except that he should know that she adores him, that she is "giving herself away" and "perfectly willing to do it for nothing," we (like the Prince) are left in no doubt about the fact that she is "letting him off." Amerigo observes that "she let him off, it seemed, even from so much as answering"; and he accordingly allows his "handsome, slightly anxious yet still more definitely 'amused' face" to register all the attention her speech deserves, but otherwise remains totally silent and unresponsive.[84] Again, at the crucial meeting in Portland Place, when the Prince is awaiting Maggie for tea and Charlotte arrives instead,[85] the impression throughout the scene is that Charlotte is leading, all the time; and the Prince is again justified in the view he had expressed to himself in an earlier scene—that he could always get what he wanted from women "without lifting a finger," that "he only had to wait with a decent patience, to be placed, in spite of himself, it might really be said, in the right."[86]

But it is at Matcham most conspicuously that Charlotte's high competence makes everything easy. She so "arranges" everything, down to the train-times for their several departures and arrivals, that it is little wonder that Amerigo should reflect again, with a still greater intensity of satisfaction, that "he had, after all, gained more from women than he had ever lost by them." They seemed all, the "wonderful creatures"—Charlotte, his wife Maggie, Mrs Assingham, even his hostess Lady Castledean—to do nothing but "combine and conspire for his advantage"; and all there was left for him to do was to justify their unspoken faith in him—"that he wasn't, as a nature, as a character, as a gentleman, in fine, below his remarkable fortune."[87]

The fatal taint in the relationship is already apparent, and becomes unmistakable before the end of the Matcham episode.

"You're terrible," Amerigo says to Charlotte when she tells him about the train-times; and this is like an answer—in anticipation, as it were—to Maggie's secret prayer at a later stage in the story, that her husband may before long tire of "Mrs Verver's too perfect competence."[88] Already at Matcham her competence is proving too perfect for his nerves, his "finer irritability"; there is a shade of revulsion, along with the admiration and delight, in the cry "You're terrible"; and the short colloquy with which the Matcham section ends is, as we have cause to remember afterwards, the first ominous sign of the crack in their golden bowl. He says to her laughingly, "How shall I ever keep anything [from you]—some day when I shall wish to?" And she replies, "Ah for things I mayn't want to know I promise you shall find me stupid."[89]

The source of the taint, the reason for the crack in the golden bowl, is threefold: first, the aestheticism we have already examined;[90] second, the purely erotic element in their passion, which is closely connected with the aesthetic; third, the "utilitarian" aspect of their relationship—which is a consequence of the other two. The three are so intimately linked that they are inseparable in experience and can barely be distinguished in analysis. The primary bond between Charlotte and the Prince, we remember, was their touchstone of taste; and we received an early insight into the sense of beauty which nourished and sustained this common view. In the passage describing the Prince's first impression of Charlotte at Mrs Assingham's,[91] his appreciation of her beauty, we recall, is conveyed by images at once erotic and commercial. These images signify an attitude simultaneously *detached* and *possessive;* and since both the detachment and possessiveness are of the kind with which we normally view things rather than persons, they are as such inimical to a real involvement in the person who is being thus viewed as a thing. This absence of the kind of involvement which is the basis of love is still more powerfully suggested by another passage in the same scene in which the Prince's recognition of Charlotte's state of "abjection" is recorded. It is as searing a comment as any to be found in James's works on male sexuality in its cruellest, most destructive aspect; and the cruelty and destructiveness are not mitigated but intensified by the characteristic grace and good humour with which the Prince conducts his reflections:

Once more, as a man conscious of having known many women, he could assist, as he would have called it, at the recurrent, the predestined phenomenon, the thing always as certain as sunrise or the coming round of saints' days, the doing by the woman of the thing that gave her away. She did it, ever, inevitably, infallibly—she couldn't possibly not do it. It was her nature, it was her life, and the man could always expect it without lifting a finger. . . . It produced for [him] that extraordinary mixture of pity and profit in which his relation with her, when he was not a mere brute, mainly consisted; and gave him in fact his most pertinent ground of being always nice to her, nice about her, nice *for* her. She always dressed her act up, of course, she muffled and disguised and arranged it, showing in fact in these dissimulations a cleverness equal to but one thing in the world, equal to her abjection. . . . She was the twentieth woman, she was possessed by her doom, but her doom was also to arrange appearances, and what now concerned him was to learn how she proposed. He would help her, would arrange *with* her—to any point in reason; the only thing was to know what appearance could best be produced and best be preserved. Produced and preserved on her part of course; since on his own there had been luckily no folly to cover up, nothing but a perfect accord between conduct and obligation.[92]

The seed of self-destruction in the relationship that is about to develop lies in the phrase about the "pity and profit," and in the repeated emphasis on the Prince's marvellous "luck" in having to do nothing about it except (like Densher in *The Wings of the Dove*) refrain from being a "brute" and co-operate in whatever Charlotte proposes. We see the destruction taken a stage further in the episode at Matcham, where the Prince's consciousness of his "luck," of his "profit," and of the beauty and virtue of co-operating with Charlotte, is never more intense; only now the "pity" is absent, having been replaced by a pleasure in which the aesthetic, the erotic and the commercial blend in images as richly evocative as any to be found in *The Golden Bowl*. There he hears "the chink of gold in his ear" when Charlotte tells the Assinghams that they are staying on to luncheon at Matcham,[93] there everything melts together "to feed his sense of beauty,"[94] the exquisite day blooms "like a large fragrant flower that he had only to gather,"[95] his freedom is "as perfect and rounded and lustrous as some huge precious pearl";[96] and when Charlotte appears at an upper window of the house,

Something in her long look at him now out of the old grey window, something in the very poise of her hat, the colour of her necktie, the prolonged stillness of her smile, touched with sudden light for him all the wealth of the fact that he could count on her. He had his hand there to pluck it, on the open bloom of the day.[97]

He does pluck it; and he and Charlotte are on that unforgettable occasion as mutual a pair as any two people have ever perhaps succeeded in being by the strength of the touchstone of taste, reinforced by passion and courage. But (as we have remarked) in the very moment, so to speak, of plucking the wonderful bloom, the signs of the imminent decay are already to be noticed. The dangerous detachment is one of them. The Prince can even at this moment jest (or half-jest) about some day wishing to "keep things" from her; she can strike him as "terrible" in her very splendour; and he can revert again and again to the "profit" *motif.* The result is that already, before the end of the Matcham episode, we have an inkling of what may be the crucial defect in a passion grounded solely in the touchstone of taste. We perceive that such a passion is ultimately external—directed in the end only to the beautiful surface of the other, making this the entire object of its delight and desire, but evading the deeper involvements and responsibilities of love. That is why it is also possessive in the sense indicated: it can so easily treat the other as a "thing"—a valuable, even a precious thing, but still a thing—because it has so little care for it as a human being. That is why, too, it can "exploit" the other, with the good conscience and perfect lack of scruple with which we have seen the Prince use Charlotte—or, rather, allow Charlotte to allow herself to be used as (he knows) she wants to be used, thereby absolving himself from all moral responsibility for the using. It is because his passion is external in this sense that, after the Matcham episode, the Prince can treat Charlotte with the refined brutality which, when she recognises it, brings tears to Maggie's eyes: keeping from Charlotte everything he "knows," leaving her to suffer the torments of fear and anxiety in solitude, sharing with her nothing of the profound inner change that he himself is undergoing all that long summer at Fawns, and finally, when he knows they are to be separated for ever, pronouncing her "stupid."

These, James tells us, are the wages of sin—the common degradation of the sinners, which in the Prince takes the form of inflicting pain, in Charlotte that of suffering it. That is the price to be paid when two human beings take the appearance for the reality, the simulacrum for the thing itself; and if in this instance the thing itself is love, the simulacrum that shone with such brilliance and splendour at Matcham may well receive the old-fashioned name of lust.[98]

Turning now from the Prince's side of the relationship to Charlotte's, we at once encounter certain familiar difficulties. As in *The Wings of the Dove* James had made it as difficult as possible to pronounce judgement on Kate Croy and her infernal design by supplying her with justifications irresistibly cogent and persuasive, so in *The Golden Bowl* he makes similar provision for Charlotte Stant. In the opening chapters of the story we learn, first from Mrs Assingham[99] and then from Maggie,[100] that she has always been alone and unprotected; and we have this indirectly but poignantly confirmed by her own declaration of her passion to the Prince. We learn, again separately from Mrs Assingham[101] and Maggie,[102] that she has "loved and lost," and from Mrs Assingham, who knows so much more about the matter than Maggie, that there has been a peculiarly "magnificent" heroism in her giving up the Prince in order that he might be free to court Maggie.[103] Presently, in the proposal scene with Adam Verver, we receive direct proof of Charlotte's remarkable honesty, courage and pride. As Kate Croy, when she had already formed her dreadful plan and desperately needed Milly's co-operation in it, had nevertheless in her "bright perversity" openly warned Milly to get out of Lancaster Gate before she was destroyed,[104] so Charlotte here, "oddly conscientious," intimates to Adam, first, that he does not perhaps know her as well as he thinks, and then, in spite of her openly expressed desire to marry, that his reasons for wanting to marry her are not perhaps as good as they might be.[105] Both Kate Croy and Charlotte Stant know what they want and know how to get it; but neither will have it cheaply. They not only take all the necessary risks but some gratuitous ones as well—partly no doubt for conscience' sake, but chiefly out of that "perversity" which is the form taken by their courage and pride; and Charlotte's offer to show Adam the Prince's telegram[106] is meant as a final, spectacular proof of this.

After the marriage our sympathies are still more strongly engaged for her in the ironic situation that develops. Charlotte shows herself to be (in the phrase Adam Verver had used at Brighton) "very very honourable" in the fulfilment of her part of the contract. She "does the worldly" for the two families not only with energy and zeal but also with grace and good will; the Ververs' complacent acceptance of her services shows at its least agreeable at this point in the story; and Charlotte's final resentment at being so conspicuously neglected by Adam and so much taken for granted by both Ververs strikes us as more than justified.[107] And after the disastrous Matcham week-end which leads to Maggie's finding out everything, when Charlotte is left alone with her fear and doubt and suffers unspeakable torments in her isolation, we hardly need Maggie's outbursts of compassion to Fanny Assingham to convince us that (as Maggie says to the Prince at the end) "it's *always* terrible for women."

The seemingly monstrous severity of Charlotte's "punishment" is accordingly very difficult to explain, let alone to justify. The completeness of her subjugation is conveyed in images which, for their sustained violence and ferocity, have no parallel in James's works. Repeatedly, Charlotte is described as a creature "in a cage": in the scene with Maggie which ends in the Judas kiss, she is a "splendid shining supple creature out of the cage";[108] at another moment, she stands in "the hard glare of nature . . . , virtually at bay and yet denied the last grace of any protecting truth."[109] Again, as *cicerone* to the visitors at Fawns, Maggie imagines her going about with "a long silk halter looped round her beautiful neck," the end of which is firmly held by her father in one of his pocketed hands. ("He didn't twitch it, yet it was there; he didn't drag her, but she came");[110] and she seems to hear Charlotte's "high coerced quaver before the cabinets in the hushed gallery."[111] The cumulative effect is horrible and terrifying; and it is reinforced by the images of desperate, back-to-wall conflict between the two women, Maggie and Charlotte, in their two crucial encounters in the last part of the book,[112] and (most of all perhaps) by the strange and fearful imaginary dialogue between Maggie and her father as they watch Charlotte conduct the visitors round the galleries. This is what Maggie imagines her father to be saying:

Yes, you see—I lead her now by the neck, I lead her to her doom, and she doesn't so much as know what it is, though she has a fear in her heart which, if you had the chances to apply your ear there that I, as a husband,have, you would hear thump and thump and thump. She thinks it *may* be, her doom, the awful place over there—awful for *her;* but she's afraid to ask, don't you see? Just as she's afraid of not asking; just as she's afraid of so many other things that she sees multiplied all about her now as perils and portents. She'll know, however—when she does know.[113]

James has made the case of Charlotte as "difficult" as possible; and to determine the nature and extent of her "guilt" is accordingly not easy.

The first indication of a moral taint in Charlotte is given in her exchange with Fanny Assingham at the Foreign Office reception, at which she virtually tells Mrs Assingham that she and Amerigo are, or are about to become, lovers. We learn that she has "an easy command" and "a high enjoyment" of her "crisis":[114] unlike Maggie, she does not "quake" but positively enjoys the dangers of her situation. Presently again we hear that she actually wants Fanny to "know" and, again, positively enjoys her knowing.[115] In the exchange itself Charlotte is as usual "magnificent," and her charges against the Ververs are unanswerable. But there is a note of defiance in it, a hardness (her face shows a "fine and slightly hard radiance"),[116] an absence of tenderness, and—most significant—an absence of the least sign of grief or even regret that the situation should be as it is; which, taken together, are revealing indeed. Charlotte *is* hard, is fundamentally un-tender. Nor does she really mind the badness of the situation because it is bad: she minds it only in so far as it affects her unpleasantly; she does not mind it at all in so far as she can triumph over it. That is why she can have such an "easy command" and "high enjoyment" of her crisis: because she is never for a moment undermined, much less disabled, by any distress or shock or grief; because she is in fact fundamentally detached from it, uninvolved in it, indeed only interested in it as a challenge—a challenge to herself to master it. In the present scene, she triumphantly succeeds; and it is the knowledge of her mastery that blends with her consciousness of her own splendid appearance and the brilliance of the whole occasion to produce in her a sense of power and pride that (we are meant to see) is charged with danger. As she stands alone on the grand staircase feeling as never before that she has been "justified of her faith,"[117] she suggests vividly a modern allegorical figure of the deadly sin of Pride placed against a symbolic background of the modern world at its worldliest:

> The air had suggestions enough . . . to constitute those conditions with which, for our young woman, the hour was brilliantly crowned. She was herself in truth crowned, and it all hung together, melted together, in light and colour and sound: the unsurpassed diamonds that her head so happily carried, the other jewels, the other perfections of aspect and arrangement that made her personal scheme a success, the *proved* private theory that materials to work with had been all she required and that there were none too precious for her to understand and use . . .

Then, as the Prince joins her,

> She had an impression of all the place as higher and wider and more appointed for great moments; with its dome of lustres lifted, its ascents and descents more majestic, its marble tiers more vividly overhung, its numerosity of royalties, foreign and domestic, more unprecedented, its symbolism of "State" hospitality both emphasised and refined. This was doubtless a large consequence of a fairly familiar cause, a considerable inward stir to spring from the mere vision, striking as that might be, of Amerigo in a crowd; but she had her reasons, she held them there, she carried them in fact, responsibly and overtly, as she carried her head, her high tiara, her folded fan, her indifferent unattended eminence; and it was when he reached her and she could, taking his arm, show herself as placed in her relation, that she felt supremely justified.[118]

This is the pitch that Charlotte maintains in all the scenes that follow, culminating in the week-end at Matcham. At Matcham, we have seen, she is as "young" and brilliant as she has ever been: she enchants the Prince as never before by her beauty, her intelligence, her good humour, and (as at the Foreign Office reception) by her easy command and high enjoyment of their crisis. And there also, in the scrap of dialogue already quoted,[119] we receive our clearest hint of the fundamental moral flaw in Charlotte:

> "How shall I ever keep anything [from you]—some day when I shall wish to?" [the Prince says].
> "Ah for things I mayn't want to know I promise you shall find me stupid."

Here, I believe, is the key to our understanding of the complex nature of Charlotte's guilt; it is confirmed in the subsequent scenes in which the kind and quality of her "stupidity" are directly and indirectly exhibited. This stupidity, we gradually come to see, consists in her refusal to recognise her guilt. Though she has repeated opportunities to "confess," she refuses each time: persistently, on each successive occasion, she refuses to humble herself by admitting—even to herself, we may presume—that she has done anything wrong; and her "stupidity" accordingly reveals itself to be a fundamental moral insensibility, a fundamental lack of grasp of the moral realities of her situation, which is at the same time "willed"—that is, deliberate and conscious. Such a failing, in a person of Charlotte's specific gifts and endowments, is deeply culpable. (For who could plead for Charlotte Stant that she was too simple to understand and must therefore be exonerated on the grounds of invincible ignorance; or, remembering her "too perfect competence," that she was too weak to act on her understanding?) With such gifts and endowments, she could have understood, and could therefore have recognised and acknowledged her guilt. But she refuses, deliberately and consciously, to do so: refuses to eat the bread of humiliation, to abase her pride before a creature like Maggie Verver whom she despises, to admit for a moment that she has "failed"; and it is for this reason that she is damned, and has to suffer the purgatorial fire of that long agonising summer.

Our first direct view of Charlotte after the move to Fawns is in her encounter with Maggie on the terrace when she challenges Maggie to say whether she knows of any wrong she, Charlotte, has done her. What we recognise as damnable here is the perfect coolness and self-possession with which Charlotte can speak the necessary lie, and the absence of any hint of a recognition of the wrong she has been guilty of, much less of any shame or penitence. She is brazening it out, and not defensively but aggressively, using all the formidable resources of her "greatness" to frighten and subdue Maggie and ensure her absolute victory in the contest:

> "I'm aware of no point whatever at which I may have failed you," said Charlotte, "nor of any at which I may have failed any one in whom I can suppose you sufficiently interested to care. If I've been guilty of some fault I've committed it all unconsciously. . . ."[120]

The episode ends appropriately with the "high publicity" of the Judas kiss, which Charlotte forces upon Maggie as the final mark of her victory.

In the scenes that follow, Charlotte's suffering in her growing isolation is poignantly exhibited; and it is in these scenes also that we receive our most explicit intimations of the reason for her suffering. It is her "stupidity," we see again and again, her infernal pride, her dogged refusal to recognise the moral reality of her condition, that condemns her to her suffering. We have already had Maggie's vision of Charlotte at one point as standing "in the hard glare of nature . . . virtually at bay and yet denied the last grace of any protecting truth."[121] In a later scene, Maggie compares the Prince's "caged" condition with Charlotte's and sees what the difference is—that he is "lurking there by his own act and his own choice" while Charlotte has had to be forced into it, against her own act and choice, resisting all the time.[122] Then there is Charlotte's imagined address to Maggie, in which her own anguish at the loss of her lover is as moving as her contempt of Maggie (and her total insensibility to Maggie's suffering) is reprehensible and—in the sense explained—"stupid." "You don't know what it is to be loved and broken with," Maggie imagines her saying,

> You haven't been broken with, because in *your* relation what can there have been worth speaking of to break? Ours was everything a relation could be, filled to the brim with the wine of consciousness; and if it was to have no meaning, no better meaning than that such a creature as you could breathe upon it, at your hour, for blight, why was I myself dealt with all for deception? why condemned after a couple of short years to find the golden flame—oh the golden flame!—a mere handful of black ashes?[123]

Finally, there is Charlotte's last despairing stand in her second and final encounter with Maggie in the garden at Fawns, in which the pride that at once ruins and sustains her is most fully exhibited. Charlotte is in anguish, knowing herself to be "doomed to a separation that was like a knife in her heart," and she has wandered out of the house on this hot afternoon in her "uncontrollable, her blinded physical quest for a peace not to be grasped."[124] Maggie, who knows all about her impending separation from the Prince, and is now filled with a boundless compassion for Charlotte, has followed her into the garden with a single object in view—"to make somehow, for her support, the last demonstration,"[125] to "allow her, . . . fairly to produce in her, the sense of highly choosing"[126]—the sense, that is, of choosing to go to America with Adam Verver, when in fact she is being forced to it and is full of bitter loathing of the plan. As Charlotte sees the other approach, she is momentarily seized with fear: has Maggie come to retract the "lie" she had told on the terrace, that she knew of no wrong Charlotte had done her; and is there to be an exposure after all? But as she perceives her rival is looking as "little dangerous," as "abjectly mild" as usual, she decides that Maggie has after all only "presented herself once more to . . . grovel"; and this gives her her cue and her inspiration to do exactly what Maggie wishes her to do—to give the appearance of "highly choosing."[127] Maggie perceives how this produces in her an "instant stiffening of the spring of pride":

> Pride indeed had the next moment become the mantle caught up for protection and perversity; she flung it round her as a denial of any loss of her freedom. To be doomed was in her situation to have extravagantly incurred a doom, so that to confess to wretchedness was by the same stroke to confess to falsity. She wouldn't confess, she didn't— a thousand times no; she only cast about her, and quite frankly and fiercely, for something else that would give colour to her having burst her bonds. Her eyes expanded, her bosom heaved as she invoked it, and the effect upon Maggie was verily to wish she could only help her to it.[128]

There follows a dialogue, the most openly hostile yet on Charlotte's side, in the course of which Charlotte once more asserts her "greatness," in the grand style with which she plays out the illusion of free choice; and it ends with Maggie's last act of self-abasement directed to the single end of ensuring that Charlotte's sense of highly choosing shall be as complete and perfect as possible:

> "How I see that you loathed our marriage! . . . How I see that you've worked against me!" [says Charlotte].
> "Oh, oh, oh!" the Princess exclaimed.
> Her companion, leaving her, had reached one of the archways, but on this turned round with a flare. "You haven't worked against me?"
> Maggie took it and for a moment kept it; held it, with closed eyes, as if it had been some captured fluttering bird pressed by both hands

to her breast. Then she opened her eyes to speak. "What does it matter
—if I've failed?"

"You recognise then that you've failed?" asked Charlotte from the
threshold.

Maggie waited; she looked, as her companion had done a moment
before, at the two books on the seat; she put them together and laid
them down; then she made up her mind.

"I've failed!" she sounded out before Charlotte, having given her
time, walked away. She watched her, splendid and erect, float down
the long vista; then she sank upon a seat, Yes she had done all.[129]

So Charlotte's pride with all its implications is the cause of her
damnation and the reason for her terrible "purgatorial" suffering
at Fawns; but it is also the groundwork of her salvation. There is
a first hint of this in one of Maggie's colloquies with Fanny Assingham at Fawns. Mrs Assingham is speaking of America, the penal
colony to which Charlotte is before long to be exiled:

> "I see the long miles of ocean and the dreadful great country, State
> after State. . . . I see the extraordinary 'interesting' place [Ameri-
> can City]—which I've never been to, you know, and you have
> —and the exact degree in which she [Charlotte] will be expected to
> be interested."
> "She *will* be," Maggie presently replied.
> "Expected?"
> "Interested."[130]

Of Charlotte's defiant intention to be "interested" we have already been given sufficient notice in her address to Maggie in their
encounter in the garden. Then, when the Prince and Maggie are
back in their house in London, we hear of Charlotte's energetic
supervision of the removal of the art-treasures from Fawns, which
(it seems) absorbs her so completely as to leave her no time for
social calls, even on her step-daughter and former lover; and this
is the immediate occasion for a pregnant remark which the Prince
addresses to Maggie. They have been speaking of Charlotte and
the life that lies before her in America: "As you say, she's splendid," he says, "but there is—there always will be—much of her
left. Only, as you also say, for others."[131]

It seems perfunctory, but it is in fact an important clue for our
understanding of the redemptive power of Charlotte's "greatness." What it chiefly intimates is that her pride, which is the
foundation of her "greatness," has given her in the most testing

situation of her life a remarkable resilence, resourcefulness, courage and resolution with which to meet it; and that this is its positive, affirmative side, as the other was negative and destructive. The Prince's remark thus also suggests the double-view we are ultimately expected to take of the case of Charlotte Stant. Because her pride is deadly and damnable, she has to suffer the torments of rejection and isolation, and the final punishment of separation and exile; and because at the same time it is a source of energy and beauty, life-giving and life-affirming, it redeems her suffering and turns her final "punishment" into a fresh opportunity for the exercise of her gifts. Both aspects, James wishes us to see, are equally real; neither cancels out the other. They simply coexist, seemingly contradictory and incompatible, yet reconciled in living experience, and as such forming one of the paradoxes of the moral life.

The redeeming power of the sin of pride is memorably figured in Charlotte when she comes with her husband on her last visit to Portland Place and speaks of her "mission" to the citizens of American City:

> The question of the amount of correction to which Charlotte had laid herself open rose and hovered for the instant only to sink conspicuously by its own weight; so high a pitch she seemed to give to the unconsciousness of questions, so resplendent a show of serenity she succeeded in making. The shade of the official, in her beauty and security, never for a moment dropped; it was a cool high refuge, like the deep arched recess of some coloured and gilded image, in which she sat and smiled and waited, drank her tea, referred to her husband and remembered her mission. Her mission had quite taken form—it was but another name for the interest of her great opportunity: that of representing the arts and the graces to a people languishing, afar off, in ignorance. . . . The difficulty now indeed was to choose, for explicit tribute of admiration, between the varieties of her nobler aspects. She carried it off, to put the matter coarsely, with a taste and a discretion that held our young woman's attention. . . . to the very point of diverting it from the attitude of her over-shadowed, her almost superseded companion."[132]

The ironic overtones here do, of course, sufficiently indicate the limitations of Charlotte's redemption by pride; yet they do not diminish its reality. Charlotte's "greatness" has remained unimpaired; and this, we learn in the last exchange between Maggie and her father, is to be her salvation. "She wasn't to be wasted," Maggie perceives: "her gifts, her variety, her power" were to be used to capacity; she was to be "great for the world that was before her"; there was to be no loss for her but only gain. She was, in short, to realise herself more fully and splendidly in the service of Adam's "idea" than she had ever before been able; and though her greatness at Matcham may have been more brilliant, her greatness in American City will be more worthwhile and enduring. And because the triumph of good over evil, especially when achieved at the cost of much suffering, is the ultimte form of success, and because the pure in heart rejoice particularly in such successes, Maggie Verver's last words to her father are "It's success, father" and his to her, "It's success."[133]

Among the many problems presented to the critic of *The Golden Bowl,* one important one (at least) remains to be considered: that of James's particular use of ambiguity in this work. Technically speaking, the ambiguity of *The Golden Bowl,* like that of *The Turn of the Screw* and *The Sacred Fount,* is a direct consequence of James's "law of successive aspects"[134] which leads him here as in all the works of the late period (and, though less rigorously, also in the main works of the early and middle periods) to present his story at every point through the consciousness of a single inter-preter, so that everything that happens is seen from that inter-preter's point of view and no other. In *The Golden Bowl* the two principal centres of consciousness are the Prince in the First Book, Maggie in the Second; the only deviations that James allows him-self are Fanny Assingham's analytical sessions with her husband, and Adam Verver's brief reflections on Maggie's happiness early in the First Book and Charlotte's on her own happiness at the grand reception later in the First Book.

As a technical device, its primary intention is to ensure the maximum economy and intensity of effect, and this it achieves wherever it is employed—in *Washington Square* and *The Portrait of a Lady* no less than in *The Awkward Age* and *The Ambassadors.* What produces the peculiar ambiguity which *The Golden Bowl* has in common with *The Turn of the Screw* and *The Sacred Fount* is the deliberate exploitation of the device to cast the shadow of a huge doubt over the validity of any given interpretation. This, as we saw, was accomplished in *The Turn of the Screw* and *The Sacred Fount* by so arranging the dialogues and interior monologues that they could with perfect self-consistency yield two distinct and, in the context, contradictory meanings, one confirming the validity of the interpreter's point of view, the other putting it in doubt. In *The Golden Bowl* the effect is accomplished in exactly the same way; and James's conscious deliberation in the matter is attested by explicit hints of, or even direct references to, the prevailing ambiguity.

As Maggie, on the night of her encounter with Charlotte on the terrace at Fawns, is made by Charlotte to pause before the window of the smoking-room where the others are playing their game of bridge, she reflects that "this picture of quiet harmonies, the positive charm of it and, as might have been said, the full significance . . . could be no more after all than a matter of interpretation, differing always for a different interpreter."[135] Fanny Assingham, in one of her conversations with Maggie, is allowed an explicit doubt about the validity of what she is "seeing": "She saw her [Maggie]—or believed she saw her—look at her chance for straight denunciation, look at it and then pass it by."[136] Even more significantly, Maggie herself is allowed a spasm of self-doubt—or rather two spasms—as radical and portentous as that of the governess in *The Turn of the Screw* asking herself at a crucial point in the story, "If he *were* innocent, what then on earth was I?" Maggie's moment comes in the same scene on the terrace with Charlotte. As Charlotte is approaching her, she "literally" catches herself "in the act of dodging and ducking," and recognises "vividly, in a single word, what she had all along been afraid of"—that Charlotte might go to Adam, tell him openly about Maggie's suspicions of her, and convince Adam that they were wickedly false:

> Such a glimpse of her [Charlotte's] conceivable idea . . . opened out wide as soon as it had come into view; for if so much as this was still firm ground between the elder pair [Charlotte and Adam], if the beauty of appearances had been so consistently preserved, it was only the golden bowl as Maggie herself knew it that had been broken. The breakage stood not for any wrought discomposure among the triumphant three—it stood merely for the dire deformity of her attitude toward them.[137]

It is this fear that decides Maggie that she must "of her own prudence" persuade Charlotte to believe that she has no quarrel with her; and so, "with a rare contraction of the heart," she proceeds to do.

It is true that we have in *The Golden Bowl* the kind of "check" that was completely absent in *The Turn of the Screw:* we have actually seen the Prince and Charlotte together at Matcham (and at Portland Place when they passionately seal their pledge[138]), and there can accordingly be no doubt about the adultery—as there could be a doubt in *The Turn of the Screw* about whether the children in fact saw the apparitions of the dead servants and had any relations with them. But there can still be a doubt about Maggie's moral attitude to what has happened, and about her view of its moral consequences. Is it really as wicked and destructive (a "wrought discomposure") as it appears to her to be; or is this merely an illusion induced principally by her desire to get her husband back from Charlotte and ensure her own happiness ("the golden bowl as she herself knew it")? The emphasis in what follows on the "prudence" of her lying to Charlotte in order to prevent her from going to Adam makes it clear that the ambiguity is intended to put Maggie's motive in doubt; and since the most ambiguous passages in the book do impugn precisely Maggie's motive (and Adam's), it is consistent that her moment of self-doubt should turn upon this.[139]

The Golden Bowl abounds in dialogues as impenetrably ambiguous as those of *The Turn of the Screw* and *The Sacred Fount.* There is, for instance, Maggie's conversation with her father on their walk in Regent's Park soon after the Matcham episode when she is at the peak of her terror about his coming to "know" what he must on no account know. Again and again Adam makes a remark or rejoinder that could mean that he does know "everything," yet could also be perfectly innocent; Maggie as the scene advances chooses more and more, by reasonings often remarkably circuitous, to interpret everything he says as a sign that he does know; and we are left with no key to the true state of affairs.[140] The same is true of that other crucial talk between Maggie and her father in the garden at Fawns. Again everything Adam says may mean nothing more than it appears to, or it may mean all that Maggie reads into it; and again the reader is left with nothing conclusive to tip the scales either way—except the fact that Adam, in this instance as in the other, in fact does what Maggie wants him to. But though these acts—the cancellation of the holiday in Spain and the return to America with Charlotte—visibly happen, they are no conclusive proof of Adam's having known what Maggie supposes him to know; and the more so since it is an important part of their ambiguity that we are in both instances uncertain whether Adam made his decision independently (as Maggie believes) or whether Maggie, however "unconsciously," put the idea into his head, and he, being the devoted father he was, responded to her suggestion. (In the talk in the garden, for instance, is it really Adam who first thinks of returning to America—or is it Maggie who insinuates the idea into his mind by first mentioning American City?)[141]

The most interesting and most baffling ambiguities, however, are those which bear on the question of the Ververs' motives. Again and again in the Second Book, as we listen to Maggie and her father talking about Charlotte or the Prince, or themselves in relation to either or both, the question arises, often very insistently: Are they really as "good" as everyone—the Prince, Charlotte, Fanny Assingham—says they are? Are their motives as disinterested as the others seem to assume, and they themselves certainly believe? What, for instance, are we to make of their attitude to Charlotte, with its constant and seemingly shameless emphasis on her "usefulness" to them? In the talk in Regent's Park, they touch on the question of their returning to Fawns. Maggie asks, "Is Charlotte really ready?" and Adam answers,

> "Oh if you and I and Amerigo are. Whenever one corners Charlotte ... one finds that she only wants to know what *we* want. Which is what we got her for!"
> "What we got her for—exactly!" [Maggie answers][142].

Later in a conversation with Fanny Assingham, Maggie has a momentary inkling of the kind of cruelty it might have been to Charlotte to know that Adam had "got her in" chiefly for the sake of her, Maggie's, happiness; but she repudiates it as a serious criticism of Adam almost as soon as it occurs to her.[143] In the garden at Fawns, again, when her father announces his decision to return to America, Maggie for a moment has a vision of Charlotte "removed, transported, doomed";[144] and soon after this, when her compassion for Charlotte leads her in imagination to

beg her father to desist from his "punishment," we have this extraordinary imagined conversation between the daughter and the
father:

> The high voice [Charlotte's] went on; its quaver was doubtless for
> conscious ears only, but there were verily thirty seconds during which
> it sounded, for our young woman, like the shriek of a soul in pain. Kept
> up a minute longer it would break and collapse—so that Maggie felt
> herself, the next thing, turn with a start to her father. "Can't she be
> stopped? Hasn't she done it *enough?*" Some such question she let
> herself ask him to suppose in her. Then it was that, across half the
> gallery—for he had not moved from where she had first seen him—
> he struck her as confessing, with strange tears in his own eyes, to sharp
> identity of emotion. "Poor thing, poor thing"—it reached straight—
> "*Isn't* she, for one's credit, on the swagger?" After which, as, held thus
> together they had still another strained minute, the shame, the pity,
> the better knowledge, the smothered protest, the divined anguish
> even, so overcame him that, blushing to his eyes, he turned short
> away.[145]

On the view of Adam as the figure of the Just God administering
a just punishment,[146] the passage makes reasonable coherent
sense. The "strange tears" in Adam's eyes and the "sharp identity
of emotion" would refer to the peculiar intimacy of his relation
with Maggie; the "shame" would presumably be Charlotte's
shame, the "pity" would be for Charlotte (or perhaps the pity of
her condition—oh, the pity of it), the "protest" that is smothered
and the "anguish" he divines would again be Charlotte's, and the
"better knowledge" (of the reality of her condition perhaps) would
be his. But the alternative interpretation presses hard here: that the
"shame" is Adam's; that, having divined Charlotte's "anguish," he
recognises (and Maggie recognises with him) that his punishment
of Charlotte is shamefully cruel; and that this is the "better knowledge" which causes him to "blush to the eyes."

The question is raised again, for the last time and most acutely,
by the exchange between Maggie and her father when he and
Charlotte come on their final visit to Portland Place before their
departure. I have already indicated[147] the interpretation that
seems to me consistent with the redemptive theme of *The Golden
Bowl;* and I will have something more to say about it presently.
Granted that this is one valid account, the ambiguity nevertheless
leaves the way open for the alternative interpretation which un-

sympathetic readers of *The Golden Bowl* have not hesitated to give. As Maggie and her father stand on the balcony looking into the room where Charlotte and the Prince are talking together for the last time, the Ververs' "collectors' " view of them is heavily emphasised:

> The two noble persons seated in conversation and at tea fell thus into the splendid effect and the general harmony: Mrs Verver and the Prince fairly "placed" themselves, however unwittingly, as high expressions of the kind of human furniture required esthetically by such a scene. The fusion of their presence with the decorative elements, their contribution to the triumph of selection, was complete and admirable; though to a lingering view, a view more penetrating than the occasion really demanded, they also might have figured as concrete attestations of a rare power of purchase. There was much indeed in the tone in which Adam Verver spoke again, and who shall say where his thought stopped? *"Le compte y est.* You've got some good things." Maggie met it afresh—"Ah, don't they look well?"[148]

Presently when Adam says of Charlotte, "She's beautiful, beautiful," Maggie detects in this "the note of possession and control"; and when at the end she says "It's success, father" and he answers "It's success,"[149] the reader is meant to see that it might be one of two kinds of success—either the good and noble kind consistent with the redemptive theme, or a success fundamentally power-seeking and acquisitive, and not the more attractive for its admixture of self-righteousness.

The ambiguities bearing on Maggie's relation to the Prince are equally striking; and the question they repeatedly raise is whether Maggie's motives are as selfless as she herself and everyone else (including the Prince) believes them to be, or whether there is not a strong taint of selfishness, indeed of greed and possessiveness, in her determination to separate him from Charlotte and draw him back to herself. In an earlier section[150] I suggested an account of Maggie's selfishness compatible with her role as scapegoat and redeemer in James's fable of salvation; but again, as in all the other instances I have cited, the ambiguities are so striking and so consistent that it is impossible to suppose that James did not intend the alternative meanings to be taken seriously. Soon after the Matcham episode, for instance, when Maggie is being the princess for the first time in her life, Fanny Assingham notes her "blameless egoism" in "using" them, the Assinghams, to capacity, and finds her "as hard . . . in spite of her fever as a little pointed diamond" showing "something of the glitter of consciously possessing the constructive, the creative hand."[151] That the egoism is "blame-less" is Fanny's view, and since her view, like everyone else's in the book, is necessarily partial, the reader is invited to wonder whether it is in fact correct. The same is true of Maggie's declara-tion to Fanny at Fawns that the Prince now understands what she wants. "I want happiness without a hole in it big enough for you to poke in your finger . . . The golden bowl—as it *was* to have been. The bowl with all our happiness in it. The bowl without the crack," she says;[152] and here it is the assurance of the tone and the inflexi-bility of purpose it expresses that creates the ambiguity. It is the same again in all the scenes between Maggie and the Prince him-self, where there is always a phrase or tone or emphasis to raise a similar doubt, right up to the last scene and the last lines of the book.

"I see nothing but *you*, "says the Prince on the closing page; and upon this follow the lines:

> And the truth of it had with this force, after a moment, so strangely lighted his eyes that as for pity and dread of them she buried her own in his breast.[153]

Mr R. P. Blackmur sees in these lines "a shade embracing a shade . . . in the shades of poetry," and is convinced that Maggie "under the presidency of [her] goodness, the sovereignty of her love, and the tyranny of her conscience" has in fact effected the "break-down" of the other three, the Prince, Charlotte and Adam— though (Mr Blackmur adds) this destructive outcome of Maggie Verver's efforts "is all the nearer to reality because it is protected and sustained by the cover of manners, by the insistence on equi-librium, the preservation of decorum."[154] If the account of the redemptive theme of *The Golden Bowl* set out in the previous chapter is correct, Mr Blackmur's "break-down" theory, if not false, is not the only possible interpretation; and the same is true of his interpretation specifically of the "pity" and "dread" in the last lines. For he appears not to have taken into account what there is in this last passage to link it intimately with the redemptive theme. Since immediately before this we have been told that Mag-gie, as the Prince re-enters the room and advances towards her, is "charged with a new horror" at the thought that he might want, or feel obliged, to "confess" to her, the pity and the dread in the last lines may surely be taken to refer to this—to the confession and repentance implied in his "I see nothing but *you*" (no longer Charlotte but only "you," Maggie), and in the light that "the truth of it"—that is, the "confessional" implication of now seeing only her—kindles in his eyes. If we recall the other crucial places in the story where Maggie has been shown to have the same impulse to "spare" the Prince,[155] it need cause no surprise that James should have chosen to emphasise this again in the closing scene as the supreme expression of the moral beauty of his heroine.

Nevertheless, as in all the other instances I have cited, the "pity and dread" does admit of an alternative interpretation; the ambiguity here does therefore at least give colour to Mr Blackmur's interpretation, just as the ambiguities in *The Turn of the Screw* and *The Sacred Fount* gave colour to Mr Wilson's; and if it is correct to suppose that all this is perfectly deliberate—that James, so far from being "unconscious" of the ambiguity (as Mr Wilson supposed), has deliberately put it there to ensure just such a double reading of some of the most crucial passages—it becomes necessary to find an explanation of the ambiguity compatible with the various themes of *The Golden Bowl* discussed in these chapters, and in particular the redemptive theme.

The explanation has in fact already been touched on. The ambiguity is perhaps best defined as a huge, elaborate metaphor for James's experience of the unavoidable, unalterable mixed motive of all human action, and the consequent dual ("ambiguous") character of all human endeavour. The selfless motive is inseparable in experience from the selfish, the beneficent action from the acquisitive, the courage and intelligence of love from the cravenness of fear, the beauty of good faith and good will from the meanness of moral evasion and the cruelty of sexual power. Nor are they merely conjoined but rather causally connected: the good is somehow the result of evil, the base is somehow a necessary condition of the noble—is, indeed, the very soil from which it springs and in which it is nurtured. If Maggie Verver had not wanted the Prince, passionately and possessively, she would have had no motive for undertaking her redemptive task with all its terrifying difficulties. If the Prince had not wanted the ease and freedom supplied by Adam Verver's money, he would have had no motive for acquiring the moral sense he lacked; if Charlotte likewise had not wanted the security from loneliness and want, the status and opportunities provided by her position as Adam Verver's wife, she would never have consented to go to American City and so would have missed her finest opportunity for the exercise of her "greatness." As for Adam Verver: if Adam had not been passionately acquisitive, he would not have made his millions; if he had not made his millions, he would not have had his limitless power at once to bestow benefits upon the three souls in his care and to exact submission or "obedience" from them to the conditions of the gift; while they—Maggie equally with the Prince and Charlotte —would have had no motive for wanting to stay in his "boat," nor therefore for making themselves, in their various ways, good enough to stay in it; and Henry James in that case would have had no story to tell.

To recognise this interdependence in human life of the good and the evil, the noble and the base, the beautiful and the sordid, is by itself perhaps no special distinction; there is no great novelist or dramatist who has not recognised it and attempted to render it in his art. James's distinction is that he invented a literary technique, the late style, which enabled him to render his sense of the fusion, or rather fusedness, of these co-existent and interdependent elements with a peculiar immediacy. In James's works the double aspect of everything in human life is never described or analysed or commented upon or in any manner directly treated. It is projected by the late style itself in a strictly poetic and dramatic mode —"enacted" in such a way as to make the experience of the fusedness directly accessible to us; and here James's achievement has no parallel in that of any other novelist, nor indeed anywhere in European literature except perhaps in the early Socratic dialogues of Plato and in Shakespeare's mature drama.

Recalling the pervasive Jamesian irony in *The Golden Bowl* and how it is directed equally against the "good" Ververs and the "bad" Prince and Charlotte; and having in mind the significant change in the tone and mood of the irony between the First and Second Books—how it is comparatively light, even light-hearted, in the First, but in the Second grows steadily grimmer and harsher until it reaches a peak of savage "unpleasantness" in the scenes relating to Charlotte—we ought to have no difficulty in discerning the profoundly pessimistic side of James's vision. "Everything is terrible, *cara*—in the heart of man," says the Prince to Maggie near the end of the story; and this sentence might be the epigraph for that side of *The Golden Bowl* which relates it to the prophetical book of the Old Testament from which the title is taken. The blandness of the Jamesian manner does not (and is not meant to) obscure the bitterness; on the contrary, it intensifies it. When Adam Verver in his loving daughter's imagination is allowed to make his savage comments on Charlotte's tormented state in the coolest, most matter-of-fact tones, what this signifies is not the brutality or diabolism of Adam Verver but the grief of Henry James, speaking through his vessel of consciousness Maggie Verver, at all that is terrible in the heart of man. Oh, the pity of it, and the horror: that the wages of sin should by their nature be so desolating; that the execution of justice should by its nature be so merciless; that pride and fear, the first so wicked and the second so mean, should be the only ground of salvation for those who cannot be saved by love; that the cost of salvation in this world, the cost in pain, terror and humiliation, should be so bitterly heavy.

This is how the dominant mood and tone of the Second Book of *The Golden Bowl* are linked with those of Ecclesiastes. The possible reasons, in James's personal life and his life as an artist, for their presence in the latest of his late works are to be briefly considered in the next chapter. Meanwhile, it remains to add that the Jamesian pessimism is, of course, only one side of the picture. The other is the faith, hope and charity embodied in the story of Maggie Verver's triumphant work of redemption; and viewed from this aspect, the scene in the last chapter, in which Maggie and her father stand together on the balcony looking at "the two noble persons" inside, brings together in a grand recapitulation all the components of James's complex vision. If Charlotte and the Prince "might have figured as concrete attestations of a rare power of purchase," if Adam Verver can say to Maggie *"Le compte y est. You've got some good things,"* and Maggie can answer "Ah, don't they look well," it is because the acquisitive passion in Adam was from the beginning, and remains to the end, the source of the limitless wealth which is the foundation of his limitless power, which in turn was the ground of their salvation. If when Adam says of Charlotte "She's beautiful, beautiful," and Maggie detects in this "the note of possession and control," the point again is that power by definition implies these qualities, and without Adam's possession and control of his vast resources they would all have been lost. Finally when Maggie, rejoicing at the knowledge that Charlotte "wasn't to be wasted," says "It's success, father" and he answers "It's success," they are summing up in that phrase the whole story of the redemption that has been accomplished, by love where that was possible, by justice where love was rendered inoperative by pride and fear. The "pessimism" is there, in the unforgettable knowledge of the price that has had to be paid—Maggie's suffering, Charlotte's, the Prince's; the "optimism" is there, in the faith that the good can nevertheless be affirmed so long as there are people willing to pay in suffering. And that is why they all emerge more wonderful and prodigious at the end than they were at the beginning. For each (to adapt a famous formula) has contributed according to his means and has received back according to his need. Adam has given his power and wisdom; Maggie has given her love, informed by intelligence and sustained by courage; the Prince has given his good faith; Charlotte has given her pride (her "greatness"). Between them they *have* in the end succeeded: in restoring the dignities, decencies and serenities of their common life, which figure the harmony and stability of the universal moral order; and in finding their individual salvation within that larger restoration.

To say this, however, is not to say that the pessimism is cancelled out by the faith and hope, or by the "success" that in the end crowns them. Tempting as this conclusion may be, especially to those who find in James's handling of the redemptive theme in *The Golden Bowl* the supreme achievement of his mature genius, what forbids it is precisely the ambiguity. Even as we listen again to Maggie's last dialogue with her father, and presently to Maggie's with the Prince in the moment of their ultimate reunion, the Jamesian ambiguity is persistently, relentlessly, impenetrably there. Certainly each exchange could have the meaning consistent with the redemptive theme; and this would seem to argue the annihilation of all the pessimistic bitterness and horror. But it could also, and as consistently, have the other meaning. The "high power of purchase" could as well signify nothing but the vulgar acquisitiveness of a vulgar American millionaire turned art-collector; the "possession and control" could signify nothing but the passion of such a man for power, in this instance reinforced by complacency and a strong streak of (perhaps "unconscious") sadism; and the talk about "success" could be nothing but the gratification, vulgar or naive or both, of the simple but cunning American pair who have outwitted the two clever Europeans, and have succeeded in getting what they want while forcing the others to take what they are given. Again, in the last scene, the "pity" and "dread" with which Maggie buries her eyes in her husband's breast can mean what I suggested; but it can also mean what Mr Blackmur thought it to mean—that Maggie "pities" the Prince because she knows that this moment marks his final subjugation to her moral "tyranny," and "dreads" her own remorse about what she had done, or the Prince's recognition of his state of subjection, or perhaps both.

But it is not really a question of alternative meanings. The question is not whether the ambiguous passages *could* have the meaning consistent with the redemptive theme: they do have that meaning. Nor need it be asked whether they could have the meaning consistent with the bitter, pessimistic, all-is-vanity view: for they do have that meaning too. If the general hypothesis about the Jamesian ambiguity in *The Golden Bowl* advanced in this chapter is valid, its presence at these crucial points in the resolution of the drama can itself then have only one meaning: that, in Henry James's total vision, the sense of the grimness and bitterness of human life is inseparably fused with the sense of its beauty and blessedness; that neither cancels out the other; and that the ambiguity is intended to express precisely this experience of their permanent, inseparable fusion.

NOTES

1. *The Golden Bowl*, p. xx.
2. *Ibid.*, I, iii, 9, pp. 317-18.
3. *The Awkward Age*, p. xxvi.
4. *Letters*, ed. Lubbock, II, p. 254.
5. *The Awkward Age*, p. xxiii.
6. *Ibid.*, pp. xxv-xxvi.

7. *The Golden Bowl*, I, iii, 7, p. 297.

8. *Ibid.*, I, iii, 9, pp. 318, 321.

9. *Ibid.*, I, i, 2, pp. 28-29.

10. *Ibid.*, I, i, 5, pp. 90-92.

11. The Prince's humility has been explicitly mentioned in the opening section of the whole book when, walking alone in Bond Street, he meditates on his qualifications and disqualifications for the "scientific" future that is in store for him with the Ververs: "He was intelligent enough to feel quite humble, to wish not to be in the least hard or voracious, not to insist on his own side of the bargain, to warn himself in short against arrogance and greed." *(The Golden Bowl*, I, i, 1, p. 14). Again: "Humble as he was, at the same time he was not so humble as if he had known himself frivolous or stupid. He had an idea . . . that when you were stupid enough to be mistaken about such a matter you did know it." *(Ibid.*, I, i, 1, p. 15). The good faith, upon which the success of Maggie Verver's act of restoration absolutely depends, is first mentioned by the Prince himself in his talk with Fanny Assingham the day before his wedding: "You apparently can't understand either my good faith or my humility," he finds himself constrained to say to her in the course of this talk (I, i, 2, p. 27). But Fanny, it seems, does understand: "Amerigo's good faith was perfect," she tells Maggie at their meeting after the antiquary's visit (II, iv, 9, p. 153); and to her husband after the Matcham week-end she says, speaking of Charlotte and the Prince: "There's nothing they're not now capable of—in their so intense good faith. . . . It's their mutual consideration, all round, that has made the bottomless gulf; and they're really so embroiled but because, in their way, they've been so improbably *good.* "(I, iii, 10-11, pp. 337, 352). It is not mentioned again until the last chapter but one when the Prince offers it as his sole word of self-justification in the moment of his reunion with Maggie: "If ever a man since the beginning of time acted in good faith—!" he says (II, vi, 2, p. 308); and needs to say no more since Maggie, it seems, perfectly grasps the point with all its implications.

12. *The Golden Bowl*, I, i, 3, pp. 42-43. See p. 397-98 below.

13. *Ibid.*, I, iii, 7, pp. 298-300.

14. *Ibid.*, I, ii, 5, pp. 175-76.

15. *Ibid.*, I, ii, 5, p. 175.

16. *Ibid.*, I, ii, 1, pp. 122-23.

17. *Ibid.*, I, iii, 6, p. 290.

18. *Ibid.*, II, iv, 1, p. 5.

19. Part II, pp. 417-18, 443-47 below.

20. *The Golden Bowl*, I, iii, 6, p. 288.

21. *Ibid.*, II, iv, 8, p. 134.

22. These details are examined in a later section (Part II, pp. 425-31 below), where it is also suggested that they justify the use of the old-fashioned word

"lust" in spite of (or indeed because of) their Jamesian complexities and refinements.

23. Or, rather, it is at once selfless and selfish; and the sense in which it is "selfish" yet is not therefore the less selfless is to be considered later (Part II, pp. 418-20).

24. *The Golden Bowl*, I, i, 3, pp. 42-43.

25. *Ibid.*, II, iv, 2, pp. 25-26.

26. *Ibid.*, II, iv, 3, pp. 50-51.

27. *Ibid.*, II, iv, 2, pp. 31, 38-39.

28. See pp. 403-06.

29. See pp. 411-13.

30. *The Golden Bowl*, II, iv, 10.

31. This phrase, it will be remembered, is actually used by Miles in *The Turn of the Screw* when the governess, kneeling by his bed after his midnight encounter with Peter Quint, is pressing him to confess what he had "done" at school . . . .

32. *The Golden Bowl*, II, v, 4, pp. 247-48.

33. *Ibid.*, II, v, 2.

34. *Ibid.*, II, v, 2, p. 206.

35. *Ibid.*, II, v, 2, p. 207.

36. *Ibid.*, II, v, 2, pp. 209-10.

37. *Ibid.*, II, v, 2, p. 208.

38. P. 396.

39. Pp. 390-91.

40. *The Golden Bowl*, II, iv, 10, p. 179.

41. Mr Percy Lubbock has made the point very beautifully in his discussion of a similar climactic moment in *The Wings of the Dove:* "Turning back, looking over the pages again, I can mark the very point, perhaps, at which the thing [i.e. the vital piece of knowledge] was liberated and I became possessed of it; I can see the word that finally gave it to me. But at the time it may easily have passed unnoticed; the enlightening word did not seem peculiarly emphatic as it was uttered, it was not announced with any particular circumstance; and yet, presently—there was the piece of knowledge that I had not possessed before." *(The Craft of Fiction*, p. 176.)

42. *The Golden Bowl*, II, vi, 2, p. 303.

43. *Ibid.*, II, vi, 2, p. 304.

44. *Ibid.*, II, vi, 2, p. 307.

45. The point is to be taken up again in its relation to Charlotte in a later section (pp. 428, 430, 435f).

46. Pp. 407 above.

47. Quoted by Quentin Anderson in *The American Henry James*, p. 5.

48. Pp. 400.

49. *The Golden Bowl*, II, iv, 10, p. 164.

50. *Ibid.*, II, iv, 10, p. 163.

51. *Ibid.*, II, v, 1, pp. 201-02.

52. *Ibid.*, II, vi, 3, p. 324.

53. *Ibid.*, II, vi, 2, pp. 310-11.

54. The point is made explicitly in the last chapter of *The Golden Bowl* when Maggie, watching her father walk out on to the balcony of the house in Portland Place, "asked herself but for a few seconds whether reality, should she follow him, would overtake or meet her there," and then recognises as she joins him "how impossible such a passage would have been to them, how it would have torn them to pieces, if they had so much as suffered its suppressed relations to peep out of their eyes." (II, vi, 3, p. 319.)

55. Frederick C. Crews, *The Tragedy of Manners: Moral Drama in the Later Novels of Henry James* (1957).

56. *Ibid.*, pp. 105-08.

57. *Ibid.*, p. 106.

58. See above. . . . [In her Preface to *The Ordeal of Consciousness* the author refers to a projected study of James's development "towards a view of life which I proposed to call 'religious-humanist,' " in which she hopes "to be able to show, on the basis of certain external evidences as well as the internal evidences provided by some of the most important novels and stories of the late period, that Henry James might be counted as one of the greatest representatives of the modern Humanist tradition." *Ordeal*, p. ix. (Ed.)]

59. Mr Stephen Spender was one of the first to draw attention to these in his in many ways admirable essay on *The Golden Bowl* reprinted in *The Question of Henry James*, ed. W. F. Dupee (1947). The conclusion he drew from them, however—that they express "abysses of despair and disbelief: *Ulysses* and *The Waste Land*"—is, I will try to show, seriously incomplete.

60. Ch. VIII [Part I], p. 396 above.

61. *The Golden Bowl*, II, v, 3, p. 231.

62. Pp. 398-99.

63. Pp. 428-31.

64. *The Golden Bowl*, II, v, 4, p. 248. Cp. p. 403 above.

65. Pp. 445ff.

66. Quentin Anderson, *The American Henry James* (Rutgers University Press, 1957).

67. The relation between the novels and the stories of the later period is more fully discussed in chapter X . . . [of *The Ordeal of Consciousness* (Ed.)].

68. *The Golden Bowl*, I, i, 1, pp. 19-20.

69. *The Wings of the Dove*, I, ii, 1, p. 63.

70. *The Golden Bowl*, I, iii, 5.

71. *Ibid.*, II, iv, 2, pp. 33-34.

72. *The Wings of the Dove*, I, iv, 2, pp. 154-59.

73. *The Golden Bowl*, II, vi, 3, p. 319.

74. *Ibid.*, I, iii, 5, p. 279.

75. *The Wings of the Dove*, I, ii, 2, pp. 85-86. The passionate episode in Venice *(ibid.,* II, ix, 1, pp. 211ff.) is, characteristically, not described directly but entirely by its effects—by evoking the enchantment that for Densher hangs upon the air of his small room for many days after Kate had come to him. We are expected in this connexion to remember James's comment on the representation of physical love in the novel in a letter to H. G. Wells: "I think the exhibition of 'Love'—functional Love—always suffers from a certain inevitable and insurmountable flat-footedness (for the readers' nerves etc.); which is only to be counterplotted by roundabout arts—as by tracing it through indirectness and tortuosities of application and effect—to keep it somehow interesting and productive . . ." *(Letters,* ed. Lubbock, II, p. 189).

76. *The Wings of the Dove*, I, ii, 2, pp. 73ff.

77. *The Golden Bowl*, I, ii, 1, pp. 122-23.

78. Cp. ch. VIII [Part I], pp. 395-96.

79. *The Golden Bowl*, I, iii, 11, p. 357.

80. *Ibid.*, II, iv, 10, p. 176. Cp. p. 457, n 139 below for further discussion of this passage.

81. *Ibid.*, II, iv, 10, p. 175.

82. *Ibid.*, I, i, 6, p. 106.

83. In this connexion it is interesting to remember that James had at least in one other important work made a dramatic issue of the difference between the European and the American (or Anglo-Saxon) attitude to the glib, wanton untruth. In *The Europeans* what finally decides Robert Acton that he cannot propose to the Baroness is the fact, simply, that she lies to him about having signed the document dissolving her marriage (or supposed marriage) to her German Prince *(The Europeans,* 11, p. 178; 12, p. 204). He finds the Baroness in a hundred ways fascinating and adorable; as a result of his European travels, he has himself adopted a score of her European attitudes, and has reconciled himself to a dozen others which he cannot adopt. But the ingrained Anglo-Saxon or "Puritan" revulsion from lying of the easy, habitual kind practised by the Baroness cannot, it seems, be exorcised by any amount of acquired European culture; nor can it be compensated for by any European virtues, however brilliant; and Robert Acton's decision is finally determined by this seemingly most trivial of considerations—that he cannot marry a woman who lies.

84. *The Golden Bowl*, I, i, 5, pp. 86-88.

85. *Ibid.*, I, iii, 4-5.

86. *Ibid.*, I, i, 3, p. 45.

87. *Ibid.*, I, iii, 9, p. 315.

88. *Ibid.*, II, iv, 8, p. 126.

89. *Ibid.*, I, iii, 9, p. 325.

90. Pp. 385-91 passim, 397-98, 406-07, 409-10, 411-14, above.

91. Pp. 397-98.

92. *The Golden Bowl*, I, i, 3, pp. 45-46.

93. *Ibid.*, I, iii, 8, p. 309.

94. *Ibid.*, I, iii, 9, p. 315.

95. *Ibid.*, I, iii, 9, p. 318.

96. *Ibid.*, I, iii, 9, p. 321.

97. *Ibid.*, I, iii, 9, pp. 319-20.

98. The cruel "unfairness" of it—that Charlotte should suffer so much for their common sin, the Prince by comparison so little—is to be considered in the next section.

99. *The Golden Bowl*, I, i, 4, p. 77.

100. *Ibid.*, I, ii, 4, pp. 161-62.

101. *Ibid.*, I, i, 4, pp. 64-65, 67-68.

102. *Ibid.*, I, ii, 4, pp. 165-66.

103. *Ibid.*, I, i, 4, p. 76.

104. *The Wings of the Dove*, I, v, 6, pp. 247-48.

105. *The Golden Bowl*, I, ii, 6, pp. 195-202.

106. *Ibid.*, I, ii, 7, p. 215.

107. *Ibid.*, I, iii, 1, 4, 5.

108. *Ibid.*, II, v, 2, p. 211.

109. *Ibid.*, II, v, 5, p. 267.

110. *Ibid.*, II, v, 4, p. 253.

111. *Ibid.*, II, v, 4, p. 259.

112. In the first encounter on the terrace, for instance, Maggie's terror of Charlotte is expressed in the picture of herself as "having been thrown over on her back with her neck from the first half broken and her helpless face staring up" *(Ibid.*, II, v, 2, p. 214).

113. *Ibid.*, II, v, 4, p. 253.

114. *Ibid.*, I, iii, 1, p. 220.

115. *Ibid.*, I, iii, 1, p. 226.

116. *Ibid.*, I, iii, 1, p. 230.

117. *Ibid.*, I, iii, 1, p. 219.

118. *Ibid.*, I, iii, 1, pp. 220, 221.

119. P. 428.

120. *Ibid.*, II, v, 2, p. 219.

121. *Ibid.*, II, v, 5, p. 267.

122. *Ibid.*, II, vi, 2, p. 298.

123. *Ibid.*, II, vi, 1, pp. 290-91.

124. *Ibid.*, II, v, 5, pp. 274-75.

125. *Ibid.*, II, v, 5, p. 271.

126. *Ibid.*, II, v, 5, p. 273.

127. *Ibid.*, II, v, 5, pp. 273-76.

128. *Ibid.*, II, v, 5, p. 275.

129. *Ibid.*, II, v, 5, pp. 279-80.

130. *Ibid.*, II, v, 5, p. 268.

131. *Ibid.*, II, vi, 2, p. 305.

132. *Ibid.*, II, vi, 3, pp. 314-15.

133. *Ibid.*, II, vi, 3, p. 322.

134. (Mrs. Krook discusses this "law" in an Appendix to *The Ordeal of Con-sciousness.* [Ed.])

135. *The Golden Bowl*, II, v, 2, p. 215.

136. *Ibid.*, II, iv, 9, p. 143.

137. *Ibid.*, II, v, 2, p. 212.

138. P. 424.

139. There is a seemingly similar moment earlier in the Second Book, which, however, is not quite the same, and is in any case much less explicit. It occurs in the scene between Maggie and the Prince which follows the breaking of the golden bowl, when the Prince says to her "You've never been more sacred to me than you were at that hour—unless perhaps you've become so at this one" (II, iv, 10, p. 425 above). Upon this follows the passage: "The assurance of his speech, she could note, quite held up its head in him; his eyes met her own so for the declaration that it was *as if something cold and momentarily unimaginable breathed upon her, from afar off, out of his strange consistency.* She kept her direction still however under that." The italicised words seem to suggest that she has a momentary doubt, very chilling to her, about the validity of the conclusions she has drawn from what the antiquary told her, which she is at that moment imparting to the Prince. If this is what the words mean (and if they do not, it is difficult to know what they do mean), the "doubt" would clearly not be of the same radical kind as the one cited above. For we know that the Prince's "strange consistency" is due to his never "really" having cared for Charlotte (see pp. 425-27 above); and since Maggie does not at this stage know it, there is no ambiguity here of the kind we are examing, but only straightforward dramatic irony.

140. *The Golden Bowl*, II, iv, 5, pp. 77ff.

141. *Ibid.*, II, v, 3, p. 238.

142. *Ibid.*, II, iv, 5, p. 83.

143. *Ibid.*, II, iv, 9, pp. 150, 152-54.

144. *Ibid.*, II, v, 3, p. 239.

145. *Ibid.*, II, v, 4, p. 257.

146. P. 421 above.

147. Pp. 439-40.

148. *The Golden Bowl*, II, vi, 3, pp. 317-18.

149. *Ibid.*, II, vi, 3, p. 322.

150. Pp. 418-20.

151. *The Golden Bowl*, II, iv, 8, p. 128. Cp. the narrator in *The Sacred Fount. . . .*

152. *Ibid.*, II, v, 1, p. 191.
153. *Ibid.*, II, vi, 3, p. 325.
154. R. P. Blackmur, Introduction to *The Golden Bowl* pp. xx-xxi (Grove Press, New York 1952).
155. Pp. 410-13 above.

Selected Bibliography

A complete listing of James's writings is to be found in *A Bibliography of Henry James*, by Leon Edel and Dan H. Laurence, London, 1957, revised 1961. The definitive biography by Leon Edel is not yet completed; four volumes have been published by Lippincott:

Henry James: The Untried Years (1843-1870). 1953.
Henry James: The Conquest of London (1870-1881). 1962.
Henry James: The Middle Years (1882-1895). 1962.
Henry James: The Treacherous Years (1895-1901). 1969.

CRITICAL BIOGRAPHIES:

Edgar, Pelham. *Henry James: Man and Author*. Boston, 1927.
Dupee, F. W. *Henry James*. New York, 1956.

BOOKS:

Anderson, Quentin. *The American Henry James*. New Brunswick, N.J.: Rutgers University Press, 1956.
Andreas, Osborne. *Henry James and the Expanding Horizon*. Seattle: University of Washington Press, 1948.
Beach, Joseph Warren. *The Method of Henry James*, rev. ed. Philadelphia: Albert Saifer, 1954.
Blackall, Jean Frantz. *Jamesian Ambiguity and "The Sacred Fount."* Ithaca, N. Y.: Cornell University Press, 1965.
Bowden, Edwin T. *The Themes of Henry James*. New Haven, Conn.: Yale University Press, 1956.
Cargill, Oscar. *The Novels of Henry James*. New York: Macmillan, 1961.

Clair, John. *The Ironic Dimension in the Fiction of Henry James*. Pittsburgh: Duquesne University Press, 1965.

Crews, Frederick C. *The Tragedy of Manners: Moral Drama in the Later Novels of Henry James*. New Haven, Conn.: Yale University Press, 1957.

Gale, Robert L. *The Caught Image: Figurative Language in the Fiction of Henry James*. Chapel Hill: University of North Carolina Press, 1964.

Holland, Laurence B. *The Expense of Vision: Essays on the Craft of Henry James*. Princeton, N. J.: Princeton University Press, 1964.

Jefferson, D. W. *Henry James and the Modern Reader*. Edinburgh: Oliver and Boyd, 1964.

Krook, Dorothea. *The Ordeal of Consciousness in Henry James*. New York: Cambridge University Press, 1962.

Lebowitz, Naomi. *The Imagination of Loving: Henry James's Legacy to the Novel*. Detroit: Wayne State University Press, 1965.

Levy, Leo B. *Versions of Melodrama: a Study of the Fiction and Drama of Henry James, 1865-1897*. Berkeley: University of California Press, 1957.

Lubbock, Percy. *The Craft of Fiction*. New York: Scribners, 1921.

McCarthy, Harold T. *Henry James: The Creative Process*. New York: Thomas Yoseloff, 1958.

Marks, Robert. *James's Later Novels: An Interpretation*. New York: William-Frederick Press, 1960.

Poirier, Richard. *The Comic Sense of Henry James: A Study of the Early Novels*. New York: Oxford University Press, 1960.

Matthiessen, F. O. *Henry James: The Major Phase*. New York: Oxford University Press, 1944.

Putt, S. Gorley. *A Reader's Guide to Henry James*. Ithaca, N. Y.: Cornell University Press, 1966.

Sharp, Sister M. Corona. *The "Confidante" in Henry James: Evolution and Moral Value of a Fictive Character*. Notre Dame, Ind.: University of Notre Dame Press, 1963.

Stevenson, Elizabeth. *The Crooked Corridor: A Study of Henry James*. New York: Macmillan, 1949.

Stone, Edward. *The Battle of the Books: Some Aspects of Henry James*. Athens, Ohio: Ohio University Press, 1964.

Ward, Joseph A. *The Imagination of Disaster: Evil in the Fiction of Henry James*. Lincoln, Neb.: University of Nebraska Press, 1961.

Wegelin, Christof. *Image of Europe in Henry James.* Dallas: Southern
     Methodist University Press, 1958.
Wiesenfarth, Joseph. *Henry James and the Dramatic Analogy.* New
     York: Fordham University Press, 1963.
Wright, Walter F. *The Madness of Art: A Study of Henry James.* Lincoln,
     Neb.: University of Nebraska Press, 1962.